S0-AVN-325

PHOTOGRAPHIS 84

PHOTOGRAPHIS 84

The International Annual of Advertising and Editorial Photography

Das internationale Jahrbuch der Werbephotographie und der redaktionellen Photographie

Le répertoire international de la photographie publicitaire et rédactionnelle

Edited by: / Herausgegeben von: / Réalisé par:

Walter Herdeg

Graphis Press Corp., Dufourstr. 107, Zurich (Switzerland)

GRAPHIS PUBLICATIONS

GRAPHIS, International bi-monthly journal of graphic art and applied art
GRAPHIS ANNUAL, The international annual of advertising and editorial graphics
GRAPHIS POSTERS, The international annual of poster art
GRAPHIS PACKAGING VOL. 4, An international survey of package design
CHILDREN'S BOOK ILLUSTRATION VOL. 3, VOL. 4, An international survey of children's book illustration
GRAPHIS DIAGRAMS, The graphic visualization of abstract data
FILM + TV GRAPHICS 2, An international survey of the art of film animation
ARCHIGRAPHIA, Architectural and environmental graphics
GRAPHIS EPHEMERA, Artists' Self-Promotion

GRAPHIS-PUBLIKATIONEN

GRAPHIS, Die internationale Zweimonatsschrift für Graphik und angewandte Kunst
GRAPHIS ANNUAL, Das internationale Jahrbuch der Werbegraphik und der redaktionellen Graphik
GRAPHIS POSTERS, Das internationale Jahrbuch der Plakatkunst
GRAPHIS PACKUNGEN BAND 4, Internationales Handbuch der Packungsgestaltung
KINDERBUCH-ILLUSTRATION BAND 3, BAND 4, Eine internationale Übersicht über die Kinderbuch-Illustration
GRAPHIS DIAGRAMS, Die graphische Visualisierung abstrakter Gegebenheiten
FILM + TV GRAPHICS 2, Ein internationaler Überblick über die Kunst des Animationsfilms
ARCHIGRAPHIA, Architektur- und Umweltgraphik
GRAPHIS EPHEMERA, Künstler-Eigenwerbung

PUBLICATIONS GRAPHIS

GRAPHIS, La revue bimestrielle internationale d'arts graphiques et d'arts appliqués
GRAPHIS ANNUAL, Le répertoire international de l'art publicitaire et l'art illustratif
GRAPHIS POSTERS, Le répertoire international de l'art de l'affiche
GRAPHIS EMBALLAGES VOL. 4, Répertoire international des formes de l'emballage
ILLUSTRATIONS DE LIVRES D'ENFANTS VOL. 3, VOL. 4, Un aperçu international des illustrations de livres d'enfants
GRAPHIS DIAGRAMS, La visualisation graphique de données abstraites
FILM + TV GRAPHICS 2, Un panorama international de l'art du film d'animation
ARCHIGRAPHIA, La création graphique appliquée à l'architecture et à l'environnement
GRAPHIS EPHEMERA, Autopromotion des artistes

Distributors / Auslieferung / Distribution:

USA: WATSON-GUPTILL PUBLICATIONS, INC., 1515 Broadway, New York, N.Y. 10036 **(ISBN: 0-8230-4003-8)**
CANADA: HURTIG PUBLISHERS, 10560-105 Street, Edmonton, Alberta T5H 2W7, tel. (403) 426-2469
FRANCE: GRAPHIS DISTRIBUTION, Milon-la-Chapelle, F-78470 St-Rémy-lès-Chevreuse, tél. 052-13-26
ITALIA: INTER-ORBIS, Via Lorenteggio, 31/1, I-20146 Milano, tel. 422 57 46
SPAIN: COMERCIAL ATHENEUM, S.A., Consejo de Ciento, 130-136, Barcelona 15, tel. 223 14 51-3
AMERICA LATINA, AUSTRALIA, JAPAN AND OTHER ASIAN COUNTRIES, AFRICA:
FLEETBOOKS S.A., c/o Feffer & Simons, Inc., 100 Park Avenue, New York, N.Y. 10017, tel. (212) 686-0888

All other countries / Alle anderen Länder / Tout autres pays:

GRAPHIS PRESS CORP., 107 Dufourstrasse, CH-8008 Zurich (Switzerland)

PUBLICATION No. 175 (ISBN 3-85709-284-X)

Contents

Inhalt

Sommaire

Abbreviations

Australia	AUS
Austria	AUT
Belgium	BEL
Brazil	BRA
Canada	CAN
Columbia	COL
Denmark	DEN
Finland	FIN
France	FRA
Germany (West)	GER
Great Britain	GBR
Italy	ITA
Japan	JPN
Netherlands	NLD
Norway	NOR
Singapore	SIN
Spain	SPA
Switzerland	SWI
USA	USA

Abkürzungen

Australien	AUS
Belgien	BEL
Brasilien	BRA
Dänemark	DEN
Deutschland	GER
Finnland	FIN
Frankreich	FRA
Grossbritannien	GBR
Italien	ITA
Japan	JPN
Kanada	CAN
Kolumbien	COL
Niederlande	NLD
Norwegen	NOR
Österreich	AUT
Schweiz	SWI
Singapur	SIN
Spanien	SPA
USA	USA

Abréviations

Allemagne occidentale	GER
Australie	AUS
Autriche	AUT
Belgique	BEL
Brésil	BRA
Canada	CAN
Colombie	COL
Danemark	DEN
Espagne	SPA
Etats-Unis	USA
Finlande	FIN
France	FRA
Grande-Bretagne	GBR
Italie	ITA
Japon	JPN
Norvège	NOR
Pays-Bas	NLD
Singapour	SIN
Suisse	SWI

Cover Design/Umschlag/Couverture: Roger Turqueti

It was the submission of photographic works by the thousands that enabled us to make the selection presented in this international overview. Here, therefore, we wish to express our sincere thanks to all who contributed—including those whose work, for various reasons, could not be included this year—and trust we may continue to count on their co-operation in future.

Dank Tausenden von eingesandten photographischen Arbeiten ist es uns möglich gewesen, die vorliegende internationale Übersicht zusammenzustellen. Wir möchten allen Einsendern herzlich danken, auch denjenigen, deren Arbeiten aus verschiedenen Gründen nicht berücksichtigt werden konnten, und hoffen, dass wir auch in Zukunft auf ihre Mitarbeit zählen dürfen.

C'est grâce aux milliers de travaux photographiques qui nous sont parvenus que nous avons pu réaliser ce panorama international. Nos remerciements les plus vifs vont à tous les artistes qui nous ont fait bénéficier de leurs envois, même et surtout s'ils n'ont pu, pour quelque raison, être admis dans la sélection finale. Nous espérons pouvoir compter à l'avenir également sur leur précieuse collaboration.

ROGER TURQUETI, who took the cover shot on this year's edition of PHOTOGRAPHIS, is a native Parisian born in 1949. It was in 1964, when he attended the Ecole Estienne (Ecole des Arts Graphiques de Paris) that photography became his favourite part of the curriculum. This passion led to the opening of his own Paris studio in 1974. With a red pepper as its only spot of colour, his still life shows the dual play of light from a single source: the curve of the black glossy plate and the smooth surface of the black plastic below reflect light that was projected through the mesh of a light box above (dimmed by us to leave the title legible).

ROGER TURQUETI, Photograph der Umschlagaufnahme, wurde 1949 in Paris geboren. Er besuchte dort die Ecole Estienne, wo das Fach Photographie seine grosse Leidenschaft wurde. Seit 1974 führt er ein eigenes Photoatelier in Paris. Sein Stilleben, welches als einzigen Farbfleck eine Paprikaschote zeigt, entstand durch das Doppelspiel der Reflexe, die mittels eines Lichtgitterkastens erzielt wurden, den er oberhalb eines glänzenden, glatten, schwarzen Plastiks und eines schwarzen, gewölbten Tellers montierte. Damit die Lesbarkeit des Buchtitels gewährleistet ist, wurde der Verlauf des Gitters von uns nach oben hin gedämpft.

ROGER TURQUETI, qui a réalisé la photo illustrant la couverture de l'édition 1984 de PHOTOGRAPHIS, est né à Paris en 1949. En 1964, il entre à l'Ecole Estienne (Ecole des Arts Graphiques de Paris), où il se découvre une passion pour la photo. Depuis 1964, il a son atelier de photo à Paris. Sa nature morte, où un poivron introduit la seule tache de couleur, est née d'un double jeu de reflets obtenus au moyen d'une boîte à lumière quadrillée sur une surface de plastique noir plane et brillante et une assiette creuse noire. Nous avons garanti la lisibilité du titre de l'ouvrage en atténuant dans la partie supérieure les reflets de la lumière quadrillée.

Stanley Mason

Preface

STANLEY MASON was born in 1917 in Alberta, Canada. After completing his studies in English literature at Oxford he moved to Switzerland, where he worked as a teacher and as the translator of many books on art and culture. A magazine editor, too, the was the assistant editor of GRAPHIS from 1963 until the end of last year. His published works include an English grammar and several volumes of poetry.

"In the future," wrote Theo van Doesburg in 1914, "there will only be one art. It will be a language that everybody will understand." Seventy years on, art is split up into a dozen or more categories, and fine art, to which van Doesburg was chiefly referring, is not understood by the man in the street at all.

Yet the movement to which van Doesburg belonged—the Dutch de Stijl—has had a powerful influence on the visual arts of our century. It led on to constructive art and to abstraction, and above all it helped to shape, through the Bauhaus philosophy, modern graphic and industrial design, establishing the dominion of functionalism, the carefully balanced but unequivocal visual utterance. The Bauhaus also helped photography to its great breakthrough as a result of the work of Moholy-Nagy and others; and photography came armed with wonderful credentials in these circumstances, since it was regarded as being pledged by its technical character to the reproduction of reality and truth.

Perhaps as a reaction to functionalism, and certainly as a reaction to photography, what is known as fine art has since drifted away into a limbo in which it finally came to the despairing conclusion that everything is art. The only difference between a heap of stones dumped by a builder and one composed by an artist is that the latter is the result of a creative act; and this distinction is of value—paradoxical as it may sound—only if we accept the myth first spread abroad by the Romantics that the creative artist is an inspired Shelleyan creature, a sort of angel miraculously walking the earth but deriving his legitimation from above. The masses have little patience with the results; they are not interested in such fine art, and can only shake their heads at its far-out productions.

Yet the masses live in a world of images denser and more ubiquitous than ever before in man's history. This visual universe that has sprung up around them consists of the images of television, of the press, of advertising. Some of these images are handmade, but most of them are photographic.

The camera, as we have seen, began with an enormous advantage over the forms of visual communication that had gone before it—drawing, painting, engraving, etc.—because it guaranteed fidelity to objective truth. In particular, it was the obvious choice for the advertising of products, since it showed the consumer exactly what he was going to get. We know today that this is all moonshine: the photographer can falsify truth almost as well as the artist. He can manipulate the objects he places before his lens, he can use the lens itself to distort them, he can tinker with the resulting films to produce double or otherwise adulterated images, he can mount his photographs in new constellations. By using special objectives, microscopic and macroscopic shots, infra-red and other techniques, he can even demonstrate to us that there is no such thing as objective truth, that our vision is only one way of seeing the world among many thousands of possible ways.

All these potentialities, which are being extended year by year, are obviously a great temptation to the photographer. Yet anyone who leafs through the present volume and compares it, say, with the first issue of PHOTOGRAPHIS in 1966, will realize that no great revolution has occurred in the meantime. Although the gates of imaginative freedom have since been opened fairly wide to the photographer, he has not fallen head over heels into the new kingdom.

We are dealing here, of course, only with advertising and editorial photography. Against the former, at least, many adherents of fine art, many secret believers in the Romantic myth and many critics of the consumer society level the charge that, by subordinating itself to the requirements of advertisers whose goals are almost purely mercenary, it forfeits the claim to being art or to having any truly lasting value. That advertising photography is not the highest form of creative activity most people will admit. On the other hand, it reflects much more faithfully than any fine art or even free photography the world we live in and the nature of our culture.

One reason why advertising photography cannot always be highly creative lies in the mode of operation of the advertising profession. For many years the photographer was a very small-part man in its scenario. He was called in when the art director had prepared his concept, and was told exactly what he had to shoot—with little or no scope for imagination or experiment on his own part. David Ogilvy, though fully aware of the value of good photography, was able to write: "If you have a remarkable idea for a photograph, it does not require a genius to click the shutter." Things have improved somewhat since then, and the Germans in particular have tried to set up the photo-designer as a more all-round man with abilities qualifying him to play a central part in the visualization process.

Advertising photography today is also beset by other dangers. The age of functionalism is beginning to totter. Graphic designers of the New Wave are putting accents into their compositions that are extraneous to the message. Lettering becomes less legible because the artist happens to think it more exciting that way. In other sectors of our culture, particularly the more popular ones, genuine utterance and moral responsibility have long gone by the board. On the rock scene inadequate voices, mediocre music and the absence of any real message are too often replaced by phoney, perspiratory passion and all the instrumentarium of lighting, noise and electronics—cheap effects are called upon to make up for an absence of substance. The progressive theatre grows steadily more eccentric, more artificial. Television lives to a large extent on a stylized brutality and sensationalism that are not even true to life. Nothing can really blind us to the fact that we are living in an age of self-indulgence, of mental dishonesty, of disorientation, of decadence. But as R. E. Martinez wrote in the preface to the very first PHOTOGRAPHIS: "To make advertising the scapegoat of our disorientation ... can only help those who are prepared to put their trust in a vain nostalgia for an allegedly golden past."

The applied photography reproduced in this and the last few volumes of PHOTOGRAPHIS, however, reveals that in this field the temptations of our age have on the whole been resisted. There are admittedly more offbeat shots today, New Wave styles have occasionally insinuated themselves into photography, postures are sometimes showy, dramatic and unnatural, light tracks appear where they serve no real end, distortion and Surrealist shifts are exploited, laminates produce an unearthly gloss, recourse is had to science-fiction settings—extraneous effects frequently not justified by the themes treated. Yet these excursions are comparatively few and rarely excessive. Many photographs serve to translate ideas into straight if skilful images: a map of Europe composed of gastronomic products for a cookery guide, or a delineation of Johnnie Walker in spilt whisky. The beautiful still lifes of cheeses, bread and wine are still there, or the shiny, high-powered shots of motorcycles in action. Imagination is used but is not allowed to run away with itself, as when metallic clothing is set off against glacial landscapes. Even in self-promotion and calendars, where pure fancy is given a longer lead, most photographers are keeping one foot on mother earth.

In a sense advertising photography is here profiting from what at first appears to be its great disability: the advertisers who are accused of clipping its wings are ensuring, in an age when temptations are great, that it does not fly too far from home. They are thus helping to preserve what has always been its primary recommendation—its credibility.

Stanley Mason

Vorwort

STANLEY MASON wurde 1917 in Alberta, Kanada, geboren. Er studierte englische Literatur in Oxford und zog später in die Schweiz, wo er als Lehrer, Übersetzer von zahlreichen Büchern über Kunst und Kultur sowie als Redakteur von Zeitschriften arbeitete. Er war von 1963–1983 in leitender Position in der Redaktion der Zeitschrift GRAPHIS tätig. Er ist Verfasser eines Englisch-Lehrgangs und hat als Lyriker mehrere Gedichtbände veröffentlicht.

«In Zukunft», schrieb Theo van Doesburg 1914, «wird es nur eine Kunstform geben. Es wird eine Sprache sein, die jeder versteht.» Siebzig Jahre danach ist Kunst in mehr als ein Dutzend Kategorien aufgesplittert, und die bildende Kunst, auf die van Doesburg vor allem anspielte, wird vom Mann auf der Strasse überhaupt nicht verstanden. Die Bewegung, der van Doesburg angehörte – der holländische de Stijl – hatte jedoch starken Einfluss auf die visuellen Künste unseres Jahrhunderts. Sie führte zur konstruktiven Kunst und zur Abstraktion, und vor allem trug sie durch die Bauhaus-Philosophie dazu bei, moderne Graphik und Produkt-Design zu formen, die Domäne des Funktionalismus zu etablieren, den sorgfältig ausgewogenen, aber unzweideutigen visuellen Ausdruck. Durch das Werk von Moholy-Nagy und anderen verhalf das Bauhaus auch der Photographie zu ihrem grossen Durchbruch, und in diesem Umfeld trat die Photographie allerbestens ausgerüstet hervor, denn durch ihren technischen Charakter wurde sie als Garant für realistische und wahrheitsgetreue Wiedergabe angesehen.

Vielleicht als Reaktion auf den Funktionalismus, sicher aber als Reaktion auf die Photographie, ist das, was unter bildender Kunst verstanden wird, vollkommen abgetrieben und an einem Punkt angelangt, an dem man zu der entmutigenden Folgerung gelangte, dass alles Kunst sei. Der einzige Unterschied zwischen einem Haufen Steine, der von einem Bauarbeiter aufgeschichtet wurde, und einem der von einem Künstler arrangiert wurde, ist, dass der letztere das Ergebnis eines kreativen Akts ist; und diese Unterscheidung ist – so paradox es klingen mag – nur dann gültig, wenn wir den zuerst von den Romantikern verbreiteten Mythos akzeptieren, gemäss welchem der kreative Künstler eine inspirierte Kreatur ist, wie eine Gestalt aus der Dichtung von Percy B. Shelley, eine Art Engel, der wunderwirkend auf der Erde einherwandelt, aber seine Legitimation von oben erhält. Was die Ergebnisse anbelangt, so hat die grosse Masse wenig Geduld; sie hat kein Interesse an dieser Art bildender Kunst, und angesichts der ausgefallenen Produktionen kann sie nur den Kopf schütteln. Die grosse Masse lebt jedoch in einer Welt der Bilder, die dichter und allgegenwärtiger ist als je zuvor in der Geschichte der Menschheit. Dieses visuelle Universum, das sich um sie herum aufgetan hat, besteht aus den Bildern des Fernsehens, der Presse, der Werbung. Einige dieser Bilder sind handgemacht, die meisten davon aber sind photographisch.

Wie wir gesehen haben, begann die Kamera gegenüber anderen Formen der visuellen Kommunikation – wie Zeichnen, Malen, Gravieren, etc. – mit einem enormen Vorteil, weil sie objektive Wahrheitstreue versprach. Sie schien insbesondere für die Produktwerbung geeignet, weil sie dem Konsumenten genau zeigte, was er bekommen würde. Wir wissen heute, dass dies alles nicht mehr zutrifft: der Photograph kann die Wahrheit fast so gut verfälschen wie der Künstler. Die Dinge, die er vor sein Objektiv stellt, kann er manipulieren, das Objektiv selbst kann ihm dazu dienen, sie zu verzerren, das Ergebnis kann er dann noch so behandeln, dass doppelte oder sonst irgendwie veränderte Bilder entstehen, er kann seine Aufnahmen so montieren, dass sich ganz neue Zusammenhänge ergeben. Durch die Verwendung spezieller Objektive, mikro- oder makroskopischer Aufnahmen, Infrarot und anderer Techniken, kann er sogar beweisen, dass es so etwas wie eine objektive Wahrheit nicht gibt, dass unsere Vision nur eine von vielen tausend Möglichkeiten ist, die Welt zu sehen.

Alle diese Möglichkeiten, die Jahr für Jahr erweitert werden, sind für den Photographen natürlich eine grosse Versuchung. Wenn man jedoch im vorliegenden Band blättert und ihn vielleicht mit der ersten Ausgabe von PHOTOGRAPHIS aus dem Jahre 1966 vergleicht, wird man feststellen, dass in der Zwischenzeit keine grosse Revolution stattgefunden hat. Obwohl dem Photographen seither die Pforten der kreativen Freiheit einigermassen weit geöffnet wurden, hat er sich nicht Hals über Kopf in das neue Himmelreich gestürzt.

Wir haben es hier natürlich nur mit Werbe- und redaktioneller Photographie zu tun. Viele Anhänger der bildenden Kunst, viele heimliche Anhänger des romantischen Mythos und viele Kritiker der Konsumgesellschaft halten der Auftrags-Photographie entgegen, dass sie durch ihre Unterordnung gegenüber den Anforderungen der Werber den Anspruch verliert, Kunst zu sein oder einen bleibenden Wert zu haben. Dass angewandte Photographie nicht die höchste Stufe kreativer Tätigkeit ist, werden die meisten zugeben. Auf der anderen Seite spiegelt sie die

Welt, in der wir leben, und das Wesen unserer Kultur sehr viel wahrheitsgetreuer wider als die bildende Kunst oder sogar die freie Photographie.

Ein Grund dafür, dass Auftrags-Photographie nicht immer sehr kreativ sein kann, liegt in der Arbeitsweise der Werbewelt. Während vieler Jahre spielte der Photograph auf dieser Bühne nur eine unbedeutende Nebenrolle. Er wurde hinzugerufen, wenn der Art Director sein Konzept vorbereitet hatte, und es wurde ihm genau gesagt, was er aufzunehmen hatte – mit wenig oder gar keinem Spielraum für Phantasie oder Experiment auf seiner Seite. Obgleich er sich des Wertes guter Photographie durchaus bewusst war, brachte David Ogilvy es fertig, folgendes zu schreiben: «Wenn man eine bemerkenswerte Idee für eine Aufnahme hat, braucht man kein Genie, um den Auslöser zu bedienen.» Seitdem haben sich die Dinge ein wenig gebessert, besonders die Deutschen haben versucht, den Begriff Photo-Designer zu etablieren, als Bezeichnung und Aufwertung für eine Person mit vielseitigeren Fähigkeiten.

Heute ist die angewandte Photographie noch durch andere Gefahren bedroht. Das Zeitalter des Funktionalismus beginnt zu schwanken. Graphik-Designer der New Wave setzen in ihre Kompositionen Akzente, die für die Aussage unwesentlich sind. Die Schrift wird weniger gut lesbar, weil es dem Künstler gerade einfällt zu glauben, dass es auf diese Weise spannender sei. In anderen Bereichen unserer Kultur, besonders in den populären, wurden echte Aussage und moralische Verantwortung längst über Bord geworfen. In der Rock-Szene werden unzulängliche Stimmen, mittelmässige Musik und das Fehlen einer wirklichen Botschaft nur allzuoft ersetzt durch unechte, schwülstige Leidenschaft und das ganze Instrumentarium von Licht, Lautstärke und Elektronik – billige Effekte, auf die zurückgegriffen wird, um das Fehlen von Substanz wettzumachen. Das progressive Theater wird immer exzentrischer, immer künstlicher. Das Fernsehen lebt grossenteils von stilisierter Brutalität und Sensationsmache, die nicht einmal dem Leben entsprechen. Nichts kann uns wirklich die Tatsache verschleiern, dass wir in einem Zeitalter materieller Genussucht, geistiger Unaufrichtigkeit, der Desorientierung, der Dekadenz leben. Wie jedoch R. E. Martinez im Vorwort zur ersten Ausgabe von PHOTOGRAPHIS 1966 schrieb: «Die Werbung zum Sündenbock für unsere Desorientierung zu machen ... kann nur jenen helfen, die bereit sind, sich einer fruchtlosen Sehnsucht nach einer vermeintlich goldenen Vergangenheit hinzugeben.»

Die angewandte Photographie, die in PHOTOGRAPHIS reproduziert ist, zeigt jedoch, dass man auf diesem Gebiet den Versuchungen unseres Zeitalters im grossen und ganzen nicht erlegen war. Es gibt zwar mehr extravagante Aufnahmen, New-Wave-Stilarten haben sich gelegentlich in die Photographie eingeschlichen, Stellungen sind manchmal auffällig, dramatisch und unnatürlich, Lichteffekte tauchen auf, wo sie unnötig sind. Verzerrung und surrealistische Richtungen werden erkundet, Laminierungen erzeugen überirdischen Glanz, Science-Fiction-Decors werden aufgeboten – überflüssige Effekte, die durch die behandelten Themen häufig nicht gerechtfertigt sind. Diese Ausflüge sind jedoch verhältnismässig selten und kaum übertrieben. Viele Aufnahmen dienen dazu, Ideen in einfache, aber gekonnte Bilder umzusetzen: eine Karte von Europa, die sich aus gastronomischen Produkten zusammensetzt, für einen kulinarischen Führer, oder verschütteter Whisky, der die Gestalt von Johnnie Walker angenommen hat. Die schönen Stilleben mit Käse, Brot und Wein sind noch immer zu finden, oder die glänzenden, rasanten Aufnahmen von Motorrädern. Ohne zu übertreiben wird Phantasie hier eingesetzt, wie bei der Aufnahme metallischer Kleidung im Zusammenspiel mit Gletscherlandschaften. Sogar bei Eigenwerbung und Kalendern bleiben die meisten Photographen mit einem Fuss auf dem Erdboden.

Auf eine Art profitiert die Werbe-Photographie hier von dem, was auf den ersten Blick ihr grosser Nachteil zu sein scheint: die Werber, die beschuldigt werden, ihre Flügel zu stutzen, sorgen dafür, dass sie in einem Zeitalter, in dem die Versuchungen gross sind, nicht zu weit davonfliegt. Sie helfen damit, das zu erhalten, was immer ihr grösster Vorzug war – ihre Glaubhaftigkeit.

Stanley Mason

Préface

STANLEY MASON, né dans l'Alberta, au Canada, en 1917, a fait ses classes de littérature anglaise à Oxford, puis s'est installé en Suisse où il a été professeur, traducteur de nombreux ouvrages d'art et de civilisation et rédacteur de divers magazines. De 1963 à 1983, il a fait partie de la direction de la rédaction du magazine GRAPHIS. Auteur d'un manuel d'anglais, il a aussi publié plusieurs recueils de poésie.

«A l'avenir, écrivait Theo van Doesburg en 1914, il n'y aura plus qu'un seul art. Ce sera un langage accessible à tous.» Soixante-dix ans après, l'art a éclaté en plus d'une douzaine de catégories, et les beaux-arts auxquels van Doesburg pensait avant tout sont hors de portée de Monsieur Tout-le-Monde. Pourtant, le mouvement dont van Doesburg se réclamait – le De Stijl hollandais – a puissamment influencé les arts visuels de notre siècle. Il a abouti au constructivisme et à l'abstraction et a surtout contribué à donner forme, par le biais de la philosophie du Bauhaus, à l'art publicitaire et à l'esthétique industrielle modernes en annonçant le règne du fonctionnalisme, d'une expression visuelle fruit d'un équilibre savamment dosé et ne tolérant pas la moindre équivoque. Le Bauhaus a également aidé la photographie à s'imposer grâce aux travaux de Moholy-Nagy entre autres; ce faisant, la photographie s'est parée d'atours extrêmement séduisants, puisque son caractère technique paraissait la vouer à la tâche combien exaltante de la reproduction pure et simple du réel et de la vérité.

C'est peut-être en réaction au fonctionnalisme et certainement en réaction au devenir de la photographie que ce que l'on est convenu d'appeler les beaux-arts s'est retiré sur une ligne de repli où la conclusion, accablante, a fini par s'imposer: tout est art. La seule différence entre un tas de pierres entassé par un maçon et le même agrégat composé par un artiste tient à l'acte créateur que manifeste le second. Or, ce distinguo ne peut être maintenu – aussi paradoxal que cela puisse sembler – qu'à condition d'adhérer au mythe romantique qui veut que l'artiste créateur est un être rimbaldien inspiré, un ange miraculeusement tombé parmi nous, mais tirant sa légitimité de ses origines célestes. Il faut bien dire que la masse ne suit pas le mouvement, n'est guère intéressé à ce genre de beaux-arts, qui suscite dans ses productions extrêmes des haussements d'épaules et des mines perplexes.
Pourtant, la masse évolue au sein d'un monde d'images dont la densité et l'omniprésence n'ont d'égales à aucune autre époque de l'Histoire. Cet univers visuel qui s'est constitué autour de nous se compose d'images télévisées, illustrées et publicitaires. Si certaines de ces images sont dessinées, la majorité est réalisée par photographie.

L'appareil photographique, nous l'avons vu, présentait d'emblée un énorme avantage par rapport aux modes traditionnels de la communication visuelle, le dessin, la peinture, la gravure, etc., en garantissant fidèlement la restitution de la vérité objective. C'était en particulier le choix qui s'imposait pour la publicité produits, puisque grâce à la photo, le consommateur était informé avec précision de ce qu'il allait acheter. Nous savons aujourd'hui que c'était là une illusion de taille et que le photographe peut falsifier la vérité presque autant que l'artiste. Il peut manipuler les objets avant de les enregistrer sur sa pellicule, il peut les déformer par des artifices d'objectif, peut traiter les films en résultant de manière à produire des images doubles ou transformées de quelque manière, ou encore assembler ses photos en des montages inédits. En recourant à des objectifs spéciaux, à des micro- et macrophotos, à l'infrarouge et à d'autres techniques, il peut même nous faire la démonstration de l'inexistence d'un réel prétendument objectif et nous convaincre que la vision humaine prime les 1001 manières de voir cet univers.

Toutes ces potentialités, dont l'arsenal s'accroît d'année en année, constituent évidemment une tentation sérieuse pour le photographe. Toutefois, à feuilleter le présent volume et à le comparer par exemple avec la première édition de PHOTOGRAPHIS en 1966, on ne trouvera pas trace d'un bouleversement qui aurait affecté la photographie depuis. Si les portes de la liberté d'imaginer se sont grandes ouvertes au photographe depuis 18 ans, il ne s'est néanmoins pas précipité la tête la première dans son nouveau royaume des trente-six mille volontés.

Nous parlons ici, bien entendu, uniquement de la photo publicitaire et illustrative. La première tout au moins est en butte aux accusations de nombre d'adeptes des beaux-arts, de partisans secrets du mythe romantique et d'une foule de critiques de la société de consommation, qui tous lui reprochent de se soumettre au diktat d'annonceurs ne poursuivant que des fins vulgaires et de déchoir par-là de son rang de forme d'art et de toute prétention à la pérennité. La plupart d'entre nous admettront que la photographie publicitaire ne constitue pas la forme suprême de l'activité créatrice. Et pourtant, elle reflète bien mieux que les beaux-arts ou même la photographie non commerciale le monde où nous vivons et la nature même de notre civilisation.

L'une des raisons pour lesquelles la photographie publicitaire ne saurait être constamment au diapason d'une créativité exaltée est à rechercher dans le mode opératoire de l'industrie publicitaire. Très longtemps, le photographe a joué un rôle effacé au sein de l'équipe publicitaire. On faisait appel à lui lorsque le directeur artistique avait mis au point sa conception de la photo à faire en suivant ses instructions. Il n'y avait là que très peu de liberté sur le plan de l'imagination ou de l'expérimentation. Et David Ogilvy pouvait alors écrire, tout en étant conscient de la valeur d'une photo de qualité: «Si vous avez une idée remarquable pour prendre un sujet en photo, vous n'avez pas besoin d'un génie pour appuyer sur le déclencheur.» Les choses ont changé en bien depuis. Les Allemands en particuliers ont donné au designer photographe un profil plus complet, qui lui fait obtenir une part prépondérante dans le processus de visualisation.

D'autres menaces encore pèsent de nos jours sur la photographie publicitaire. L'âge du fonctionnalisme semble toucher à sa fin. Les artistes Nouvelle Vague introduisent dans leurs réalisations des accents étrangers au message. Les textes perdent en lisibilité par la volonté d'artistes qui trouvent cette manière de faire bien plus excitante. Dans d'autres secteurs de notre culture, notamment dans les plus populaires, l'authenticité de l'expression et la responsabilité morale ont depuis longtemps passé par-dessus bord. Sur la scène du rock, des voix inexpérimentées, une musique médiocre et l'absence d'un message vrai sont trop souvent remplacées par le déchaînement forcené de passions en faux-fuyants, dégoulinant de sueur, et tout l'arsenal de l'éclairage, du bruit et de l'électronique – autant d'effets bon marché tendant à faire oublier l'absence de toute substance. Le théâtre progressiste devient toujours plus excentrique, plus artificieux. La télévision vit dans une large mesure de l'évocation d'une brutalité stylisée et d'un sensationnalisme en porte-à-faux par rapport au réel. Rien ne saurait nous masquer le fait que nous vivons à une époque où triomphent la satisfaction égoïste des instincts, la malhonnêteté intellectuelle, la désorientation, la décadence. Retenons pourtant ce que R. E. Martinez écrivait dans la préface du tout premier annuel PHOTOGRAPHIS: «Faire de la publicité le bouc émissaire de notre désorientation... ne peut servir que ceux qui sont disposés à placer tous leurs espoirs dans la vaine nostalgie d'un âge d'or qui aurait prétendument existé.»

Les travaux de photographie appliquée reproduits dans PHOTOGRAPHIS nous enseignent heureusement que dans ce domaine, les tentations de notre époque ont été en général surmontées. Reconnaissons qu'il y a bien plus de clichés hors des sentiers battus de nos jours, que des styles Nouvelle Vague s'immiscent occasionnellement dans la photographie, que les postures adoptées sont parfois démonstratives, dramatiques et peu naturelles, que des raies de lumière apparaissent parfois sans aucune justification, que les effets de distorsion et de déplacement surréaliste sont savamment exploités, que la technique des paraglyphes donne des effets de transposition surnaturels, que des décors de science-fiction ajoutent des éléments extrinsèques souvent nullement justifiés par le sujet. Dans l'ensemble, toutefois, ces intrusions sont comparativement rares et rarement excessives. Un grand nombre des photos réalisées servent à transposer des idées dans des images directes mais ingénieuses – une carte de l'Europe composée des produits gastronomiques nationaux, pour un livre de cuisine, ou la silhouette de Johnnie Walker composée à l'aide de whisky renversé. On trouve toujours de superbes natures mortes de fromages, de pain et de vin, ou encore des photos action de motos gros cubes reluisantes. L'imagination a son rôle à jouer, mais ne peut l'emporter au paradis du délire. Exemple, ces vêtements métallisés contrastés avec des paysages de glaces. Même dans la publicité autopromotionnelle et dans les calendriers la plupart des photographes gardent au moins un pied sur terre.

En un certain sens, la photographie publicitaire tire ici profit de ce qui, à première vue, semble constituer sa faiblesse majeure: le rôle joué par les annonceurs. Vilipendés parce qu'ils sont censés couper les ailes aux artistes, ceux-ci contribuent tout de même, à une époque de tentations grandissantes, à empêcher les nouveaux Icares de voler trop haut. Ce faisant, ils nous aident à préserver ce qui a toujours été au cœur de la photographie publicitaire: sa crédibilité.

Index to Photographers
Verzeichnis der Photographen
Index des Photographes

Index to Designers
Verzeichnis der Gestalter
Index des Maquettistes

Index to Art Directors
Verzeichnis der künstlerischen Leiter
Index des Directeurs Artistiques

Index to Agencies and Studios
Verzeichnis der Agenturen und Studios
Index des Agences et Studios

Index to Publishers
Verzeichnis der Verleger
Index des Editeurs

Index to Advertisers
Verzeichnis der Auftraggeber
Index des Clients

■ Entry instructions may be requested by anyone interested in submitting samples of exceptional graphics or photography for possible inclusion in our annuals. No fees involved. Closing dates for entries:
GRAPHIS ANNUAL (advertising and editorial art and design): 31 January
PHOTOGRAPHIS (advertising and editorial photography): 30 June
GRAPHIS POSTERS (an annual of poster art): 30 June
Write to: Graphis Press Corp., Dufourstrasse 107, 8008 Zurich, Switzerland

■ Einsendebedingungen können von jedermann angefordert werden, der uns Beispiele hervorragender Photographie oder Graphik zur Auswahl für unsere Jahrbücher unterbreiten möchte. Es werden keine Gebühren erhoben.
Einsendetermine:
GRAPHIS ANNUAL (Werbe- und redaktionelle Graphik): 31. Januar
PHOTOGRAPHIS (Werbe- und redaktionelle Photographie): 30. Juni
GRAPHIS POSTERS (ein Jahrbuch der Plakatkunst): 30. Juni
Adresse: Graphis Verlag AG, Dufourstrasse 107, 8008 Zürich, Schweiz

■ Tout intéressé à la soumission de travaux photographiques et graphiques recevra les informations nécessaires sur demande. Sans charge de participation.
Dates limites:
GRAPHIS ANNUAL (art graphique publicitaire et rédactionnel): 31 janvier
PHOTOGRAPHIS (photographie publicitaire et rédactionnelle): 30 juin
GRAPHIS POSTERS (annuaire sur l'art de l'affiche): 30 juin
S'adresser à: Editions Graphis SA, Dufourstrasse 107, 8008 Zurich, Suisse

Editor and Art Director: Walter Herdeg
Assistant Editor: McIver A. H. Campbell
Project Managers: Romy Herzog, Heinke Jenssen
Designers: Marino Bianchera, Martin Byland, Ulrich Kemmner
Art Assistants: Peter Wittwer, Walter Zuber

1

Magazine Advertisements
Newspaper Advertisements

Zeitschriften-Inserate
Zeitungs-Inserate

Annonces de revues
Annonces de presse

1

PUT WHAT YOU WANT TO SELL MOST ON THE WAY TO THE MAXELL TAPE.

2

3

PHOTOGRAPHER / PHOTOGRAPH / PHOTOGRAPHE:

1 Henry Pierre Schultz
2, 3 Dennis Chalkin
4 Hickson-Bender

ART DIRECTOR / DIRECTEUR ARTISTIQUE:

1 Felix Zimmermann
2, 3 Cathie Campbell
4 Bob Bender

AGENCY / AGENTUR / AGENCE – STUDIO:

1 Gisler & Gisler
2, 3 Scali, McCabe, Sloves
4 Lord Sullivan & Yoder

1 A room becomes "the hard-rock café that never closes" with a high-fidelity music rack by *Philips*. Double spread in full colour. (SWI)
2, 3 Dealers can boost their sales of other products by exploiting facts from research about the buyers of *Maxell* audio tapes—who are also interested in other quality products (Fig. 2), especially those displayed near the tapes, and who (Fig. 3) buy twice as many records as the average buyer. Double spreads in black and white. (USA)
4 Which came first, the chicken or the egg? There is no question of precedence, or an alternative, to what *Harter* offers with its office-seating line in 18 models: form plus comfort. (USA)

1 Ein Raum wird zu «einem Hard-Rock-Café, das niemals schliesst» mit einer HiFi-Anlage von *Philips*. Mehrfarbige Doppelseite. (SWI)
2, 3 Händler können ihre Verkäufe ankurbeln, indem sie von der Tatsache profitieren, dass Käufer von *Maxell*-Tonbandkassetten auch an weiteren Qualitätsprodukten interessiert sind, die man am besten in der Nähe der gut sichtbar ausgestellten Kassetten plaziert (Abb. 2). «*Maxell*-Tonbandkassetten-Käufer erwerben doppelt soviele Grammophon-Platten als andere» (Abb. 3). Doppelseiten in Schwarzweiss. (USA)
4 «Was kam zuerst – das Huhn oder das Ei, Form oder Komfort?» *Harter* bietet beides gleichzeitig bei allen 18 Bürostuhlmodellen. (USA)

1 La chambre se mue en «café-concert hard rock qui ne ferme jamais», grâce à une chaîne stéréo *Philips*. Double page polychrome. (SWI)
2, 3 Les revendeurs peuvent décupler leur chiffre d'affaires en misant sur le fait que les acheteurs de cassettes d'enregistreurs *Maxell* s'intéressent aussi à d'autres produits de qualité que l'on a intérêt à placer au voisinage immédiat des cassettes bien exposées (fig. 2). «Les acheteurs de cassettes *Maxell* achètent deux fois plus de disques que les autres clients» (fig. 3). Doubles pages noir et blanc. (USA)
4 «Qu'est-ce qui était là d'abord, la poule ou l'œuf – la forme ou le confort?» Les deux, du moins dans les 18 modèles *Harter*. (USA)

4

JOOP GREYPINK
PHOTOGRAPHY
0211 · 30 87 34
JOOP GREYPINK IS REPRESENTED BY
MORLE SCHUSTER

5

JOOP GREYPINK
PHOTOGRAPHY
0211 · 30 87 34
JOOP GREYPINK IS REPRESENTED BY
MORLE SCHUSTER

6

la véritable élégance
est celle qui ne se voit pas.
L'élégance du compact PENTAX
est de tout faire, avec discrétion -
le réglage de la lumière : automatique
la mise au point : automatique. L'éclairage
d'appoint : Flash intégré.
Même l'avancement de la pellicule
est automatique : moteur en option
Comme tous les grands, c'est dans
le cœur qu'il tient le plus de place
COMPACT PENTAX. Que peut-il lui manquer?
PENTAX
PC35AF

7

Jetzt im Duopack.
Kodacolor II
FILM FÜR FARBBILDER
FILM POUR EPREUVES COULEUR
110
Kodak
Kodak

8

PHOTOGRAPHER / PHOTOGRAPH:

5, 6 Joop Greypink
7 Daniel Fauchon
8 Jiri Vurma
9, 10 Noboru Murata
11 James Lauritz

ART DIRECTOR / DIRECTEUR ARTISTIQUE:

5, 6 Joop Greypink
7 Anne de Peyerhimoff / D. Robert
8 Ernst Herzog
9, 10 Shin Yoshida
11 Eddy Greenwood

DESIGNER / GESTALTER / MAQUETTISTE:

8 Ernst Herzog
9, 10 Toru Suzuki / Hisashi Honma

AGENCY / AGENTUR / AGENCE – STUDIO:

7 Robert & Partners
8 Advico
11 Kutt, Skinner, Bennett

5, 6 A photographer's self-promotional advertisement specially shot for the magazine *Select* as full-page insertions. (BRD)
7 Full-page magazine advertisement in full colour for a *Pentax* camera. (FRA)
8 Full-page advertisement for a *Kodak* sales promotion on dual film packs. (SWI)
9, 10 Newspaper ads in black and white by the Japan Newspapers' and Editors' Association. Theme: the dialogue between newspapers and their readers. (JPN)
11 Double spread advertising *Kodak* films, "The Professionals". (AUS)

5, 6 Eigenwerbungs-Anzeigen des Photographen mit Aufnahmen, die speziell für die Zeitschrift *Select* hergestellt wurden. (BRD)
7 Ganzseitige, mehrfarbige Zeitschriften-Anzeige für eine *Pentax*-Kamera. (FRA)
8 Ganzseitige Anzeige mit Angebot für *Kodak*-Filme im Duopack. Mehrfarbig. (SWI)
9, 10 Schwarzweisse Zeitungs-Inserate der Japan Newspapers' and Editors' Association. Themen dieser Anzeigen ist der Dialog zwischen Zeitung und Lesern. (JPN)
11 Doppelseitige Anzeige für *Kodak*-Filme, «Die Professionellen». (AUS)

5, 6 Annonces autopromotionnelles du photographe, illustrées de clichés réalisés pour le magazine *Select*. (BRD)
7 Annonce de magazine polychrome, pleine page, pour un appareil photo *Pentax*. (FRA)
8 Annonce pleine page pour un paquet de deux films *Kodak*. Polychromie. (SWI)
9, 10 Annonces de journaux noir et blanc pour la Japan Newspapers' and Editors' Association, sur le thème du dialogue nécessaire avec les lecteurs. (JPN)
11 Annonce double page pour les films *Kodak*, «les professionnels». (AUS)

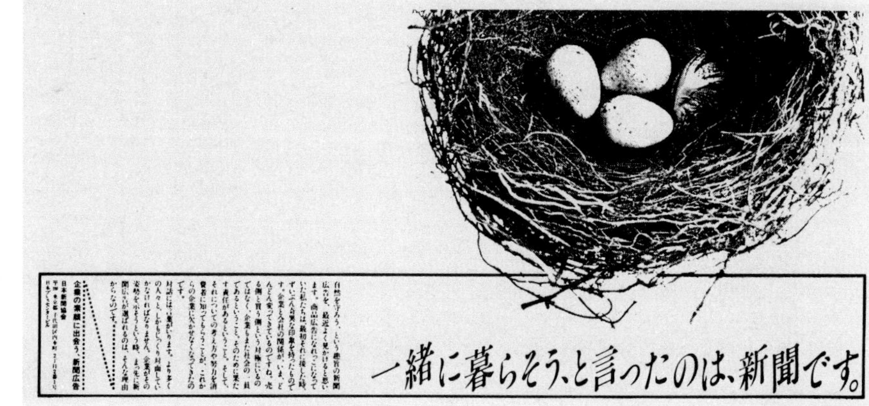

9

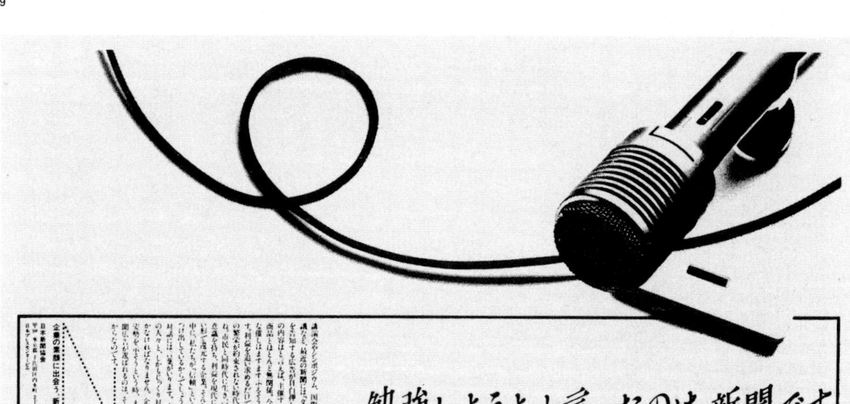

10

Advertisements/Anzeigen/Annonces

Horizon as key to color dimension. Kodak Ektachrome 64 professional film.

Photography has the power to record images, some of them irresistible, some of them not. The impact so often depends on the subtlety and dimension of color.

Those very nuances that make the difference in truly memorable photography.

Kodak Ektachrome 64 professional film is a nonpareil for general photography. Excellent color, improved sharpness and low graininess give superb image quality.

Balanced for daylight, electronic or blue flash, this film gives clean highlights under every circumstance.

It can be processed in your own darkroom, giving complete control over the creative process.

Kodak Ektachrome 64 professional film comes in a range of sizes, including 135 and 120 rolls, 35mm long rolls and sheets in three sizes.

The Professionals.

11

12

13

PHOTOGRAPHER / PHOTOGRAPH / PHOTOGRAPHE:

12 Image Bank
13 Alf Dietrich
14 Walo Kuhn/Swissairphoto
15, 16 Jay Maisel

DESIGNER / GESTALTER / MAQUETTISTE:

12–14 Ernst Baechtold

ART DIRECTOR / DIRECTEUR ARTISTIQUE:

12–14 Ernst Baechtold
15, 16 Anne Prochaska

AGENCY / AGENTUR / AGENCE – STUDIO:

12–14 GGK
15, 16 Vansant Dugdale & Co.

Ein Bild von einem Auftrag, den uns jeder erteilen kann.

Diese Flugaufnahme haben wir bei Sévery aus 80 m Höhe gemacht. Den Auftrag hätten Sie uns erteilen können. Denn auch für Sie gehen wir in die Luft, wenn Sie eine Flugaufnahme vom schönsten Fleckchen Erde haben möchten. Von einem ganz bestimmten Gebäude. Von einer Gemeinde. Von der Firma. Von einem Ferienort. Von der Sportanlage. Oder von irgend etwas. Für eine Broschüre. Für den Geschäftsbericht. Oder für die Empfangshalle, das Sitzungszimmer oder die Schulungsräume. Oder für eine Ausstellung. Oder für ein Inserat.

Vielleicht finden Sie die Flugaufnahme, die Sie brauchen, aber auch in unserem Archiv. Es umfasst etwa 50 000 Flugfotos aus der ganzen Schweiz, schwarzweiss oder farbig. Von den Anfängen der Fliegerei bis zur Gegenwart. Von den Aufnahmen können Sie Vergrösserungen in jedem Format haben. So gross wie die grösste Wand des grössten Zimmers.
Rufen Sie uns an. Oder kommen Sie bei uns vorbei. Wir möchten uns gern ein Bild von Ihren Ideen machen.

swissair Photo+Vermessungen AG
Postfach, 8035 Zürich, Stampfenbachstrasse 75, Telefon 01 363 33 33.

14

15

12, 13 Full-colour double spreads advertise specific *Swissair* routes: Fig. 12 shows a painted doorway in Lisbon, and Fig. 13 displays the national cheeses of countries on its European route. (SWI)
14 A double spread ad that typifies another *Swissair* service: aerial photography and surveys. (SWI)
15, 16 Actual size of shot, used as shown, in double-spread ad from a campaign in trade magazines for *Westinghouse* defence systems. (USA)

12, 13 Beispiele von doppelseitigen *Swissair*-Anzeigen. Abb. 12: Eine portugiesische Tür; Abb. 13: Berühmte Käse-Herstellerländer auf der *Swissair*-Europa-Route. (SWI)
14 *Swissair* bietet mit dieser Anzeige ihre Luftaufnahmen- und Vermessungsdienste an. (SWI)
15, 16 Aufnahme in Originalgrösse und vollständige doppelseitige Anzeige aus einer Fachzeitschriften-Kampagne für *Westinghouse*-Verteidigungssysteme. (USA)

12, 13 Exemples d'annonces *Swissair* sur double page. Fig. 12: une porte portugaise; fig. 13: des pays connus pour leur production fromagère sur la route européenne de *Swissair*. (SWI)
14 Dans cette annonce, *Swissair* offre ses services de photographie et cartographie. (SWI)
15, 16 Photo au format original et annonce double page complète pour une campagne *Westinghouse* destinée à vanter dans les revues spécialisées les mérites de divers systèmes de défense. (USA)

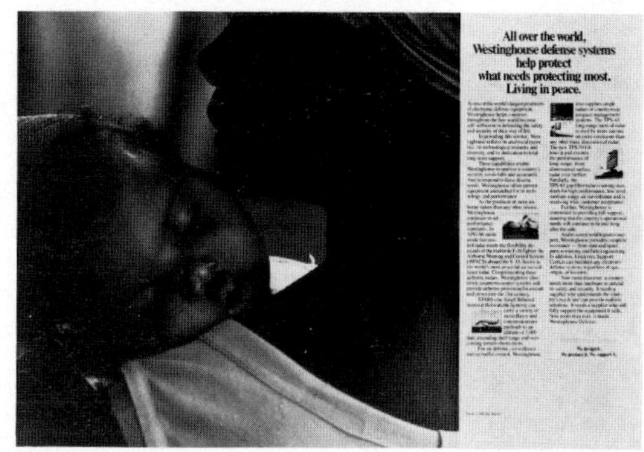

16

17

18

17, 18 Travellers are led to compare the many negatives of doing their own driving with all the joys of leaving that to a locomotive of the West German Federal Railway, by its campaign of colour ads in magazine double spreads. Fig. 17 recalls the saying that "Travellers should not be delayed", and Fig. 18 signposts the "Last exit before motorway". (GER)
19 Interest rates grow annually, too, in Post Office banking: colour double spread. (GER)
20 To attract entrants for a competition aimed at young "science reporters", this plug-and-nib motif was used in a full-page colour ad by a foundation for explorative youth. (GER)
21 Full-page colour ad for *Singapore Airlines*: good food's a good deal for businessmen. (SWI)
22 Finger-painting that highlights the colour range of TV sets made by *Mediator*. (SWI)
23 To emphasize that its schedules are not affected by winter weather, the Swiss Federal Railway illustrated a snowed-in car. For legal reasons, an old model was used. (SWI)

17, 18 Reisende sollten überlegen, ob sie die vielen Nachteile des Autofahrens in Kauf nehmen oder lieber die Vorteile der Deutschen Bundesbahn geniessen wollen. Doppelseitige, mehrfarbige Anzeigen aus einer Werbekampagne der DB. (GER)
19 «Sparen mit wachsendem Zins» als Anreiz, ein Sparkonto bei der Bundespost zu eröffnen. (GER)
20 Bekanntgabe eines Wettbewerbs der «Stiftung Jugend forscht», für den Manuskripte unter dem Motto «Wissenschaft aus der Feder» eingesandt werden sollen. (GER)
21 Mehrfarbige Anzeige, welche für die Langstreckenflüge der *Singapore Airlines* wirbt. (SWI)
22 Beispiel aus einer Anzeigen-Kampagne für *Mediator*-Fernsehgeräte, in der besonders auf die verschiedenen vorhandenen Farbausführungen hingewiesen wird. (SWI)
23 Ganzseitige Anzeige der Schweizerischen Bundesbahnen, deren Fahrpläne auch im Winter «nicht aus dem Takt fallen». Aus rechtlichen Gründen wurde absichtlich ein altes VW-Modell verwendet. (SWI)

20

21

19

PHOTOGRAPHER / PHOTOGRAPH:

17, 18 Clive Davies
20 Holger Matthies
21 Willie Tang
22 Daniel Gendre

DESIGNER / GESTALTER / MAQUETTISTE:

17, 18 Matthias Kersten
20 Holger Matthies
22 Dominik Burckhardt
23 Mathias Bapst

ART DIRECTOR / DIRECTEUR ARTISTIQUE:

17, 18 Alan Telfer-Layton
20 Peter Sternberg
21 John Finn
22 Dominik Burckhardt
23 Mathias Bapst

AGENCY / AGENTUR / AGENCE – STUDIO:

17, 18 McCann-Erickson GmbH
19 Lintas
21 Batey Advertising
22 Burckhardt, Lüdi
23 Young & Rubicam

17, 18 Les voyageurs sont invités à un moment de réflexion: pourquoi accepter les nombreux inconvénients d'un déplacement en voiture, alors que le train n'offre que des avantages? Annonces double page polychromes pour une campagne des Chemins de fer fédéraux allemands. (GER)
19 «L'épargne à intérêt croissant», voilà ce que promet l'ouverture d'un compte PTT. (GER)
20 Annonce d'un concours de la Fondation «Jugend forscht» (La Jeunesse fait de la recherche), invitant les jeunes à soumettre des manuscrits scientifiques pour publication. (GER)
21 Annonce polychrome en faveur des vols des long-courriers de *Singapore Airlines*. (SWI)
22 Exemple d'une campagne d'annonces pour les téléviseurs *Mediator* où l'on met l'accent sur la diversité des coloris disponibles. (SWI)
23 Annonce pleine page des Chemins de fer fédéraux suisses, dont les horaires cadencés ne varient pas en fonction des intempéries. Vieux modèle VW, pour des raisons juridiques. (SWI)

Advertisements/Anzeigen/Annonces

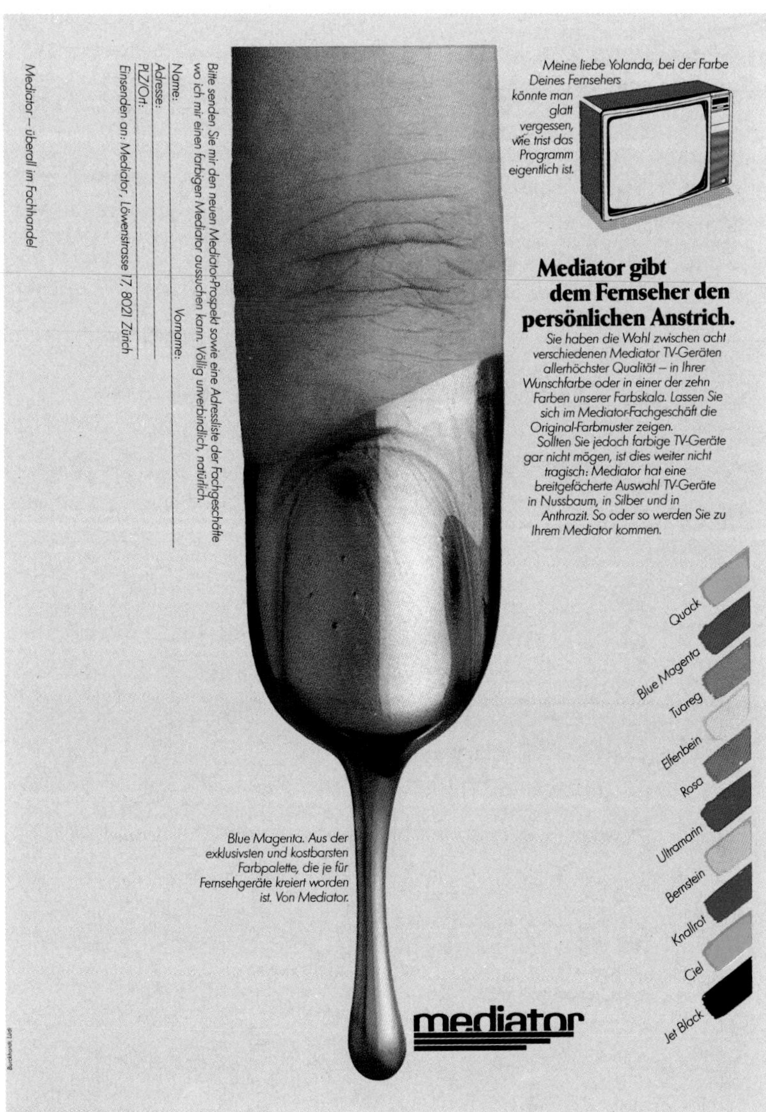

22

23

皐風晴童。

24

Advertisements/Anzeigen/Annonces

25

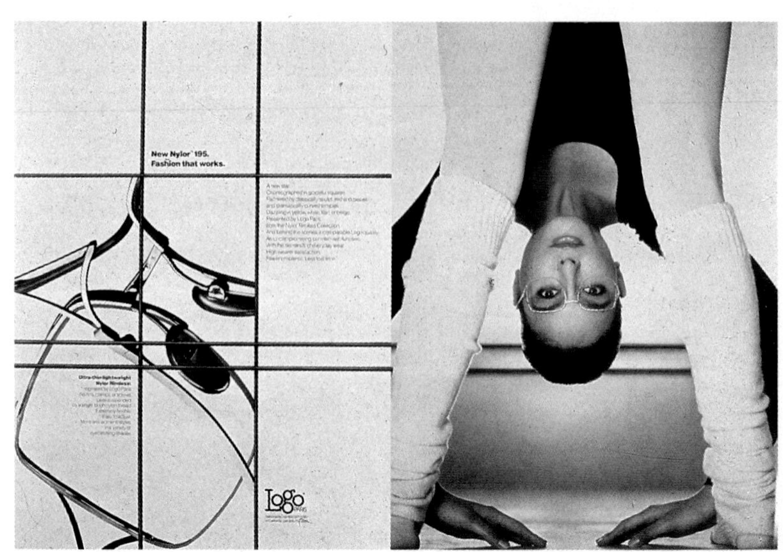

26

PHOTOGRAPHER / PHOTOGRAPH / PHOTOGRAPHE:

24 Hiroyuki Yamamoto
25 Ronnie Poon
26 Michael Utterbach/George Brown
27–29 Stone & Staccati

DESIGNER / GESTALTER / MAQUETTISTE:

24 Kyoko Chiba
26 Cassie Leng
27–29 Jerry Berman/Sidjakov Berman & Gomez

ART DIRECTOR / DIRECTEUR ARTISTIQUE:

24 Kazuo Saito
25 Kris Knight
26 Cassie Leng
27–29 Jerry Berman

AGENCY / AGENTUR / AGENCE – STUDIO:

24 Yomiko Advertising Inc.
25 Macy's Advertising
26 Humpal, Leftwich & Sinn
27–29 Jolene Hammons Advertising

24 Full-page advertisement for the sale of private apartments surrounded by greenery. (JPN)
25 From a series of double-spread ads in full colour for *Macy's* Gift Department, here displaying stoneware carrying the "Normandy" motif. (USA)
26 The rimless "Nylor" glasses stay in place, even head-over-heels ... at exercise. (USA)
27–29 From a series of full-page advertisements in full colour for products that, as in Fig. 26, are "dependable in every situation": those made by *Dependable Furniture*. (USA)

24 Ganzseitige Anzeige für den Verkauf von im Grünen gelegenen Eigentumswohnungen. (JPN)
25 Aus einer Serie von doppelseitigen Anzeigen mit mehrfarbigen Aufnahmen für *Macy's* Geschenkabteilung; hier für Steingut-Geschirr mit dem Design «Normandie». (USA)
26 Die randlose Brille «Nylor» hält auch bei Ballettübungen mit «hängendem Kopf». (USA)
27–29 «*Dependable* Möbel sind in jeder Situation zuverlässig.» Aus einer Serie von ganzseitigen, mehrfarbigen Anzeigen für *Dependable Furniture*. (USA)

24 Annonce pleine page pour la vente d'appartements en copropriété en zone de verdure. (JPN)
25 Exemple d'une série d'annonces double page illustrées de photos polychromes, pour le département cadeaux de *Macy's*, ici pour de la vaisselle de grès de la gamme «Normandie». (USA)
26 Les lunettes sans monture «Nylor» restent en place même la tête en bas. (USA)
27–29 «Les meubles *Dependable* sont à l'épreuve de toute situation.» Exemples d'annonces polychromes pleine page publiées dans une série réalisée pour *Dependable Furniture*. (USA)

27

28

29

30

31

32

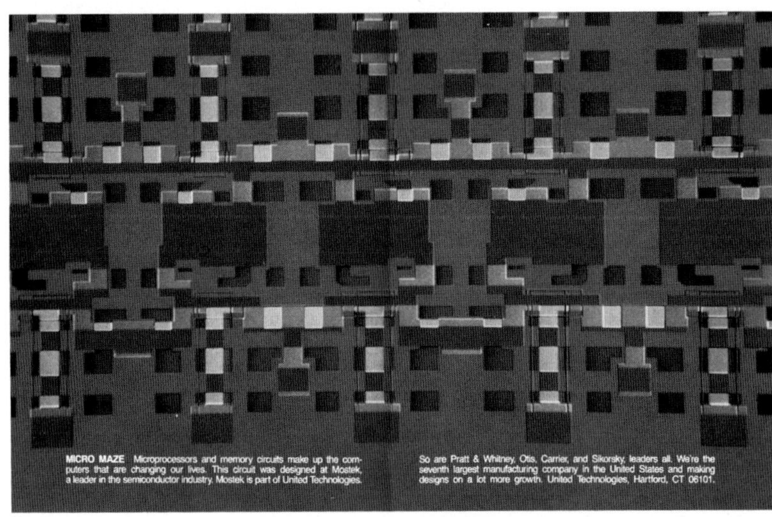

33

Advertisements/Anzeigen/Annonces

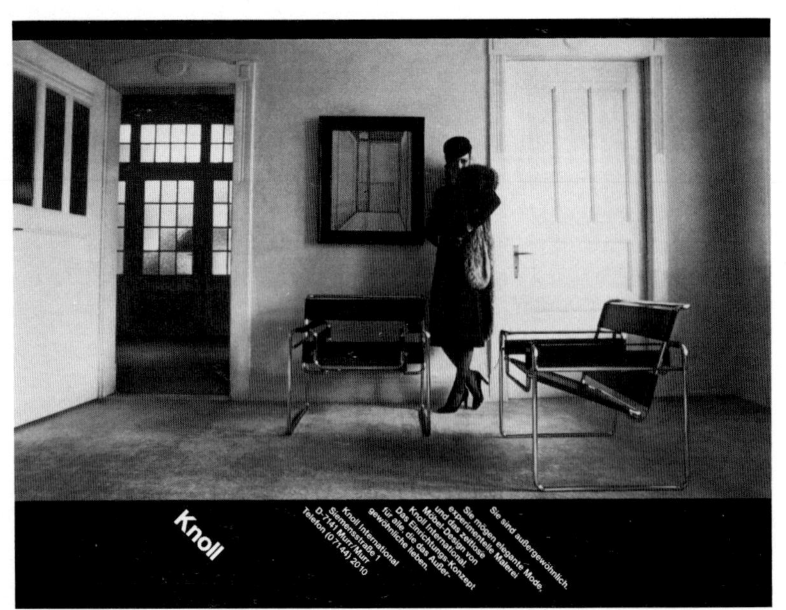

34

35

36a

PHOTOGRAPHER / PHOTOGRAPH:

30 Werner Eisele
31 Pierre Berger
32, 33 Jay Maisel
34 Richard Schenkirz
35 Jacques Primois
36, 36a Hickson-Bender

DESIGNER / GESTALTER:

31 Manfred Siegler/ Dorothea Steinhof
32, 33 William Wondriska
34, 35 Rudolf Beck

ART DIRECTOR:

30 Wolfgang Brüggemann
31 Paul Bodo Köchel
32, 33 Gordon Bowman
34, 35 Wolf Kaiser
36, 36a Doug Fisher

36

30 This full-colour double spread by *Kodak* announces its most sensitive film. (GER)
31 Full-colour double spread for plastic window-frames that "let the forest be". (GER)
32, 33 Corporate campaign in full-colour double spreads by United Technologies Corporation. The illustrations relate to the specific work done by some of its companies. (USA)
34, 35 Two-colour spreads for *Knoll International* furniture aimed at potential buyers of exceptional taste, a liking for experimental painting and also for timeless design. (GER)
36, 36a In this illustration for a full-page ad (Fig. 36a), the leaping salmon symbolize design ideas spawned by *Nevamar* with its decorative laminates for covering surfaces. (USA)

AGENCY / AGENTUR / AGENCE:

30 Lintas
31 COMmunication Agency Köchel GmbH
32, 33 United Technologies/ In House
36, 36a Lord Sullivan & Yoder

30 Doppelseitige Anzeige für einen extrem lichtempfindlichen Farbnegativfilm von *Kodak*. (GER)
31 Doppelseitige Anzeige aus einer Kampagne für *Kömmerling*-Kunststoff-Fensterrahmen. (GER)
32, 33 Mehrfarbige, doppelseitige Anzeigen aus einer Image-Kampagne der United Technologies Corp., der mehrere Firmen angehören. Themen sind die verschiedenen Unternehmensbereiche. (USA)
34, 35 Zwei Anzeigen für Möbel von *Knoll International*. Appelliert wird an den exklusiven Geschmack der Käufer(innen). Abb. 34: Blau/schwarz; Abb. 35: Gelb/schwarz. (GER)
36, 36a Aufnahme und vollständige ganzseitige Anzeige für *Nevamar*-Boden- und Wandbeläge. Die springenden Lachse symbolisieren die phantasievollen Design-Ideen der Firma. (USA)

30 Annonce double page pour un film négatif couleur ultrasensible de *Kodak*. (GER)
31 Annonce double page: campagne pour les châssis de fenêtres *Kömmerling* en plastique. (GER)
32, 33 Annonces polychromes double page pour une campagne de prestige de la United Technologies Corp. Thème: les divers domaines d'activité de ce groupe d'entreprises. (USA)
34, 35 Deux annonces pour les meubles *Knoll International*. On s'y adresse au goût infaillible de la clientèle éclairée. Fig. 34: bleu, noir; fig. 35: jaune, noir. (GER)
36, 36a Photo et annonce pleine page complète pour les sols et revêtements *Nevamar*. Le saut des saumons symbolise les idées originales de l'entreprise en matière de design. (USA)

37

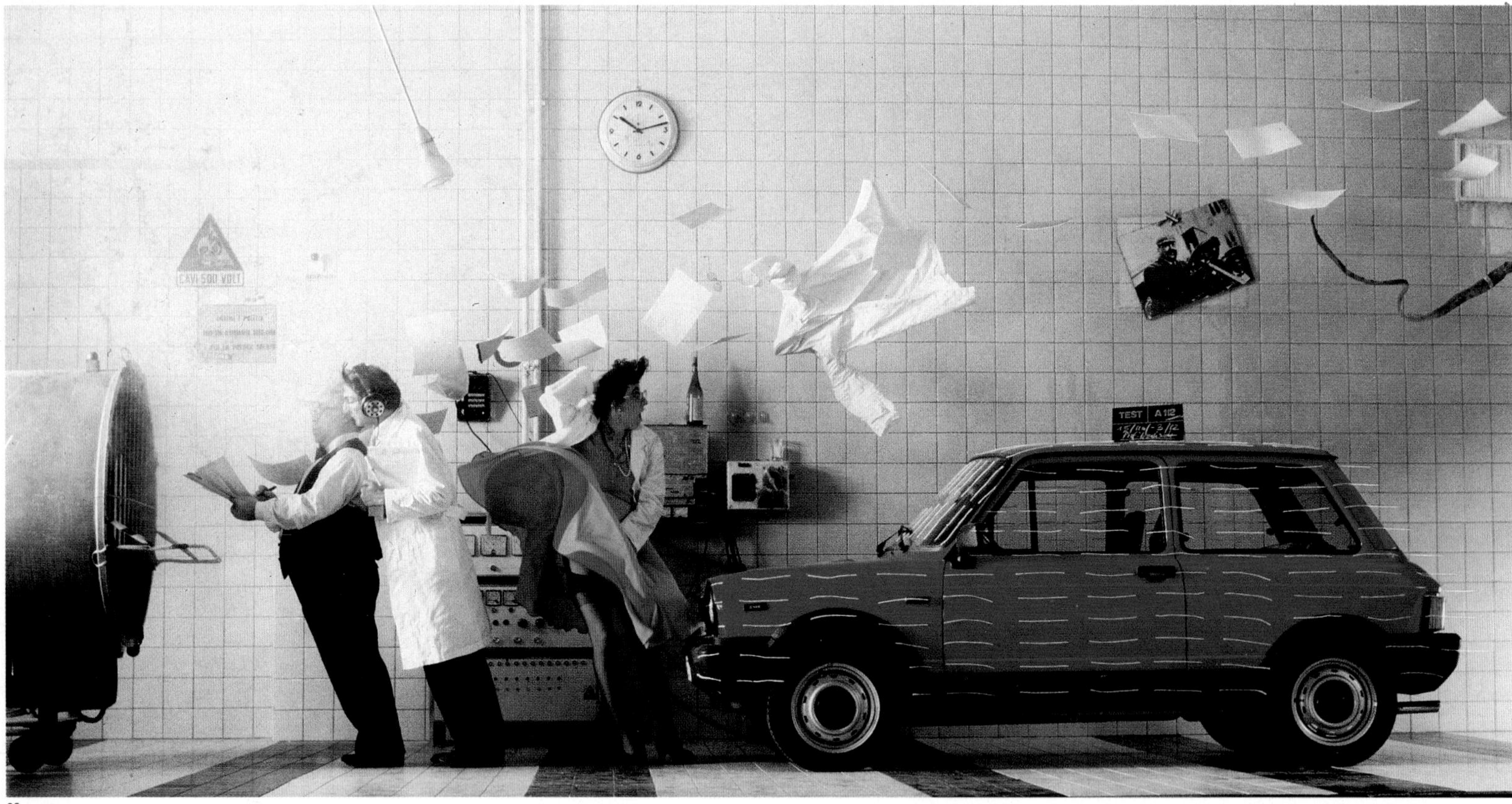

38

PHOTOGRAPHER / PHOTOGRAPH / PHOTOGRAPHE:

37–39 Ben Oyne
40 Ramón Giovanni
41 Tom Martin
42 Robert Keeling
43 Peter Hendrie

DESIGNER / GESTALTER / MAQUETTISTE:

37–39 Uli Weber
40 Ramón Giovanni
42 Jeff Barnes
43 Garry Emery

39

Advertisements/Anzeigen

ART DIRECTOR:

37–39 Uli Weber
40 Ramón Giovanni
41 Callie Crosby
42 Jeff Barnes
43 Garry Emery

AGENCY / AGENTUR / AGENCE:

37–39 Leonhardt & Kern
40 Ramón Giovanni
41 Lenac, Warford, Stone
42 Barnes Design Office
43 Emery Vincent Associates

40

41

42

43

37–39 The ad campaign in double spreads for *Lancia*: Fig. 37 shows "the car that really belongs in the Museum of Modern Art", and Fig. 38 illustrates how it is as quick as the wind in reaching high speed. (GER)
40 A full-page ad for *Kodak* film. Yellow on blue. (COL)
41 Full-page advertisement for *Yamaha* skis. White suit with red. (USA)
42 Black-and white ad for the opening of *City*, a store in Chicago. (USA)
43 Full-page ad visualizing the protection given by *Glaxo* drugs for skin diseases: green "Bearded Dragon" on human skin. (AUS)

37–39 Aus einer Kampagne mit doppelseitigen Anzeigen für *Lancia*. Abb. 37: «Das Auto, das eigentlich ins Museum of Modern Art gehört.» Abb. 38 weist auf die speziell windschlüpfrige Karosserie des «Aprilia»-Modells hin. (GER)
40 Ganzseitige Zeitschriften-Anzeige für *Kodak*. Gelb auf Blau. (COL)
41 *Yamaha* wirbt mit dieser ganzseitigen Anzeige für Skis. (USA)
42 Ganzseitige Schwarzweiss-Anzeige für die Eröffnung eines Geschäfts. (USA)
43 Mehrfarbige, ganzseitige Zeitschriften-Anzeige für Medikamente gegen Hauterkrankungen. «Bärtiger Drache» auf menschlicher Haut. (AUS)

37–39 Annonces double page dans une campagne pour *Lancia*. Fig. 37: «L'auto qui devrait en somme figurer au Musée d'art moderne.» La fig. 38 met en évidence le profil particulièrement aérodynamique du modèle «Aprilia». (GER)
40 Annonce de magazine pleine page pour *Kodak*. Jaune sur bleu. (COL)
41 Dans cette annonce pleine page, *Yamaha* fait de la pub pour ses skis. (USA)
42 Annonce noir-blanc pleine page pour l'ouverture d'un magasin. (USA)
43 Annonce de magazine polychrome, pleine page, pour des remèdes contre les dermatoses. «Dragon barbu» sur peau humaine. (AUS)

PHOTOGRAPHER / PHOTOGRAPH:

44 Jean-Paul Seaulieu
45 Stak Aivaliotis
46 Alexander Carroux
47 Ian Giles
48 Ilmari Kostiainen

DESIGNER / GESTALTER:

46 Atelier Barth
48 Kari Torkler

ART DIRECTOR:

44 Eric Derchain
45 Rob Morris
46 Klaus Barth
47 Gordon Smith
48 Kari Torkler

AGENCY / AGENTUR / AGENCE:

44 Tobago
45 Brignull Le Bas
46 Atelier Barth
47 Gold Greenlees Trott Ltd
48 Asanti Konttinen Torkler Oy

44

45

46

47

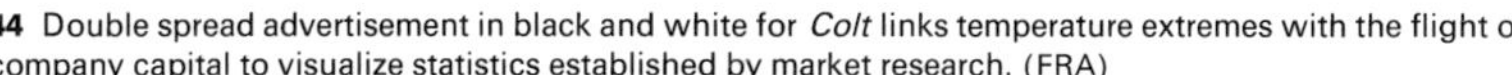

44 Double spread advertisement in black and white for *Colt* links temperature extremes with the flight of company capital to visualize statistics established by market research. (FRA)
45 Full-page newspaper ad in black and white for *Scandinavian Airlines* announcing its new EuroClass for businessmen. (GBR)
46 Full-page trade ad by BASF announces new dyes to bulk buyers. Brown, bronze, blue. (GER)
47 Full-page newspaper ad in black and white: the London Docklands Development Corporation exaggerates the hectic to-and-fro of business travel outside its area. (GBR)
48 Full-page magazine ad in full colour used by the Finnish Art Directors' Club to advertise its 1981 annual, which had this illustration on its dust jacket. (FIN)

44 Doppelseitige Anzeige in Schwarzweiss. Dank *Colt*-Ventilatoren sollen die Angestellten effizienter arbeiten, soll das Kapital weniger «davonfliegen». (FRA)
45 Ganzseitiges Zeitungsinserat für die skandinavische Luftlinie SAS, zur Einführung einer Spezialklasse für Geschäftsleute. (GBR)
46 Ganzseitige Fachzeitschriften-Anzeige für Lederflüssigfarbstoffe. Mehrfarbig. (GER)
47 Die London Docklands werden mit diesem Inserat als Geschäftsdomizil angepriesen. (GBR)
48 Mit dieser Aufnahme wirbt der Finnische Art Directors Club für das Jahrbuch 1981. Das Photo wurde auch für den Umschlag des Buches verwendet. (FIN)

44 Annonce double page, noir et blanc. Grâce aux ventilateurs *Colt*, les employés sont censés travailler mieux, et les capitaux fuir un peu moins. (FRA)
45 Annonce de journal pleine page pour la compagnie aérienne scandinave SAS, annonçant l'introduction d'une classe spéciale pour hommes d'affaires. (GBR)
46 Annonce de revue professionnelle, pleine page, polychrome: colorants cuir liquides. (GER)
47 Annonce de journal pleine page invitant les firmes à se domicilier à London Docklands. (GBR)
48 Cette photo, qui figure en couverture de l'annuaire 1981 de l'Art Directors Club finlandais, sert à faire de la publicité pour cette publication. (FIN)

48

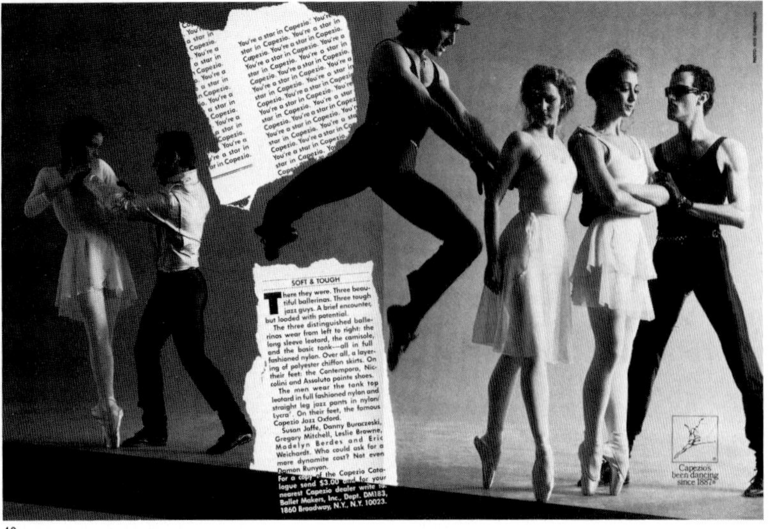

SOFT & TOUGH
There they were. Three beautiful ballerinas. Three tough jazz guys. A brief encounter, but loaded with potential.
The three distinguished ballerinas wear from left to right: the long sleeve leotard, the camisole, and the basic tank—all in full fashioned nylon. Over all, a layering of polyester chiffon skirts. On their feet: the Contempora, Niccolini and Assoluto pointe shoes.
The men wear the tank top leotard in full fashioned nylon and straight leg jazz pants in nylon/Lycra®. On their feet, the famous Capezio Jazz Oxford.
Susan Jaffe, Danny Buraczeski, Gregory Mitchell, Leslie Browne, Madelyn Berdes and Eric Weichardt. Who could ask for a more dynamite cast? Not even Damon Runyon.
For a copy of the Capezio Catalogue send $3.00 and for your nearest Capezio dealer write to: Ballet Makers, Inc., Dept. DM183, 1860 Broadway, N.Y., N.Y. 10023.
Capezio's been dancing since 1887®

49

You're a Star in Capezio®
Valentina Kozlova and Leonid Kozlov, graduates of the Bolshoi Ballet School, danced as principals with the Bolshoi Ballet Company. Since then, they have danced around the world. And now, they add a new chapter to their saga as principals with the New York City Ballet.
Valentina wears the shirred neck leotard in Silky Stretch nylon/Lycra®, Chiffon Wrap Skirt, Hold and Stretch Tights and her beloved Capezio® toe shoes. Leonid wears the cotton/Lycra® Tank with the new nylon Performance Weight Tights and the famous Russian Ballet Slippers.
Gifted, vital, striking: they will be adding more dramatic chapters to an already remarkable story.
For your Capezio Catalogue, send $1.00 and for your nearest Capezio dealer, write to: Ballet Makers, Inc., Dept. DM683, 1860 Broadway, New York, New York 10023.
Capezio's been dancing since 1887®

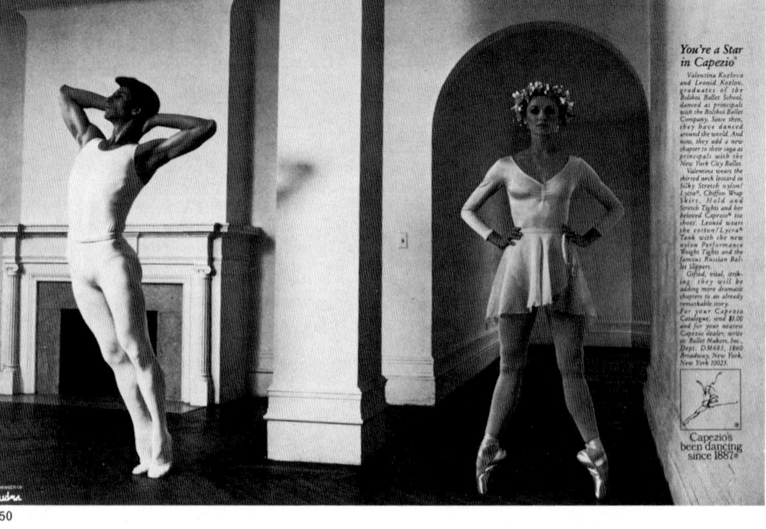

50

49, 50 Double-page magazine spreads in full colour advertising ballet clothes and shoes by *Capezio* (see also Fig. 52). All the models were recruited from renowned ballet corps: Fig. 49, the seven-member ensemble, "Soft & Tough" (below, as a newspaper tearout, is the only ad copy); Fig. 50, "The Kozlovs", two members of the Bolshoi Ballet. (USA)

51 From the advertising campaign, "Express yourself softly", for clothes by *Kathryn Conover*, here in pink with white in dim bluish light. (USA)

52 "You're a star in *Capezio*": another double-spread magazine advertisement for these ballet clothes (see Figs. 49, 50), here worn by seven members of the Paul Taylor Dance Company. (USA)

53, 53a Double-page magazine spread for a manufacturer of clothing. (JPN)

49, 50 Doppelseitige, mehrfarbige Zeitschriften-Anzeigen für Ballettbekleidung samt Schuhen von *Capezio*. Gezeigt werden berühmte Tanztruppen; Abb. 49: Die siebenköpfige Tanztruppe «Soft & Tough». Der ganze Werbetext ist im unteren ausgerissenen Stück Zeitung enthalten. Abb. 50: «Die Kozlovs», ein russisches Tänzerpaar des Bolschoi Balletts. Siehe auch Abb. 52. (USA)

51 Aus einer Anzeigenkampagne für *Kathryn-Conover*-Bekleidung: «Drück dich sanft aus.» Kleider in Rosa mit Weiss; bläuliches Dämmerlicht. (USA)

52 «*Capezio* macht dich zum Star.» Eine weitere doppelseitige Anzeige für Ballettbekleidung, getragen von sieben Mitgliedern der Paul Taylor Dance Company. Siehe auch Abb. 49, 50. (USA)

53, 53a Doppelseitige Zeitschriften-Anzeige für eine Bekleidungsfirma. (JPN)

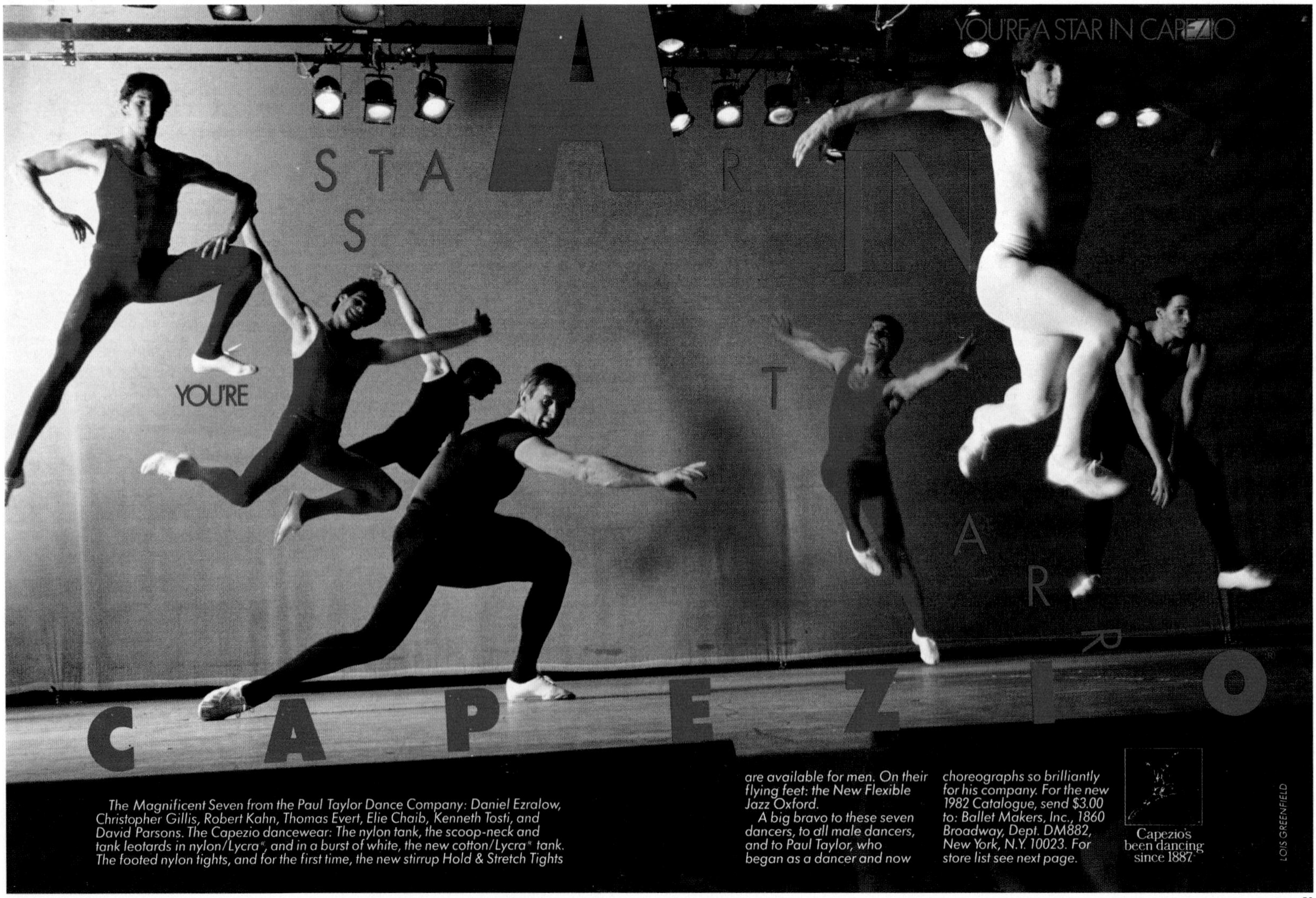
YOU'RE A STAR IN CAPEZIO
YOU'RE
A
STAR
IN
CAPEZIO
The Magnificent Seven from the Paul Taylor Dance Company: Daniel Ezralow, Christopher Gillis, Robert Kahn, Thomas Evert, Elie Chaib, Kenneth Tosti, and David Parsons. The Capezio dancewear: The nylon tank, the scoop-neck and tank leotards in nylon/Lycra®, and in a burst of white, the new cotton/Lycra® tank. The footed nylon tights, and for the first time, the new stirrup Hold & Stretch Tights are available for men. On their flying feet: the New Flexible Jazz Oxford.
A big bravo to these seven dancers, to all male dancers, and to Paul Taylor, who began as a dancer and now choreographs so brilliantly for his company. For the new 1982 Catalogue, send $3.00 to: Ballet Makers, Inc., 1860 Broadway, Dept. DM882, New York, N.Y. 10023. For store list see next page.
Capezio's been dancing since 1887®
LOIS GREENFIELD

52

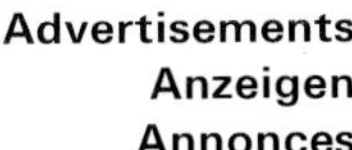

51

PHOTOGRAPHER / PHOTOGRAPH / PHOTOGRAPHE:

49, 50, 52 Lois Greenfield
51 Deborah Turbeville
53, 53a Keiichi Hagiwara

DESIGNER / GESTALTER / MAQUETTISTE:

49, 50, 52 Frank Young
53, 53a Hiroshi Ninomiya/Yoshiko Kuwabara

ART DIRECTOR / DIRECTEUR ARTISTIQUE:

49, 50, 52 Frank Young
51 David Wenman
53, 53a Hiroshi Ninomiya

AGENCY / AGENTUR / AGENCE – STUDIO:

49, 50, 52 Ovesey & Co.
51 David Wenman

49, 50 Annonces polychromes de magazines, sur double page, pour les tenues et chaussons de ballet *Capezio*. On y présente des corps de ballet célèbres: fig. 49, les sept danseurs de la compagnie «Soft & Tough», le texte publicitaire figurant sur le bout de journal arraché; fig. 50: «Les Kozlov», un couple de danseurs du Bolchoï. Voir aussi la fig. 52. (USA)
51 Exemple d'annonce dans une campagne en faveur des robes *Kathryn Conover*. «Exprime-toi doucement.» Robes roses, avec du blanc; lumière crépusculaire bleue. (USA)
52 «*Capezio* fait de toi une star.» Une autre annonce double page pour des tenues de ballet portées cette fois-ci par sept danseurs de la Paul Taylor Dance Company. Cf. 49, 50. (USA)
53, 53a Annonce de magazine double page pour une maison de confection. (JPN)

53a

53

Advertisements/Anzeigen/Annonces

PHOTOGRAPHER / PHOTOGRAPH:

54, 55 Ballo & Ballo
56, 58 Jean-Paul Seaulieu
57, 59, 60 Jost Wildbolz

DESIGNER / GESTALTER:

57 Kreativ-Team Ulrich & Fehlmann
59, 60 Franz Merlicek

ART DIRECTOR:

56, 58 Marc Ayrault
59, 60 Franz Merlicek

AGENCY / AGENTUR / AGENCE:

54, 55 G & R Pubblicità
56, 58 R2 C
57 Kreativ-Team Ulrich & Fehlmann
59, 60 Demner & Merlicek

54

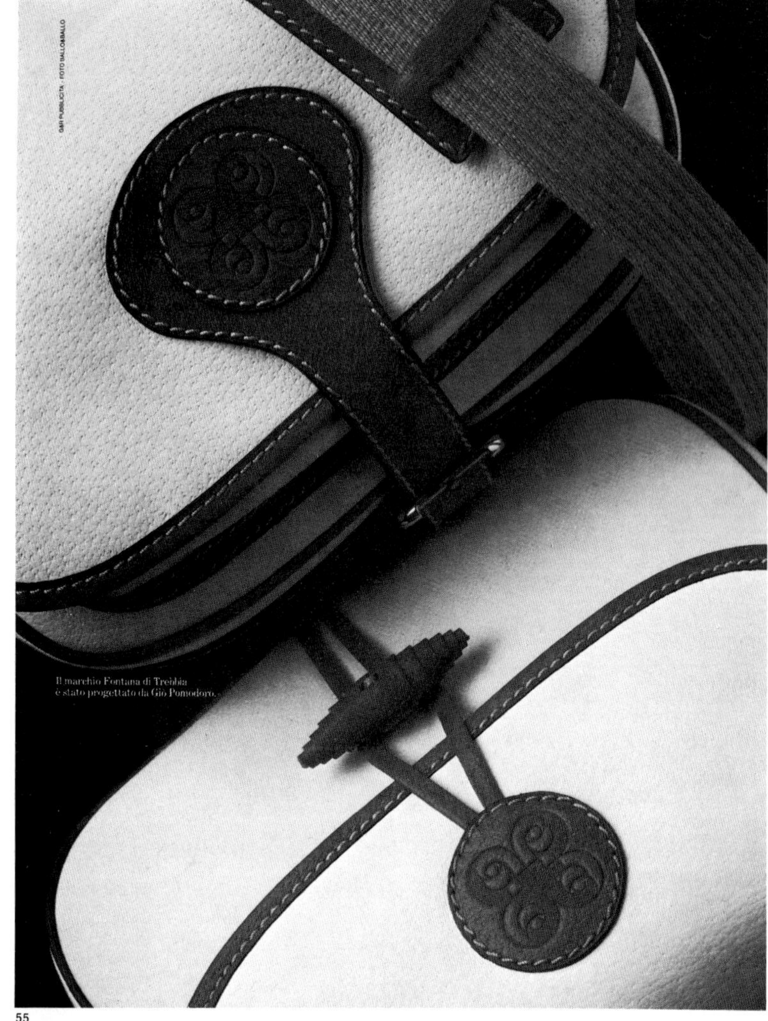

55

56

54, 55 The double-spread ad and its full-colour page which highlight the exclusive points that distinguish handbags by *Fontana di Trebbia*: choice leathers in choice colours, plus the perfection of detail and technique. (ITA)
56 The illustration to an ad in a French magazine for a *Skiss* combi ski suit. (FRA)
57 Cover of a three-page gatefold ad in magazines to advertise *Sawaco* silk undies. Soft tones of brown and beige with brand name in white. (SWI)
58 Illustration of full-page ad in full color for an exclusive sable poncho by *Splitz*. This shot was taken against a background of stark black and white. (FRA)
59, 60 From a series of full-page ads in black and white for *Lady Manhattan* fashion clothes for women. Here, the theme of both ads was classical music. (AUT)

54, 55 Ganzseitige, mehrfarbige Aufnahme und vollständige doppelseitige Zeitschriften-Anzeige für Taschen von *Fontana di Trebbia*. Hervorgehoben wird die Exklusivität des Leders und der Farben, die perfekte Detail-Verarbeitung und technische Raffinesse. (ITA)
56 Aufnahme aus einer Zeitschriften-Anzeige für einen Skianzug der Marke *Skiss*. (FRA)
57 Vorderseite einer dreiseitigen Zeitschriften-Anzeige für Seidenunterwäsche der Marke *Sawaco*. Zarte Braun- und Beige-Töne, Markenname weiss. (SWI)
58 Zeitschriften-Anzeige für einen Zobel-Poncho der gehobenen Preisklasse von *Splitz*. (FRA)
59, 60 Aus einer Serie von ganzseitigen Zeitschriften-Anzeigen in Schwarzweiss für *Lady-Manhattan*-Kleider. Das zentrale Thema der Kampagne ist klassische Musik. (AUT)

54, 55 Photo polychrome pleine page et annonce de magazine double page complète pour les sacs *Fontana di Trebbia*. On y souligne le caractère exclusif du cuir et des coloris, le raffinement de l'exécution de détail et le nec-plus-ultra technique de ces articles de grand prix. (ITA)
56 Photo illustrant une annonce de journal: publicité pour une tenue de ski marque *Skiss*. (FRA)
57 Première page d'une annonce de magazine sur trois pages pour les dessous en soie de *Sawaco*. Divers bruns et beiges atténués, nom de la marque en blanc. (SWI)
58 Annonce de magazine pour un poncho de zibeline de grand prix fabriqué par *Splitz*. (FRA)
59, 60 Exemples d'annonces de magazines noir et blanc, pleine page, dans une campagne réalisée pour les vêtements *Lady Manhattan*. La campagne tout entière est axée sur un thème central: la musique classique. (AUT)

57

58

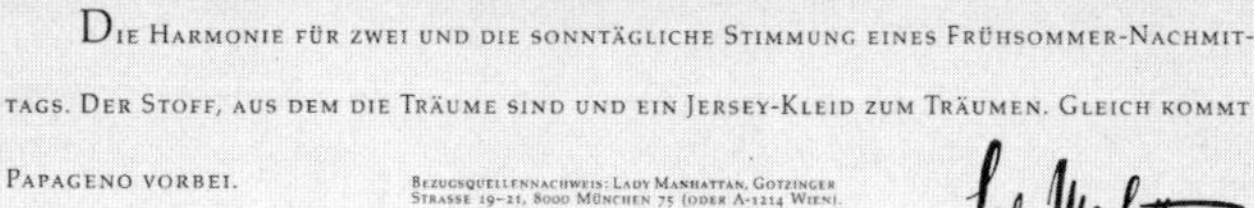

59

Lieben Sie Klassik? Klassisch das Plissee der Bluse mit dem samtenen Band. Samten auch das Licht, die Stimmung, der Augenblick. Wenn Herbert den Taktstock weglegt, hat er die Lady ganz klassisch im Arm. Und das Konzert im Ohr.

Bezugsquellennachweis: Lady Manhattan, Gotzinger Strasse 19–21, 8000 München 75 (oder A-1214 Wien).

Lady Manhattan.

60

Advertisements/Anzeigen/Annonces

61 Full-page advertisement in full colour for *Bulova* watches. (USA)
62 Magazine advertising for *Lassale* watches in full-colour. (FRA)
63 Full-page advertisement in a colour campaign for *Omega* watches. (JPN)
64 Gold jewellery with precious and semi-precious stones on white ground, with blind-embossed logotype. Full-page ad for *Bulgari.* (FRA)
65, 66 Illustration and complete advertisement for *Dupont* fountain pen. (USA)

61 Ganzseitiges Inserat mit mehrfarbiger Aufnahme für *Bulova*-Uhren: «Ein prägnantes Gesicht verdient ein ebensolches zweites.» (USA)
62 Zeitschriftenwerbung für *Lassale*-Uhren. Ganzseitige Farbaufnahme. (FRA)
63 Ganzseitiges Inserat aus einer Kampagne für *Omega*-Uhren. In Farbe. (JPN)
64 Goldschmuck mit verschiedenfarbigen Edel- und Halbedelsteinen auf weissem Grund mit blindgeprägtem Markennamen; ganzseitige Anzeige für *Bulgari.* (FRA)
65, 66 Aufnahme und vollständiges Inserat für einen Füllfederhalter. (USA)

61 Annonce pleine page illustrée d'une photo couleur, pour les montres *Bulova*: «Un visage hors pair, cadran de montre idoine.» (USA)
62 Publicité magazines des montres *Lassale.* Photo couleur pleine page. (FRA)
63 Annonce pleine page dans une campagne des montres *Oméga.* En couleur. (JPN)
64 Annonce pleine page pour la bijouterie *Bulgari*: or, pierreries. (FRA)
65, 66 Photo et annonce complète pour un stylo nec plus ultra. (USA)

PHOTOGRAPHER:

61 Henry Wolf
62 Alexis Stroukoff
63 Yoshiaki Ohkura
64 RKM
65, 66 Clint Clemens

DESIGNER / GESTALTER:

63 Ryuichi Inaba
64 René H. Bittel
65, 66 Keith Lane

61

62

63

64

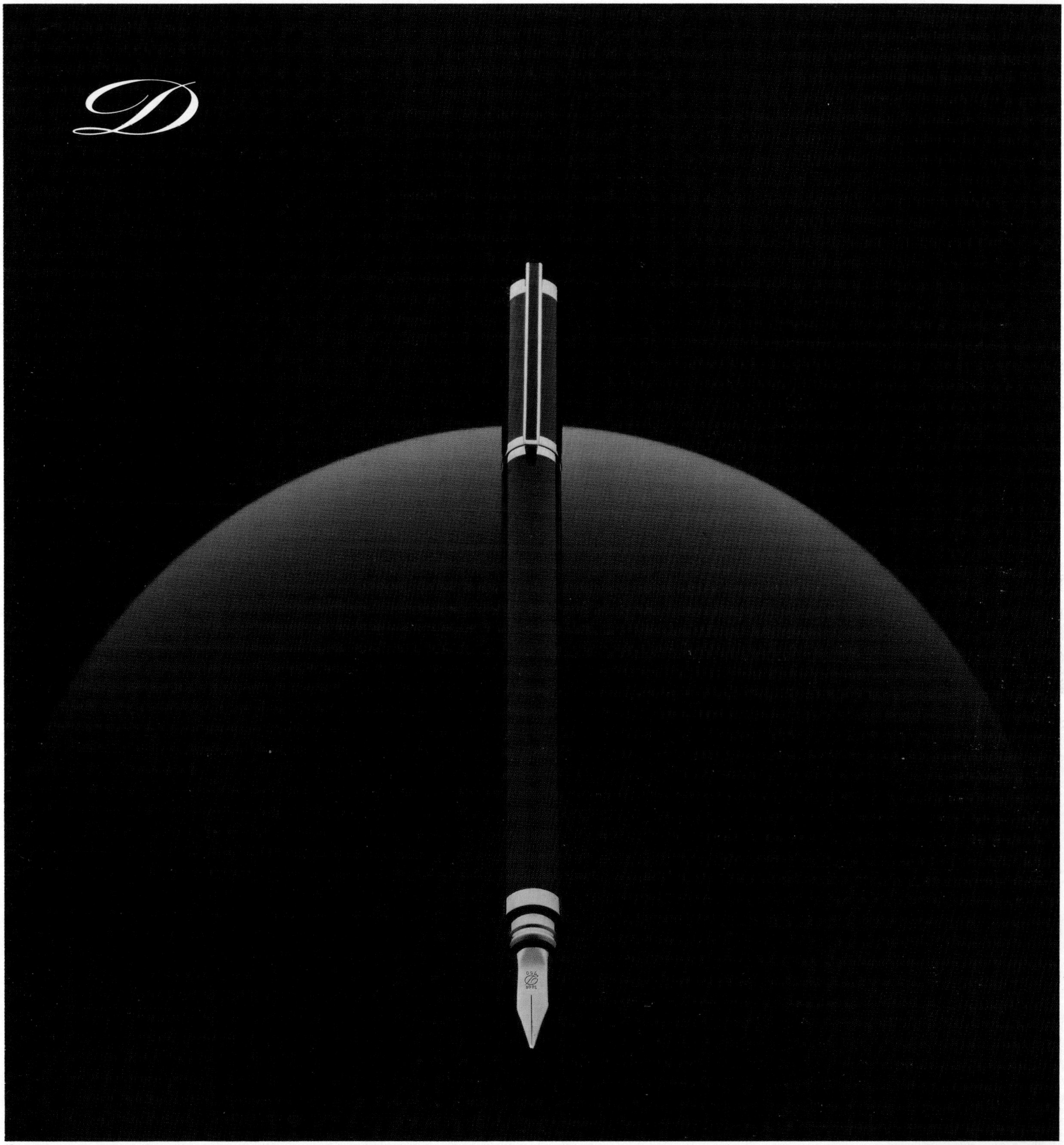

65

ART DIRECTOR / DIRECTEUR ARTISTIQUE:

63 Hizonobu Shindo
64 René H. Bittel
65, 66 Keith Lane

AGENCY / AGENTUR / AGENCE – STUDIO:

61 Henry Wolf Productions
63 McCann-Erickson Hakuhodo Inc.
64 Kenyon & Eckhardt SA
65, 66 Emerson, Lane Fortuna

66

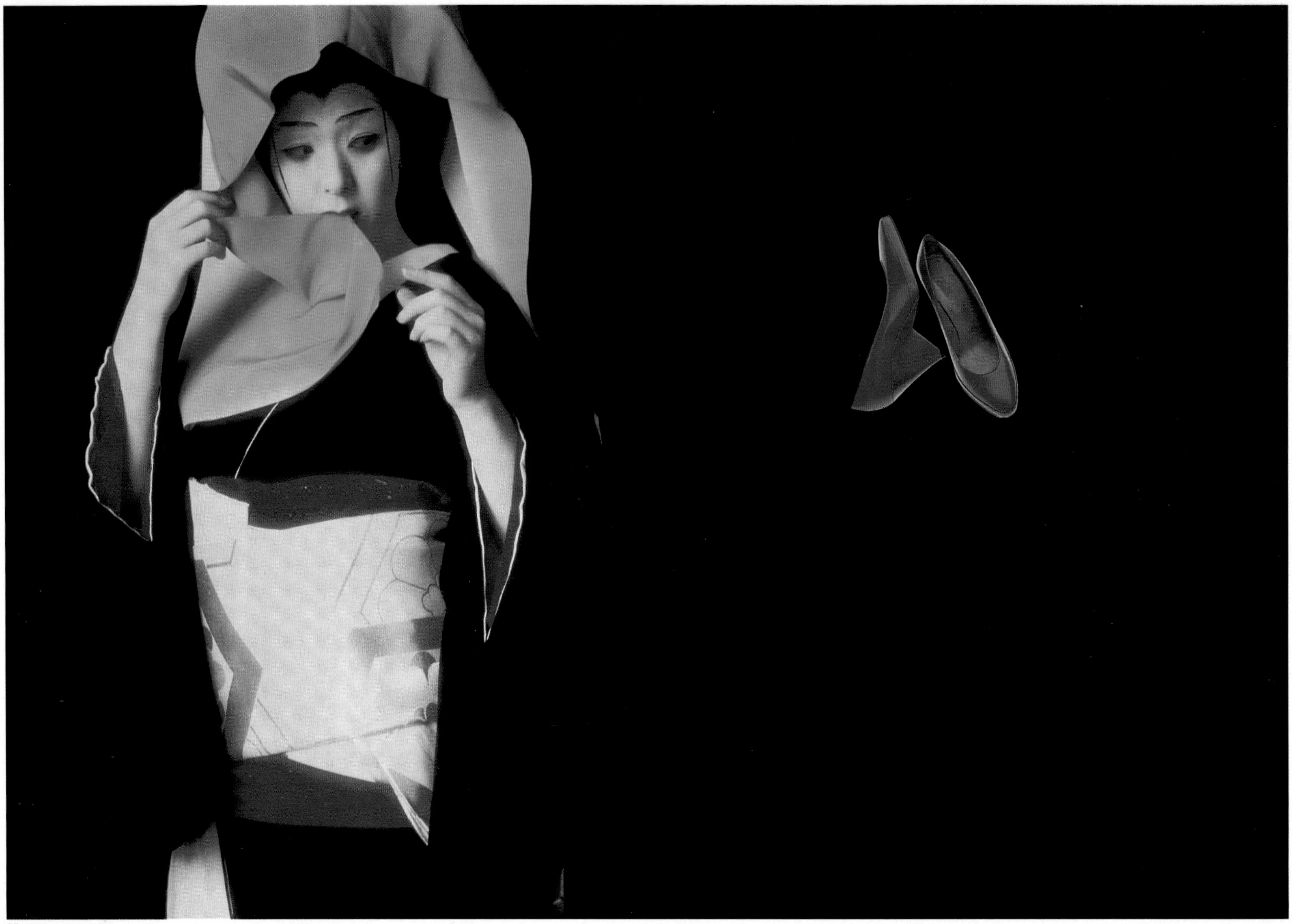

67

PHOTOGRAPHER / PHOTOGRAPH:

67, 68 Komaro Hoshino
69–71 Uwe Ommer

DESIGNER / GESTALTER / MAQUETTISTE:

67, 68 Komaro Hoshino
69–71 Michel Pahin

ART DIRECTOR / DIRECTEUR ARTISTIQUE:

67, 68 Josiane Chanderon
69–71 Uwe Ommer

AGENCY / AGENTUR / AGENCE – STUDIO:

67, 68 R & D Campbell-Ewald

68

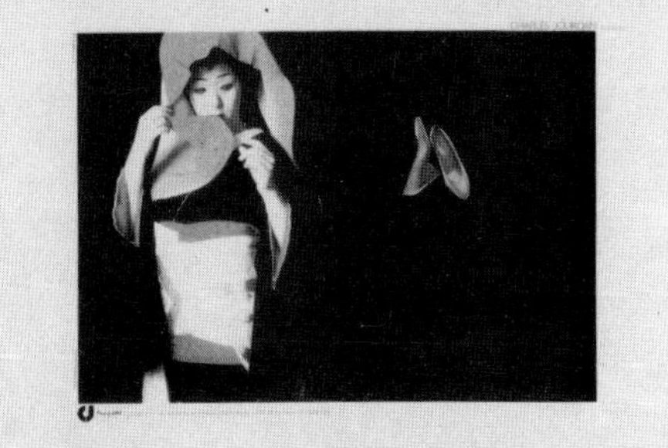

67a

69

70

Advertisements/Anzeigen/Annonces

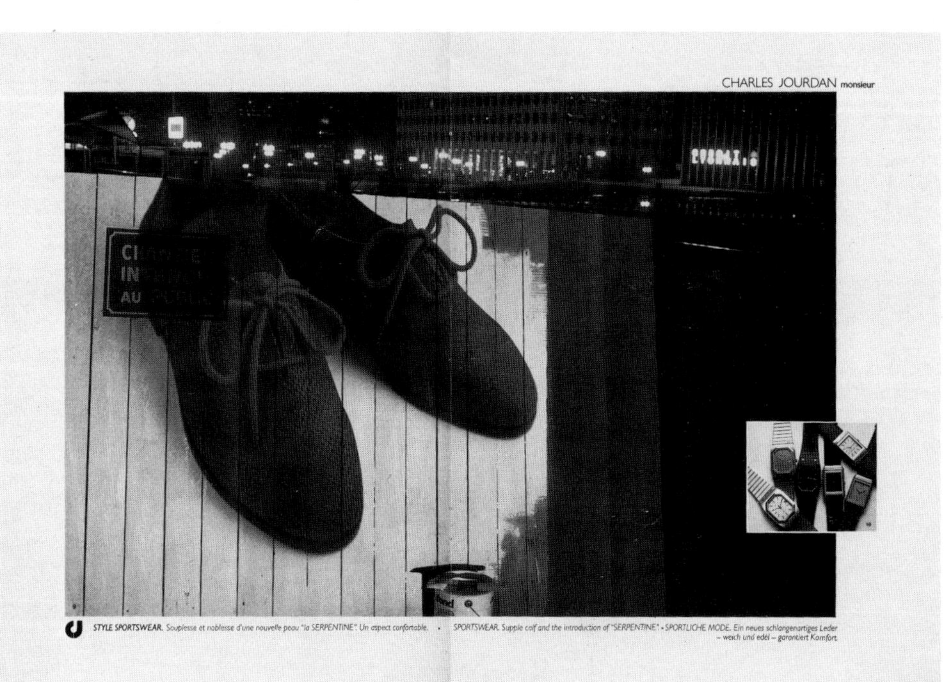

71

67, 67a, 68 Examples from an advertising campaign of magazine double spreads for *Charles Jourdan* shoes. (FRA)
69–71 Double spreads in full colour from a campaign for men's shoes and accessories by *Charles Jourdan*. Fig. 69 is for classical "City" models, Fig. 70 for boots, while Fig. 71 also shows watches that match with shoes for casual wear. (FRA)

67, 67a, 68 Beispiele aus einer Werbekampagne mit doppelseitigen Zeitschrifteninseraten für Schuhe von *Charles Jourdan*. (FRA)
69–71 Doppelseiten mit Farbaufnahmen aus einer Kampagne für Herrenschuhe und Zubehöre von *Charles Jourdan*. In Abb. 69 geht es um «City-Mode» mit klassischen Formen, in Abb. 70 um Stiefel und in Abb. 71 um sportliche Mode mit passenden Uhren. (FRA)

67, 67a, 68 Exemples d'annonces de magazines double page dans une campagne publicitaire pour les chaussures *Charles Jourdan*. (FRA)
69–71 Doubles pages, illustrations couleur, pour une campagne en faveur des chaussures et accessoires messieurs *Charles Jourdan*: le style ville à la fig. 69, les bottes à la fig. 70, le style sportif avec montres assorties à la fig. 71. (FRA)

72

73

PHOTOGRAPHER / PHOTOGRAPH / PHOTOGRAPHE:

72, 73 Lord Snowdon
74 Sarah Moon
75 Myron
77 Gösta Peterson

DESIGNER / GESTALTER / MAQUETTISTE:

72, 73 Charles Banuchi
75 Tyler Smith
77 Gösta Peterson

74

75

76

ART DIRECTOR / DIRECTEUR ARTISTIQUE:

72, 73 John C. Jay
74 Robert Delpire
75 Tyler Smith
77 Barbara Richer

AGENCY / AGENTUR / AGENCE – STUDIO:

72, 73 Bloomingdale's Adv. Dept.
74 Ideodis
75 Tyler Smith
77 Announcebureau

72, 73 Full-page newspaper ad in black and white for men's clothes from *Bloomingdale's* department store, New York: film stars Ben Cross and Ian Charleson. (USA)
74 Full-colour double-spread magazine ad for *RoC* sun creams and oils. (FRA)
75 Soft-focus shot from full-colour launch campaign in American magazines advertising a new line of Italian sportswear and clothing. (USA)
76 Full-page magazine ad, in shades of grey, for *Grey Flannel* men's cologne. (USA)
77 Full-colour double spread in magazines advertising men's fashions by *Gianfranco Ruffini*. Pastels with designer's logo overprinted in pink. (USA)

72, 73 Ganzseitige Zeitungsinserate in Schwarzweiss für Herrenmode des New Yorker Kaufhauses *Bloomingdale's*. Die Modelle sind zwei amerikanische Filmstars. (USA)
74 Doppelseitige Zeitschriftenanzeige für *RoC*-Sonnenschutzprodukte. (FRA)
75 Aus einer Anzeigenkampagne für die Einführung einer neuen Sportbekleidungs-Linie in den Vereinigten Staaten. Weichgezeichnete Farbaufnahme. (USA)
76 Ganzseitiges Inserat in Grautönen für *Grey Flannel* Eau-de-Toilette für Herren. (USA)
77 Doppelseitiges Zeitschrifteninserat für Herrenmode von *Gianfranco Ruffini*. Aufnahme in zurückhaltenden Farben, Markenaufdruck pink. (USA)

72, 73 Annonces de journaux pleine page, en noir et blanc, pour le département de confection hommes des grands magasins newyorkais *Bloomingdale's*. Les modèles sont deux vedettes du cinéma américain. (USA)
74 Annonce de magazine double page pour les produits solaires *RoC*. (FRA)
75 Annonce pour le lancement d'une gamme de vêtements de sports aux Etats-Unis. (USA)
76 Annonce pleine page, en grisés, pour l'eau de toilette messieurs *Grey Flannel*. (USA)
77 Annonce de magazine double page pour les modes masculines *Gianfranco Ruffini*. Photo couleur aux tons adoucis, marque imprimée en rose. (USA)

77

78

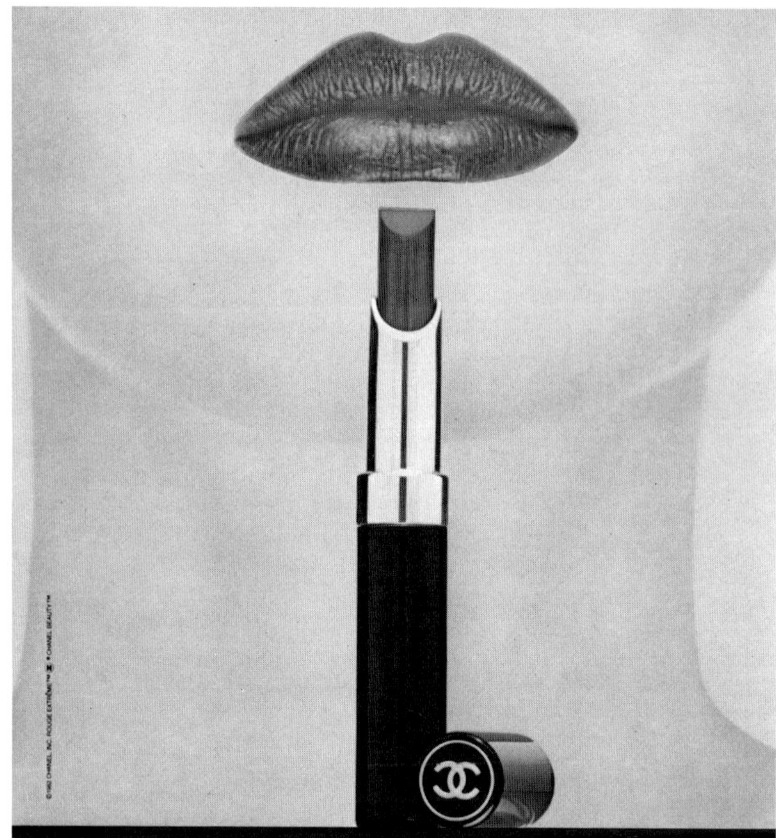
CHANEL
INTRODUCING ROUGE EXTRÊME. DARING NEW HIGH-INTENSITY LIPCOLOUR.
CONCENTRATED TO MAKE A LASTING IMPRESSION.

79

80

81

78, 80, 81 Full-page illustrations from a magazine campaign advertising pearls and jewellery. In full colour. (GER)
79 Full-page magazine advertisement to introduce a new lipstick, "Rouge Extrême" by *Chanel*. Black, gold and bright deep red on ground of very light beige. (USA)
82 Full-colour double spread in magazines for "faceless" *Omega* watches with round dials that show only the hands. (FRA)
83 The black pearls, from Tahiti, are the products advertised by *Graff* in this magazine double spread. (FRA)

78, 80, 81 Ganzseitige Farbaufnahmen aus einer Inseratenkampagne für Perlen, Edelsteine und Schmuck. (GER)
79 Zeitschrifteninserat für die Einführung von «Rouge-Extrême»-Lippenstiften aus dem Hause *Chanel*. Leuchtendes, tiefes Rot, Gold und Schwarz, Haut und Hintergrund in sehr hellem Beige. (USA)
82 Doppelseitiges Inserat für *Omega*-Uhren. Farbaufnahme. (FRA)
83 Schwarze Perlen aus Tahiti sind Gegenstand dieser doppelseitigen Anzeige eines Schmuckhändlers. (FRA)

78, 80, 81 Photos couleur pleine page dans une campagne d'annonces pour des perles, pierres précieuses et bijoux. (GER)
79 Annonce de magazine pour le lancement des rouges à lèvres «Rouge Extrême» de *Chanel*. Rouge foncé lumineux, noir et or, peau et arrière-plan beige très clair. (USA)
82 Annonce double page des montres *Oméga*. Photo couleur. (FRA)
83 Les perles noires de Tahiti constituent le sujet de cette annonce double page d'un bijoutier. (FRA)

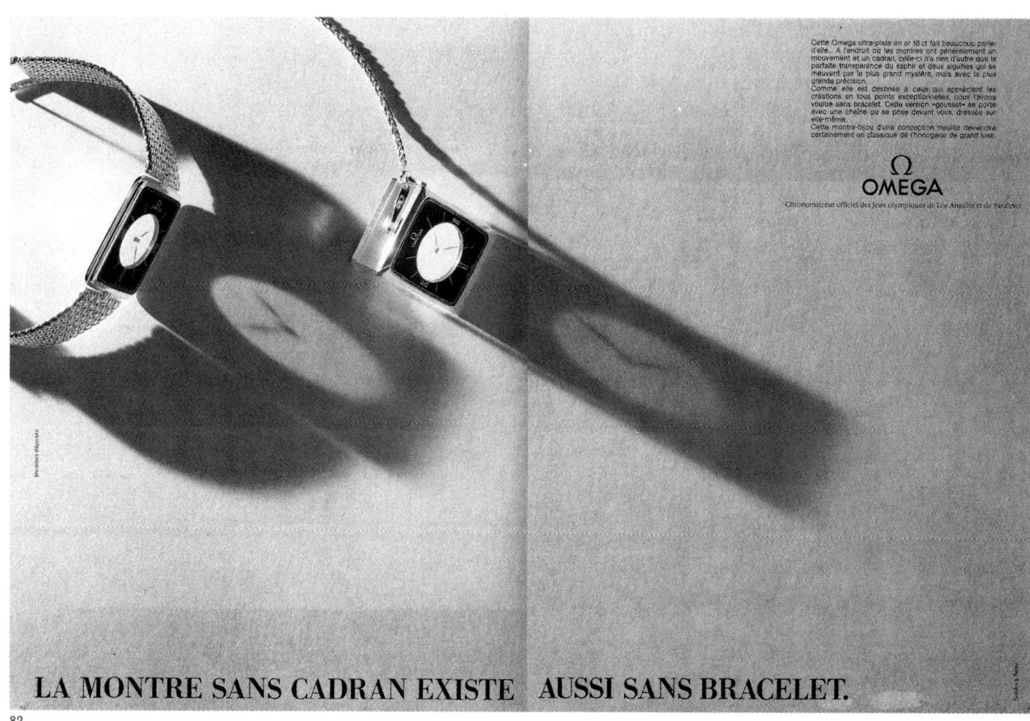

82

PHOTOGRAPHER / PHOTOGRAPH / PHOTOGRAPHE:

78, 80, 81 Otto Hoernisch
79 Hiro
82 Ruedi Hofstetter
83 James Wedge

DESIGNER / GESTALTER / MAQUETTISTE:

78, 80, 81 Otto Hoernisch
79 Bernard Cumming
82 Beat Keusch
83 Ted Vaughn

ART DIRECTOR / DIRECTEUR ARTISTIQUE:

78, 80, 81 Otto Hoernisch
79 Bernard Cumming
82 Beat Keusch
83 Ted Vaughn

AGENCY / AGENTUR / AGENCE – STUDIO:

79 Doyle Dane Bernbach
82 Stalder & Suter
83 LansdownEuro

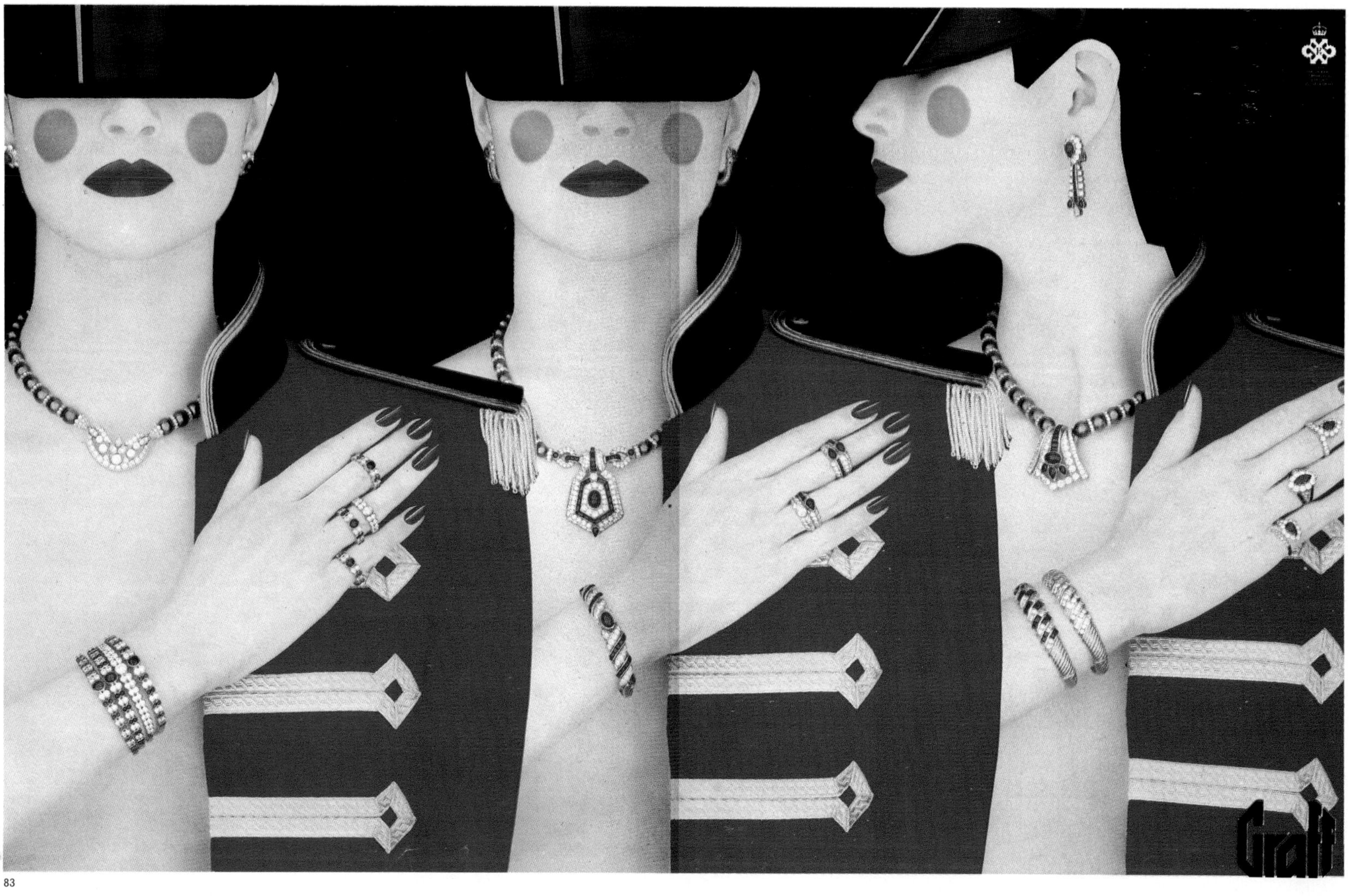

83

PHOTOGRAPHER / PHOTOGRAPH:

84 Paolo Roversi
87–89 Les Goldberg

DESIGNER / GESTALTER / MAQUETTISTE:

84 Jacqueline & Franck Salier
87–89 Sharon L. Occhipinti

ART DIRECTOR / DIRECTEUR ARTISTIQUE:

84 Jacqueline & Franck Salier
87–89 Sharon L. Occhipinti

AGENCY / AGENTUR / AGENCE – STUDIO:

84 J & F Salier
87–89 Doyle Dane Bernbach

84

Advertisements/Anzeigen/Annonces

84 Full-colour magazine ad for *Tiktiner* fashion clothes. The ground repeats the light beige of the complexion and the grey-green tones of the clothes. (FRA)
85, 86 Full-page samples from a campaign advertising furs by *Galanos* which tells New Yorkers which two local stores stock them. (USA)
87–89 Full-page magazine ads from a campaign highlighting "the look of silk" that can be atteined with *Ceylon* yarns of *Fortrel* polyester. The campaign showed how noted American fashion designers achieved this look, in various ways, emphasizing the feel of silk by using Chinese characters. (USA)

84 Zeitschriften-Inserat für *Tiktiner*-Mode. Das helle Beige der Haut und der graugrüne Ton der Kleidung wiederholen sich im Hintergrund. (FRA)
85, 86 Beispiele aus einer Werbekampagne für *Galanos*-Pelze, mit Angabe der New Yorker Geschäfte, die diese Pelze führen. Aufnahmen in Schwarzweiss. (USA)
87–89 Aus einer Kampagne mit ganzseitigen Inseraten für Mode aus *Ceylon*, einem Stoff aus *Fortrel*-Polyester, der wie echte Seide aussehen soll. Unterstrichen wird dieser Anspruch durch den Markennamen und die chinesischen Schriftzeichen. (USA)

84 Annonce de magazine pour les modes *Tiktiner*. Le beige clair de la peau et le vert gris du vêtement se répètent à l'arrière-plan. (FRA)
85, 86 Exemples de photos noir-blanc dans une campagne en faveur des fourrures *Galanos*, avec indication des dépositaires newyorkais. (USA)
87–89 Campagne d'annonces pleine page pour les modes en *Ceylon*, un tissu polyester *Fortrel* semblable à la soie, d'où le nom de la marque et les caractères chinois. (USA)

87

GALANOS
neiman-marcus
bergdorf goodman

85

GALANOS
neiman-marcus
bergdorf goodman

86

絹以上に絹、セイロン
Wilroy gets the look of silk from Ceylon.
And nothing's lost in translation. Wilroy created this blouse in an elegant crepe de chine from Klopman Textured Wovens, division of Burlington Industries. Made of Ceylon™ yarn of Celanese Fortrel® polyester.
CELANESE CEYLON

88

絹以上に絹、セイロン
Jerell's Sweetheart gets the look of silk from Ceylon.
And nothing's lost in translation. Jerell's Sweetheart, division of Jerell, Inc. created this peplum dress in a satin stripe from Manes. Made with Ceylon™ yarn of Celanese Fortrel® polyester.
CELANESE CEYLON

89

90

91

92

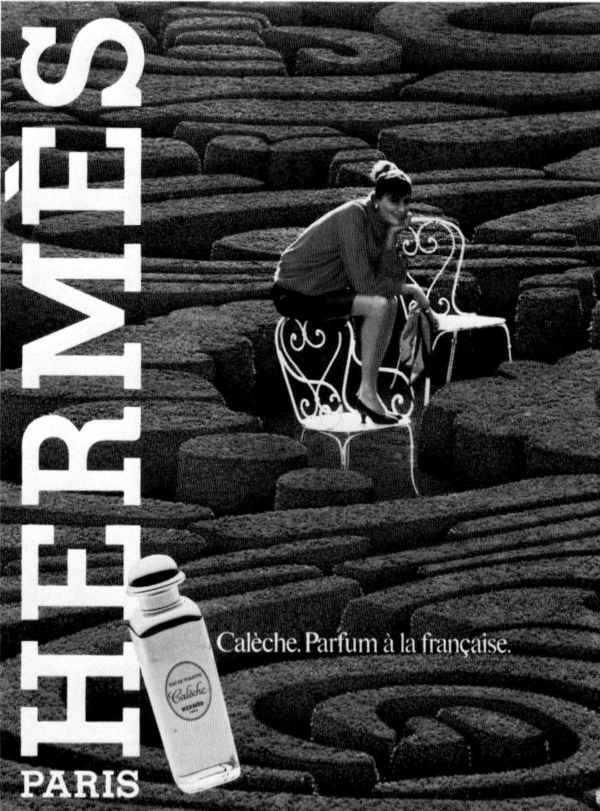

93

90 Sample of an advertising campaign by *Shiseido*, a Japanese manufacturer of toilet articles (see also Figs. 94–97), here for cosmetics. (JPN)
91 From a campaign advertising *Mustang* jeans and sportswear. This photographed portrait of the artistes as young "in" people of today, shot by themselves, shows the Swiss mime group "Mummenschanz". (GER)
92 Full-page fashion ad by *Studio-V*, in black and white. (FRA)
93 Full-page advertisement for perfume with French flair from *Hermès*. (FRA)
94–97 More samples (as in Fig. 90) of advertising by *Shiseido*: here, full pages devoted to illustrations of its "crystal-clear" soaps. (JPN)

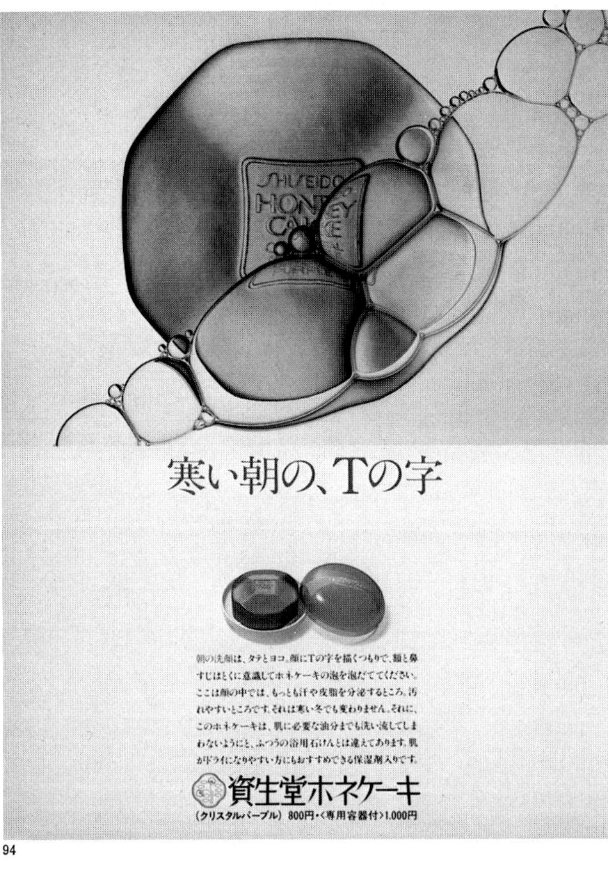

94

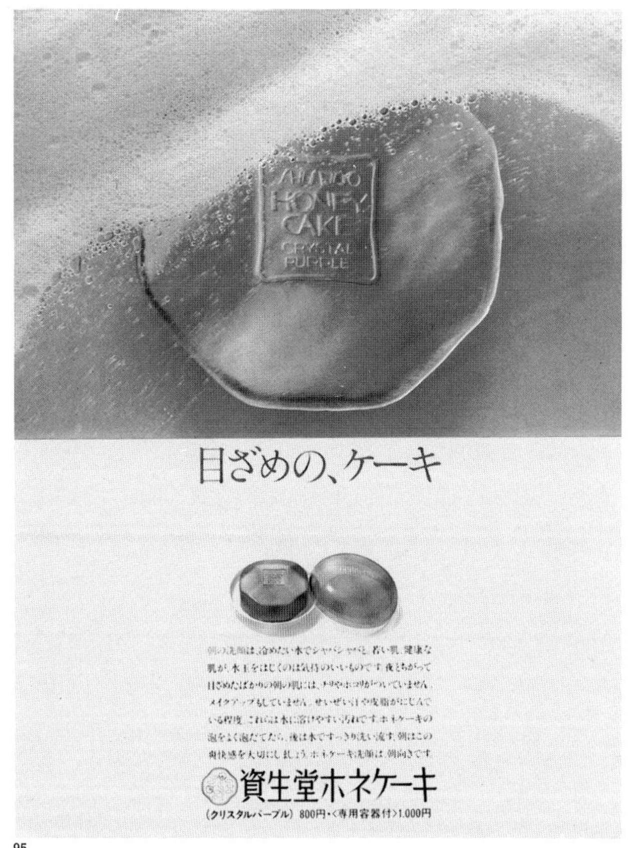

95

肌は、スケートリンク

資生堂ホネケーキ

(クリスタルパーブル) 800円・〈専用容器付〉1,000円

96

97

PHOTOGRAPHER / PHOTOGRAPH:

90 Sachiko Kuru
91 Ingolf Thiel
92 Susumu Yasui
93 Gilles Bensimon
94–97 Masao Sakamoto

DESIGNER / GESTALTER:

90 Kazuhiko Tajima
91 Uli Weber
94–97 Mitsuru Ito

ART DIRECTOR:

90 Kenji Tanaka
91 Uli Weber
92 Irie & Atsuko
93 Patrick Stenz
94–97 Atsutoshi Saisho

AGENCY / AGENTUR / AGENCE:

91 Leonhardt & Kern
93 CFRP

90 Beispiel aus einer Inseraten-Kampagne für Make-up-Artikel des japanischen Kosmetikkonzerns *Shiseido.* (JPN)
91 Aus einer Kampagne für *Mustang*-Jeans und -Sportbekleidung unter dem Motto: «Leute von heute, von sich selbst photographiert.» Hier die Gruppe «Mummenschanz», die 1983 auf Deutschland-Tournee war. (GER)
92 Ganzseitiges Inserat in Schwarzweiss für Mode von *Studio-V.* (FRA)
93 Mehrfarbige Anzeige für ein «französisches» Parfum von *Hermès.* (FRA)
94–97 Beispiele aus einer Serie mit ganzseitigen Anzeigen für «kristallklare» Seife von *Shiseido.* (JPN)

90 Annonce figurant dans une campagne en faveur des produits de maquillage du groupe cosmétique japonais *Shiseido.* (JPN)
91 Elément d'une campagne publicitaire pour les jeans et vêtements de sport *Mustang* placée sous la devise des «gens d'aujourd'hui photographiés par eux-mêmes.» Ici, le groupe «Mummenschanz» (tournée allemande 1983). (GER)
92 Annonce pleine page, noir et blanc, pour les modes *Studio-V.* (FRA)
93 Annonce polychrome pour un parfum «français» de *Hermès.* (FRA)
94–97 Exemples d'une série d'annonces pleine page en faveur des savons *Shiseido* réputés avoir la «clarté du cristal». (JPN)

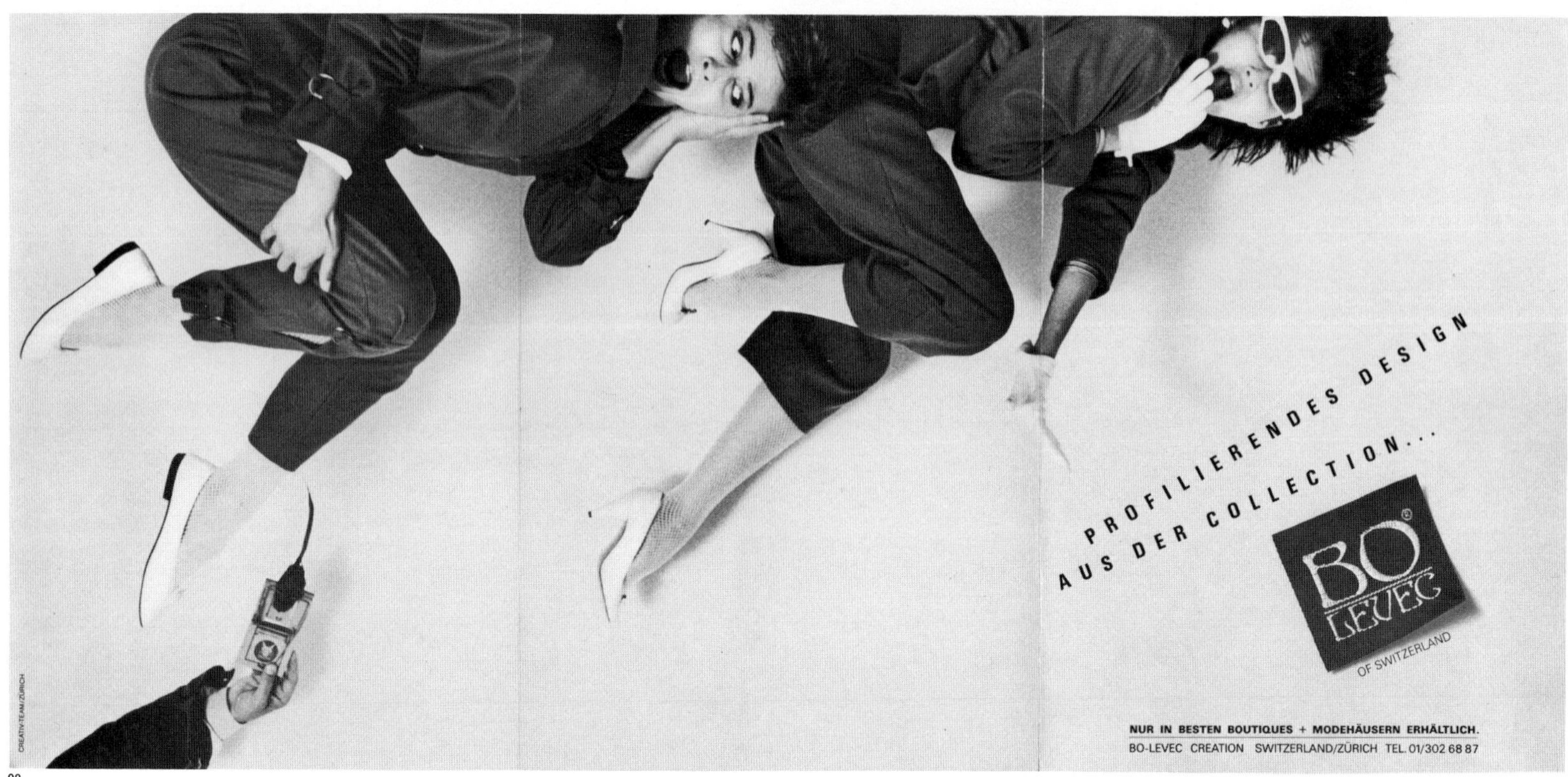

98

99

98, 99 Samples from a series of magazine advertisements using photography in black and white for fashion collections created by *Bo-Levec.* (SWI)
100 Full-colour double spread in magazines advertising luggage that is "the soul of travel", as made by *Louis Vuitton* of Paris. (FRA)
101 Typical full-colour double spread of magazine campaign by *Dior.* The models are the focal point in this advertising for the full range of clothes and accessories. (USA)

98, 99 Beispiele aus einer Inseratenserie in Zeitschriften, im Rahmen einer Werbekampagne mit Schwarzweissaufnahmen, für Mode der Marke *Bo-Levec.* (SWI)
100 «*Louis Vuitton.* Die Seele der Reise.» Doppelseitiges Inserat mit Farbaufnahme für Koffer und Taschen von *Louis Vuitton.* (FRA)
101 Beispiel aus einer Serie von doppelseitigen Inseraten mit Farbaufnahmen für Artikel aus dem Hause *Dior.* Mittelpunkt der Kampagne sind die drei «Diors». (USA)

98, 99 Annonces de magazines figurant dans une série noir et blanc où sont vantées les modes commercialisées sous la marque *Bo-Levec.* (SWI)
100 Cette annonce double page au slogan percutant, illustrée d'une photo couleur, sert à la publicité des sacs de voyage et valises *Louis Vuitton.* (FRA)
101 Exemple des annonces double page parues dans une série illustrée de photos couleur pour des accessoires *Dior.* Au centre de cette campagne figurent les «trois Dior». (USA)

PHOTOGRAPHER / PHOTOGRAPH:

98, 99 Giorgio Balmelli
101 Richard Avedon

DESIGNER / GESTALTER / MAQUETTISTE:

98, 99 William Bolleter

ART DIRECTOR / DIRECTEUR ARTISTIQUE:

98, 99 William Bolleter
101 Rochelle Udell

AGENCY / AGENTUR / AGENCE – STUDIO:

98, 99 Creativ-Team Ltd.
100 The Creative Business
101 J. Walter Thompson

Il y a des voyageurs de talent. Ils abordent le voyage comme un art.

C'est pour eux que Louis Vuitton fait des bagages car il faut à ces connaisseurs le savoir-faire d'un artisan pour leur façonner les meilleurs instruments.

Les compagnons-malletiers de Louis Vuitton répètent depuis plus d'un siècle les gestes sûrs et précis qui font d'une malle, d'une valise ou d'un sac des bagages résistants, fonctionnels et raffinés. Ces hommes de métier travaillent des matériaux choisis avec intransigeance. Depuis toujours, ils réalisent aussi des bagages sur mesure.

Cette conception du bagage est unique. Louis Vuitton la maintient depuis 1854.

A Paris et dans les grandes villes du monde.

LOUIS VUITTON

100

Meet the Diors: the Wizard, the Mouth, and Oliver.

Christian Dior

Dior for Men: Footwear, Hosiery, Sportshirts, Beachwear, Scarves & Mufflers, Gloves, Clothing & Outerwear, Ready-to-Wear, Dress Shirts, Neckwear, Underwear, Accessories, Nightwear, Eyewear, Sweaters, Robes, Loungewear & Activewear, Umbrellas.

Dior for Women: Furs, Intimate Apparel, Robes, Intimates, Scarves, Small Leather Goods, Jewelry, Gloves, Knit Hats & Mufflers, Footwear, Sportswear, Separates, Handbags & Luggage, Umbrellas & Rain Hats, Eyewear, Beachwear, Belts, Legwear, Activewear, Bed Linens.

Christian Dior Fragrances for Men & Women. Christian Dior Makeup.

Like all good things, one Dior leads to another.

101

PICK A ROAD.
ANY ROAD.
We believe that when you ride, your motorcycle shouldn't be the one deciding which roads you'll take.
Which is why we offer the new Honda CB1000 Custom.
Its famous DOHC engine puts all the horsepower you'll ever need right in your hand. With a dual-range transmission that lets you pump that power through the drive shaft two different ways. Five speeds in low for quick acceleration. Or five speeds in high for effortless cruising.
You can fine tune the air-adjustable suspension to make it as firm or as soft as you want. And TRAC™ our exclusive Torque Reactive Anti-dive Control, helps reduce fork compression during braking without altering the feel of the brakes.
The result is a motorcycle that's at home anywhere but home. Charging from curve to curve. Touring from coast to coast. Or cruising from stoplight to stoplight.
The CB1000 Custom.
At $3648,* it takes the gamble out of picking the right motorcycle.
HONDA
FOLLOW THE LEADER
HONDA

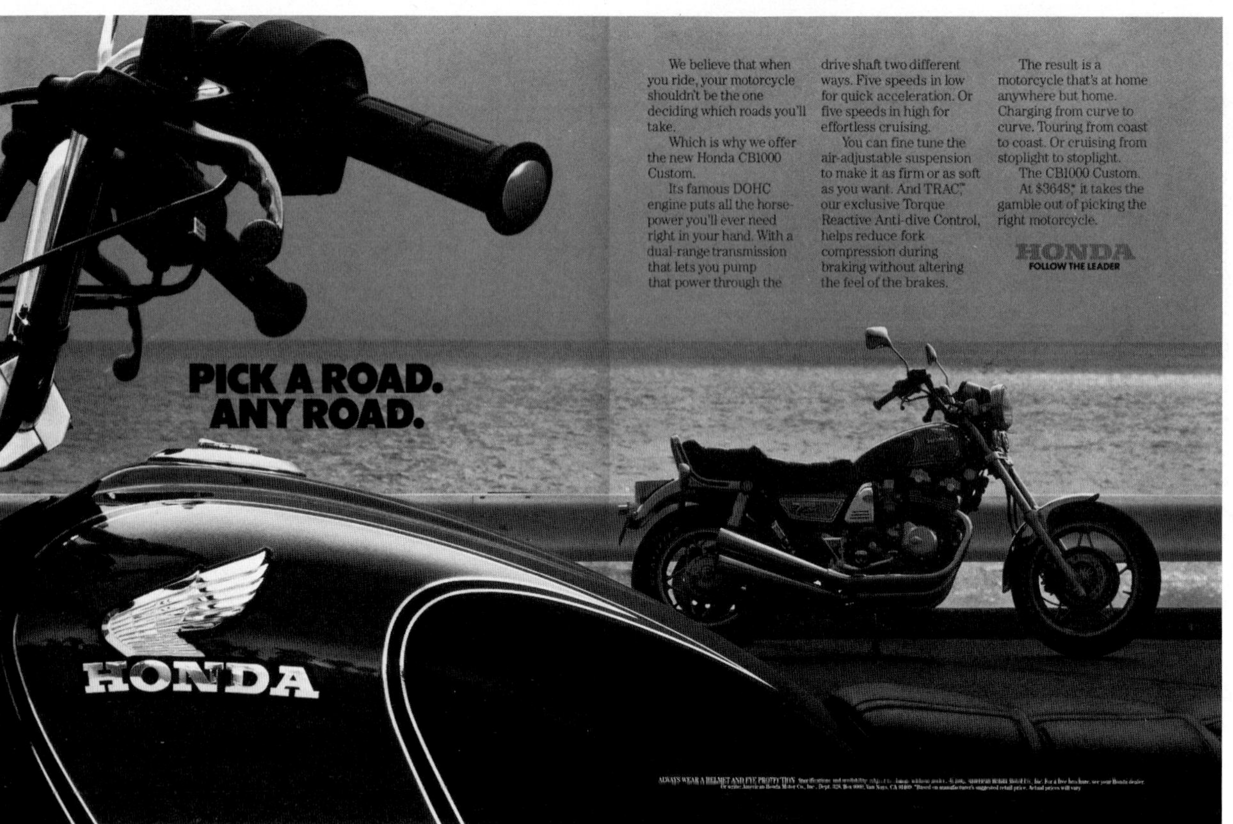

102

PHOTOGRAPHER / PHOTOGRAPH:

102 Steve Sakai
103 Manfred Rieker Studio
104 Cailor/Resnick
105, 106 David Deahl

DESIGNER / GESTALTER:

103 Wolfgang Fetzer
104 Barbara Bowman
105, 106 Dick Lemon

ART DIRECTOR:

102 Richard Polk
103 Wolfgang Groffy
104 Jeff Vogt/Anthony Angotti
105, 106 Dick Lemon

AGENCY / AGENTUR / AGENCE:

102 Dailey & Associates
103 Team/BBDO
104 Ammirati & Puris Art Studio
105, 106 Zechman & Assoc.

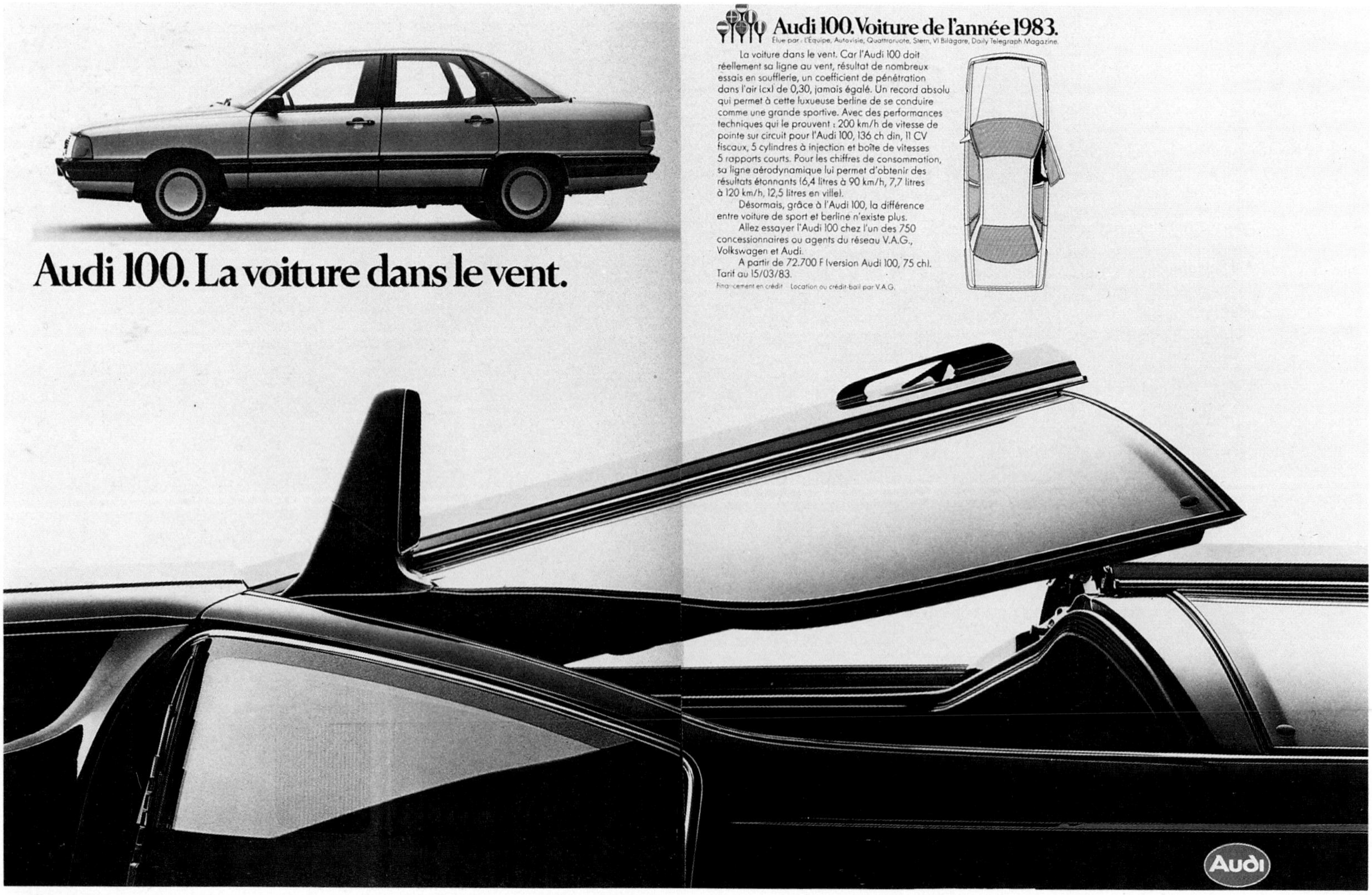
Audi 100. La voiture dans le vent.
Audi 100. Voiture de l'année 1983.
Élue par : L'Équipe, Autovisie, Quattroruote, Stern, VI Bilägare, Daily Telegraph Magazine.
La voiture dans le vent. Car l'Audi 100 doit réellement sa ligne au vent, résultat de nombreux essais en soufflerie, un coefficient de pénétration dans l'air (cx) de 0,30, jamais égalé. Un record absolu qui permet à cette luxueuse berline de se conduire comme une grande sportive. Avec des performances techniques qui le prouvent : 200 km/h de vitesse de pointe sur circuit pour l'Audi 100, 136 ch din, 11 CV fiscaux, 5 cylindres à injection et boîte de vitesses 5 rapports courts. Pour les chiffres de consommation, sa ligne aérodynamique lui permet d'obtenir des résultats étonnants (6,4 litres à 90 km/h, 7,7 litres à 120 km/h, 12,5 litres en ville).
Désormais, grâce à l'Audi 100, la différence entre voiture de sport et berline n'existe plus.
Allez essayer l'Audi 100 chez l'un des 750 concessionnaires ou agents du réseau V.A.G., Volkswagen et Audi.
A partir de 72.700 F (version Audi 100, 75 ch). Tarif au 15/03/83.
Financement en crédit Location ou crédit-bail par V.A.G.
Audi

103

104

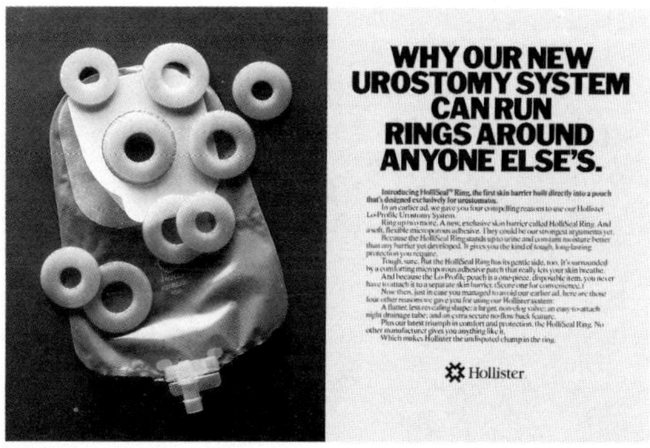

105

106

102 Full-colour double spread from a national advertising campaign by *Honda* that was launched to introduce its new motorcycle model. (USA)
103 Full-colour magazine double spread for the *Audi* highlights its aerodynamic points. (FRA)
104 Illustration in ad for a BMW sports model, "epitome of truth in packaging". (USA)
105, 106 Double-spread ad for a medical product and the illustration that emphasized its newly developed ring seals. (USA)

102 Doppelseitige Zeitschriften-Anzeige für die Einführung eines neuen Modells in der Reihe der *Honda*-Motorräder. Mehrfarbige Aufnahme. (USA)
103 Die Aerodynamik des *Audi 100* ist das Hauptthema dieses doppelseitigen Inserats. (FRA)
104 Inserat für ein BMW-Sport-Coupé der Luxus-Klasse, «der Inbegriff ehrlicher Verpackung». (USA)
105, 106 Vollständige doppelseitige Anzeige und Aufnahme für einen medizinischen Bedarfsartikel, hier mit besonderer Betonung der neu entwickelten Ringe. (USA)

102 Annonce de magazine double page à l'occasion du lancement d'un nouveau modèle de moto *Honda*. Photo en polychromie. (USA)
103 Thème de cette annonce double page: les caractéristiques aérodynamiques de l'*Audi 100*. (FRA)
104 Annonce pour un coupé sport de luxe BMW, «incarnation de la vérité de l'emballage». (USA)
105, 106 Annonce double page complète et photo pour un équipement médical; l'accent est mis ici sur les anneaux de conception nouvelle. (USA)

Advertisements/Anzeigen/Annonces

PHOTOGRAPHER / PHOTOGRAPH / PHOTOGRAPHE:

107 Gerald Farber
108 Yasuo Kizu
109 Andreas Heiniger
110 Somei Kaneto
111 Taku Aramasa

DESIGNER / GESTALTER / MAQUETTISTE:

107 Cindy Sikorski/Joe Minnella
108 Yasumi Numajiri
110 Kazuhiko Otsuki

107 A full-page colour ad sums up the interests of American youngsters and their mothers—baseball and nutrition—by showing a fielder's glove with banana fingers. (USA)
108 Ad in Japanese magazine for an *American Brand* food product. (JPN)
109 Double-spread magazine ad for *Lycra* corduroy material. (BRA)
110 One of a series of magazine double spreads shot in colour for *Onward* sportswear: here, in Japan, at the Lakeland Golf Club. (JPN)
111 Full-page newspaper ad in black and white announcing the annual Paris presentation of fashion collections from the house of *Hanai*, Tokyo. (JPN)

107 Ganzseitiges Inserat mit Farbaufnahme für Bananen, hier als besonders wertvolle Nahrung für den sportlichen Nachwuchs hervorgehoben. (USA)
108 Zeitschrifteninserat für Nahrungsmittel der Marke *American Brand*. (JPN)
109 Doppelseitiges Zeitschrifteninserat für Cord-Stoffe aus *Lycra*. (BRA)
110 Aus einer Serie von doppelseitigen Zeitschrifteninseraten mit Farbaufnahmen für *Onward*-Sportmode, auf dem Gelände des japanischen Golf-Clubs Lakeland aufgenommen. (JPN)
111 Zeitschrifteninserat mit ganzseitiger Schwarzweissaufnahme für die Ankündigung der jährlichen Pariser Präsentationstermine der Kollektionen aus dem Hause *Hanai*, Tokio. (JPN)

107 Annonce pleine page illustrée d'une photo couleur: les bananes y sont présentées comme un aliment essentiel pour les performances des jeunes sportifs. (USA)
108 Annonce de magazine pour les produits alimentaires *American Brand*. (JPN)
109 Annonce de magazine double page pour les côtelés velours en *Lycra*. (BRA)
110 Annonce de magazine double page illustrée en couleur dans une série réalisée pour les modes sports *Onward* sur le terrain du club de golf japonais de Lakeland. (JPN)
111 Annonce de magazine (photo pleine page noir et blanc) indiquant les dates de la présentation annuelle à Paris des collections du couturier *Hanai* de Tōkyō. (JPN)

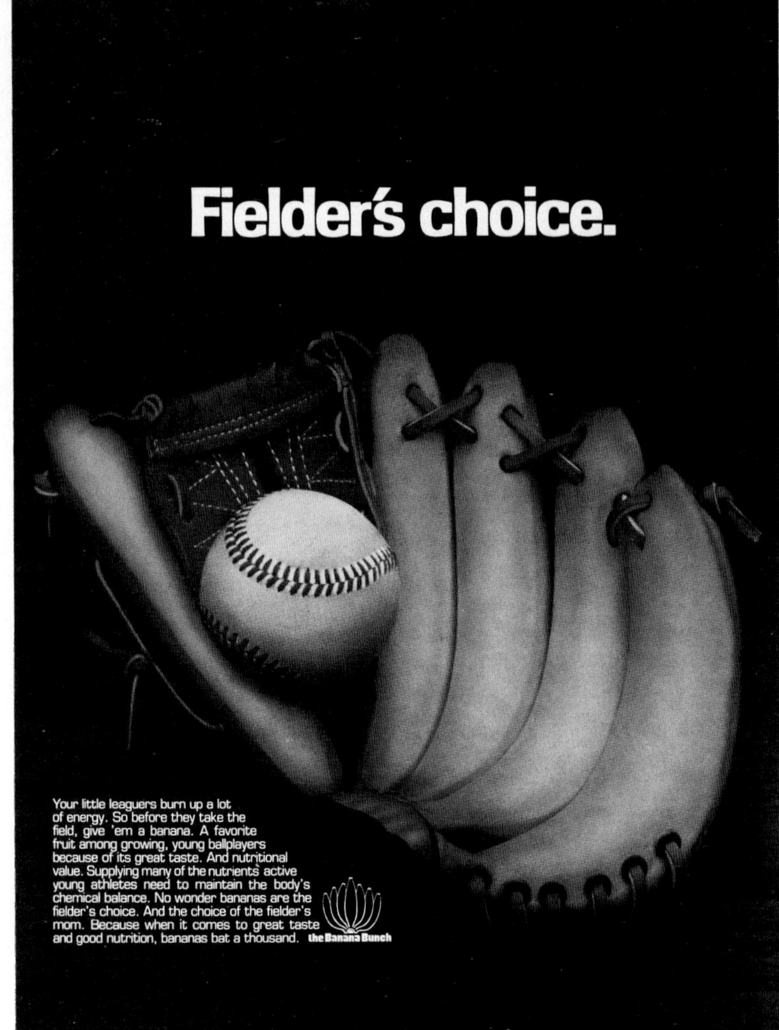

107

PACIFIC WEST
surfboards santa monica, ca

サンドイッチを食べるときは、裸足になりましょう。

ロスからサンタモニカを左へ。ハイウエイワンを南へ1時間。波がハイになっていく。ハンチントンビーチ、レドンドビーチ、国境を越えてティファナ。あのビッグ・ウエンズデイのステージだ。波があっても、無くても、延々と続くビーチは楽しい。ラジオカセットを聴きながら、潮風に吹かれ、まどろむ。サンドイッチがとてもおいしい。マスタードとマヨネーズをあわせてねったアメリカンタイプ。マヨネーズはマイルドであっさりしたものがいい。日本で手に入るのは、あのキユーピーマヨネーズ(アメリカン)。サンドイッチをLAスタイルにした。

★★ キユーピーマヨネーズ American

108

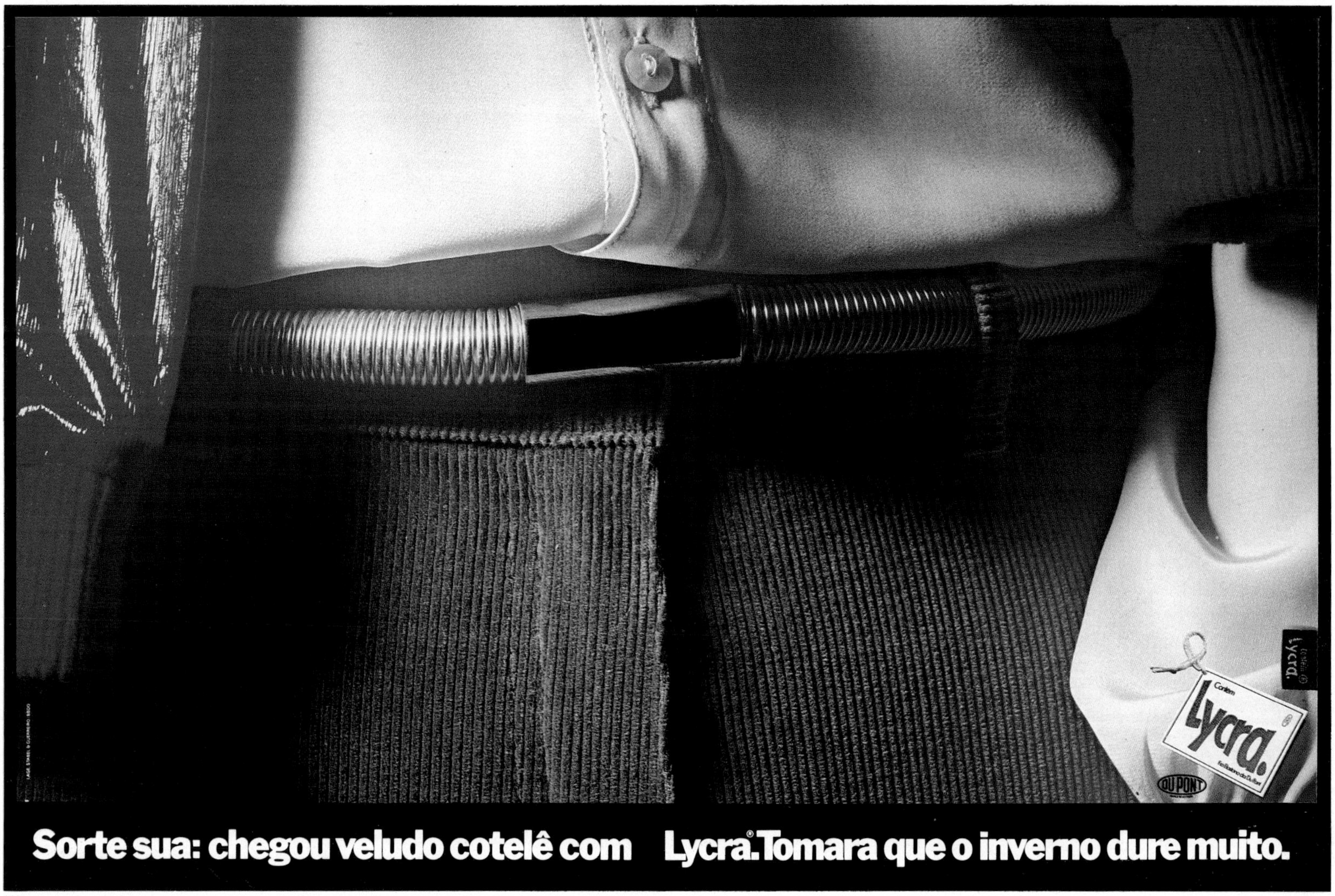
Sorte sua: chegou veludo cotelê com Lycra® Tomara que o inverno dure muito.
Lycra
DU PONT

109

ART DIRECTOR / DIRECTEUR ARTISTIQUE:

107 Cindy Sikorski/Joe Minnella
108 Gan Hosoya
109 Magy Imoberdorf
110 Kenji Sekido
111 Yasuyuki Uno

AGENCY / AGENTUR / AGENCE – STUDIO:

107 W. B. Doner & Co.
109 Lage, Stabel & Guerreiro/BBDO

Onward.
Fashion Being
ゴルフは、地球を相手にするスポーツだ。
レイクランド
Lakeland
オンワード樫山

110

HANAI YUKIKO

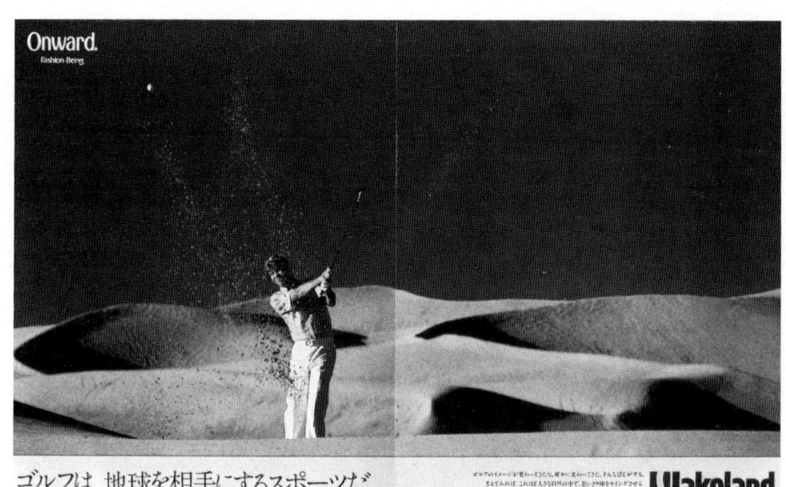

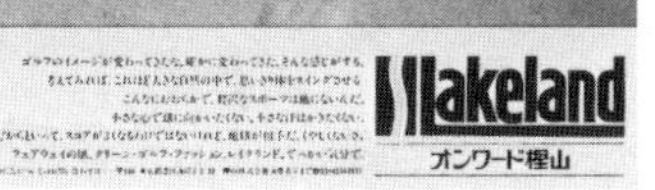

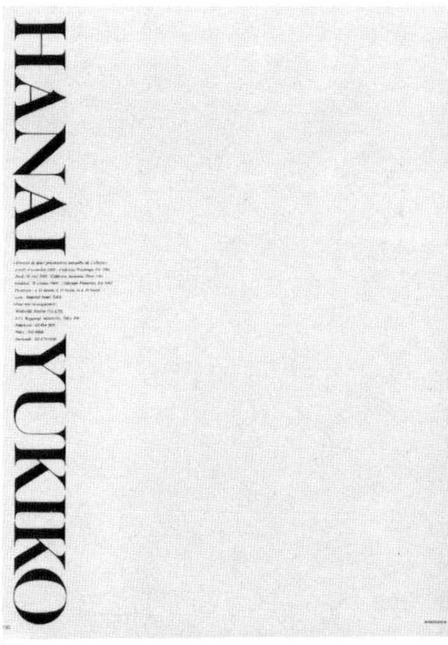

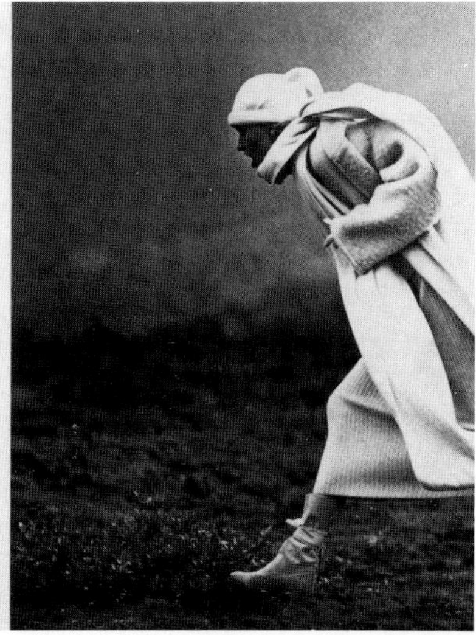

111

So we're stretching our whole fleet for you.

Five whole feet.

PREFERRED POOL

45

AVAILCO

AVAZ 256981

TTX 153280

In tough times, there is something to be said for agility.

At AVAILCO (where the smart money rides in piggyback leasing) we realized that conditions in our industry were not about to improve automatically, so we set about improving them ourselves.

A major commitment of both brains and money is now at work converting our entire fleet of Preferred Pool trailers from 40-footers to 45-footers. Within the year the job will be done, and you'll be able to call on the industry's only 100% 45-foot trailer fleet. You'll find it to be about 10,000 strong, clean as a whistle, newly serviced, and ready to roll with that added cube to add to your profitability.

If you'd like more information about what AVAILCO's major vote of confidence in the future of this industry can mean to you, contact Ron Tackbary, President, 312-787-1817.

That's him stretching.

You'll feel good to stretch, too.

AVAILCO

112

Unwrapping the American businessman

Government is acting to cool its regulatory fervor, but it's obvious the going is not going to be easy.

Overregulation of business continues to choke off opportunities for entrepreneurs, investors and workers alike, as it sharply drives up the cost of U.S. goods and services here and abroad.

One official estimate is that regulations have been adding a whopping $100 billion a year to the cost of doing business in this country.

At Ingersoll-Rand our concern is productivity. We make thousands of high quality machines and tools that America needs to revitalize its industries. Everything from giant coal mining equipment to needle bearings used in front-wheel-drive cars.

We know that true revitalization also requires an ongoing fight for regulatory reform—and sanity.

Only by continuing to unwrap the American businessman can we regain the competitive edge. And get our economy out of its bind.

INGERSOLL-RAND®

For information about Ingersoll-Rand products, write to us at Woodcliff Lake, NJ 07675.

113

Advertisements/Anzeigen/Annonces

112 Double spread of a full-colour gatefold ad by a transport company showing new, extended length of its trailers—hidden by the flap, which said only that "It feels good to stretch". (USA)
113 A double spread for a plea by *Ingersoll-Rand* to cut business free from red tape. (USA)
114 Ad for *Shiseido* sun creams and oils. Model, on sandy ground, has a golden tan. (JPN)
115–118 Double spreads from a *Ford* ad campaign, "We have lots to tell you". Specific points were detailed: aerodynamic design, in Figs. 117 and 118; an illuminated make-up mirror, in Fig. 116; and, in Fig. 115, an ignition key with a built-in lamp. (GER)

112 Doppelseitiges Inserat für ein Transportunternehmen, welches das Ausmass seiner Lastwagen verlängert hat. Die «Verlängerung» des Inserats durch eine Klappe unterstreicht diese Aussage. (USA)
113 Die Befreiung des US-Geschäftsmannes von zu grosser staatlicher Einflussnahme auf die Wirtschaft ist Thema dieses doppelseitigen Inserats des Maschinenherstellers *Ingersoll-Rand.* (USA)
114 Inserat für *Shiseido*-Sonnenschutzprodukte. Goldbraune Haut, sandfarbener Hintergrund. (JPN)
115–118 Aus einer Kampagne mit doppelseitigen Anzeigen für *Ford.* Abb. 117: Einführung des *Ford Sierra*; Abb. 115, 116: Vorteile des *Granada* bei Nacht; Abb. 118: Die Stromform des *Escort.* (GER)

112 Annonce double page pour un transporteur ayant augmenté les dimensions de ses trains routiers, ce qui est visualisé par le prolongement de l'annonce sur un rabat. (USA)
113 Cette annonce double page d'*Ingersoll-Rand* (construction mécanique) traite de la libération du businessman américain des contraintes étatiques qui l'enserrent de toutes parts. (USA)
114 Annonce pour les produits solaires *Shiseido.* Peau brun doré, fond sable. (JPN)
115–118 Campagne d'annonces double page pour *Ford.* Fig. 117: introduction de la *Ford Sierra*; fig. 115, 116: avantages de la *Granada*, la nuit; fig. 118: aérodynamique de l'*Escort.* (GER)

114

PHOTOGRAPHER / PHOTOGRAPH:
112 François Robert
113 Pete Elliott
114 Somei Kaneto
115, 116, 118 Dennis Manarchy
117 Duane Fouraker

DESIGNER / GESTALTER:
112 Larney Walker
113 John Dolby
114 Shuji Kawasaki
115, 116, 118 Claus Koch
117 Desmond Cremer/ Mervin Rees

ART DIRECTOR:
112 Larney Walker
113 John Dolby
114 Reikichi Nakayama
115–118 Claus Koch

AGENCY / AGENTUR / AGENCE:
112, 113 BBDM, Inc.
115–118 J. Walter Thompson GmbH

115

116

117

118

The National Federation of Coffee Growers of Colombia, 140 E. 57th Street, N.Y., N.Y. 10022

Will the popularity of Colombian Coffee go to their heads?

Nope.
Even though most Americans are convinced that Colombian Coffee is the best in the world. And even though Juan Valdez® and his partner are on television all the time, success won't change them.
But their success could change you. By offering a 100% Colombian Coffee brand your sales could pick up immediately. Not to mention all of the extra profits you'll reap.
Meanwhile, Juan will remain unaffected by it all. He remarks "We like the traditional life of Colombia much better than Hollywood. So you never have to worry about us moving out to Tinseltown."

100% Colombian Coffee

120

120–122 Double spreads in full colour from a comprehensive advertising campaign in trade magazines for Columbian coffee. This informed the trade how to profit from the success of an extensive campaign of television commercials and the popularity of its male and mule stars—both symbolizing the advertiser's logotype. (USA)
123, 124 Double spreads in colour advertising veterinary products by *Bayer*. Here, on the campaign theme: "We care about animals, but we think about people." (BRA)

120–122 Beispiele aus einer Fachzeitschriften-Kampagne für kolumbianischen Kaffee, mit den Stars der Fernsehwerbung, die auch im Markenzeichen enthalten sind. Abb. 120: «Wird die Popularität des kolumbianischen Kaffees ihnen zu Kopf steigen?»; Abb. 121: «Auf dem Weg zum Erfolg»; Abb. 122: «Ein Juan ist nicht genug» – als Anspielung auf die Popularität der Kampagne. (USA)
123, 124 Doppelseitige Anzeigen mit Farbaufnahmen aus einer Werbekampagne für veterinärmedizinische Produkte von *Bayer*. «Wir kümmern uns um das Tier, aber wir denken an den Menschen.» (BRA)

120–122 Exemples d'une campagne de revues professionnelles pour le café de Colombie, avec les deux vedettes de la publicité télévisée qui se retrouvent aussi dans la marque déposée. Fig. 120: «La popularité du café colombien va-t-elle leur monter à la tête?» Fig. 121: «Sur la voie du succès.» Fig. 122: «Un Juan ne suffit pas» – allusion au succès de la campagne. (USA)
123, 124 Annonces double page, photos couleur, dans une campagne pour les produits vétérinaires de *Bayer*. «Nous nous occupons de l'animal, mais nous pensons à l'homme.» (BRA)

121

122

PHOTOGRAPHER / PHOTOGRAPH:

120–122 Larry Robbins
123, 124 Miro

DESIGNER / GESTALTER / MAQUETTISTE:

120–122 Mark Hughes

ART DIRECTOR / DIRECTEUR ARTISTIQUE:

120–122 Mark Hughes
123, 124 Elio Mirrado

AGENCY / AGENTUR / AGENCE – STUDIO:

120–122 Doyle Dane Bernbach
123, 124 CBBA

A vaca, essa maravilhosa máquina de transformar capim em leite.

A produção brasileira de leite pasteurizado atinge a impressionante cifra de 2,5 bilhões de litros por ano.

Esses números, porém, estão longe de serem suficientes: representam aproximadamente 7 milhões de litros por dia ainda pouco para a nossa população. E para apoiar o nosso desenvolvimento pecuário que a Bayer não mede esforços em seu Departamento Veterinário.

Operando três unidades industriais, a Bayer produz uma completa linha de produtos veterinários, que ajudam a engrossar os rebanhos por todo o país, multiplicando e melhorando as raças, criando empregos, fixando o homem no campo.

Para vencer essa luta, a Bayer traz para o Brasil toda sua experiência e tecnologia internacionais na pesquisa e produção de medicamentos.

Alem disso, todo um trabalho de adequação às nossas condições e necessidades é feito pelos nossos técnicos brasileiros.

So para se ter uma idéia, o desenvolvimento de um produto custa 10 milhões de dólares e demora de 8 a 10 anos. E depois de todo esse investimento, de cada 10.000 drogas pesquisadas apenas uma ou duas chegam a ser comercializadas. Não é só o leite que os produtos veterinários da Bayer ajudam a produzir. É a lingüiça, é a omelete, é a picanha, é o frango com polenta, é a feijoada.

E mais a roupa de lã e o sapato de couro. E mais os dólares com a exportação de tudo isso. E o que é melhor, protegem a saúde de todos nós.

Cuidando do animal, mas pensando no homem.

123

Cuidando do animal, mas pensando no homem.

Quanto melhor a saúde dos nossos animais, melhor será a saúde da nossa gente. Pensando nisso é que a Bayer não mede esforços em seu Departamento Veterinário, para estar sempre junto aos criadores e veterinários, na luta pela melhoria e pelo incremento dos rebanhos nacionais. Além de trazer para o Brasil seus produtos e experiências já aprovados em todo o mundo, a Bayer investe aqui em pesquisas e testes próprios, procurando adequar soluções específicas para os problemas da criação nacional. Constantemente realiza convênios científicos com instituições oficiais e particulares, promove campanhas junto aos criadores e homens do campo, apoia os veterinários em seus esforços por uma pecuária mais avançada e esclarecida. Alguns dos produtos Bayer há muitos anos são parte integrante do dia-a-dia das fazendas e granjas brasileiras.

É o caso do famoso bernicida, larvicida e inseticida Nevugon, grande amigo das vacas, ovelhas, cavalos, porcos e galinhas.

É o caso mais recente de Bayo-n-ox, o mais eficiente promotor de crescimento para aves e suínos. É o caso de Tiguvon Spot-on, o moderno eliminador dos bernes.

Hoje somos 120 milhões de brasileiros, que precisam ser alimentados. A pecuária, ao lado da agricultura, representa papel fundamental nessa tarefa.

Incumbindo-se ainda, através da exportação, de trazer divisas vitais para a economia do país. É por tudo isso que a Bayer se dedica aos animais com todo amor e carinho.

124

125

127

126

128

A good Stilton from Sainsbury's will make your mouth water. (Not your eyes.)

If you associate Stilton with a strong sharp smell you've probably been associating with the wrong kind of Stilton.

A good Stilton should have a mellow taste and smell, with no trace of bitterness.

The blueing should explode from the centre of the cheese but not quite reach the edge.

The texture should be crumbly, but not dry.

There's quite an art in producing fine Stilton and only three counties in England are allowed to do it.

(Most of Sainsbury's Stilton comes from the Vale of Belvoir around Melton Mowbray.)

A Stilton takes at least eleven weeks to make.

The cheese is pierced three times with copper rods to encourage the blueing, and there's a complicated ritual of turning to keep the cheese evenly moist.

Our inspectors check every batch with a cheese iron to make sure the Stilton is perfect.

And we have strict controls on the amount of blueing we'll accept.

At this time of year, we sell Stilton in jars, halves and quarters, though perhaps our most popular size is the Stilton disc you see in the picture.

(Buy one now and it will keep happily in the bottom of the refrigerator until Christmas.)

Of course, if you're buying your Stilton at Sainsbury's you should also look at our port.

It's outstanding value.

We sell a Vintage Character, Ruby and Tawny and every bottle carries a numbered seal of quality from the Institute of Port in Portugal.

Perhaps the most suitable to drink with Stilton is our Vintage Character – a blend of fine ports matured for years in oak casks.

At only £3.48 a bottle, it's one item on our shelves you shouldn't pass.

Good food costs less at Sainsbury's.

129

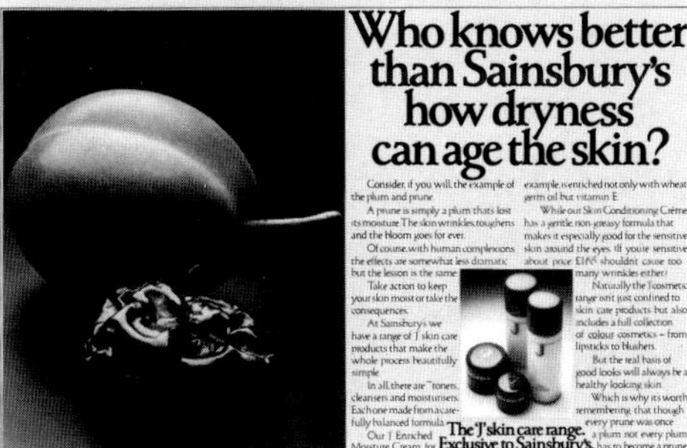

130

Advertisements/Anzeigen/Annonces

PHOTOGRAPHER / PHOTOGRAPH:

125, 126 Brigitte Richter
127–130 Martin Thompson
131 Derek Seagrim

ART DIRECTOR / DIRECTEUR ARTISTIQUE:

125, 126 Manfred Offermann
127–130 Ron Brown
131 David Harrison

AGENCY / AGENTUR / AGENCE – STUDIO:

125, 126 Young & Rubicam GmbH
127–130 Abbott Mead Vickers/SMS Ltd.
131 Davidson Pearce Ltd.

125, 126 Full-page colour ads for very dry sherry from *Gonzales Byass.* Sun-glasses and shoe red, ground in black and white. (GER)
127–130 The photographic illustrations and complete double spreads of magazine advertisements by *Sainsbury's* department store, for Stilton cheese and skin-care products. (GBR)
131 Double-spread announcement of a new cookery section in the *Observer* magazine. (GBR)

125, 126 Ganzseitige Zeitschriften-Anzeigen aus einer Kampagne mit Farbaufnahmen für sehr trockenen Sherry von *Gonzales Byass.* Schuhe und Sonnenbrille in leuchtendem Rot. (GER)
127–130 Aufnahmen und vollständige Doppelseiten aus einer *Sainsbury*-Inseraten-Kampagne in Zeitschriften, hier für Stilton-Käse und Hautpflegeprodukte. (GBR)
131 Doppelseitiges Zeitschriften-Inserat mit Ankündigung einer Folge von kulinarischen Köstlichkeiten aus elf europäischen Ländern, die während zehn Wochen im Magazin der Zeitung *Observer* in Wort und Bild präsentiert werden. (GBR)

125, 126 Annonce de journal pleine page dans une campagne illustrée de photos couleur pour un xérès très sec de *Gonzales Byass.* Chaussures et lunettes de soleil rouge vif. (GER)
127–130 Photos et doubles pages complètes d'une série d'annonces de magazines pour *Sainsbury,* ici pour le fromage Stilton et les produits de soins pour le corps. (GBR)
131 Annonce de magazine double page annonçant la publication, durant dix semaines, dans le magazine du journal *Observer,* d'une série de recettes gastronomiques venant de onze pays européens et illustrées par le texte et par l'image. (GBR)

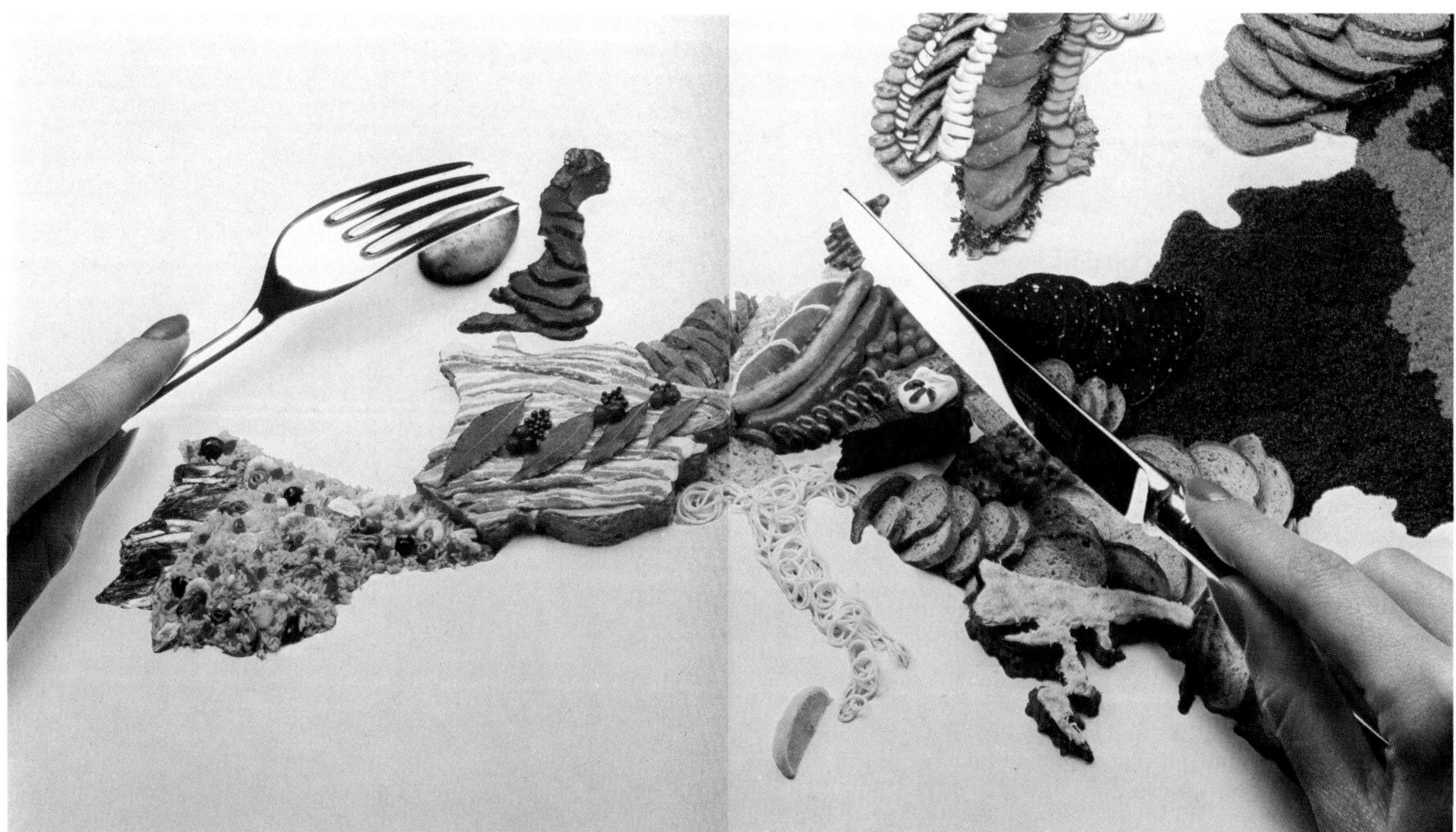

The Observer Guide to European Cookery starts March 28.

Week by week, for 10 weeks, in a pull-out section of the Magazine, we'll be taking you on a cook's tour of Europe.

Jane Grigson, Observer magazine cookery writer and author of 'The Vegetable Book' and 'Food with the Famous,' will outline the culinary delights of 11 countries.

From Portugal to Russia. And from French country cooking to Hungarian goulash.

With mouth-watering photographs taken 'in situ', and dozens of detailed recipes.

There will be features on each country's drink, where to sample its food in restaurants, and where to buy the right ingredients and utensils to be a good Eurocook yourself.

Each week, too, you have the chance to win a competition.

Pull out and keep each part of the Guide in our special binder.

And start cooking your way across Europe.

131

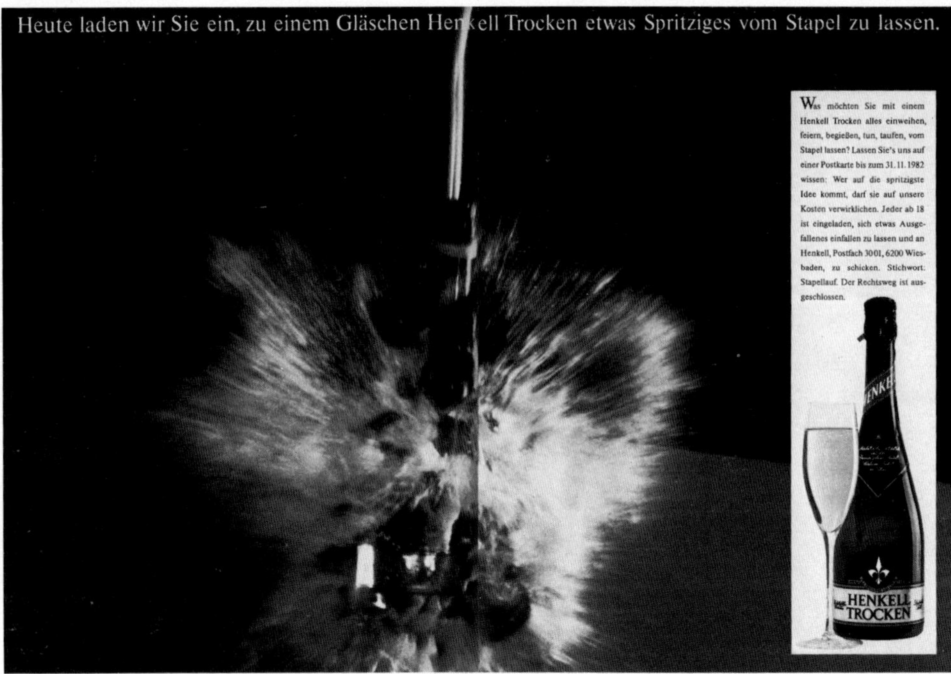

132

132 Double-spread magazine ad for *Henkell* champagne-type wine. Green bottle is shown launched against red and black of ship's side. (GER)
133 Full-page magazine ad for tomato concentrate. Red on white. (SWI)
134 Full-page advertisement in magazines. Coffee-coloured headline, newsprint on cup underlined in red, white ground. (GER)
135–137 Double-spread and two full-page advertisements in colour campaign for *Hero* preserved foods. The headlines in Figs. 136 and 137 are overprinted on green and raspberry ground, respectively. (SWI)

132 Doppelseitige, mehrfarbige Zeitschriften-Anzeige für *Henkell-Trocken*-Sekt. Auf dem Ausschnitt rechts wird der Leser aufgefordert, seine Ideen für einen Grund zum Sekttrinken der Firma einzuschicken. (GER)
133 Ganzseitige Zeitschriften-Anzeige für Tomatenpurée. In Farbe. (SWI)
134 Die Deutsche Kaffeegesellschaft assoziiert Kaffee mit Klatsch: «heiss, aktuell und in aller Munde». (GER)
135–137 Mehrfarbige Anzeigen aus einer Kampagne für *Hero*-Konserven. Slogans in Abb. 136, 137 auf grünem respektive himbeerrotem Grund. (SWI)

132 Annonce de magazine double page, en polychromie, pour le mousseux *Henkell Trocken*. Le coupon de droite permet de participer à un concours en indiquant une bonne raison de boire du mousseux. (GER)
133 Annonce de magazine pleine page pour une purée de tomates. (SWI)
134 La Deutsche Kaffeegesellschaft associe le café aux cancans: «brûlant, d'actualité, dans toutes les bouches». (GER)
135–137 Annonces polychromes dans une campagne en faveur des conserves *Hero*. Slogans 136 et 137 sur fond vert respectivement framboise. (SWI)

PHOTOGRAPHER / PHOTOGRAPH
132 Christian von Alvensleben
133, 135–137 Marjolaine Dutoit
134 Dirk Olaf Wexel

DESIGNER / GESTALTER / MAQUETTISTE:
133 Renato Ferrara
134 Rainer Osterwalder
135–137 Mario Ferrara

ART DIRECTOR:
132 Christine & Rainer de Rooy
133 H. Brütsch
134 Rainer Osterwalder
135–137 Renato Ferrara

AGENCY / AGENTUR:
132 TBWA
133, 135–137 Adolf Wirz AG
134 Heye, Needham & Partner

Die mit mehr Früchten... ist die mit weniger Zucker.

mehr Früchte, weniger Zucker
Delicia
Himbeeren
Framboises
Hero

Hero Delicia ist die fruchtigste Confitüre*. Weil sie viel mehr Früchte enthält und viel weniger Zucker. Und daher 20% weniger Kalorien. Hero Delicia gibt es in 11 verschiedenen Sorten. Und keine von ihnen hat Farbstoffe.

* Ohne Konservierungsmittel. Und trotzdem haltbar.

Hero
Freude am Essen

135

133

134

136

137

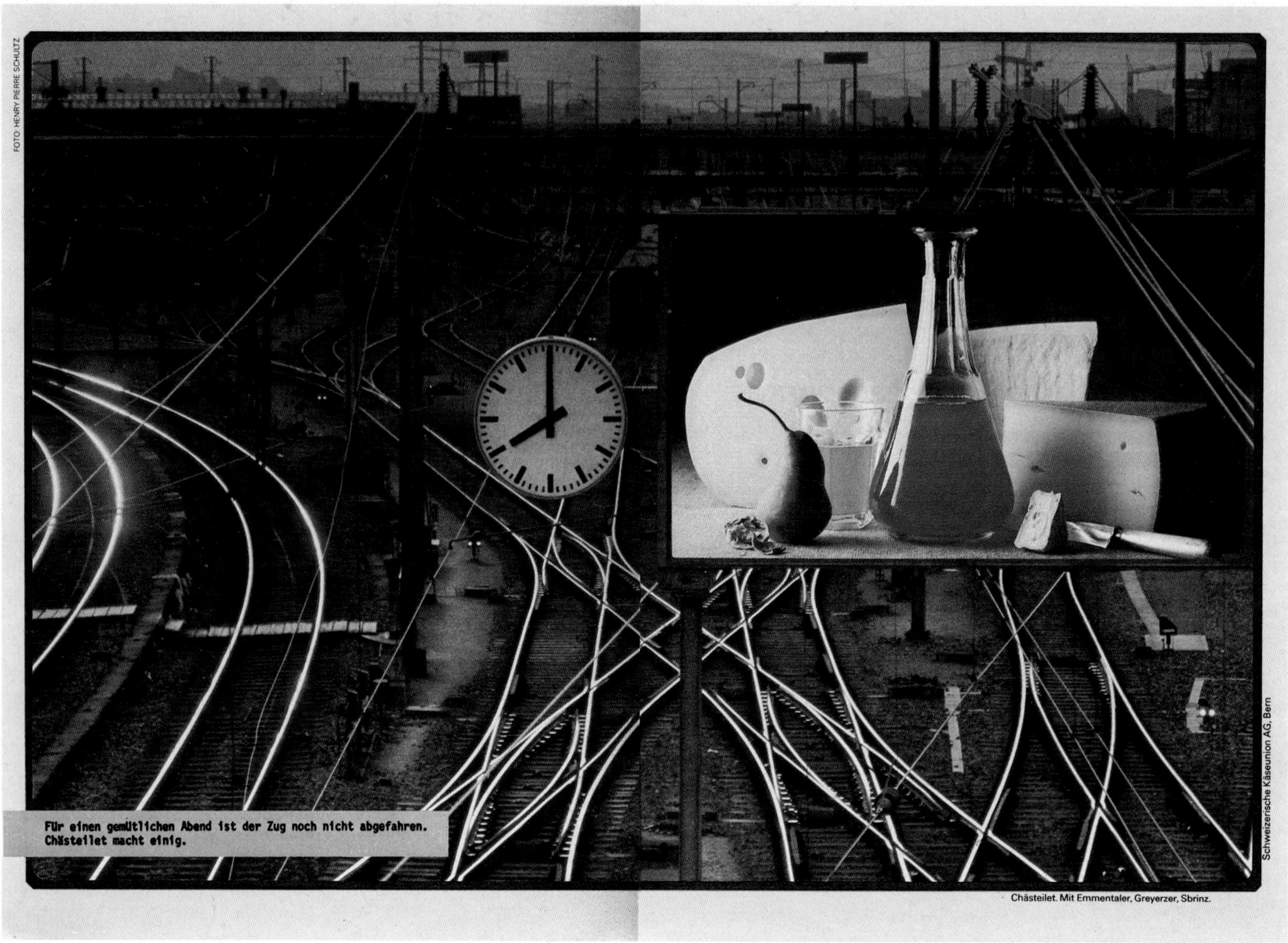
FOTO: HENRY PIERRE SCHULTZ
Für einen gemütlichen Abend ist der Zug noch nicht abgefahren.
Chästeilet macht einig.
Schweizerische Käseunion AG, Bern
Chästeilet. Mit Emmentaler, Greyerzer, Sbrinz.

138

PHOTOGRAPHER / PHOTOGRAPH:

138 Henry Pierre Schultz
139 Senji Urushibata
140, 141 Axel Gnad

DESIGNER / GESTALTER / MAQUETTISTE:

138 Fredy Steiner
139 Hiromi Shimazaki/Yoji Tanaka
140, 141 Christine & Rainer de Rooy

ART DIRECTOR / DIRECTEUR ARTISTIQUE:

138 Fredy Steiner
139 Masaaki Izumiya/Senji Urushibata
140, 141 Christine & Rainer de Rooy

AGENCY / AGENTUR / AGENCE – STUDIO:

138 Gisler & Gisler
140, 141 TBWA

KÜHL FLOSS DER FRISCHE MATEUS ROSÉ.
SEIN FEINES MOUSSEUX PERLTE ÜBER DIE
ZUNGE. DU KONNTEST DIE STILLE SPÜREN.

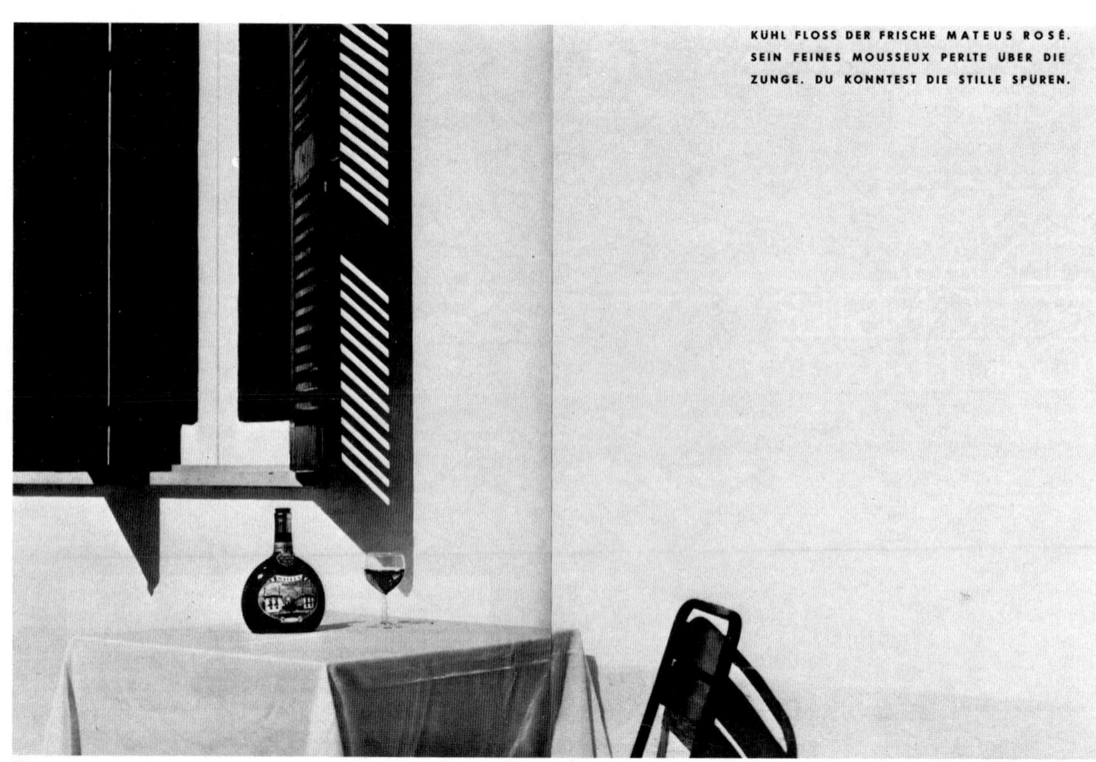

140

146

147

142–144 Samples from a series of full-page magazine advertisements in full colour for *Snow Brand*, a Japanese butter. (JPN)
145 Shot composed for a Barcelona beer, but the advertisement was not used. (SPA)
146, 147 Detail of the photograph and the complete full-page advertisement from a campaign series for *Caballero* cigarettes: "Taste for two." (NLD)

142–144 Beispiele aus einer Serie von ganzseitigen Anzeigen mit Farbaufnahmen für Butter der Marke *Snow Brand*. (JPN)
145 Aufnahme für ein Bier aus Barcelona. Das Inserat ist nicht erschienen. (SPA)
146, 147 Detail der Aufnahme und vollständiges ganzseitiges Inserat aus einer Kampagne für *Caballero*-Zigaretten: «Geschmack für zwei.» (NLD)

142–144 Exemples d'annonces pleine page illustrées en couleur dans une série réalisée pour la publicité du beurre *Snow Brand*. (JPN)
145 Photo pour une bière de Barcelone. L'annonce correspondante n'a pas paru. (SPA)
146, 147 Détail de la photo et annonce complète sur page entière, dans une campagne en faveur des cigarettes *Caballero*: «du goût pour deux.» (NLD)

PHOTOGRAPHER / PHOTOGRAPH:

142–144 Yoichi Sato
145 Lluis Brunet
146, 147 Aldo Fallai

DESIGNER / GESTALTER / MAQUETTISTE:

142–144 Hideo Mukai/Ai Ienaka
145 Lluis Brunet

ART DIRECTOR / DIRECTEUR ARTISTIQUE:

142–144 Hideo Mukai
146, 147 Jan van der Ven

AGENCY / AGENTUR / AGENCE – STUDIO:

142–144 Mukai & Assoc.
146, 147 Prad B.V.

149

Advertisements/Anzeigen/Annonces

PHOTOGRAPHER / PHOTOGRAPH / PHOTOGRAPHE:

148 Raymond Meier
149–151 Detlef Trefz

DESIGNER / GESTALTER / MAQUETTISTE:

148 Rolf Kälin

ART DIRECTOR / DIRECTEUR ARTISTIQUE:

148 Fredi Bosshard
149–151 Wolf Lommel/Annette Meisen

AGENCY / AGENTUR / AGENCE – STUDIO:

148 Adolf Wirz AG
149–151 TBWA

148 Full-page magazine ad for apple juice, showing the yellow liquid and its green bottle on white ground. It refers to the new requirement for on-pack declaration of a product's composition. Here the declaration was summed up by the campaign logo, which was projected into the shadow of the glass. Its slogan declares "Fabulous apple juice". (SWI)
149–151 Details of the photographs and one complete double spread from a magazine campaign advertising *Grand Marnier.* (GER)

148 Mehrfarbige, ganzseitige Zeitschriften-Anzeige für Apfelsaft. Bezug genommen wird auf den bundesrätlichen Beschluss, dass die Zusammensetzung von Lebensmitteln künftig deklariert werden muss. Das Signet «Fabelhaft ist Apfelsaft» wurde in den Schatten des Glases hineinprojiziert. (SWI)
149–151 Zwei doppelseitige Aufnahmen und eine vollständige doppelseitige Zeitschriften-Anzeige aus einer Kampagne für *Grand Marnier.* (GER)

148 Annonce de magazine polychrome sur page entière pour un jus de pomme. On s'y réfère à un arrêté fédéral imposant l'indication de la composition des denrées alimentaires sur les conditionnements. Le slogan «Le jus de pommes, c'est épatant» a été projeté dans l'ombre portée par le verre. (SWI)
149–151 Deux photos double page et une annonce de magazine complète sur deux pages pour une campagne en faveur du *Grand Marnier.* (GER)

148

150

PETITS MOMENTS.

Grand Marnier Cordon Rouge
Cognac prägt seinen Charakter.

GRAND MARNIER.

151

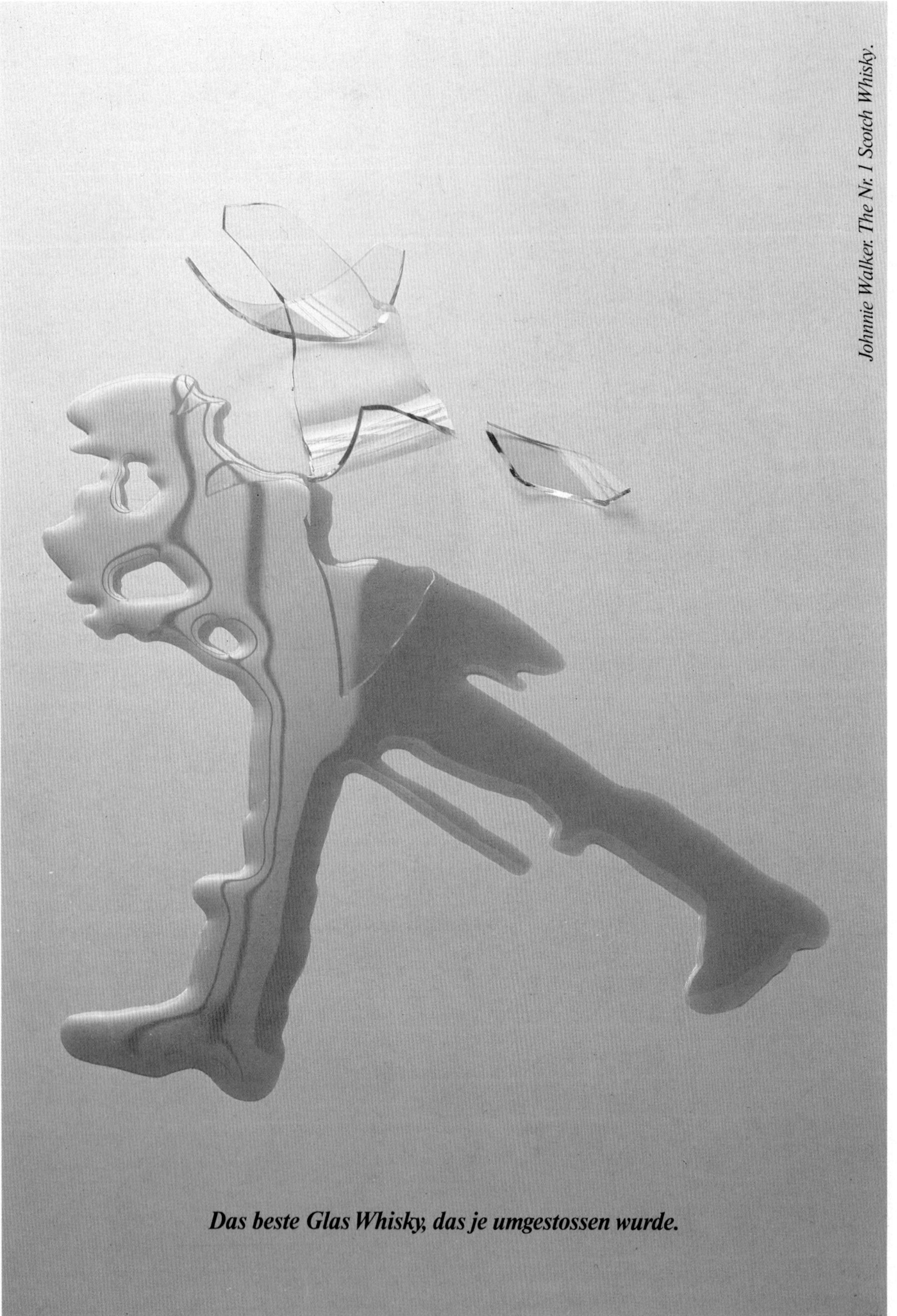

152

PHOTOGRAPHER / PHOTOGRAPH:

152 J. Tapprich
153, 154 Yoichi Sato
155 R. Spengler
156 Harald Schlüter

DESIGNER / GESTALTER / MAQUETTISTE:

152, 155 Mathias Bapst
153, 154 Hideo Mukai/Ai Ienaka
156 Erasmus Schlammer

ART DIRECTOR / DIRECTEUR ARTISTIQUE:

152, 155 Mathias Bapst
153, 154 Hideo Mukai
156 Harald Schlüter

AGENCY / AGENTUR / AGENCE – STUDIO:

152, 155 Young & Rubicam
153, 154 Mukai & Associates
156 Harald Schlüter GmbH

152, 155 Full-page advertisements from a long-term colour campaign for *Johnnie Walker* whisky. The theme of Fig. 152: "The best drop of whisky ever dropped." (SWI)
153, 154 Samples from a series of full-page colour advertisements for baking fat. Yellow on white and on black ground. (JPN)
156 From a colour campaign of full-page advertisements for flavours made by *Haarmann & Reimer.* Orange on white ground. (USA)

152, 155 Ganzseitige Inserate aus einer langfristigen Werbekampagne für *Johnnie-Walker*-Whisky. Das wohlbekannte Markenzeichen ist in beiden Fällen Mittelpunkt. (SWI)
153, 154 Beispiele aus einer Serie von ganzseitigen Inseraten für Backfette. In Farbe. (JPN)
156 Aus einer Kampagne mit ganzseitigen Inseraten für Aroma-Stoffe von *Haarmann & Reimer,* hier für süsse Nachspeisen. Die Herzform ist das Hauptelement aller Illustrationen, im Einklang mit dem Slogan: «Am Herzen des guten Geschmacks.» (USA)

152, 155 Annonces pleine page pour une campagne de longue durée orchestrée par le whisky *Johnnie Walker.* La marque déposée bien connue figure dans les deux cas au centre de l'intérêt. (SWI)
153, 154 Exemples d'une série d'annonces pleine page pour des graisses de cuisson. Couleur. (JPN)
156 Campagne d'annonces pleine page pour les arômes *Haarmann & Reimer* utilisés ici pour des desserts sucrés. Le slogan «Au cœur du bon goût» est illustré dans toutes les illustrations par un élément en forme de cœur. (USA)

クッキーを手づくりでつくる。なんとなくリッチな気持ちになりますね。それにコツさえ覚えると意外に簡単にできるのです。そこでコツをひとこと。キメ細かく、軽く焼き上げるためには小麦粉をよくふるっておくことです。空気を入れてやるのとほかの材料とよくなじませて、ムラなく仕上げるためです。粉をまぜ込むときは、手早く、絶対に練らないことです。口あたりがよく、ホロッと崩れるようなクッキー独特の感じにならないからです。生地はラップに包んで冷蔵庫で少なくとも1時間以上は休ませてください。粉っぽさがなくなり、扱いやすくなります。ボードにも抜き型にも、強力粉を振ること。焼き上がり時間を揃えるため型の大きさは揃えてください。

●雪印ケーキ用マーガリン(無塩)　ホイップしたり、充分にねり込んだりするお菓子づくりのマーガリン。風味が好評です。
●雪印ショートニング　コーン油でつくられた植物性の調理用油脂です。パンやケーキは組織が均一になってふっくら焼きあがり、クッキーは軽く、さっくりした歯ざわりになります。

雪印ショートニング
雪印 ケーキ用 マーガリン

153

マドレーヌは、その名の通りフランス生まれのお菓子ですが、日本でも親しまれているケーキのひとつです。写真のようなマドレーヌ型だけを入手すれば意外にホームメイドでおいしくつくれるのです。まず、卵に砂糖を入れて泡立て、あの独特の香りをつけるため、おろしたレモンの皮をまぜ合わせます。これに、ふるった小麦粉とベーキングパウダーを加えてまぜ合わせます。最後に溶かしたケーキ用マーガリンを少しずつ回し入れてさっくり合わせます。これで、もうタネはできあがりです。つぎにマドレーヌ型にバターをぬり、小麦粉をふってさかさにして余分な粉をおとし、タネを型の9分目ほど流しこみ、20〜30分おいてからオーブンで焼けば出来上がりです。

●雪印ケーキ用マーガリン(無塩)　ホイップしたり、充分にねり込んだりするお菓子づくりのマーガリン。風味が好評です。
●雪印ショートニング　コーン油でつくられた植物性の調理用油脂です。パンやケーキは組織が均一になってふっくら焼きあがり、クッキーは軽く、さっくりとした歯ざわりになります。

雪印ショートニング
雪印 ケーキ用 マーガリン

154

155

156

Advertisements
Anzeigen
Annonces

PHOTOGRAPHER / PHOTOGRAPH:

157, 158 Richard Avedon
159, 160 Henry Wolf
161 Bishin Jumonji

DESIGNER / GESTALTER / MAQUETTISTE:

159, 160 Henry Wolf
161, 162 Tsuguya Inoue/Yu Ueda

ART DIRECTOR / DIRECTEUR ARTISTIQUE:

157, 158 Catherine Minesco
159, 160 Henry Wolf
161, 162 Tsuguya Inoue

AGENCY / AGENTUR / AGENCE – STUDIO:

157, 158 Richard Avedon Inc.
159, 160 Henry Wolf Productions

157

158

159

160

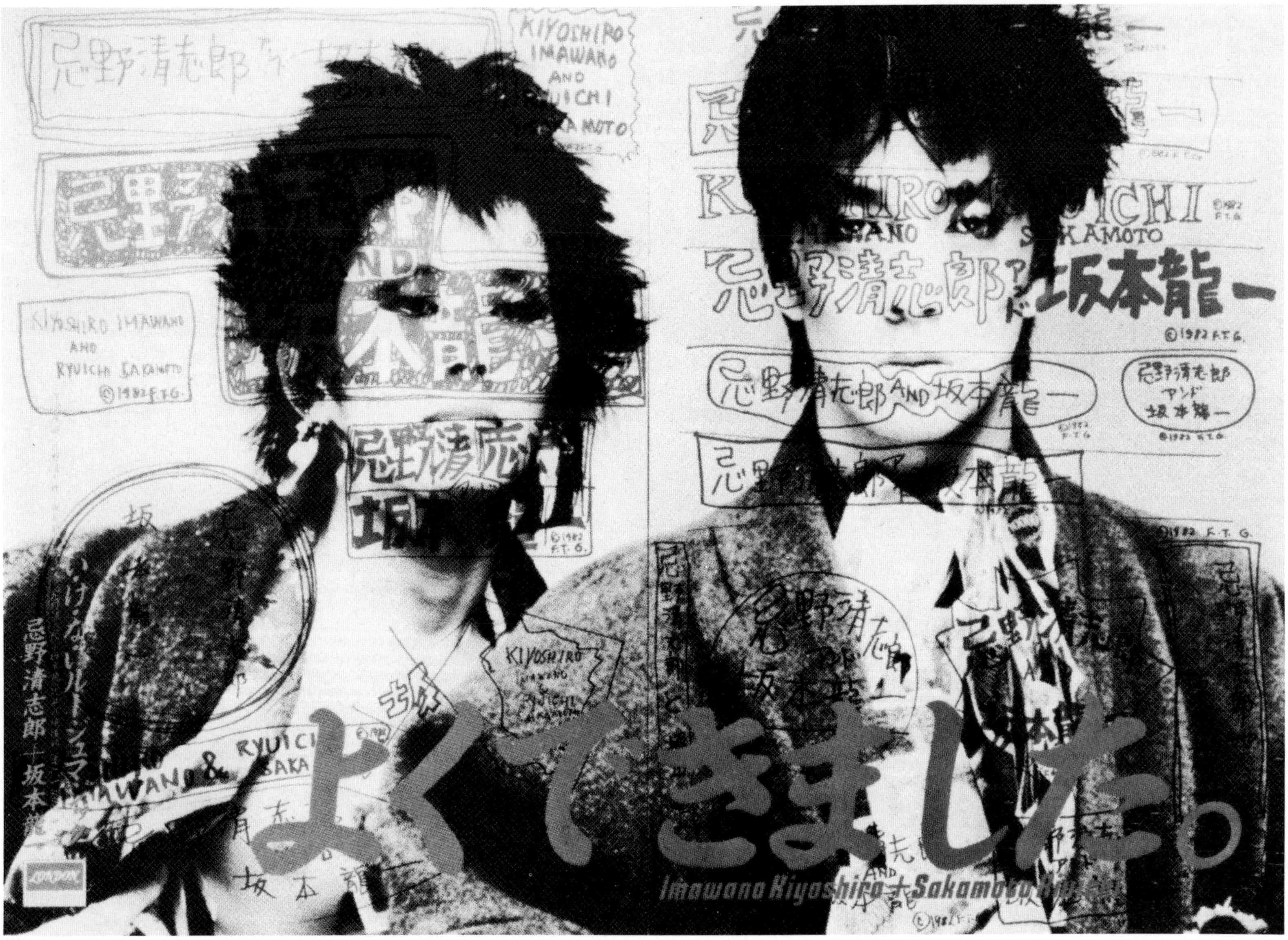

161

162

157, 158 Lena Horne and Liz Taylor are the stars who modelled for a star photographer in this campaign to attract tourists to a star city. (USA)
159, 160 Full-page magazine ads for diamond jewellery by *Van Cleef & Arpels*. Fig. 159 with emeralds, beige tones on white ground. Fig. 160 with saphires, black and lilac on black ground. (USA)
161, 162 Magazine advertising in Japan for *London Records*. Fig. 161 shows two of its Japanese recording stars. (JPN)

157, 158 Aus einer Touristik-Kampagne der Stadt New York: «New York liebt Sie. Wir freuen uns, dass Sie hier sind.» (USA)
159, 160 Ganzseitige Anzeigen mit Farbaufnahmen, aus einer Werbekampagne für den Juwelier *Van Cleef & Arpels*. (USA)
161 Doppelseitige Zeitschriftenanzeige von *London Records* für zwei japanische Schallplattenstars. (JPN)
162 Ein weiteres Inserat für Produktionen der London Records K. K. (JPN)

157, 158 Annonces figurant dans une campagne touristique en faveur de New York: «New York vous aime. Nous sommes heureux de votre séjour parmi nous.» (USA)
159, 160 Annonces pleine page illustrées en couleur, dans une campagne publicitaire du bijoutier *Van Cleef & Arpels*. (USA)
161 Annonce de magazine double page de *London Records* pour deux vedettes japonaises du disque. (JPN)
162 Une autre annonce pour les productions de London Records K. K. (JPN)

2

Booklets

Folders

Catalogues

Programmes

Broschüren

Faltprospekte

Kataloge

Programme

Brochures

Dépliants

Catalogues

Programmes

165

Booklets/Prospekte/Brochures

163

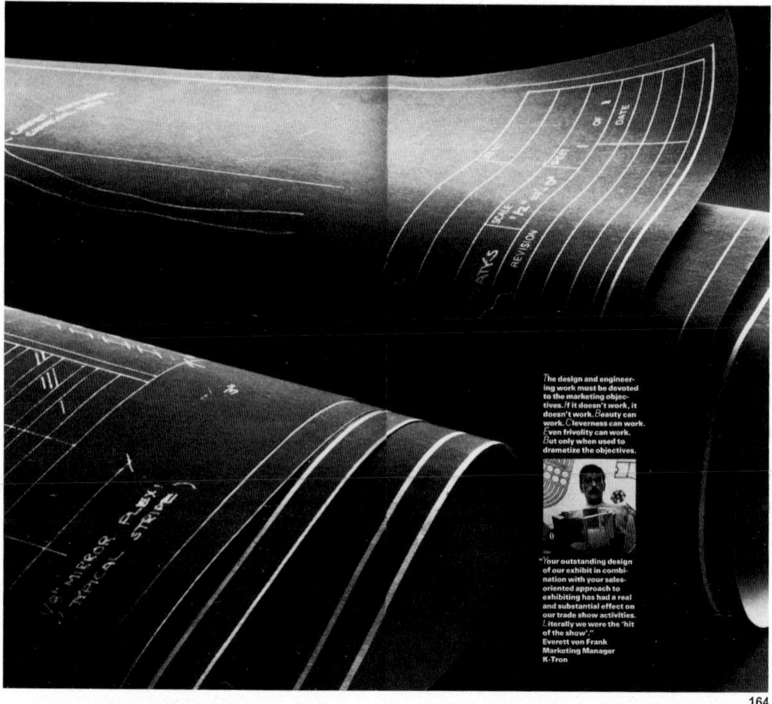

164

166

PHOTOGRAPHER / PHOTOGRAPH / PHOTOGRAPHE:

163, 164 Philip Porcella
165 Nikolay Žurek
166 Don Sparks

DESIGNER / GESTALTER / MAQUETTISTE:

163, 164 Bruce McIntosh/Robert Cipriani
165 G. Smith
166 Valerie Hepler

ART DIRECTOR / DIRECTEUR ARTISTIQUE:

163, 164 Bruce McIntosh/Robert Cipriani
165 Nikolas Sidjakov
166 Don Sparks

AGENCY / AGENTUR / AGENCE – STUDIO:

163, 164 Robert Cipriani Associates
165 Sidjakov Berman & Gomez
166 Sparks Studio

163, 164 Samples of the double spreads in black and white from a promotional booklet for *Admore*, designer of exhibits and stands for trade shows. Thoroughness is its theme. (USA)
165 Double-spread from a promotional booklet for *Diablo*, manufacturer of ribbon cartridges and printwheels. Mainly black, with coloured highlights, on blue ground. (USA)
166 Full page from a self-promotional booklet for photographer Don Sparks. (USA)

163, 164 Doppelseiten mit Schwarzweissaufnahmen aus einer Broschüre von *Admore*, Gestalter von Ausstellungs-Ständen. Thema ist die Planung, die allen Aspekten Rechnung tragen muss. (USA)
165 Doppelseitige Farbaufnahme aus einer Broschüre für *Diablo*, Hersteller von Typenrädern und Farbbandkassetten für Schreibmaschinen. (USA)
166 Ganzseitige Aufnahme aus einer Eigenwerbungsbroschüre des Photographen Don Sparks. (USA)

163, 164 Doubles pages illustrées en noir et blanc, dans une brochure réalisée pour *Admore*, concepteur de stands d'exposition. Sujet: le planning tenant compte de tous les aspects. (USA)
165 Photo couleur double page, dans une brochure pour *Diablo*, fabricant de marguerites et cassettes à ruban pour machines à écrire. (USA)
166 Photo pleine page illustrant une brochure autopromotionnelle du photographe Don Sparks. (USA)

167

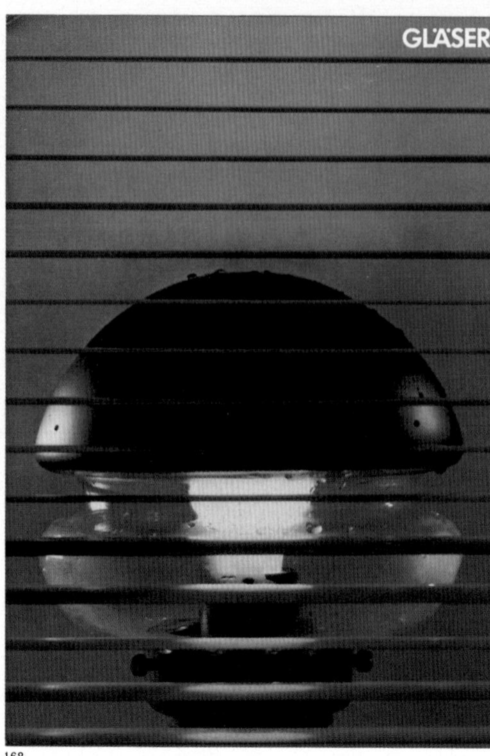

168

169

167–169 Complete pages from a catalogue for lamps from *Brillantleuchten.* (GER)
170 Cover page of a *Steelcase* booklet about its tables. Full-colour photograph on slate grey ground with white overprinting. (USA)
171 Full-colour page in shades of green from a promotional booklet for *Valentine Graphics.* It was used to visualize the entrée into full-course printing and ancillary services. (AUS)
172, 173 Detail of the photograph and complete double-spread in a catalogue of home textiles by *West Point Pepperell.* Fig. 173 shows its unusual format. (USA)

167–169 Ganzseitige Aufnahmen aus einem Katalog für *Brillantleuchten.* (GER)
170 Umschlagseite einer Broschüre für *Steelcase,* Hersteller von Tischen. Farbaufnahme, Hintergrund schiefergrau, Schrift weiss. (USA)
171 Ganzseitige Farbaufnahme in Grüntönen aus der Eigenwerbungsbroschüre eines Druckers: «Wir halten das Entrée für ebensowichtig wie den Hauptgang.» (AUS)
172, 173 Aufnahme und Doppelseite aus einer Broschüre des Heimtextilienherstellers *West Point Pepperell,* mit dem Titel «Perspektive». Abb. 173 zeigt das ungewöhnliche Format. (USA)

170

171

172

PHOTOGRAPHER / PHOTOGRAPH:

167–169 Nikolay Žurek
170 Craig Vanderlende
171 John Pollard
172, 173 Joe Standart

DESIGNER / GESTALTER / MAQUETTISTE:

167–169 Fritz Haase
170 Fletcher R. Sliker/David Perkins
171 Garry Emery
172, 173 James Sebastian/Michael McGinn/Jim Hinchee

ART DIRECTOR:

170 David Perkins
171 Garry Emery
172, 173 James Sebastian

AGENCY / AGENTUR / AGENCE – STUDIO:

167–169 Fritz Haase
170 David Perkins & Associates
171 Emery Vincent Associates
172, 173 Designframe, Inc.

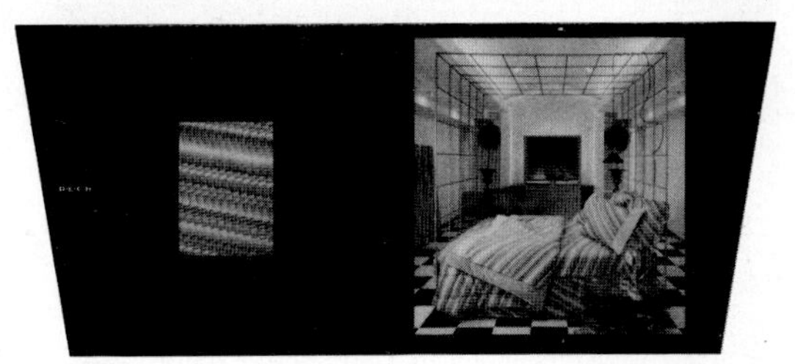

173

167–169 Photos pleine page illustrant un catalogue pour les éclairages *Brillantleuchten*. (GER)
170 Couverture d'une brochure réalisée pour *Steelcase*, fabricant de tables. Photo couleur, fond ardoisé, texte blanc. (USA)
171 Photo couleur pleine page, tonalités vertes, pour la brochure autopromotionnelle d'une imprimerie: «Nous attachons autant d'importance au hors-d'œuvre qu'au plat de résistance.» (AUS)
172, 173 Photo et double page d'une brochure de *West Point Pepperell*, fabricant de tissus d'intérieur, intitulée «Perspective». La fig. 173 révèle le format inhabituel. (USA)

174

Booklets/Prospekte/Brochures

176

177

178

175

PHOTOGRAPHER / PHOTOGRAPH / PHOTOGRAPHE:

174, 175 Dennis DeProis/Fred Kaplan
176–178 Reven T. C. Wurman
179 Dennis Gray
180 John Curtis

DESIGNER / GESTALTER / MAQUETTISTE:

174, 175 Jerry Berman
176–178 Richard Saul Wurman
179 Betty Barsamian/Michael Manwaring
180 Bill Cloutman/Tim Ryan

ART DIRECTOR / DIRECTEUR ARTISTIQUE:

174, 175 Jerry Berman
176–178 Richard Saul Wurman
179 Richard Silverstein
180 Bill Cloutman/Tim Ryan

AGENCY / AGENTUR / AGENCE – STUDIO:

174, 175 Sidjakov Berman & Gomez
179 The Office of Michael Manwaring
180 Brewster Advertising

174, 175 Inside double spread and the cover of a full-colour booklet on baseball and the San Francisco Giants, used to promote ticket sales. (USA)
176–178 Covers from a series of guidebooks published by *Access Press*. In a handy (tall pocket) format, they are full of detailed information. (USA)
179 Cover of full-colour folder about baseball and the Oakland A's team. (USA)
180 Full-colour cover of a booklet for *Maximum*, maker of wind and weather instruments. Tones of brass and gold. (USA)

174, 175 Doppelseite und Umschlag einer Werbebroschüre für die Baseball-Mannschaft San Francisco Giants, zur Förderung des Kartenverkaufs. In Farbe. (USA)
176–178 Umschläge von Stadt- bzw. Inselführern aus einer von *Access Press* veröffentlichten Reihe im praktischen, schlanken Taschenformat. (USA)
179 Umschlag einer mehrfarbigen Broschüre für eine Baseball-Mannschaft. (USA)
180 In Gold- und Gelbtönen gehaltener Umschlag für eine kleinformatige Broschüre von *Maximum*, Hersteller von meteorologischen und anderen Messgeräten. (USA)

174, 175 Double page et couverture d'une brochure publicitaire pour l'équipe de baseball San Francisco Giants, pour la promotion des ventes de billets. En couleur. (USA)
176–178 Couvertures de guides de villes et d'îles, dans une série publiée aux Editions *Access Press* dans un format réduit pratique. (USA)
179 Couverture d'une brochure polychrome pour une équipe de base-ball. (USA)
180 Couverture aux tons or et jaune pour une brochure au petit format de *Maximum*, fabricant d'instruments de mesure pour la météo et d'autres usages. (USA)

179

180

PHOTOGRAPHER / PHOTOGRAPH:

181 Daniel Gendre
182–184 Peter Häfliger
185, 186 Gauthier Fleuri

DESIGNER / GESTALTER / MAQUETTISTE:

181 Rolf Kälin
182–184 Christian Lang
185, 186 Alain Pontecorvo/
Richard Dupuy

ART DIRECTOR / DIRECTEUR ARTISTIQUE:

181 Fredi Bosshard
182–184 Christian Lang

AGENCY / AGENTUR / AGENCE – STUDIO:

181 Adolf Wirz AG
182–184 Werbung Ciba-Geigy
185, 186 Quatre H/RSC & G

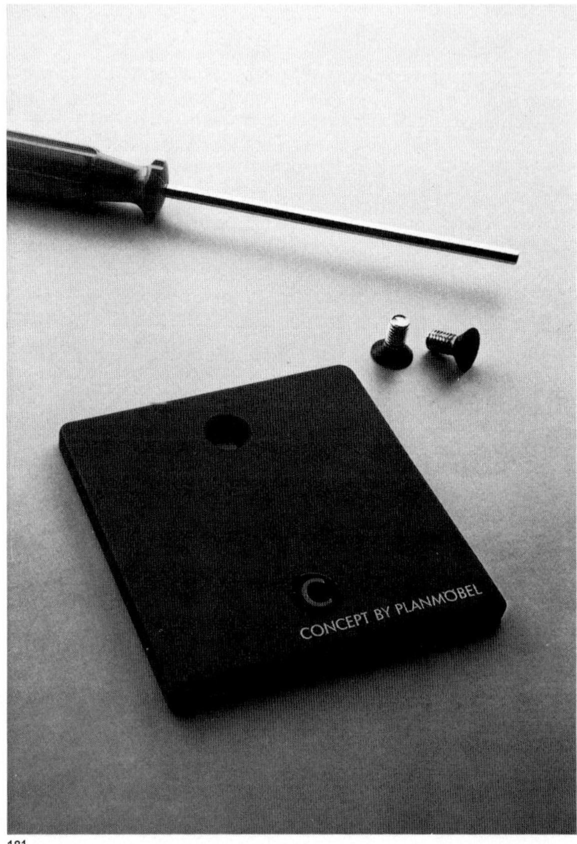

181

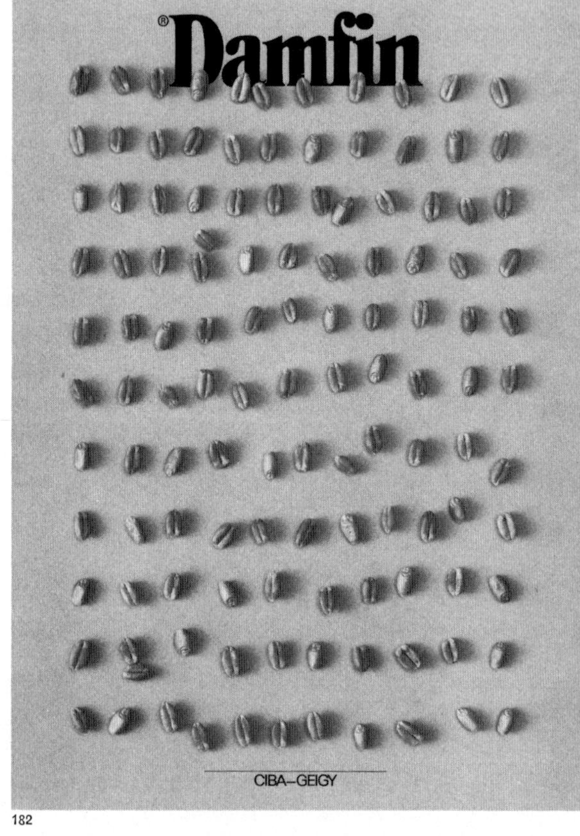

182

181 Cover of a full-colour booklet on office furniture by *Planmöbel.* (SWI)
182 Embossed cover of a *Ciba-Geigy* colour booklet on *Damfin,* an insecticide for protecting stored agricultural produce such as grain: light brown on beige. (SWI)
183, 184 Fronts of folders for a *Geigy* analgetic, *Rengasil.* The R is cut out of light brown wood and a green fabric. (SWI)
185, 186 Full-page and double-spread photographs from a hard-cover *Citroën* album. The snow tracks in Fig. 186 are greyish green, on greyish blue ground. (FRA)

181 Umschlagseite einer Broschüre für *Planmöbel.* In Farbe. (SWI)
182 Im Prägedruck hergestellter Umschlag einer *Ciba-Geigy*-Broschüre für *Damfin,* ein Vorratsschutzmittel. Hellbraune Körner auf beigefarbenem Grund. (SWI)
183, 184 Vorderseiten von Faltprospekten für *Rengasil,* ein Analgetikum von *Geigy.* Hellbraunes und grünes R. (SWI)
185, 186 Ganzseitige Aufnahme und Beispiel der doppelseitigen Aufnahmen aus einem Katalog für *Citroën.* Abb. 186: graugrüne Spuren auf graublauem Grund. (FRA)

181 Couverture d'une brochure consacrée aux ameublements *Planmöbel.* (SWI)
182 Couverture gaufrée d'une brochure *Ciba-Geigy* pour *Damfin,* un agent protecteur de denrées alimentaires entreposées. Grains brun clair sur fond beige. (SWI)
183, 184 Rectos de dépliants réalisés pour l'analgésique *Rengasil* de *Geigy.* R brun clair et vert. (SWI)
185, 186 Photo pleine page et exemple des photos double page d'un catalogue réalisé pour *Citroën.* Fig. 186: empreintes gris vert sur fond bleu gris. (FRA)

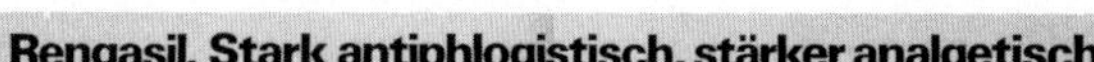

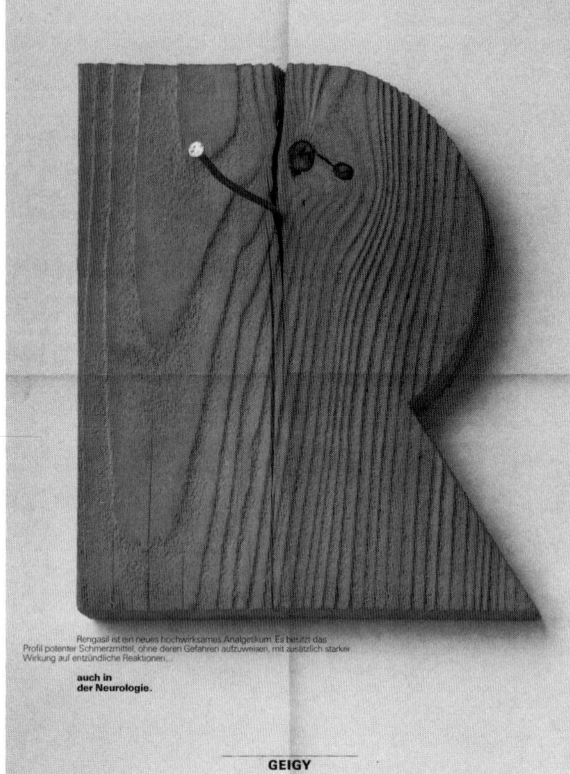

183

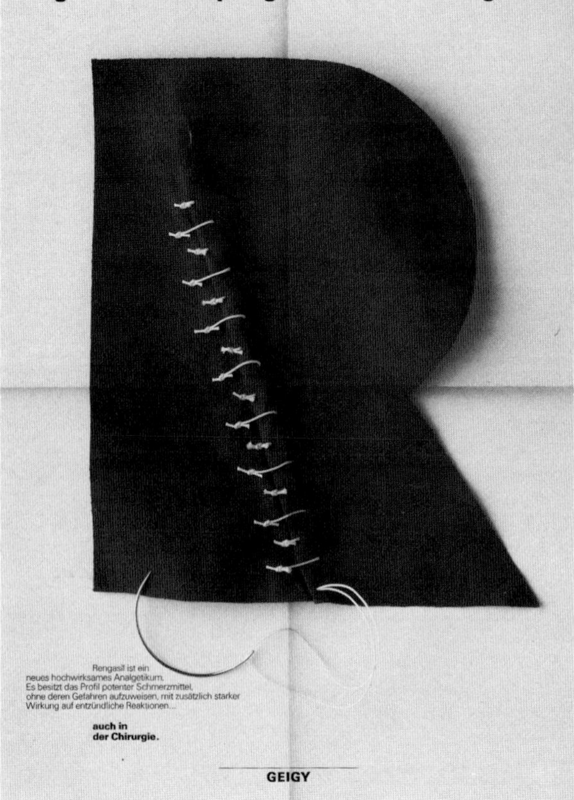

184

185

Booklets/Prospekte/Brochures

186

187

PHOTOGRAPHER / PHOTOGRAPH / PHOTOGRAPHE:

187–193 Terutaka Hoashi

DESIGNER / GESTALTER / MAQUETTISTE:

187, 189, 191–193 Hiroshi Iwata
188, 190 Mami Asano

ART DIRECTOR / DIRECTEUR ARTISTIQUE:

187–193 Hiroshi Iwata

AGENCY / AGENTUR / AGENCE – STUDIO:

187–193 Dentsu Inc.

Booklets/Prospekte/Brochures

187, 191, 192 Cover and complete folder for the *Yamaha* motorcycle model TR1. (JPN)
188–190, 193 The covers of folders for four other *Yamaha* models which, except in Fig. 190, are shown while being driven. The folders themselves are illustrated with photographs and drawings that accompany technical descriptions. Fig. 188: Stretches of green grass are seen at top and bottom; Fig. 190: Mainly black and white, as driver approaches his machine through fog. The *Yamaha* logo and the type of model is placed consistently on the cover of all folders: overprinted vertically, on the left. (JPN)

187, 191, 192 Vorderseite und vollständiger Prospekt für das *Yamaha*-Motorrad-Modell TR1. (JPN)
188–190, 193 Titelbilder von vier weiteren *Yamaha*-Modellen. Ausser beim Modell der Abb. 190 werden alle Fahrzeuge während der Fahrt vorgeführt. Die Prospekte selber enthalten gezeichnete und photographierte Illustrationen nebst dem technischen Beschrieb. Abb. 188: Oben und unten sind grüne Rasenstreifen sichtbar; Abb. 189: Hier wird die Eignung für jedes Gelände demonstriert; Abb. 190: Schwarzweiss überwiegt; der Fahrer nähert sich dem Motorrad aus dem Nebel. Das *Yamaha*-Signet, der Schriftzug und die Bezeichnung des Modells sind auf allen Prospektvorderseiten konsequent aussen links plaziert. (JPN)

187, 191, 192 Recto du prospectus et prospectus complet: la moto *Yamaha* modèle TR1. (JPN)
188–190, 193 Photos de quatre autres modèles *Yamaha* placées en tête des dépliants correspondants contenant les données techniques, des photos et des dessins. Sauf pour la 190, toutes les motos sont représentées en pleine course. Fig. 188: en haut et en bas, on voit des bandes de gazon vert; fig. 189: démonstration d'une moto tout-terrain; fig. 190: ici, le noir et blanc domine; le motard s'approche de la moto à la lumière des phares brouillards. L'emblème *Yamaha*, le nom stylisé de la marque et la désignation du modèle apparaissent systématiquement du côté gauche du recto de ces dépliants. (JPN)

188

189

190

191

192

193

194

195

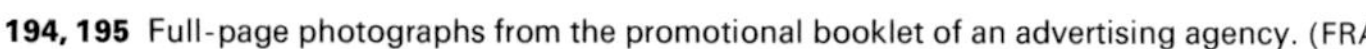

194, 195 Full-page photographs from the promotional booklet of an advertising agency. (FRA)
196 Cover of catalogue to the exhibition "Heribert Brehm: Fantastic Photography". (GER)
197 Inside spread of the unfolded card calling for 1983 entries from graphic designers to the annual Communication Graphics Show of the American Institute of Graphic Arts. (USA)
198 The exhibit from a photographic exhibition in Cologne's "Amerikahaus" that was used on the invitation to *Kodak's* programme of international culture during the 1982 Photokina. (GER)

194, 195 Ganzseitige Aufnahmen aus der Broschüre eines Werbeberatungsbüros. (FRA)
196 Umschlag des Katalogs zur Ausstellung «Heribert Brehm: Fantastische Fotografie». (GER)
197 Innenseite der auseinandergefalteten Einladung für Einsendungen zum jährlichen Graphik-Design-Wettbewerb des American Institute of Graphic Arts. (USA)
198 Aufnahme aus einer Photoausstellung im Kölner Amerikahaus, hier für die Einladung zum Internationalen *Kodak* Kulturprogramm anlässlich der Photokina 1982 verwendet. (GER)

194, 195 Photos pleine page pour la brochure d'un bureau de conseils en information. (FRA)
196 Couverture du catalogue de l'exposition «Heribert Brehm: Photographie fantastique». (GER)
197 Page intérieure de l'appel d'envois déplié de l'American Institute of Graphic Arts invitant à participer au concours annuel d'art graphique de cette organisation. (USA)
198 Photo figurant dans une exposition photo à la Maison d'Amérique de Cologne, utilisée ici pour l'invitation au programme culturel *Kodak* dans le cadre de la Photokina 1982. (GER)

197

196

198

PHOTOGRAPHER / PHOTOGRAPH:

194, 195 André Edouard/Didier Ferry
196 Heribert Brehm
197 Henry Wolf
198 James B. Wood

DESIGNER / GESTALTER / MAQUETTISTE:

194, 195 Michel Redon
196 Heribert Brehm
197 Henry Wolf

ART DIRECTOR / DIRECTEUR ARTISTIQUE:

196 Heribert Brehm
198 Bob Bowen

AGENCY / AGENTUR / AGENCE – STUDIO:

194, 195 Studio des Grands Augustins
197 Henry Wolf Productions

199

PHOTOGRAPHER / PHOTOGRAPH:

199 Miguel Martinez/
Ramon Miquel
200 Michael Steinke
201 Xavier Miserachs
202 Ray Massey
203 Bernard Vidal

DESIGNER / GESTALTER / MAQUETTISTE:

200 Gerd Lange

ART DIRECTOR / DIRECTEUR ARTISTIQUE:

199, 201–203 Dominique Hauptmann/
Patrick Levillain
200 Gerd Lange

AGENCY / AGENTUR / AGENCE – STUDIO:

200 IRM Werbeagentur GmbH

200

201

199, 201–203 Photographs from a promotional catalogue for various photographers. Fig. 199: Double spread by photographers Miguel Martinez and Ramon Miguel for a lemon drink; Fig. 201: Full-page photograph by Xavier Miserachs, specialist in almost surreal shots; Fig. 202: As the viewer tends to assume that light always falls from above, Ray Massey exploited that tendency in this trick shot, here viewed upside down. Held by a clamp, the glass was let into an aquarium and tilted, releasing the air bubbles seen here. The effect of this illusion was increased by special lighting; Fig. 203: Photograph by Bernard Vidal for *Givenchy.* (FRA)
200 Colour photograph in shades of green used in a folder for a paper mill. (SWI)

199, 201–203 Aus einem Werbekatalog für verschiedene Photographen. Abb. 199: Doppelseitige Aufnahme für ein Zitronengetränk; Abb. 201: Ganzseitige Farbaufnahme von Xavier Miserachs; Abb. 202: Hier machte sich Ray Massey die allgemeine Vorstellung, dass Licht immer von oben kommt, zunutze. Das Photo steht auf dem Kopf, das Glas wurde in ein Aquarium eingelassen (oben mit einer Klammer festgehalten); was entweicht, sind Luftblasen. Spezielle Beleuchtung verstärkt die Illusion; Abb. 203: Für *Givenchy*-Parfums. (FRA)
200 Aufnahme in Grüntönen für den Faltprospekt einer Papierfabrik. (SWI)

199, 201–203 Photos illustrant le catalogue publicitaire d'un collectif de photographes. Fig. 199: photo double page des photographes Miguel Martinez et Ramon Miguel, pour une boisson au jus de citron; fig. 201: photo couleur pleine page de Xavier Miserachs, spécialiste du cliché quasi surréaliste; fig. 202: ici, Ray Massey joue sur l'expérience courante de la lumière venue d'en haut: la photo est inversée, le verre est accroché à l'aide d'une trombone au bord d'un aquarium, les bulles d'air montent, un éclairage spécial renforce l'illusion; fig. 203: photo de Bernard Vidal pour les parfums *Givenchy.* (FRA)
200 Cette photo en diverses teintes vertes illustre le dépliant d'un fabricant de papier. (SWI)

202

203

204

Booklets/Prospekte/Brochures

204 Double spread from a promotional booklet for the Froelich / Greene Litho Corp. These and all other pages show works by photographer Neil Selkirk. (USA)
205–207 Two complete full-colour double spreads and a full-page photograph from a catalogue that the Kestner Museum in Hanover published to mark the centenary of *Rosenthal* porcelain. Fig. 207: This photograph, shot from above, is of the tea-pot in the "Drop" service designed by Luigi Colani. (GER)

PHOTOGRAPHER / PHOTOGRAPH:

204 Neil Selkirk
205–207 Helmut Groh/Michael Tessmann/Dieter Urmann

DESIGNER / GESTALTER / MAQUETTISTE:

204 Marla Dekker
205–207 Klaus Wolowiec

ART DIRECTOR / DIRECTEUR ARTISTIQUE:

204 Peter Harrison
205–207 Klaus Wolowiec

AGENCY / AGENTUR / AGENCE – STUDIO:

204 Pentagram Design
205–207 HA Kommunikation

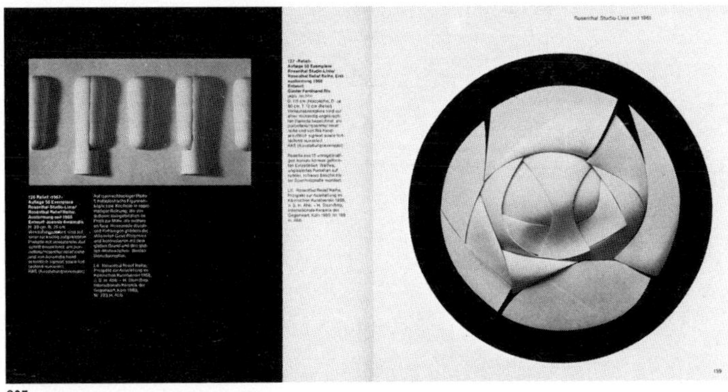

205

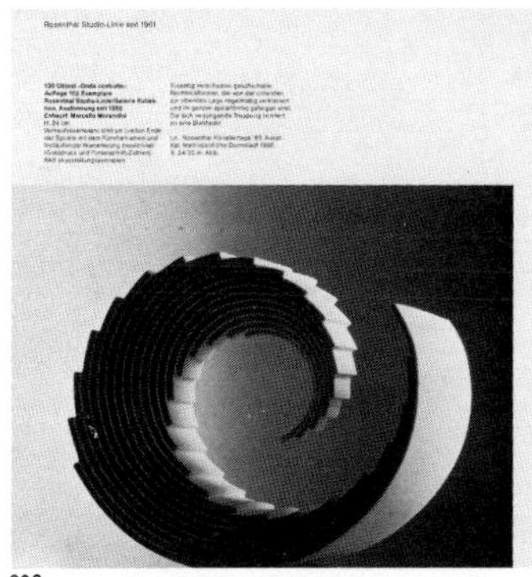

206

204 Doppelseite aus einem Eigenwerbungskatalog der Froelich / Greene Litho Corporation mit Aufnahmen des Photographen Neil Selkirk. (USA)
205–207 Zwei vollständige, mehrfarbige Doppelseiten und eine ganzseitige Aufnahme aus dem Katalog des Kestner-Museums Hannover, welcher anlässlich des hundertjährigen Bestehens des Porzellanherstellers *Rosenthal* herausgegeben wurde. Abb. 207: Die Kanne des Teeservices «Drop» – von Luigi Colani – von oben aufgenommen. (GER)

204 Double page d'un catalogue autopromotionnel de la Froelich / Greene Litho Corporation, avec des clichés du photographe Neil Selkirk. (USA)
205–207 Deux pages doubles complètes, en polychromie, et une photo pleine page tirées d'un catalogue du Musée Kestner de Hanovre publié à l'occasion du centenaire de la manufacture de porcelaine *Rosenthal*. Fig. 207: la théière du service à thé «Drop» – une création Luigi Colani – vue d'en haut. (GER)

207

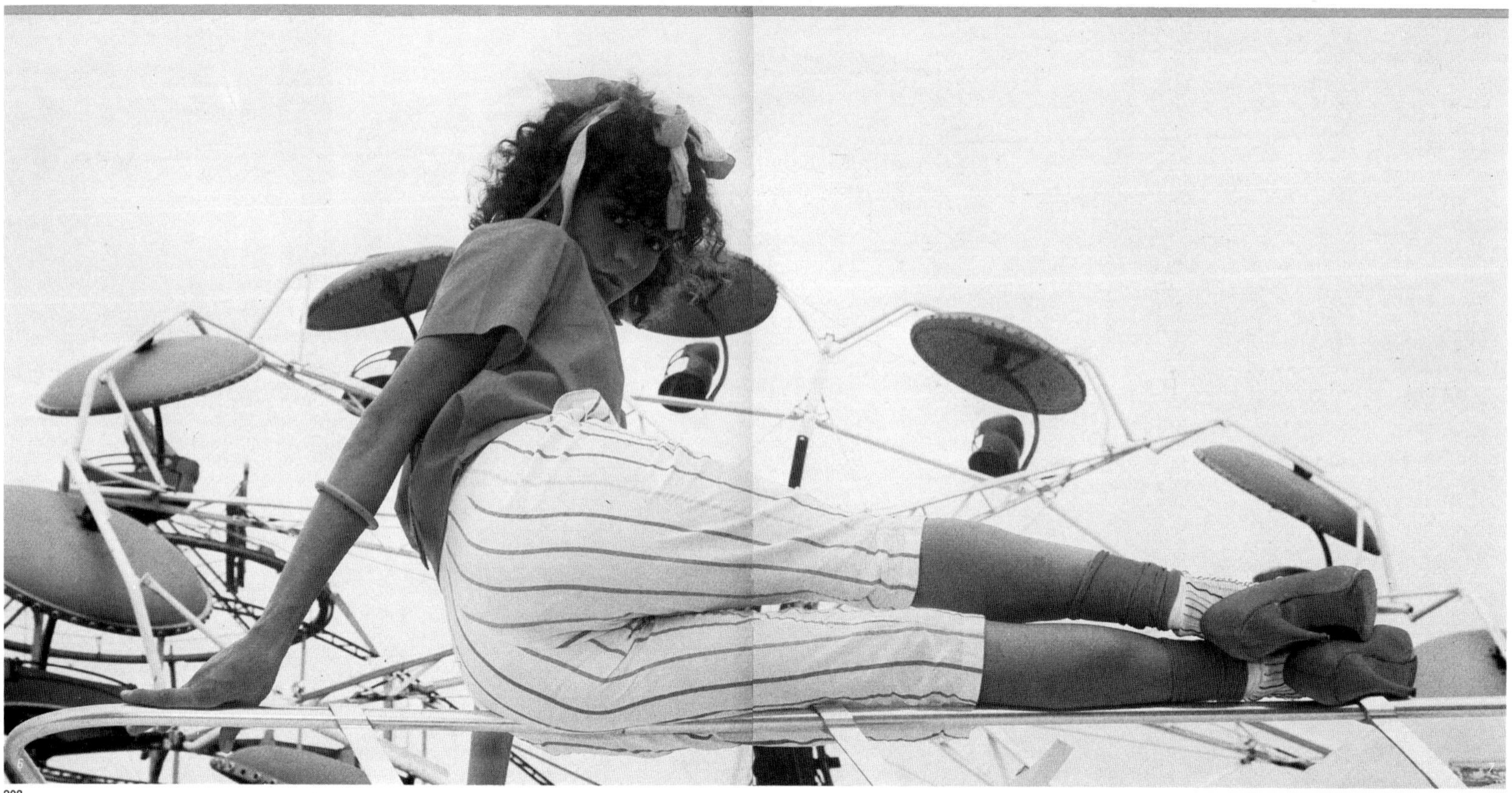

208

Booklets/Prospekte/Brochures

210

211

209

PHOTOGRAPHER / PHOTOGRAPH:

208, 209 Jean Pierre Metayer
210 Siegbert Kercher
211 Verita Monselles
212 Alberto Del'Orto

DESIGNER / GESTALTER / MAQUETTISTE:

208, 209 Michael Bierut
210 Siegbert Kercher
211 Verita Monselles
212 Guy Valais

ART DIRECTOR / DIRECTEUR ARTISTIQUE:

208, 209 Massimo Vignelli
211 Giuliano
212 Joel Desgrippes

AGENCY / AGENTUR / AGENCE – STUDIO:

208, 209 Vignelli Associates
210 Telefunken/Werbeabt.
211 Fotogrammatre
212 Desgrippes Beauchant Gobé

208, 209 Double-spread and full-page photo from a *Santa Cruz* fashion booklet. (USA)
210 From a *Telefunken* booklet: red dress and stockings, shoes blue on white ground inset with fields of red and blue tones. (GER)
211 Cover of the catalogue for spring / summer fashions by *Bagarry*. Shawls shown in soft tones achieved by using vegetable dyes. (ITA)
212 Double spread from the catalogue for a ready-wear collection by *Lanvin*. (FRA)

208, 209 Doppelseite und ganzseitige Aufnahme aus einem *Santa-Cruz*-Modeprospekt. (USA)
210 Aufnahme aus einem Prospekt für *Telefunken*. Kleidung ganz in Rot, Hintergrund in verschiedene Farbfelder aufgeteilt. (GER)
211 Umschlag des Frühjahr / Sommer-Katalogs für Mode der Marke *Bagarry*. Schals in Tönen, die man durch Pflanzenfärbungen erreichen kann. (ITA)
212 Doppelseite aus einem Katalog für eine Prêt-à-Porter-Kollektion von *Lanvin*. (FRA)

208, 209 Double page et photo pleine page d'un prospectus de mode *Santa Cruz*. (USA)
210 Photo illustrant un prospectus *Telefunken*. Vêtements rouges; le fond de l'image se compose de divers secteurs de couleurs différentes. (GER)
211 Couverture du catalogue printemps / été des modes *Bagarry*. Foulards aux teintes obtenues au moyen de colorants végétaux. (ITA)
212 Double page du catalogue d'une collection de prêt-à-porter *Lanvin*. (FRA)

Le Prêt-à-Porter LANVIN est et sera toujours LANVIN. L'inspiration vient de la grande maison et les modèles sont diffusés dans le monde entier.

212

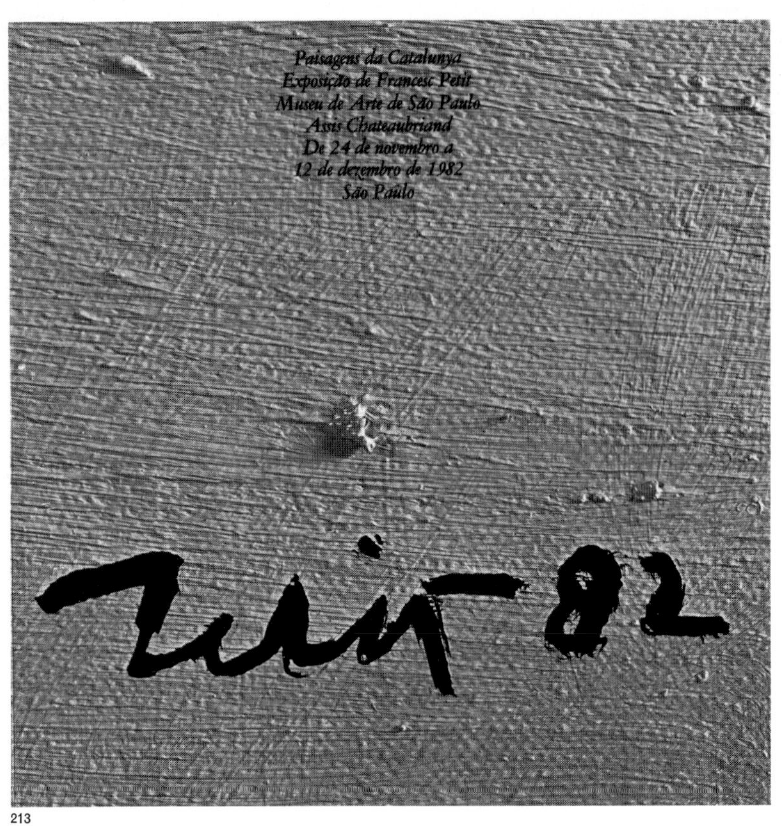

213

214

215

216

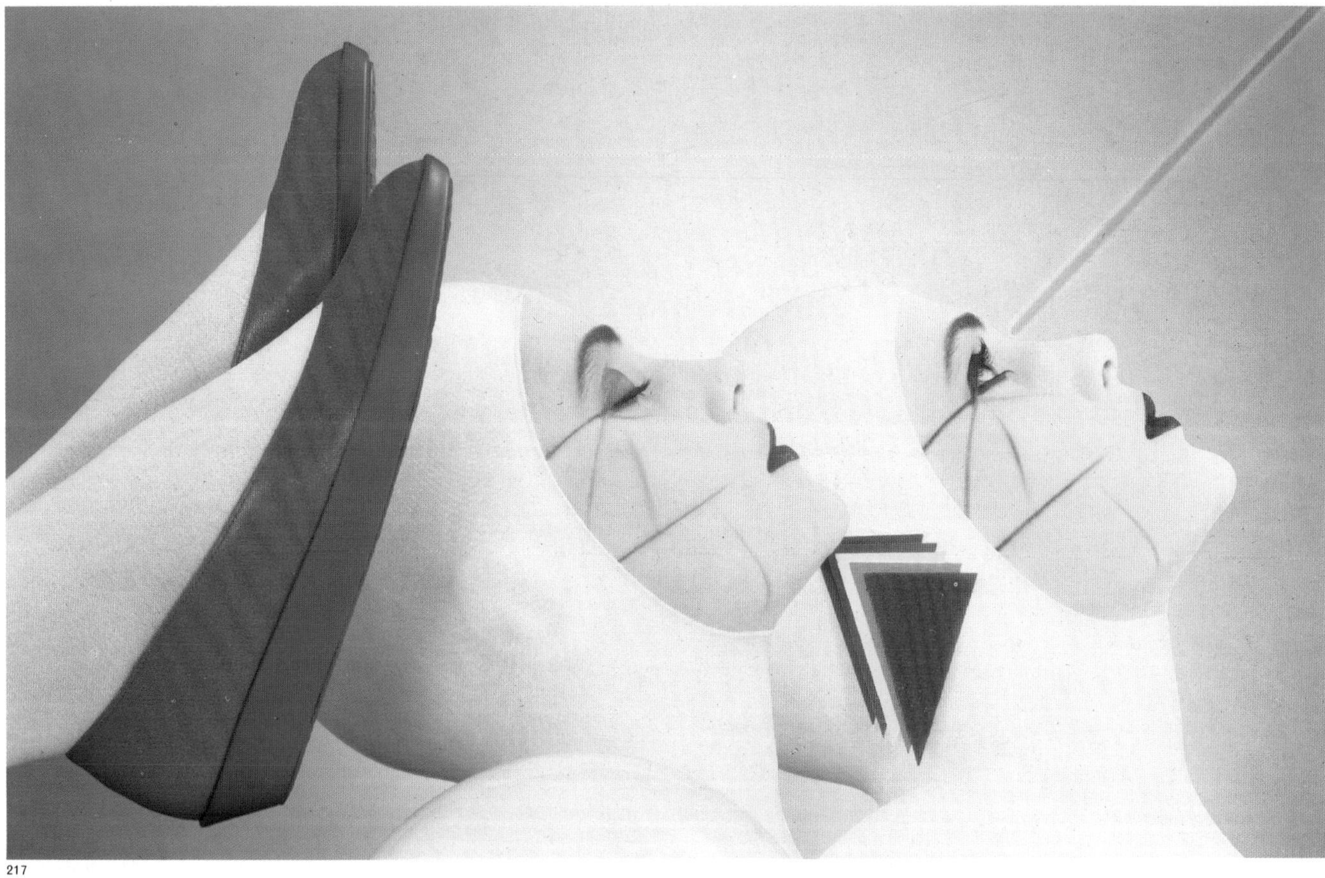

217

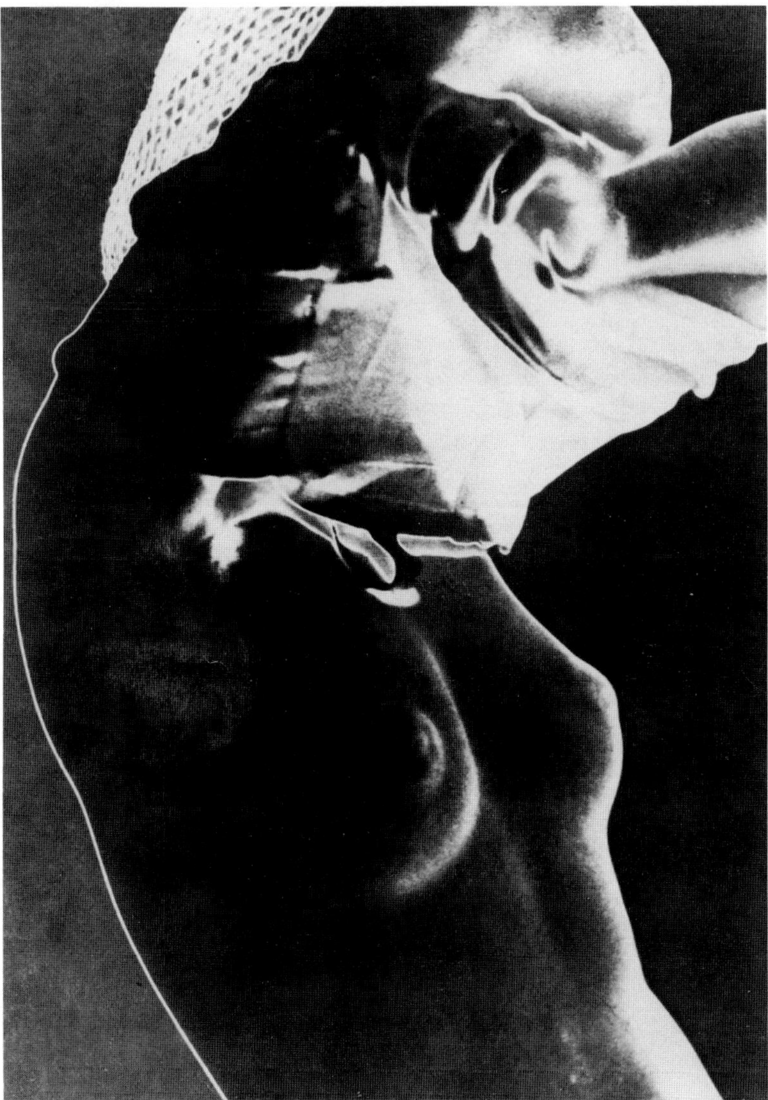

218

PHOTOGRAPHER / PHOTOGRAPH:

213 Francesc Petit
214 Tim Nighswander
215, 216 H. G. Tropper
217 Jean-Marc Scialom
218 Gertrude Fehr

DESIGNER / GESTALTER / MAQUETTISTE:

213 Francesc Petit
214 Lawrence Yang
215, 216 Madeleine Bujatti

ART DIRECTOR / DIRECTEUR ARTISTIQUE:

213 Francesc Petit
214 Lawrence Yang
215, 216 Madeleine Bujatti
217 Dominique Hauptmann/
Patrick Levillain

AGENCY / AGENTUR / AGENCE – STUDIO:

213 DPZ
214 Lawrence Yang Design
215, 216 Atelier Bujatti

213 Cover of a catalogue for an exhibition at the Museu de Arte in São Paulo. Extreme close-up of canvas painted in ochre, signature and print in black. (BRA)
214 Complete cover of a booklet on printing and paper by *Champion International.* (USA)
215, 216 Full front pages of leaflets from papermaker *Leykam-Mürztaler.* (AUT)
217 Sample of work by fashion photographer Jean-Marc Scialom, from an agent's album. (FRA)
218 Front side, in black and white, of an invitation card for an exhibition of photographs by Gertrude Fehr, held at the Musée de l'Elysée in Paris. (FRA)

213 Umschlag des Katalogs für eine Kunstausstellung im Museu de Arte, São Paulo. Grossaufnahme einer hellbraun bemalten Leinwand, Signatur und Schrift schwarz. (BRA)
214 Vollständiger Umschlag eines Prospekts für Papier von *Champion International.* (USA)
215, 216 Vorderseiten von Prospekten für den Papierhersteller *Leykam-Mürztaler.* (AUT)
217 Aufnahme des Modephotographen J.-M. Scialom, aus dem Katalog einer Agentur. (FRA)
218 Schwarzweiss-Aufnahme für die Vorderseite einer Einladungskarte zu einer Photoausstellung von Gertrude Fehr im Musée de l'Elysée, Paris. (FRA)

213 Couverture du catalogue d'une exposition d'art au Museu de Arte de São Paulo. Gros plan d'une toile peinte en brun clair, signature et texte en noir. (BRA)
214 Couverture complète d'un prospectus pour un papier *Champion International.* (USA)
215, 216 Rectos de prospectus du fabricant de papier *Leykam-Mürztaler.* (AUT)
217 Photo du photographe de mode J.-M. Scialom, dans le catalogue d'une agence. (FRA)
218 Photo noir et blanc pour le recto d'un carton d'invitation à une exposition des photos de Gertrude Fehr au Musée de l'Elysée de Paris. (FRA)

219

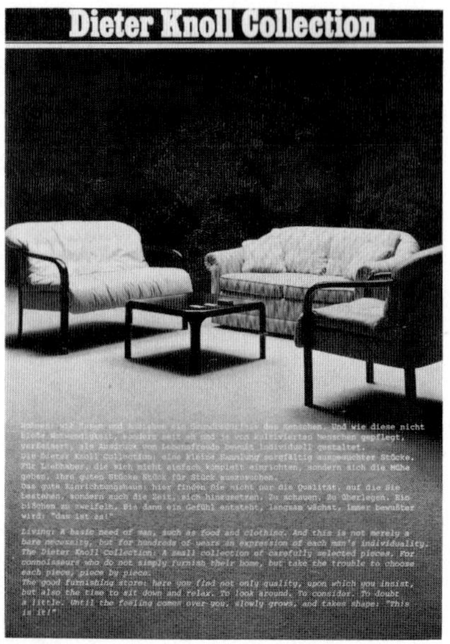

220

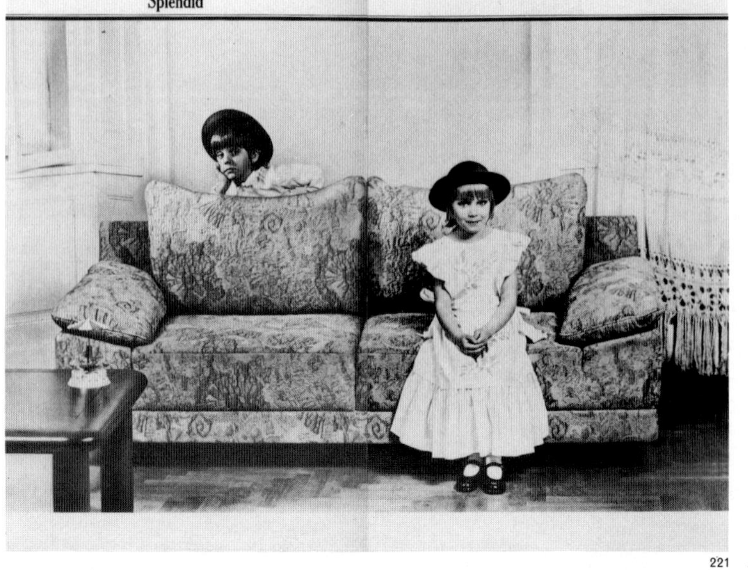

221

Booklets/Prospekte/Brochures

PHOTOGRAPHER / PHOTOGRAPH:

219 Don Sparks
220, 221 Rudolf Schenkirz

DESIGNER / GESTALTER / MAQUETTISTE:

219 Valerie Hepler/S&S Graphics Inc.
220, 221 Fritz Haubmann

ART DIRECTOR / DIRECTEUR ARTISTIQUE:

219 Don Sparks
220, 221 Fritz Haubmann

AGENCY / AGENTUR / AGENCE – STUDIO:

219 Sparks Studio
220, 221 Demner & Merlicek

219 Double spread, here almost actual size, from the self-promotional booklet by photographer Don Sparks. See also Fig. 166. (USA)
220, 221 Cover page, in shades of beige, brown and green, and a black-and-white double spread of a large-format catalogue for furniture in the *Dieter Knoll Collection.* (AUT)

219 Doppelseitige Aufnahme (beinahe Originalgrösse) aus einem Eigenwerbungsprospekt des Photographen Don Sparks. Siehe auch Abb. 166. (USA)
220, 221 Umschlagseite in Beige-, Braun- und Grüntönen und Doppelseite mit Schwarzweiss-Aufnahme aus einem grossformatigen Katalog für Möbel der *Dieter Knoll Collection.* (AUT)

219 Photo double page (au format approximativement original) figurant dans un prospectus autopromotionnel du photographe Don Sparks. Cf. la fig. 166. (USA)
220, 221 Couverture aux tons beiges, bruns, verts et double page illustrée en noir et blanc d'un catalogue au grand format des meubles de la *Dieter Knoll Collection.* (AUT)

222

▼206614 Anzug aus Baumwoll-Chintz, gefüttert. Schalkragen und Stickerei auf dem Rückenteil der Jacke. Hose mit modischer V-Passe am Bund, Schubtaschen. 100% Baumwolle. 370 Violett, 280 Petrol, 300 Cherry.
206636 Jacke aus Baumwoll-Chintz, gefüttert, mit Schalkragen und Stickerei auf dem Rückenteil. 100% Baumwolle. 370 Violett, 280 Petrol, 300 Cherry.

▼189834 Strick-Pullover mit Schneeflocken und eingestickter Gold-Lurex-Sonne, Fledermausärmel. 87% Polyacryl, 13% Viscose. 100 Weiß, 260 Navy.

223

224

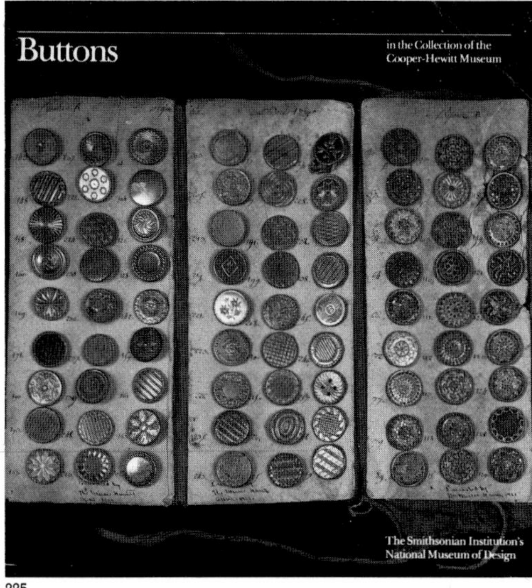

225

226

227

PHOTOGRAPHER / PHOTOGRAPH / PHOTOGRAPHE:

222 Myron
223 Hans Ulrich
226, 227 Jochen Harder

DESIGNER / GESTALTER / MAQUETTISTE:

222 Tyler Smith
223 Kreativ-Team Ulrich & Fehlmann
224, 225 Leslie Smolan
226, 227 Bib Wies

ART DIRECTOR / DIRECTEUR ARTISTIQUE:

222 Tyler Smith
223 Hans Ulrich
224, 225 Leslie Smolan

AGENCY / AGENTUR / AGENCE – STUDIO:

222 Tyler Smith
223 Kreativ-Team Ulrich & Fehlmann
224, 225 Gottschalk & Ash Int'l
226, 227 Loden-Frey/Werbeabt.

222 From a promotional booklet consisting solely of extreme close-up shots in full colour (here in shades of grey). All double spreads, they indicate client requirements for quality lithography from National Bickford Foremost. (USA)
223 Double spread from a leporello fashion folder that introduced the 1982 winter collection of *Marc B.* (GER)
224, 225 Black-and-white double spread with colour cover of the Smithsonian Institution catalogue for a button collection exhibited at the Cooper-Hewitt Museum in New York. (USA)
226, 227 Double spreads in full colour from a booklet on festive fashions by *Loden-Frey*. The cold, metallic colours of the clothes harmonize with the glacial landscape in the background of all the photographs. (GER)

222 Beispiel der ausschliesslich aus doppelseitigen Farbaufnahmen (hier in Grautönen) bestehenden Broschüre des Lithographen National Bickford Foremost. Die Aufnahmen geben gleichzeitig Aufschluss über die Kunden. (USA)
223 Aus einem Leporello-Prospekt für die Vorstellung der Kollektion von *Marc B.* für den Winter 1982. (GER)
224, 225 Doppelseite in Schwarzweiss und mehrfarbiger Umschlag des Katalogs für die Ausstellung der Knopfsammlung des National Museums of Design, New York. (USA)
226, 227 Doppelseiten aus einem Prospekt für festliche Kleidung von *Loden-Frey*. Die kalten, metallischen Farben der Kleidung harmonieren mit den Gletscherlandschaften, die den Rahmen für alle Aufnahmen bilden. (GER)

222 Exemple des photos couleur double page qui composent la brochure entière de l'atelier de litho National Bickford Foremost. Ces photos (ici, en grisés) renseignent en même temps sur les clients qui les ont commandées. (USA)
223 Dépliant en accordéon accompagnant la présentation de la collection *Marc B.* pour l'hiver 1982. (GER)
224, 225 Double page noir et blanc et couverture polychrome du catalogue réalisé pour l'exposition de boutons du National Museum of Design de New York. (USA)
226, 227 Doubles pages d'un prospectus *Loden-Frey* présentant une collection de costumes et robes du soir. Les couleurs froides, métalliques sont apparentées à celles des glaciers qui ont fourni le décor de ces photos. (GER)

228

229

PHOTOGRAPHER / PHOTOGRAPH:

228, 229 Herbert Novak
230 Cyril Kobler
231, 232 John Horvers
233, 234 Jim Wood/Geoff Stein
235 Jost Wildbolz

DESIGNER / GESTALTER / MAQUETTISTE:

228, 229 Herbert Novak
230 Julien van der Wal
231, 232 David Gauger/Mark Derena
233, 234 Cheryl Heller/Sandy Runneon
235 Reinhold Flax

ART DIRECTOR / DIRECTEUR ARTISTIQUE:

228, 229 Dieter Frey
230 Julien van der Wal
231, 232 David Gauger
233, 234 Cheryl Heller
235 Reinhold Flax

AGENCY / AGENTUR / AGENCE – STUDIO:

228, 229 Wündrich-Meissen
230 VDW
231, 232 Gauger Sparks Silva, Inc.
233, 234 HBM Design Group
235 Ender Werbung

231

232

233

234

Booklets
Prospekte
Brochures

230

228, 229 Colour double spreads from a catalogue for *Puma* sports shoes, photographed on grit of an outdoor tennis court and on the floor of a volleyball hall. (GER)
230 Full-colour shot for a double spread in a booklet on sun-glasses. Ropes white and red. (FRA)
231, 232 Two double spreads from a catalogue of *Sawyer* sheepskin coats and jackets—with a front side that forms a gatefold here, opening up to reveal more models of warm wear. (USA)
233, 234 Cover and double spread from a catalogue of footwear by *Herman.* (USA)
235 Double spread in full colour from a large-format booklet on sportswear fashions by the textile manufacturer *Mäser.* (SWI)

228, 229 Doppelseiten aus einem Schuhkatalog für *Puma*-Tennis- respektive Volleyballschuhe. Die Photos wurden auf einem Tennis-Sandplatz und in einer Volleyballhalle gemacht. (GER)
230 Mehrfarbige, doppelseitige Aufnahme aus einem Prospekt für Sonnenbrillen. (FRA)
231, 232 Zwei Doppelseiten aus einem Prospekt für *Sawyer*-Schaffellmäntel und -jacken. Beide Detailaufnahmen sind ausklappbar; auf der Rückseite werden weitere Modelle vorgestellt. (USA)
233, 234 Umschlag und Doppelseite aus einem Katalog des Schuhfabrikanten *Herman.* (USA)
235 Doppelseitige, mehrfarbige Aufnahme aus einem grossformatigen Prospekt für sportliche Mode des Textilunternehmens *Mäser.* (SWI)

228, 229 Doubles pages d'un catalogue de chaussures *Puma* pour le tennis et le volley. Les photos ont été réalisées sur un court de sable et dans une salle de volley respectivement. (GER)
230 Photo polychrome sur deux pages illustrant un prospectus de lunettes solaires. (FRA)
231, 232 Deux doubles pages d'un prospectus réalisé pour les manteaux et jaquettes de mouton *Sawyer.* Les deux photos de détail sont dépliables; au verso figurent d'autres modèles. (USA)
233, 234 Couverture et page double d'un catalogue pour le fabricant de chaussures *Herman.* (USA)
235 Photo polychrome sur deux pages, dans un prospectus au grand format réalisé pour la mode sportive de l'entreprise textile *Mäser.* (SWI)

m/ä/s/e/r
...die mit dem m

Camouflage. Die Kollektion zum Kombinieren und Variieren. Dazu die modischen Blousons. Durchdachte, funktionelle Details – effektvolle Mode.

The camouflage look: for mixing and matching. Add to that the stylish and functional jackets.

Camouflage. Pour une nouvelle façon de s'habiller aux jeux d'influences et de subtilité. A porter avec des blousons. Une histoire de détails autor de formes élémentaires et éprouvées. Une mode raffinée.

235

Courtland Matte is a free-sheet
coated web paper, whose
consistent roll quality
and strength
bring users a high hourly
rate of impressions and reliable
in-line foldability. These characteristics
make Courtland Matte
a cost-effective
web paper.

236

Booklets/Prospekte/Brochures

236–239 Complete double spread and full-page photographs in a promotional booklet to celebrate the launch of a new product, with champagne. Such shots were used by *Champion Papers* in seven spreads, the left half of each being devoted to facts about its new product. This was announced by the cover close-up of the champagne and its label: "Courtland Matte", described as "A sparkling white matte coated web paper". (USA)

236–239 Vollständige Doppelseite und ganzseitige Farbaufnahmen aus einem Eigenwerbungsprospekt des Papierherstellers *Champion Papers*. Eine neue Papierqualität wird im Prospekt vorgestellt, die mit Champagner begrüsst werden soll. Insgesamt bestehen sieben Doppelseiten, auf welchen rechts Aufnahmen zum Thema Champagner abgebildet sind, auf den gegenüberliegenden Seiten werden Erläuterungen zur neuen Papierqualität «Courtland Matte» gegeben. (USA)

236–239 Page double complète et photos couleur pleine page, dans un prospectus autopromotionnel du papetier *Champion Papers*. On y présente une nouvelle qualité de papier fêtée au champagne. La prospectus comprend sept doubles pages illustrées sur la page de droite de photos ayant trait au champagne. Les pages de gauche contiennent des explications relatives au nouveau papier «Courtland Matte». (USA)

237

238

PHOTOGRAPHER:

236–239 Tohru Nakamura

DESIGNER / GESTALTER:

236–239 Dan Friedman

ART DIRECTOR:

236–239 Colin Forbes/
Dan Friedman

AGENCY / AGENTUR / AGENCE:

236–239 Pentagram Design

239

240

PHOTOGRAPHER / PHOTOGRAPH:

240 Terry Heffernan/Jim Sadlon
241 John Senzer
242 Dieter Zembsch
243 Al Satterwhite

DESIGNER / GESTALTER / MAQUETTISTE:

240 Kit Hinrichs
241 Richard Danne/Gary Skeggs
242 Dieter Zembsch

ART DIRECTOR / DIRECTEUR ARTISTIQUE:

241 Richard Danne
242 Dieter Zembsch
243 Al Satterwhite

AGENCY / AGENTUR / AGENCE – STUDIO:

240 Jonson Pedersen Hinrichs & Shakery
241 Danne & Blackburn, Inc.
242 Zembsch' Werkstatt

240 Poster-size call for entries to an exhibition of California Graphic Design held by the American Institute of Graphic Arts (which also used it as an invitation card). The car's bumper reflects the San Francisco skyline. (USA)
241 Cover of a promotional booklet by the Fashion Institute of Technology in New York. Black and reds on beige ground with white border, FIT logo on green. (USA)
242–244 Full-colour leading pages showing photographs in shades of white. Fig. 243: The cover of this booklet, published by the German television channel ARD. (GER)
245 Shot from a self-promotional booklet by photographer Al Satterwhite. (USA)

240 Einladungskarte (und Einsendungseinladung in Plakatgrösse) des American Institute of Graphic Arts (AIGA) für die Ausstellung «California Graphic Design». Auf der Stossstange ist das Spiegelbild der Silhouette von San Francisco sichtbar. (USA)
241 Umschlagvorderseite eines mehrfarbigen Prospektes des Fashion Institute of Technology (FIT) in New York. (USA)
242–244 Mehrfarbige Leitblätter mit Ton-in-Ton-Aufnahmen aus dem ARD-Jahrbuch 1982. Abb. 243: Schutzumschlag der Broschüre. (GER)
245 Aufnahme aus einem Eigenwerbungsprospekt des Photographen Al Satterwhite. (USA)

240 Carton d'invitation (et appel d'envois au format d'une affiche) de l'American Institute of Graphic Arts AIGA pour l'exposition «California Graphic Design». La silhouette de San Francisco se reflète dans le pare-chocs. (USA)
241 Recto d'un prospectus polychrome publié par le Fashion Institute of Technology (FIT) de New York. (USA)
242–244 Feuillets polychromes illustrés en aplats, en tête des chapitres de l'annuaire ARD pour 1982. Fig. 243: jaquette de la brochure. (GER)
245 Photo tirée d'une brochure autopromotionnelle du photographe Al Satterwhite. (USA)

241

242

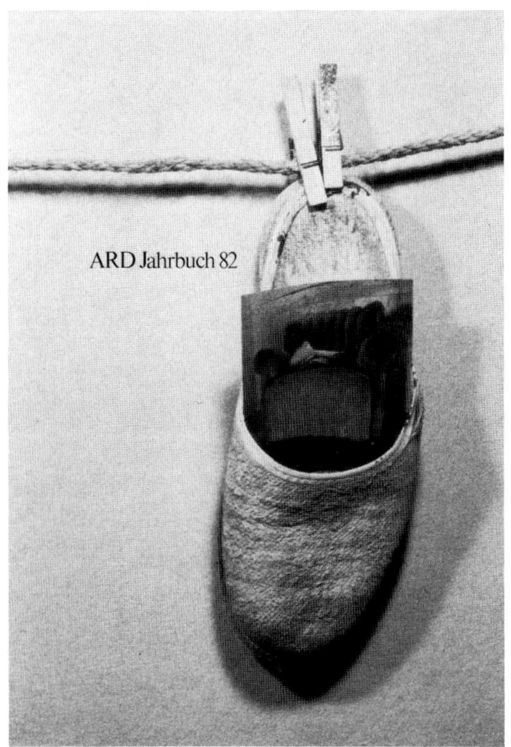

243

244

245

PHOTOGRAPHER / PHOTOGRAPH / PHOTOGRAPHE:
244–249 Peter Hendrie

DESIGNER / GESTALTER / MAQUETTISTE:
244–249 Garry Emery

ART DIRECTOR / DIRECTEUR ARTISTIQUE:
244–249 Garry Emery

AGENCY / AGENTUR / AGENCE – STUDIO:
244–249 Emery Vincent Associates

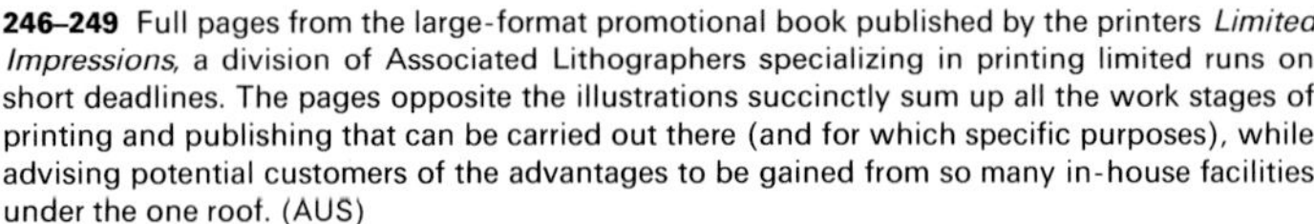

246–249 Full pages from the large-format promotional book published by the printers *Limited Impressions*, a division of Associated Lithographers specializing in printing limited runs on short deadlines. The pages opposite the illustrations succinctly sum up all the work stages of printing and publishing that can be carried out there (and for which specific purposes), while advising potential customers of the advantages to be gained from so many in-house facilities under the one roof. (AUS)

246–249 Ganzseitige, mehrfarbige Aufnahmen aus einem Eigenwerbungsprospekt der Druckerei *Limited Impressions*, einer auf kleine Auflagen und kurze Lieferzeiten spezialisierte Abteilung der Vereinigten Lithographen-Gesellschaft. Auf den gegenüberliegenden Seiten der Aufnahmen im Prospekt werden die verschiedenen Arbeitsgänge aufgeführt und die Vorteile, welche eine Herstellung von A bis Z im selben Hause bietet. (AUS)

246–249 Photos polychromes sur pages entières illustrant un prospectus autopromotionnel de l'imprimerie *Limited Impressions*, un département de la Société des Lithographes Réunis spécialisé dans les petits tirages et les délais de livraison rapides. En regard de ces photos on trouve l'exposé des diverses étapes d'exécution et des avantages inhérents à une fabrication dont toutes les étapes se font sous le même toit. (AUS)

246

247

248

250 Photograph on the cover of a *Bang & Olufsen* booklet. It was also used in a house organ and as a book cover. (DEN)
251, 252 Detail and complete photograph used for an *Etaflex* booklet and in a *Kodak* exhibition. The model wears matching make-up for this real-life portrait of the cat, which was coloured that way from birth. (GER)

250 Aufnahme für die Vorderseite eines Prospektes von *Bang & Olufsen*. Sie wurde auch als Buchumschlag und für eine Hauszeitschrift verwendet. (DEN)
251, 252 Detail und vollständige Aufnahme, die für *Etaflex*-Prospekte und Ausstellungen von *Kodak* verwendet wurde. Die Katze ist naturgetreu abgebildet; sie wurde so geboren. (GER)

250 Photo pour le recto d'un prospectus de *Bang & Olufsen*. La même photo a été utilisée comme couverture de livre et pour une revue d'entreprise. (DEN)
251, 252 Détail et photo complète utilisée pour les prospectus et expositions *Etaflex* de *Kodak*. Photo réaliste du chat, qui est ainsi de naissance. (GER)

250

251

Booklets/Prospekte/Brochures

PHOTOGRAPHER / PHOTOGRAPH / PHOTOGRAPHE:

250 Poul Ib Henriksen
251, 252 Conny J. Winter

DESIGNER / GESTALTER / MAQUETTISTE:

250 Poul Ib Henriksen
251, 252 Conny J. Winter

ART DIRECTOR / DIRECTEUR ARTISTIQUE:

250 Poul Ib Henriksen
251, 252 Hans W. Rolli

AGENCY / AGENTUR / AGENCE – STUDIO:

250 Poul Ib Henriksen

252

253

253 From a *Nestlé* booklet, here for *Crunch* bar of milk chocolate. (USA)
254, 255 Full-colour double spreads from a book-type catalogue showing examples of Scandinavian designs: here, upholstered furniture—from the *Vatne Lenestolfabrik*, Norway, and a range developed by two Danish architects in co-operation with *Magnus Olesen*. (DEN)
256, 257 Full-page photograph and complete double spread from a booklet in black and white by the International Zen Dojo Centre of Hawaii. (USA)
258 Invitation to the presentation of collections by international fashion designers in Japan. Stockings and shoes red, otherwise white and blue shades. White lettering. (JPN)

253 Aufnahme aus einer Broschüre von *Nestlé*, hier für *Crunch*-Milchschokolade-Stengel. (USA)
254, 255 Mehrfarbige Doppelseiten aus einem in Buchform erschienenen Katalog mit Beispielen skandinavischen Designs, hier Polstermöbel der *Vatne Lenestolfabrik*, Norwegen, und ein von zwei dänischen Architekten in Zusammenarbeit mit der *Magnus Olesen* entwickeltes Programm. (DEN)
256, 257 Ganzseitige Aufnahme und vollständige Doppelseite aus einer Broschüre des Internationalen Zen-Dojo-Zentrums in Hawaii. Schwarzweiss. (USA)
258 Einladung zu einer Kollektions-Präsentation internationaler Modeschöpfer in Japan. Strümpfe und Schuhe rot, übrige Aufnahme in Weiss- und Blaugrautönen. Weisser Schriftzug. (JPN)

253 Photo d'une brochure de *Nestlé* illustrant les barres de chocolat au lait *Crunch*. (USA)
254, 255 Doubles pages polychromes d'un catalogue (publié en volume) du design scandinave: meubles rembourrés de la *Vatne Lenestolfabrik* norvégienne et programme élaboré par deux architectes danois en collaboration avec l'entreprise *Magnus Olesen*. (DEN)
256, 257 Photo pleine page et double page complète d'une brochure du Centre international zen-dojo de Hawaii. Noir et blanc. (USA)
258 Invitation à une présentation des collections de grands couturiers internationaux au Japon. Bas et chaussures rouges, reste de la photo blanc et gris bleu. Texte blanc. (JPN)

254

255

256

He sees through delusions like looking through the spinning blades of a propeller.
—Tanouye Tenshin

Mushin (No-mind or Absolute Mind) is life in its absolute form, an expression of its natural harmony, and a mark of a life which has achieved perfection. It is the most dynamic and creative state of being which is nevertheless experienced as a profound tranquility. One fully experiences things as they are without being spun around by them and naturally acts according to the Way. Yamaoka Tesshu said:

When two standpoints are crossed, there is no need to ward off. The best move is to return to the origin like the lotus flower blooming in the fire. Then the energy of heaven-soaring spirits springs spontaneously from the Original Nature.

Sitting in *zazen* provides the easiest conditions for experiencing *mushin*. To abide in this state amidst the clamor of the world is infinitely more difficult. For this, *shugyo* (the deepest possible spiritual training) is necessary. *Shugyo* is like taking a lump of raw iron ore, throwing it in fire and water, and pounding it, over and over again until a flawless sword is made. A fencing master once trained a student by hitting him at every opportunity. After some years the student learned to keep alert and dodge the blows successfully. But the master still was not satisfied. One day when the master was cooking, the student tried to hit him over the head from behind. Without intention the master blocked the blow with the cover of a pot and opened his student's mind to the working aspect of *mushin*.

One undergoes *shugyo* not to gain anything but to lose the attachments accumulated since birth. Losing day by day, one attains a greater degree of maturity. One can see unity in opposition and can expect and not expect at the same time. Ultimately when all that is not real falls away, a person lives and dies as one with the life of the Universe.

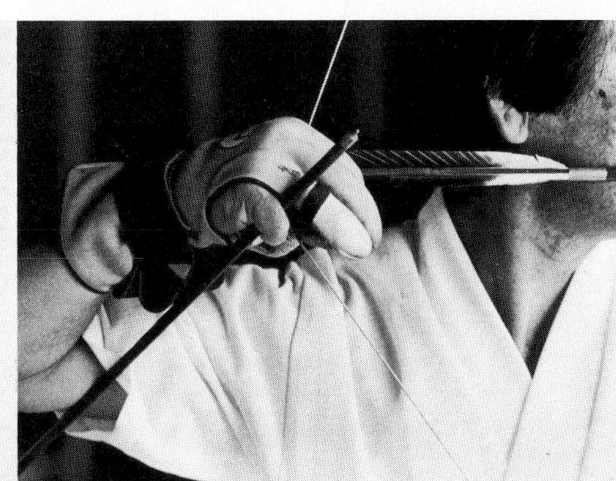

257

PHOTOGRAPHER / PHOTOGRAPH:

253 David Deahl
254, 255 Steen Bjerregard
256, 257 Masahiko Wada
258 Masanobu Fukuda

DESIGNER / GESTALTER / MAQUETTISTE:

253 David Deahl
256, 257 Kuni Hayashi
258 Gengo Hasegawa

ART DIRECTOR / DIRECTEUR ARTISTIQUE:

253 David Deahl
254, 255 Ib Clausen
256, 257 Kuni Hayashi
258 Gengo Hasegawa

AGENCY / AGENTUR / AGENCE – STUDIO:

253 Leo Burnett
254, 255 Design Forum ApS
256, 257 The Curator
258 Daiko

WHITE AVENUE

258

Booklets
Prospekte
Brochures

259

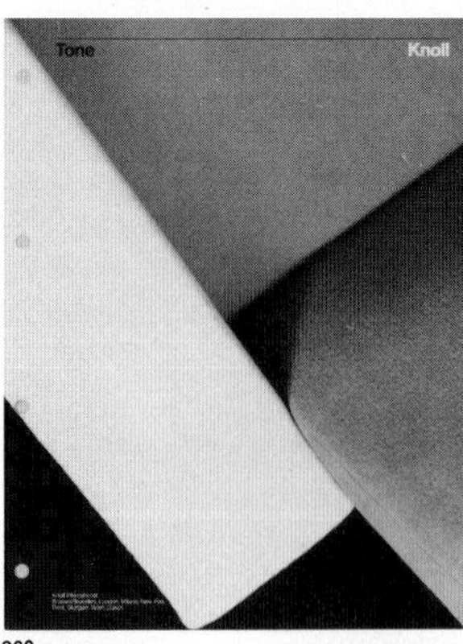

260

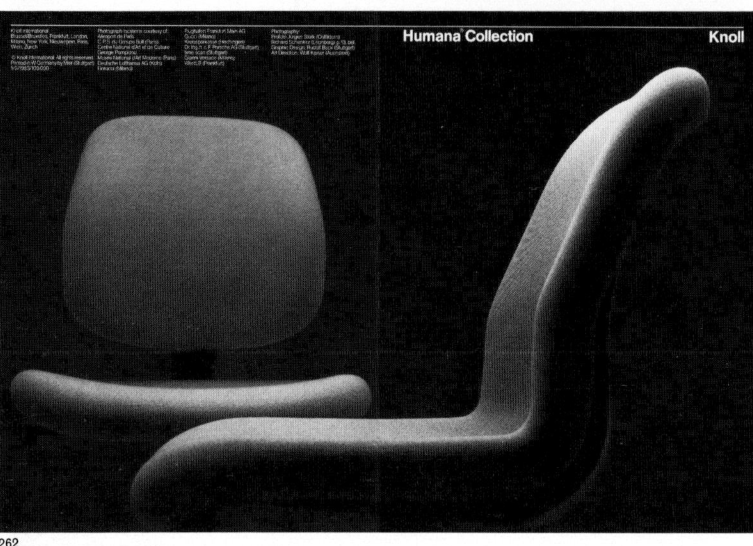

262

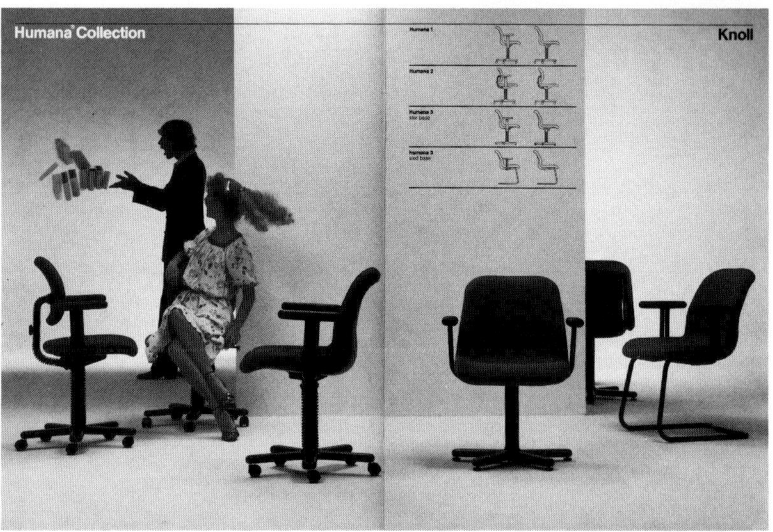

263

259–261 Opened gatefold, a front page and a detail of its photography as used in a catalogue by *Knoll.* Fig. 261 shows the detail of a *Sottsass* model in Fig. 259. (GER)
262, 263 Complete cover and a double spread from a catalogue for another *Knoll* collection. (GER)
264 Front side of an opened gatefold in full colour for marble table-tops by *Knoll.* (GER)

259–261 Auseinandergefalteter Prospekt, vollständiger Umschlag und Aufnahme für einen *Knoll*-Katalog. Abb. 261 ist eine Detailaufnahme eines *Sottsass*-Modells in Abb. 259. (GER)
262, 263 Vollständiger Umschlag und Doppelseite aus einem Katalog für *Knoll International.* (GER)
264 Vorderseite eines Faltprospekts für *Knoll.* Farbaufnahme von Marmorplatten. (GER)

259–261 Prospectus déplié, couverture complète et photo d'un catalogue *Knoll.* La Fig. 261 représente un détail de la photo du modèle *Sottsass* reproduit à la fig. 259. (GER)
262, 263 Couverture complète et page double d'un catalogue de *Knoll International.* (GER)
264 Recto d'un dépliant *Knoll.* Photo couleur de plaques de marbre. (GER)

PHOTOGRAPHER / PHOTOGRAPH / PHOTOGRAPHE:

259–261 Wolfgang Zwietasch
262, 263 Jürgen Störk
264 Richard Schenkirz

DESIGNER / GESTALTER / MAQUETTISTE:

259–264 Rudolf Beck

ART DIRECTOR / DIRECTEUR ARTISTIQUE:

259–264 Wolf Kaiser

264

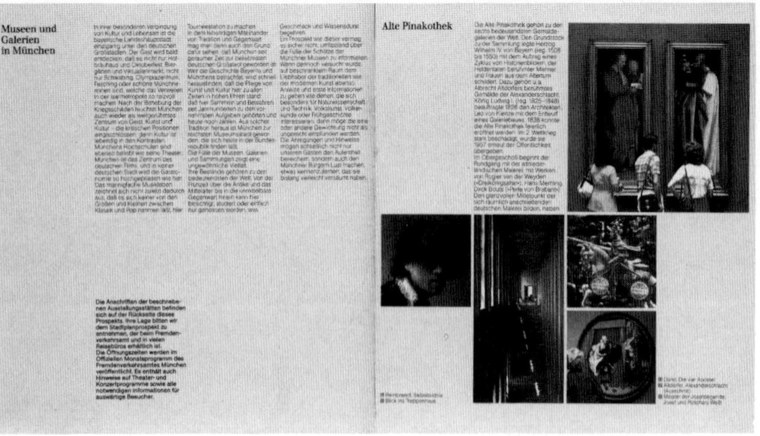

265

266

267

Booklets/Prospekte/Brochures

265, 266 Double spread from a catalogue of museums and galleries in Munich. (GER)
267 Photograph used to illustrate the cover of a catalogue for *Macy's* department store. (USA)
268, 269 Two of four photographs in black and white on the cover of a booklet "Disturbed Unity" giving "Information about psychological disturbances". Fig. 268 relates to a report on neurotic depression, and Fig. 269 is in connection with alcoholism. (GER)
270, 271 Double spreads from a high-format *Geigy* booklet devoted to a round-table discussion by American doctors about the use of its drug *Lopressor* in cases of hypertension. (USA)

265, 266 Doppelseiten aus einem Katalog über Museen und Galerien in München. (GER)
267 Aufnahme für die Umschlagseite eines Katalogs für das Kaufhaus *Macy's*. (USA)
268, 269 Zwei von vier Schwarzweiss-Aufnahmen für den Umschlag einer Broschüre mit dem Titel «Gestörte Einheit – Informationen über seelische Störungen». Abb. 268 bezieht sich auf einen Bericht über neurotische Depression, Abb. 269 auf einen Beitrag zum Thema Alkoholkrankheit. (GER)
270, 271 Doppelseiten aus einer schmalen Broschüre von *Geigy*, die einer medizinischen Fachdiskussion über Blutdruckprobleme und dem *Geigy*-Medikament *Lopressor* gewidmet ist. (USA)

265, 266 Doubles pages d'un catalogue des musées et galeries d'art munichois. (GER)
267 Photo de couverture pour un catalogue des grands magasins *Macy's*. (USA)
268, 269 Deux des quatre photos noir et blanc pour la couverture d'une brochure intitulée «Rupture de l'unité de l'être – informations sur les troubles psychiques.» La fig. 268 concerne un rapport sur la dépression névrotique, la fig. 269 un article sur la pathologie de l'alcoolisme. (GER)
270, 271 Doubles pages d'une petite brochure *Geigy* consacrée à un débat médical sur les problèmes de l'hypertension et au médicament hypotenseur *Geigy* commercialisé sous le nom de *Lopressor*. (USA)

PHOTOGRAPHER / PHOTOGRAPH:

265 Bjarne Geiges/Jürgen Hinrichs
266 Bjarne Geiges
267 Ronnie Poon
268, 269 Christoph Rau/Margot Vogel

DESIGNER / GESTALTER / MAQUETTISTE:

265, 266 Ernst Kösslinger
268, 269 Hans Jürgen Rau/Harald Trosch
270, 271 Bob Paganucci

ART DIRECTOR / DIRECTEUR ARTISTIQUE:

265, 266 Manfred Heimann
267 Dennis Walker/Brian Farrow/Kris Knight
268, 269 Hans Jürgen Rau
270, 271 Bob Paganucci

AGENCY / AGENTUR / AGENCE – STUDIO:

267 Macy's Advertising
268, 269 Studio Rau
270, 271 Salpeter Paganucci, Inc.

268

269

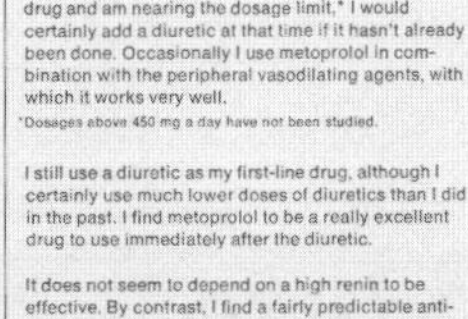

When to use Lopressor®, metoprolol tartrate

Dr. Lonigro: **Do you use metoprolol as a first-step or a second-step drug for treatment of hypertension?**

Dr. Turkington: My use of metoprolol has been almost exclusively as a second-step drug. There are a few exceptions. For example, a person who seems to have primarily an adaptive hypertensive reaction to a stressful situation might be treated with metoprolol initially, possibly just for a limited time. Also some patients who run an extremely high renin profile might be considered for first-step therapy with metoprolol.

But basically I think it's important to avoid the type of tolerance that can develop in patients who are treated exclusively with beta blockers. Almost all my patients have been treated initially with a diuretic and then, subsequently, with the addition of metoprolol or another beta blocker.

Dr. Lonigro: How do the rest of you feel about this approach?

Dr. Hartman: I also use metoprolol primarily as a second-step drug, concomitantly with a diuretic. If I use it as a first-step drug and am nearing the dosage limit,* I would certainly add a diuretic at that time if it hasn't already been done. Occasionally I use metoprolol in combination with the peripheral vasodilating agents, with which it works very well.

*Dosages above 450 mg a day have not been studied.

Dr. Persoff: I still use a diuretic as my first-line drug, although I certainly use much lower doses of diuretics than I did in the past. I find metoprolol to be a really excellent drug to use immediately after the diuretic.

It does not seem to depend on a high renin to be effective. By contrast, I find a fairly predictable anti-hypertensive response to metoprolol in most patients.

Dr. Kincaid: I too almost always use a diuretic as the first-line drug. The only situation where I might use metoprolol by itself, rather than in combination with a diuretic, is in patients with ischemic heart disease.* Patients with this condition and minimal hypertension often respond to the use of a beta blocker alone.

*Following abrupt cessation of therapy with certain beta blockers, exacerbations of angina pectoris and, in some cases, myocardial infarction have been reported. Even in the absence of overt angina pectoris, when discontinuing therapy, metoprolol should not be withdrawn abruptly, and patients should be cautioned against interruption of therapy without the physician's advice.

Dr. Lonigro: To play the devil's advocate for a moment, and to present my own point of view, one could make a case for beta blockade as the first therapy to be used in a step-care plan. Dr. Turkington alluded to this by mentioning patients who have high renin, which may reflect a decrease in intravascular volume.

There might be good reason not to use a diuretic as the first drug of choice in those patients. There are those who suggest that a patient with compromised intravascular volume might suffer ill effects from the use of a diuretic as the first drug. Therefore, beta blockade may be a better form of intial therapy for such individuals.

This doesn't preclude the use of concomitant therapy at a later stage of treatment, but as the intial therapeutic approach to these patients, one can make a

7

270

When to use Lopressor®, metoprolol tartrate

Dr. Lonigro: **Do you use metoprolol as a first-step or a second-step drug for treatment of hypertension?**

Dr. Turkington: My use of metoprolol has been almost exclusively as a second-step drug. There are a few exceptions. For example, a person who seems to have primarily an adaptive hypertensive reaction to a stressful situation might be treated with metoprolol initially, possibly just for a limited time. Also some patients who run an extremely high renin profile might be considered for first-step therapy with metoprolol.

But basically I think it's important to avoid the type of tolerance that can develop in patients who are treated exclusively with beta blockers. Almost all my patients have been treated initially with a diuretic and then, subsequently, with the addition of metoprolol or another beta blocker.

Dr. Lonigro: How do the rest of you feel about this approach?

Dr. Hartman: I also use metoprolol primarily as a second-step drug, concomitantly with a diuretic. If I use it as a first-step drug and am nearing the dosage limit,* I would certainly add a diuretic at that time if it hasn't already been done. Occasionally I use metoprolol in combination with the peripheral vasodilating agents, with which it works very well.

*Dosages above 450 mg a day have not been studied.

Dr. Persoff: I still use a diuretic as my first-line drug, although I certainly use much lower doses of diuretics than I did in the past. I find metoprolol to be a really excellent drug to use immediately after the diuretic.

It does not seem to depend on a high renin to be effective. By contrast, I find a fairly predictable anti-hypertensive response to metoprolol in most patients.

Dr. Kincaid: I too almost always use a diuretic as the first-line drug. The only situation where I might use metoprolol by itself, rather than in combination with a diuretic, is in patients with ischemic heart disease.* Patients with this condition and minimal hypertension often respond to the use of a beta blocker alone.

*Following abrupt cessation of therapy with certain beta blockers, exacerbations of angina pectoris and, in some cases, myocardial infarction have been reported. Even in the absence of overt angina pectoris, when discontinuing therapy, metoprolol should not be withdrawn abruptly, and patients should be cautioned against interruption of therapy without the physician's advice.

Dr. Lonigro: To play the devil's advocate for a moment, and to present my own point of view, one could make a case for beta blockade as the first therapy to be used in a step-care plan. Dr. Turkington alluded to this by mentioning patients who have high renin, which may reflect a decrease in intravascular volume.

There might be good reason not to use a diuretic as the first drug of choice in those patients. There are those who suggest that a patient with compromised intravascular volume might suffer ill effects from the use of a diuretic as the first drug. Therefore, beta blockade may be a better form of intial therapy for such individuals.

This doesn't preclude the use of concomitant therapy at a later stage of treatment, but as the intial therapeutic approach to these patients, one can make a

7

271

3

Editorial Photography
Magazine Covers
Trade Magazines
Book Covers
Annual Reports
Corporate Publications

Redaktionelle Photographie
Zeitschriften-Umschläge
Fachzeitschriften
Buchumschläge
Jahresberichte
Firmenpublikationen

Photographie rédactionnelle
Couvertures de périodiques
Revues professionnelles
Couvertures de livres
Rapports annuels
Publications d'entreprise

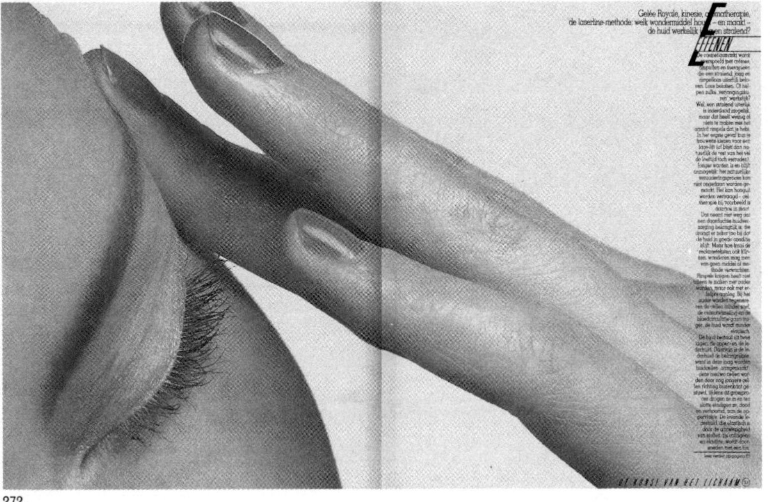

272

273

272–274 Full-colour double spreads in the Dutch magazine *Avenue* for its article on various aspects of body care. Figs. 272 and 274 relate to various methods of skin treatment, while Fig. 273 refers to the importance of fitness. (NLD)
275 From a magazine double spread: how *Vogue* showed liquid lipstick. (FRA)
276 Full-colour double spread in the Dutch magazine *Avenue* for an article on bathing suits that was headlined "Surface Tension". (NLD)

272–274 Mehrfarbige Doppelseiten aus einem Artikel in der holländischen Zeitschrift *Avenue* über verschiedene Aspekte der Körperpflege. Abb. 272 und 274 handeln von unterschiedlichen Möglichkeiten der Hautpflege; Abb. 273 erklärt die Bedeutung von Fitness. (NLD)
275 Aus einer Doppelseite der Zeitschrift *Vogue*. Hier für flüssigen Lippenstift. (FRA)
276 Mehrfarbige Doppelseite aus einem Artikel in der Zeitschrift *Avenue* über Bade-Anzüge: «Oberflächenspannung.» (NLD)

272–274 Doubles pages polychromes d'un article publié dans le magazine hollandais *Avenue* sur divers aspects de l'hygiène du corps. Les fig. 272 et 274 illustrent différentes méthodes de soins de la peau; la fig. 273 explique la signification du concept de forme physique. (NLD)
275 Détail d'une page double de *Vogue;* on y présente du rouge à lèvres liquide. (FRA)
276 Double page polychrome d'un article de modes de bain paru dans le magazine *Avenue:* «Tension superficielle.» (NLD)

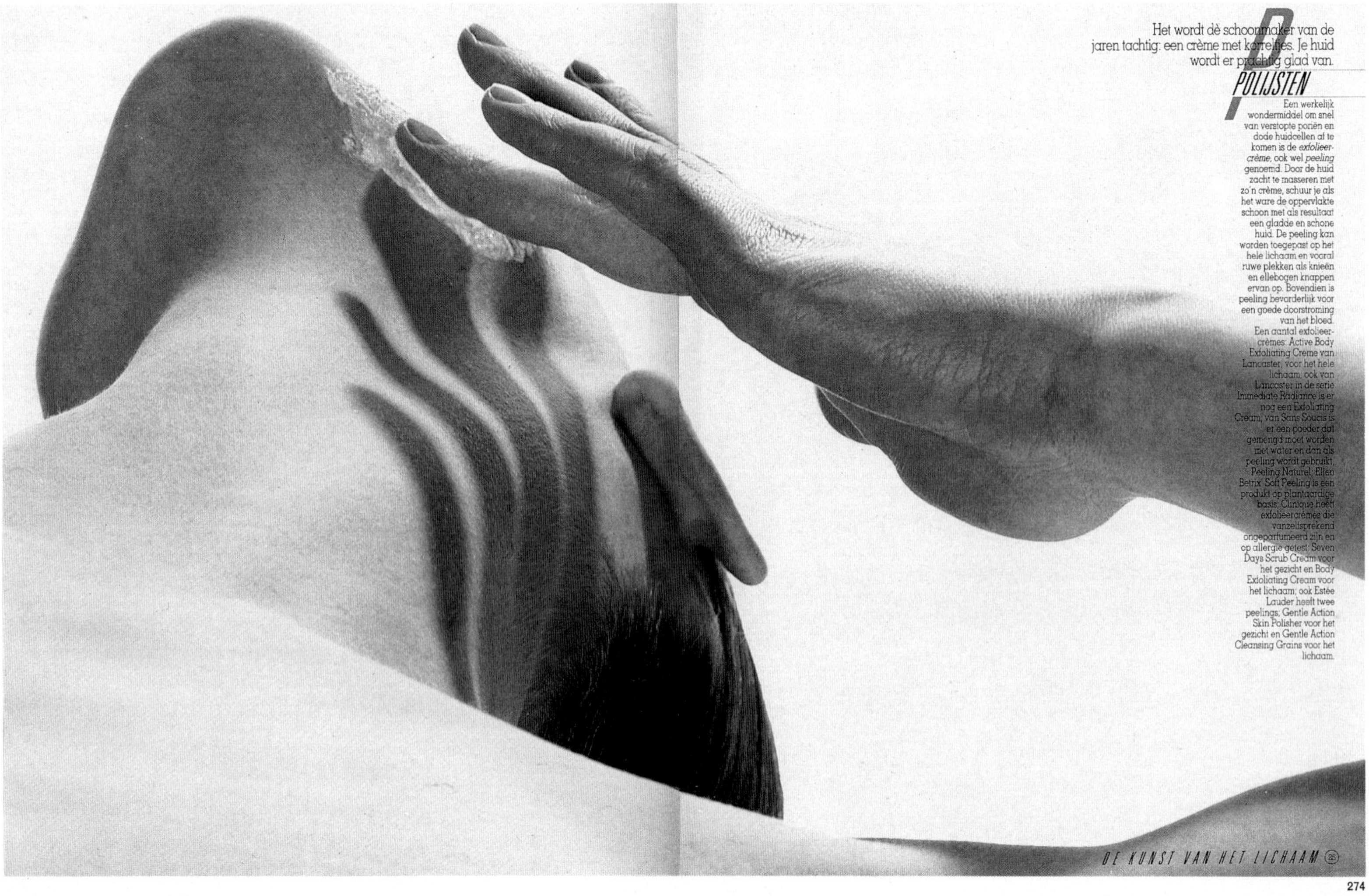

Het wordt dè schoonmaker van de jaren tachtig: een crème met korreltjes. Je huid wordt er prachtig glad van.

POLIJSTEN

Een werkelijk wondermiddel om snel van verstopte poriën en dode huidcellen af te komen is de *exfolieer-crème,* ook wel *peeling* genoemd. Door de huid zacht te masseren met zo'n crème, schuur je als het ware de oppervlakte schoon met als resultaat een gladde en schone huid. De peeling kan worden toegepast op het hele lichaam en vooral ruwe plekken als knieën en ellebogen knappen ervan op. Bovendien is peeling bevorderlijk voor een goede doorstroming van het bloed.
Een aantal exfolieer-crèmes: Active Body Exfoliating Creme van Lancaster, voor het hele lichaam; ook van Lancaster in de serie Immediate Radiance is er nog een Exfoliating Cream; van Sans Soucis is er een poeder dat gemengd moet worden met water en dan als peeling wordt gebruikt, Peeling Naturel; Ellen Betrix Soft Peeling is een produkt op plantaardige basis; Clinique heeft exfolieercrèmes die vanzelfsprekend ongeparfumeerd zijn en op allergie getest: Seven Days Scrub Cream voor het gezicht en Body Exfoliating Cream voor het lichaam; ook Estée Lauder heeft twee peelings; Gentle Action Skin Polisher voor het gezicht en Gentle Action Cleansing Grains voor het lichaam.

DE KUNST VAN HET LICHAAM

274

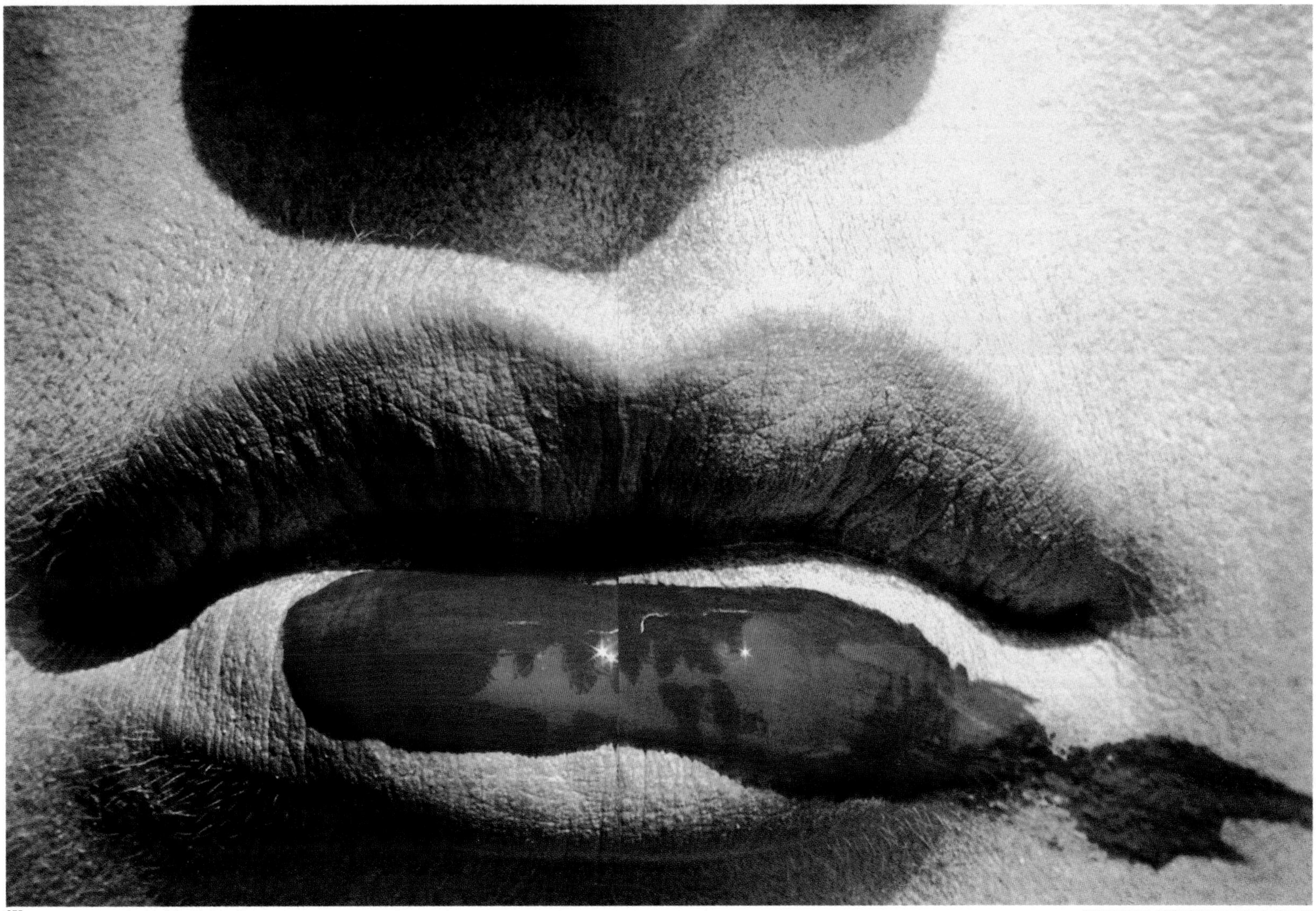

275

PHOTOGRAPHER / PHOTOGRAPH:

272–274 Boudewijn Neuteboom
275 Helmut Newton
276 Rob van Uchelen

DESIGNER / GESTALTER / MAQUETTISTE:

272–274 Louis Voogt
276 Yoke Westerman

ART DIRECTOR:

272–274, 276 Hans van Blommestein
275 Jocelyn Kargère

PUBLISHER / VERLEGER / EDITEUR:

272–274, 276 De Geillustreerde Pers
275 Condé Nast SA

276

277

278

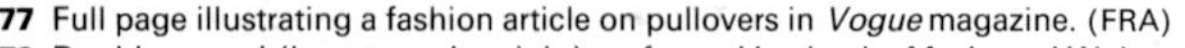

277 Full page illustrating a fashion article on pullovers in *Vogue* magazine. (FRA)
278 Double spread (here turned upright) on fur and leather in *Mode und Wohnen.* (GER)
279 Double spread introducing an article in *Gala* magazine on festive fashions for children, who are dressed in black with white and red trimmings. (GER)
280 Black-and-white double spread in an article on furs published by *Vogue.* (FRA)
281, 282 Double spreads from the men's magazine *Lui.* The colour shots illustrate an article on gifts, for women, with details and sources listed on a separate page. (GER)
283 Tarzan and Jane models show evening dresses in this *Vogue* full-colour spread. (FRA)

277 Ganzseitige Aufnahme aus einem Modebeitrag in *Vogue* über Pullover. (FRA)
278 Doppelseite (hier als Hochformat) zum Thema Pelz und Leder, aus *Mode und Wohnen.* (GER)
279 Einführende Doppelseite zu einem Beitrag über festliche Kindermode in der Zeitschrift *Gala.* Kleider schwarz mit weissen und roten Applikationen. (GER)
280 Doppelseitige Schwarzweissaufnahme aus einem Artikel über Pelze, erschienen in *Vogue.* (FRA)
281, 282 Doppelseiten aus dem Herrenmagazin *Lui.* Die Farbaufnahmen illustrieren einen Beitrag mit Geschenkvorschlägen. Angaben und Bezugsquellen befinden sich auf einer Extra-Seite. (GER)
283 Tarzan und Jane standen Pate für diesen Modebeitrag über Abendkleider in *Vogue.* (FRA)

277 Photo pleine page dans un article de *Vogue* consacré à la mode pullovers. (FRA)
278 Double page (ici format à la française) de *Mode und Wohnen:* cuir et fourrures. (GER)
279 Double page initiale d'un article du magazine *Gala* où il est question de vêtements de fête pour enfants. Robes noires, applications blanches et rouges. (GER)
280 Photo double page en noir et blanc dans un article de *Vogue* sur fourrures. (FRA)
281, 282 Doubles pages du magazine masculin *Lui.* Les photos couleur illustrent un article avec des idées de cadeaux. Références et fournisseurs figurent sur une page spéciale. (GER)
283 Tarzan et Jane ont inspiré cet article de *Vogue* sur les tenues de soirée. (FRA)

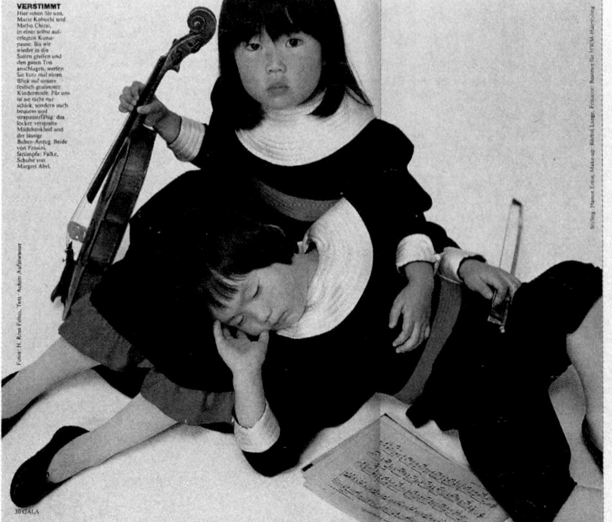

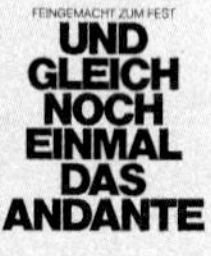

279

280

PHOTOGRAPHER / PHOTOGRAPH / PHOTOGRAPHE:

277 Albert Watson
278 Sylvain Corrodi
279 H. Ross Feltus
280 Norman Parkinson
281, 282 Gerhard Vormwald
283 Bill King

ART DIRECTOR / DIRECTEUR ARTISTIQUE:

277, 280, 283 Jocelyn Kargère
278 Heidrun Schell
279 Gudrun Hänsel
281, 282 Karl-Heinz Wendlandt

PUBLISHER / VERLEGER / EDITEUR:

277, 280, 283 Condé Nast SA
278 Lütze Verlag GmbH
279 Gala Verlag GmbH
281, 282 NewMagazines Verlagsgesellschaft mbH

281

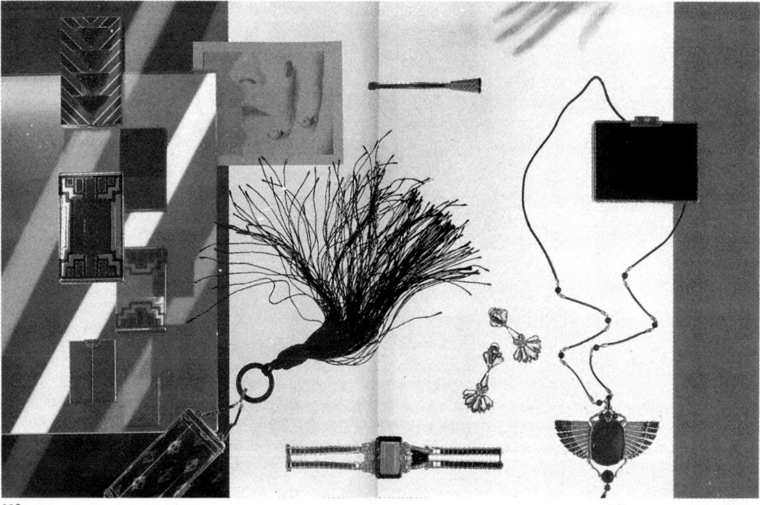

282

Lady Jane, chez Ricci, brille la nuit comme un ciel tropical. Broderies, dentelles, lamés illuminent les bustes et les jupes. Les drapés sculptent, les tulles s'envolent en jupes-nuages, les couleurs clair-de-lune risquent de réveiller le bipède chez le Comte de Greystoke, Pair du Royaume. Ci-contre, longue robe bustier paréo en lamé d'Etro. Nina Ricci par Gérard Pipart. Sandales Walter Steiger pour Nina Ricci. Boucles d'oreilles, collier et bracelets Nina Ricci. Coiffure John Sahag. Maquillage Elizabeth Arden.

NINA RICCI
et le paréo lumière.

Chez Jean-Louis Scherrer, c'est la jungle le jour, la jungle le soir. Page de droite, long fourreau à dos nu en tulle noir rebrodé par Lesage de motifs tigrés de paillettes et de strass serpentant en "voie lactée". Bijoux Jean-Louis Scherrer. Coiffure John Sahag. Maquillage Harriet Hubbard Ayer.

JEAN-LOUIS SCHERRER
et la voie lactée.

382

283

Le pull noir qui dévoile un peu de peau et le pantalon court. Une silhouette qui suit le corps. Le pull est en laine fine, décolleté bateau avec sa large bande de côtes qui couvre le haut des bras (Yvan et Marzia, 260 F). Il est rentré dans un corsaire écossais marine, vert et jaune (Agnès B., 790 F). Foulard de soie (Hermès). Lunettes (Scooter). Ceinture élastique (Yvan et Marzia). Gants (Guibert Frères). Gourmettes (Agatha). Ballerines (Carel).

133

Le col roulé noir, avec la jupe droite nouvelle longueur, et la taille bien prise dans une large ceinture. Le pull est en Lambswool (Caroll, 260 F), il épouse de près le corps, il est rentré dans une jupe gris chiné en covercoat, des poches qui décollent (D. Jagot pour Georges Rech, 610 F). Ceinture (Cacharel). Béret (La Samaritaine). Boucles d'oreille (Scooter). Broche (Agatha). Gants (Hermès). Collant (Christian Dior). Escarpins (Maud Frizon).

284

La robe de tricot, bien moulante, grand V sur le devant, grand V dans le dos. Une silhouette très dessinée et tonique. Ici robe-fourreau, en laine mélangée noire superbement pointillée de blanc (Jacqueline Jacobson pour Dorothée Bis, 890 F). Béret noir bien campé (La Samaritaine). Haute ceinture taille fine en cuir noir et gants en filet blanc et chevreau noir (Azzedine Alaïa). Collant (Christian Dior). Escarpins à talon haut et fin (Maud Frizon).

136

Le tailleur noir, bien cintré, et porté à même la peau. Une silhouette très nette et mince. Ici le tailleur est en gabardine de coton, un col tailleur, un double boutonnage à la taille, une jupe très droite (Emmanuelle Khanh, 1540 F). Pour ponctuer cette superbe austérité, cette sobriété très féminine, ce dépouillement bien séduisant: un large collier de chien, plusieurs rangs de fines perles de culture (Técla) et des gants en daim (Hermès).

137

285

PHOTOGRAPHER / PHOTOGRAPH / PHOTOGRAPHE:

284–286 Peter Lindbergh
287, 288 Daniel Jouanneau/Vogue Paris

ART DIRECTOR / DIRECTEUR ARTISTIQUE:

284–286 Walter Rospert
287, 288 Jocelyn Kargère

PUBLISHER / VERLEGER / EDITEUR:

284–286 Marie Claire
287, 288 Condé Nast SA

284–286 Complete pages from an article in *Marie Claire*, which printed them entirely in black and white, incorporating the text in small blocks next to the illustrations. This gave the look of an early film to the article's theme: typical Parisian fashions. (FRA)
287 Full-page colour shot illustrating a *Vogue* article on risotto recipes. (FRA)
288 Fashion accessories such as shoes and watches, illustrated by this full-page colour shot, were the theme of a *Vogue* article. (FRA)

284–286 Aus einem in der Zeitschrift *Marie Claire* erschienenen Modebeitrag, der ausschliesslich aus ganzseitigen Schwarzweiss-Aufnahmen mit kleinen Textblocks besteht. Das Thema ist typische Pariser Mode; die Aufnahmen (alle schwarzweiss) wirken wie Bilder aus einem ausdrucksvollen Schwarzweiss-Film über Paris. (FRA)
287 Ganzseitige Farbaufnahme aus einem Beitrag in *Vogue*, mit Risotto-Rezepten. (FRA)
288 Modische Accessoires wie Schuhe, Uhren und Handtaschen, sind Thema des Artikels, aus dem diese ganzseitige Farbaufnahme stammt. Erschienen in *Vogue*. (FRA)

284–286 Extrait d'un article de mode paru dans le magazine *Marie Claire* et composé entièrement de photos noir et blanc pleine page et de petites légendes compactes. Le sujet: le mode parisienne type; les photos donnent l'impression d'être tirées d'un film noir et blanc consacré à Paris. (FRA)
287 Photo couleur pleine page pour un article de *Vogue*, avec des recettes de risotto. (FRA)
288 Les accessoires de mode – chaussures, montres, sacs à main – constituent le sujet de l'article de *Vogue* d'où est tirée cette photo pleine page. (FRA)

287

286

288

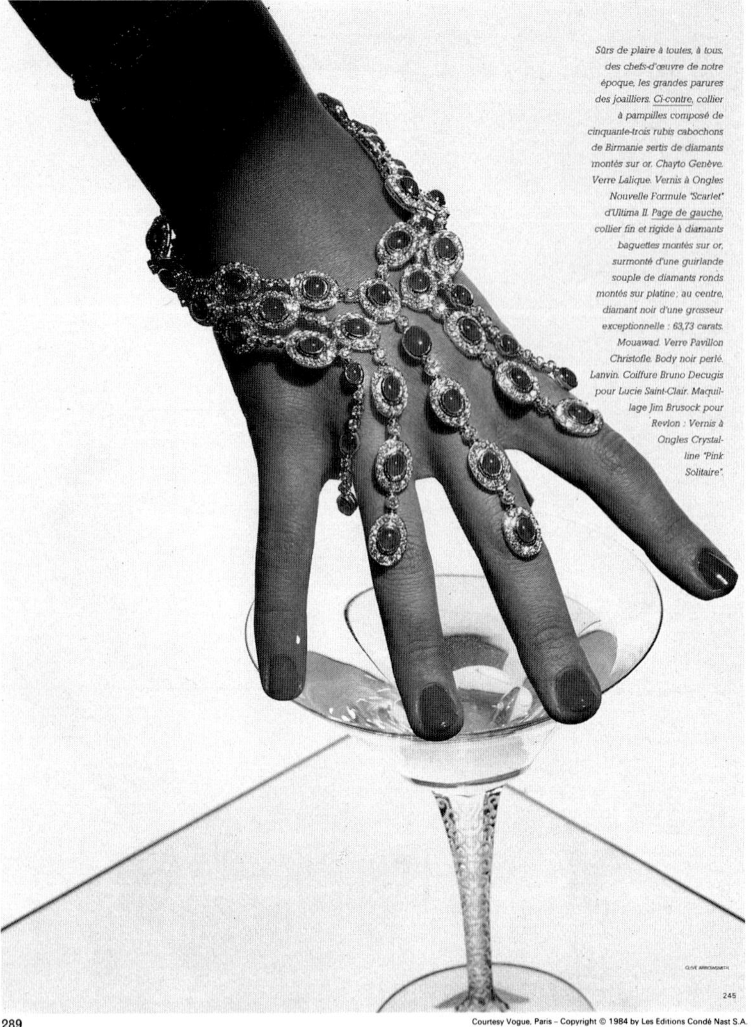

289

290

291

Editorial Photography

PHOTOGRAPHER / PHOTOGRAPH / PHOTOGRAPHE:

289–291 Clive Arrowsmith
292 Daniel Jouanneau/Vogue Paris

ART DIRECTOR / DIRECTEUR ARTISTIQUE:

289–292 Jocelyn Kargère

PUBLISHER / VERLEGER / EDITEUR:

289–292 Condé Nast SA

289–291 Full-colour pages from an article in *Vogue* magazine on the lasting value of jewels. These were shown in necklaces (Fig. 289) of rubies and diamonds, (Fig. 290) of saphires and diamonds, and (Fig. 291) of emeralds and saphires. (FRA)
292 The blue of the iris blossom is matched here by the saphire in a diamond-studded ring. Illustration from a series on jewelled rings in *Vogue* magazine, which showed them next to flowers of matching colour. (FRA)

289–291 Aus einem Beitrag in der Zeitschrift *Vogue* über den bleibenden Wert von Edelsteinen. In Farbe. Abb. 289: Halsschmuck mit Rubinen und Diamanten; Abb. 290: Rundes Collier mit Saphiren und Diamanten; Abb. 291: Halsschmuck mit Smaragden und Saphiren. (FRA)
292 Das Blau der Irisblüte korrespondiert mit dem Saphir des brillantenbesetzten Rings. Aufnahme aus einer Serie über Ringe mit Edelsteinen, arrangiert mit entsprechenden Blüten, erschienen in der Zeitschrift *Vogue*. (FRA)

289–291 Illustrations pour un article du magazine *Vogue* mettant en relief la sécurité d'investissement qu'offrent les pierres précieuses. En couleur. Fig. 289: rivière de diamants et rubis; fig. 290: rivière ronde de diamants et saphirs; fig. 291: collier d'émeraudes et de saphirs. (FRA)
292 Le bleu de la fleur d'iris correspond à celui du saphir de cette bague sertie de diamants. Photo figurant dans une série publiée dans le magazine *Vogue*, où des bagues ornées de pierres précieuses sont regroupées avec des fleurs. (FRA)

293

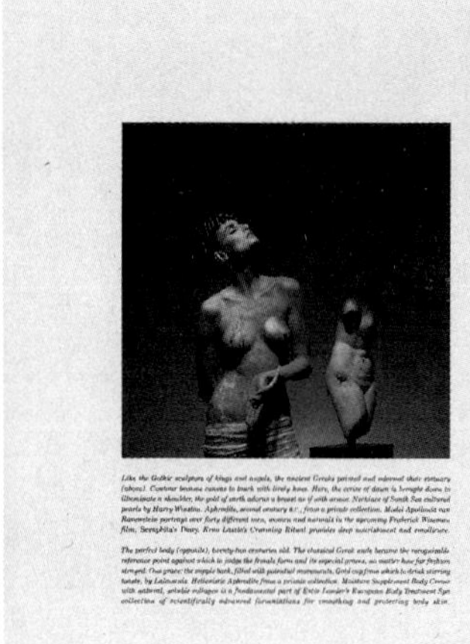

294

293–295 Double spreads in full colour from the magazine *Town & Country* for an article on "The Artful Body". Skin-care products were an integral feature of the illustrations. Fig. 293: The woman's body is powdered pink. Fig. 294: The model on the left is multicoloured and, on the right, has a streak of turquoise. Fig. 295 shows a surrealistic composition. (USA)
296, 297 Full-page illustration and a double spread from a magazine article on beauty care published in *Marie Claire*. The model is Isabella Rossellini, the daughter of Ingrid Bergman. (FRA)
298 Double spreads from a series illustrated by such interpretations of Marilyn Monroe photographs. This *Marie Claire* series featured the trench-coat. (FRA)

293–295 Doppelseiten für einen Artikel in *Town & Country* über den Körper als Kunst, wobei hier Hautpflegeprodukte die Gestaltungsmittel waren. Abb. 293: Als Pendant zu Jean Arps Torso der Körper der Frau, rosa geschminkt – ein uraltes Mittel zur Intensivierung des Ausdrucks; Abb. 294: Torso der Aphrodite (200 v. Chr.), Körper in der kleinen Abbildung mehrfarbig, mit türkisgrüner Masse in der grossen; Abb. 295: surrealistische Komposition. (USA)
296, 297 Ganzseitige Aufnahme und Doppelseite aus einem Artikel über Schönheitspflege, mit Isabella Rossellini als Modell; erschienen in *Marie Claire*. (FRA)
298 Doppelseite aus einer Serie von Aufnahmen, bei denen bereits vorhandene Photos von Marilyn Monroe interpretiert wurden. Thema des Artikels ist der Trenchcoat. Aus *Marie Claire*. (FRA)

293–295 Doubles pages d'un article de *Town & Country* sur le corps en tant qu'objet d'art transfiguré par les produits cosmétiques. Fig. 293: un corps féminin maquillé de rose, vieille technique expressive, en contrepoint au torse de Jean Arp; fig. 294: torse d'Aphrodite (200 av. J.-C.); le corps sur la petite photo est polychrome, le trait sur la grande est en turquoise; fig. 295: composition surréaliste. (USA)
296, 297 Photo pleine page et double page d'un article sur les soins de beauté utilisant Isabella Rossellini comme objet de démonstration, dans *Marie Claire*. (FRA)
298 Double page faisant partie d'une série de photos interprétant des clichés existants de Marilyn Monroe. Sujet de l'article: les trench-coats. Dans *Marie Claire*. (FRA)

295

PHOTOGRAPHER / PHOTOGRAPH:

293–295 Victor Skrebneski
296–298 Peter Lindbergh

DESIGNER / GESTALTER / MAQUETTISTE:

293–295 Melissa Tardiff

ART DIRECTOR / DIRECTEUR ARTISTIQUE:

293–295 Melissa Tardiff
296–298 Walter Rospert

PUBLISHER / VERLEGER / EDITEUR:

293–295 Hearst Corporation
296–298 Marie Claire

296

297

298

299 Full-colour double spread from *Penthouse* magazine illustrating a humorous short story about an occasional waiter—who leaned on the door mock-up for this shot. (AUS)
300 One of the Amyn Nasser photographs used in the article on him in the French magazine *Photologie.* It devoted several pages to this member of the "new generation" of American photographers. (CAN)
301–303 Full-colour double spreads from the Japanese magazine *Wig.* The theme, hair, is combined here with various fruit and vegetables. (JPN)

299 Doppelseite aus der australischen Ausgabe des Magazins *Penthouse* mit mehrfarbiger Aufnahme zu einer humoristischen Kurzgeschichte über einen Gelegenheitskellner. Der Kellner stützt sich mit den Schultern auf der Türattrappe auf. (AUS)
300 Aufnahme aus einem mehrseitigen Artikel über den Photographen Amyn Nasser in der französischen Fachzeitschrift *Photologie.* Dieses Photo leitet den Artikel ein; für den Umschlag der betreffenden Ausgabe ist ebenfalls eine Aufnahme Amyn Nassers verwendet worden, der zur «neuen Generation» der amerikanischen Photographen gehört. (CAN)
301–303 Drei doppelseitige, mehrfarbige Aufnahmen aus der japanischen Zeitschrift *Wig.* Das Thema Haar wird mit Früchten und Gemüse kombiniert. Abb. 303: Verschiedene Extremitäten gucken unter einem Haufen Tomaten hervor. (JPN)

299 Double page de l'édition australienne du magazine *Penthouse* illustrée d'une photo polychrome pour une nouvelle humoristique dont le héros est un extra. On le voit ici s'appuyer des épaules contre une porte factice. (AUS)
300 Photo illustrant un article de plusieurs pages que le magazine français *Photologie* consacre au photographe Amyn Nasser, représentant en vue de la «nouvelle génération» des photographes d'Amérique. (CAN)
301–303 Trois photos double page en polychromie pour le magazine japonais *Wig.* Le sujet, la chevelure, est associé à des fruits et légumes. (JPN)

When a casual waiter makes his confession, he lets slip quite a mouthful . . .

SPILLING THE BEANS

HUMOR BY ADAM BOWEN

It was Beef'n'Burgundy Nite at the biggest bowls club in the southern suburbs. In the Wally Gribble Memorial Auditorium hundreds of mums and dads were hoeing into baked dinners and enjoying the onstage talents of Ken and His Magic Violin.

In the huge and sweltering multi-racial kitchen I piled six more red-hot plates of grey, leathery beef swamped in murky brown gravy on to my tray. Dolores slapped a hunk of pumpkin, 15 bullet-like peas and two lumps of spud on to each plate and I was off, backwards through the double doors and into the packed auditorium, which was throbbing to the wanton sounds of I'll Take You Home Again Kathleen.

A voice from the throng called out: "Waiter!"

I feigned deafness and beetled across the puce and violet carpet towards table 12, eager to dispense my tempting trayload before the whole lot congealed. On arrival, I started dumping "Beautifully Braised Slices of Beef Swimming in Succulently Savory Sauce Sicilienne, Accompanied by Country Fresh Vegetables Baked to Perfection" into every empty space on the paper tablecloth.

"But I ordered pork," croaked a woman.

"Never mind, Madam. The beef's lovely," I replied enthusiastically, squeezing rapidly through the minute space between the backs of plastic chairs.

"Waiter!" cried an elderly gent who resembled Frank Hyde with severe sunburn.

"Yes, sir?"

"Is this beef rare?" We both stared at his portion of grisly, gravy-saturated brown death.

"Well, sir . . . it's . . . unusual."

I confess. I'm a casual waiter. I'm with the Silver Service Staff Agency. Have tuxedo will travel to hotels, motels, clubs, pubs, restaurants and private functions. I'll pour champagne at terribly trendy 21sts, I'll pick up

PHOTOGRAPHY BY GRAEME DAVEY

299

Editorial Photography

300

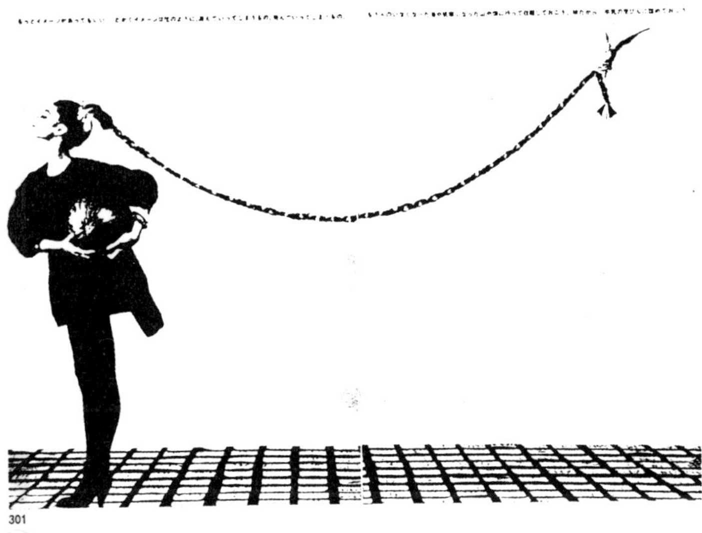

301

302

PHOTOGRAPHER / PHOTOGRAPH:

299 Graeme Davey
300 Amyn Nasser
301–303 Taiji Hirokawa

DESIGNER / GESTALTER / MAQUETTISTE:

299 Stephen Costello

ART DIRECTOR / DIRECTEUR ARTISTIQUE:

299 Stephen Costello
300 Amyn Nasser/David Glover
301–303 Tomoyuki Ono

AGENCY / AGENTUR / AGENCE – STUDIO:

301–303 Green Oasis Co., Ltd.

PUBLISHER / VERLEGER / EDITEUR:

299 Australian Penthouse
300 Photologie
301–303 Japan Wig Industrial Association

303

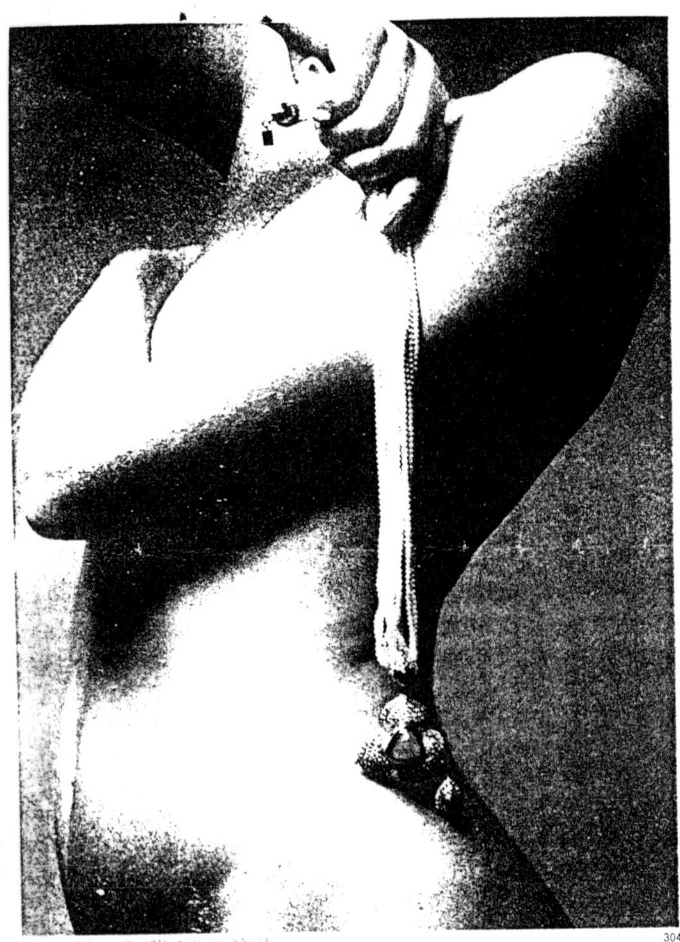

304

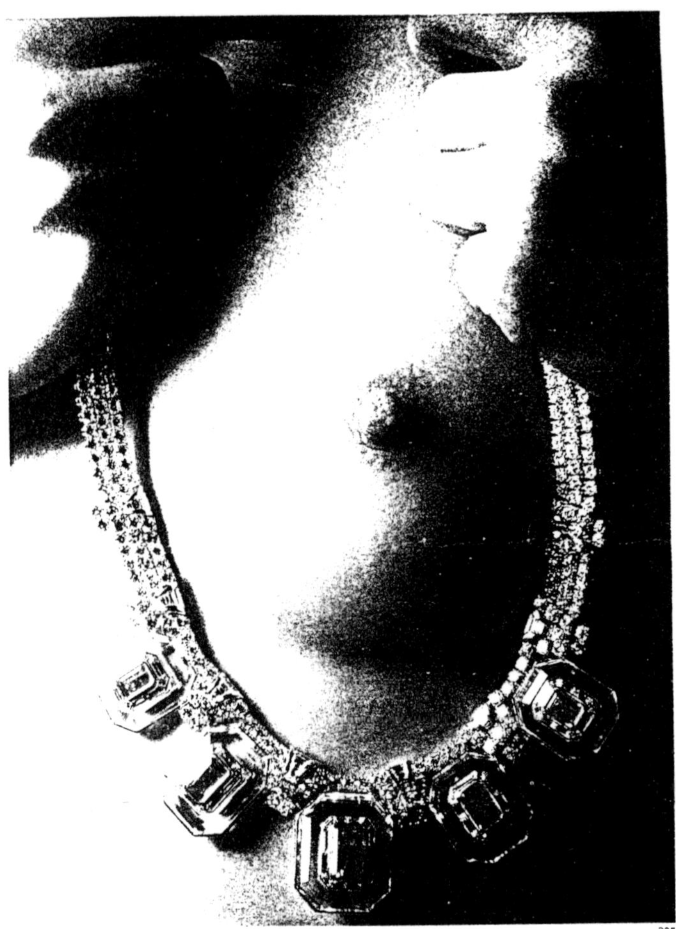

305

307

308

304–306 From an article in *Vogue* that alternated double spreads in black-and-white photography, on fashion, and those in full colour, on jewellery. Fig. 304: Central motif of this pearl necklace is its ruby, surrounded by emeralds and diamonds set in gold. Fig. 305: The pendants of this diamond and gold necklace are large emeralds set in gold with rock crystals. Fig. 306: A double spread showing costly bejewelled watches. (FRA)
307–309 Full-page photographs and a double spread from a *Vogue* article on cosmetics and perfumes. Here, cream jars in soft shades of beige (Figs. 307 and 308), and a powder-box of black glass (reflecting a greyish violet) with gold-coloured "fir cone". (FRA)

304–306 Aus einem Beitrag in *Vogue*, in dem abwechselnd eine Doppelseite mit Modeaufnahmen in Schwarzweiss und eine Doppelseite mit Farbaufnahmen von Schmuck präsentiert wird. Abb. 304: das zentrale Motiv der Perlenkette ist ein Rubin, umgeben von Smaragden und Brillanten auf Gold; Abb. 305: diamantbesetztes Collier aus Gold mit Smaragden in Gold und Bergkristall eingefasst. (FRA)
307–309 Ganzseitige Aufnahmen und Doppelseite aus einem Artikel in *Vogue* über Kosmetik und Parfums. Creme-Töpfchen in zarten Beigetönen (Abb. 307 und 308) und Puderdose aus schwarzem Glas (hier mit grauvioletter Spiegelung) mit goldfarbenem «Tannenzapfen». (FRA)

304–306 Illustrations d'un article paru dans *Vogue* où alternent une double page de photos de mode en noir et blanc et une double page de photos de bijoux en couleur. Fig. 304: le motif central de ce collier de perles est un rubis cabochon entouré d'émeraudes et de brillants enchâssés dans l'or; fig. 305: collier de diamants monté sur or, avec de grosses émeraudes enchâssées dans l'or et le cristal de roche; fig. 308: montres serties de pierreries. (FRA)
307–309 Photos pleine page et double page d'un article paru dans *Vogue*, où il est question de cosmétiques et de parfums. On voit ici des petits pots de crème aux teintes beiges délicates (fig. 307 et 308) et un poudrier en verre noir (ici aux reflets gris violet) garni d'un «cône» doré. (FRA)

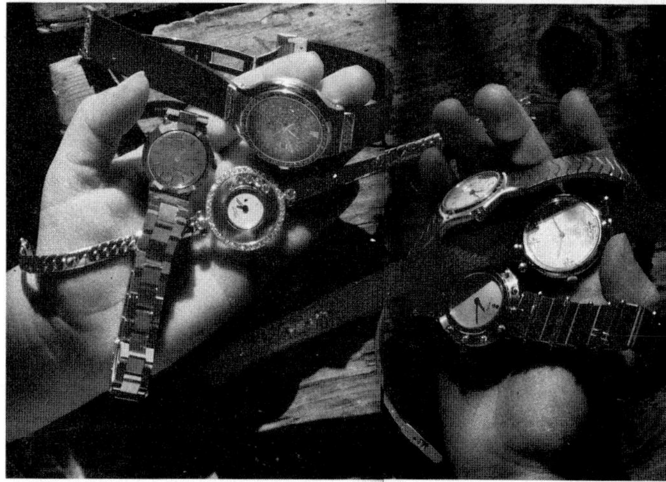

306

PHOTOGRAPHER / PHOTOGRAPH / PHOTOGRAPHE:

304–306 Jeanloup Sieff
307–309 Daniel Jouanneau/Vogue Paris

ART DIRECTOR / DIRECTEUR ARTISTIQUE:

304–309 Jocelyn Kargère

PUBLISHER / VERLEGER / EDITEUR:

304–309 Condé Nast SA

LES FARDS-ECLAT

Ce sont ceux qui déposent sur le visage et le décolleté des éclats perlés, dorés ou nacrés. Fantaisies d'un soir, les gels pailletés font scintiller les paupières, recouvrent les sourcils d'une poussière d'argent ou créent des effets miroitants sur le décolleté. Bourjois propose, pour faire pétiller les soirées, "Les Comètes", trois gels pailletés (or, cuivre et nacré) présentés dans des mini-tubes transparents. Michel Deruelle offre une palette de cinq coloris : or, argent, bleu, vert et rouge pour réhausser d'une note lumineuse un taffetas rouge ou un satin bleu. Pensez "or" pour un maquillage délicatement lamé, légèrement champagnisé. Yves Saint Laurent propose "Les Ors", deux fards dorés (un "Fard Brillant Or" et un "Vernis Laque Or") pour réhausser les lèvres et les ongles d'un éclat mordoré. Un halo qui brille tout autour des yeux, c'est l'effet que l'on obtient avec l'Ombre Satinée "Pépite" de Guerlain. En matière de beauté, un rien anime, un rien éteint... Or, la beauté fait grand usage de ces riens. La poudre en fait partie. Il faut savoir en jouer. Aujourd'hui, elle se superpose pour ajouter à la couleur un velouté impalpable ou un éclat subtilement irisé. C'est le but de "Galaxie" de Caron, une poudre blanche légèrement pailletée, transparente, presque invisible mais cependant lumineuse. Pour les carnations plus mates, Caron a créé, dans le même esprit, "Vesta", une nuance mordorée également pailletée. Une grande nouveauté : les "Poudres Libres Scintillantes" de Barbara Gould qui confèrent au visage, aux épaules ou au décolleté un éclat soyeux. Trois nuances aux noms évocateurs : "Aurore Lamée", "Equinoxe d'Or" et "Alizé Mauve".

Ci-contre, le poudrier Arpège de Lanvin spécialement réédité pour Noël 1983 : de forme ronde légèrement aplatie sur le dessus et orné d'une "pomme de pin" dorée, il se compose de deux coupelles identiques de plein verre noir. Il cache, à l'intérieur, une houppette en cygne. Selon vos désirs, il deviendra poudrier, bonbonnière ou baguier.

309

MY FUR LADY

LEFT. Persian broadtail jacket with a mink collar, £1,000, Paul Furs, 147 Notting Hill Gate, W11. Chantilly lace picture hat trimmed with black taffeta and an osprey aigrette, £300 to order, Stephen Jones Millinery. Cultured pearl, diamond and carved crystal necklace, £11,250; matching earrings, £4,425; all from Boucheron. White Thirties dress with silver embroidery, £140, Ben Thrift, stall Z6, Antiquarius. Black silk lace gloves, £15, Jo Dalby, stall X2, Antiquarius. Black suede and pewter satin shoes, £83, Chloé, 173 New Bond Street, W1. The maid wears a jet and paste necklace and matching earrings, £36, The Studio. Black and white beaded Twenties dress, £250, Mr Gubbins, Antiquarius. Brown satin shoes with bronze buckles, £90, Manolo Blahnik, 49 Old Church Street, SW3. Black suede gloves, £50, Chloé.

RIGHT. Grey chinchilla jacket, £4,600, Riva Furs, 67-69 George Street, W1. Black shako toque, edged with pewter brocade and trimmed with silver plated coq feathers, £350 to order, Stephen Jones Millinery. Diamond line necklace, £20,250; diamond drop earrings, £20,550; all from Collingwood, 46 Conduit Street, W1. Fuchsia silk satin shirt, £306, Emanuel Ungaro, 153a New Bond Street, W1. Black wool skirt from a selection at Margaret Howell. Black suede gloves from a selection at Jo Dalby, stand X2, Antiquarius. Cigarette holder, £95, The Purple Shop, Antiquarius. Purple glasses from a selection at Eat Your Heart Out, 360 King's Road, SW3.

310

Editorial Photography

PHOTOGRAPHER / PHOTOGRAPH / PHOTOGRAPHE:

310 John Bishop
311 Shuzo Koguchi
312 Graham Monro
313 Robert Amft
314 Gary S. Wolfson/Scott Robinson

ODD MAN IN?

THE FOREIGNER IN A JAPANESE COMPANY

By Eiko Fukuda

Kazuo Ido, the personnel manager for Seibu Department Stores, is a busy man. Recruiting for Japan's largest and fastest-growing multi-channel retailer is no simple task and he has little time to spare for interviews. He pauses just long enough between sentences to sweep back his hair in an impatient gesture and then continues to make his point:

"It's absolutely ridiculous," he says, "if our materials are from China, our designs from France, and our packaging done in Korea, why should all our people be from Japan? Retailing depends on quality imports and we need buyers who can see beyond a brand name. In our case, we also need experts in the art field to promote our various cultural activities. With our overseas network and production sharing philosophy, it makes good sense for Seibu to hire foreigners."

A latecomer to the eclectic world of Japanese department stores, Seibu has made its mark by becoming the trendiest of trendsetters in recent years. The Seibu Group extends its name to other fields of business including urban development, life insurance, and chemical industries, but merchandising provides the backbone of its $9.6 billion annual sales. Seibu is

17

311

312

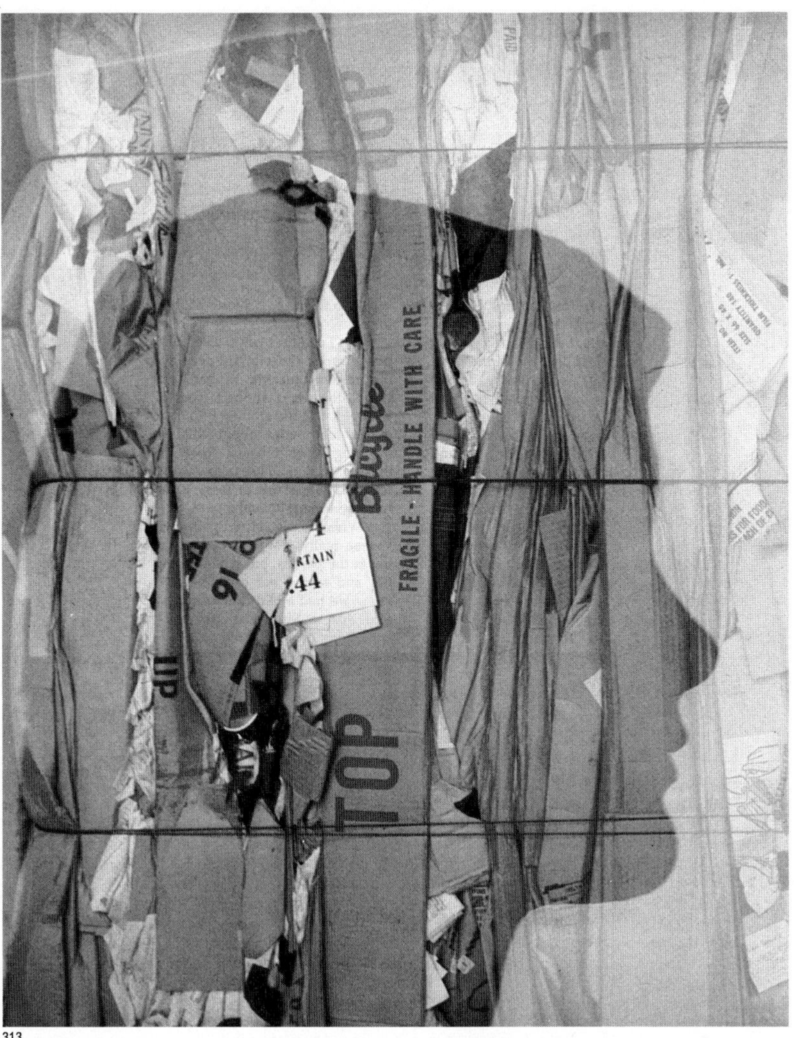

313

310 Double spread from an article about fur fashions in *The Tattler* magazine. (GBR)
311 The in-flight magazine of Japan Airlines, *Winds*, used this double spread to introduce an article on the experience of a foreigner in a Japanese firm. (JPN)
312 A *Penthouse* double spread for its article on a wild-water expedition. (AUS)
313 Full-page colour illustration to a love story in a text book on literature. (USA)
314 From the Russian-language magazine *America*, for a story on American champions. (USA)

310 Doppelseite für einen Artikel über Pelzmode in dem Magazin *The Tattler.* (GBR)
311 Einleitende Doppelseite zu einem Artikel in *Winds*, eine Publikation der Japan Airlines. Das Thema: Die Erfahrungen eines Ausländers in einem japanischen Unternehmen. (JPN)
312 Doppelseite für einen Beitrag über Wildwasser-Expeditionen, in *Penthouse.* (AUS)
313 Illustration zu einer Liebesgeschichte in einem Literatur-Lehrbuch. (USA)
314 Für einen Artikel in der Zeitschrift *Amerika*, die für die UdSSR bestimmt ist. (USA)

310 Double page pour un article sur les fourrures à la mode, dans *The Tattler.* (GBR)
311 Double page initiale d'un article de *Winds*, une publication de Japan Airlines. On y parle des expériences d'un Occidental travaillant chez des Japonais. (JPN)
312 Double page d'un article sur les expéditions en rivière, dans *Penthouse.* (AUS)
313 Illustration d'une histoire d'amour dans un manuel de littérature. (USA)
314 Pour un article de l'édition russe du magazine *Amerika.* (USA)

DESIGNER / GESTALTER / MAQUETTISTE:

310 Michael Roberts
311 Mona Kesa Meyer
312 Stephen Costello
313 Hal Kearny

ART DIRECTOR / DIRECTEUR ARTISTIQUE:

310 Michael Roberts
311 Mona Kesa Meyer
312 Stephen Costello
313 Hal Kearny

AGENCY / AGENTUR / AGENCE – STUDIO:

311 Emphasis, Inc.

PUBLISHER / VERLEGER / EDITEUR:

310 Condé Nast Publications Ltd.
311 Japan Air Lines
312 Australian Penthouse
313 Scott, Foresman
314 U.S. International Communication Agency

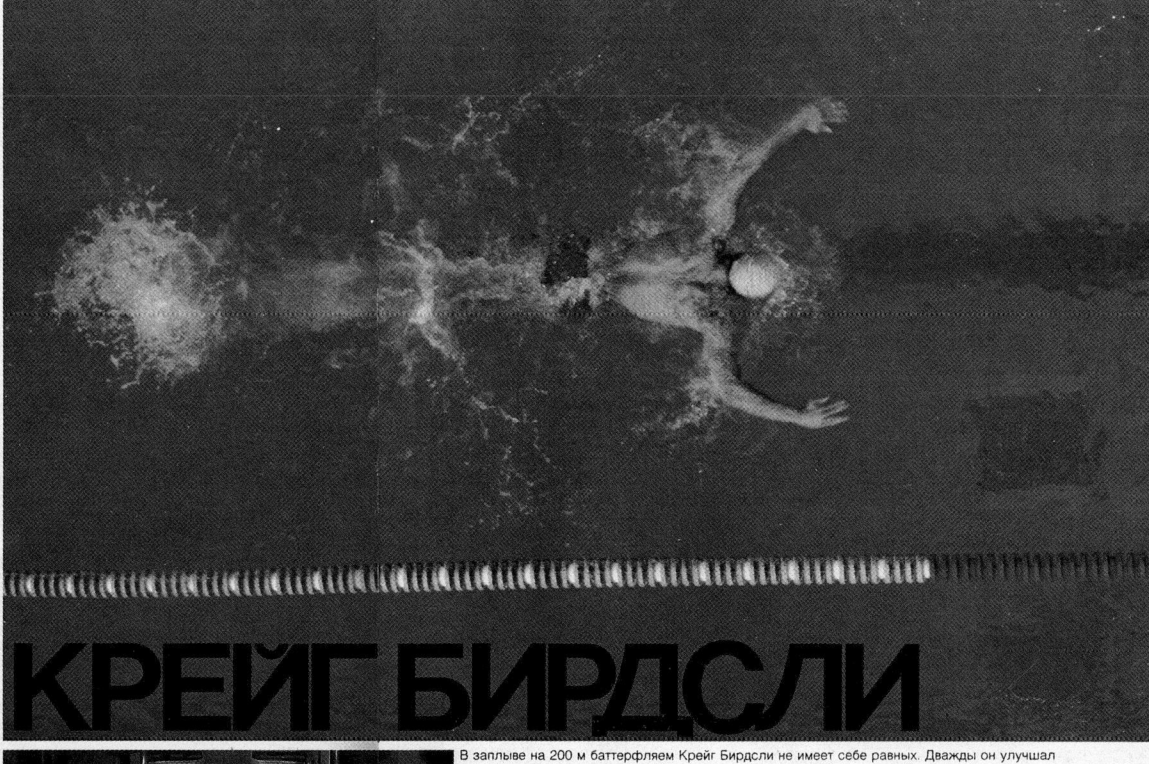

КРЕЙГ БИРДСЛИ

В заплыве на 200 м баттерфляем Крейг Бирдсли не имеет себе равных. Дважды он улучшал мировой рекорд, сняв с него в общей сложности 1,22 сек. Его нынешний рекорд на этой дистанции — 1.58,01. Возможно, что Бирдсли сумел бы еще больше прославить свое имя в спорте, будь дистанция баттерфляя — этого самого трудного вида спортивного плавания — подлиннее. В общей сложности на тренировках Крейг проплывает 6000 м, из них на баттерфляй приходится 2000 м, которые он проходит почти с такой же скоростью, как на соревнованиях. Крейг недавно получил во Флоридском университете в Гейнсвилле степень бакалавра по деловому администрированию и в недалеком будущем намеревается стать компаньоном своего отца, владельца цепи магазинов аудиооборудования в Нью-Йорке. В настоящее же время Крейг живет во Флориде и усиленно готовится к Олимпиаде 1984 года, которая состоится в Лос-Анджелесе.

29

314

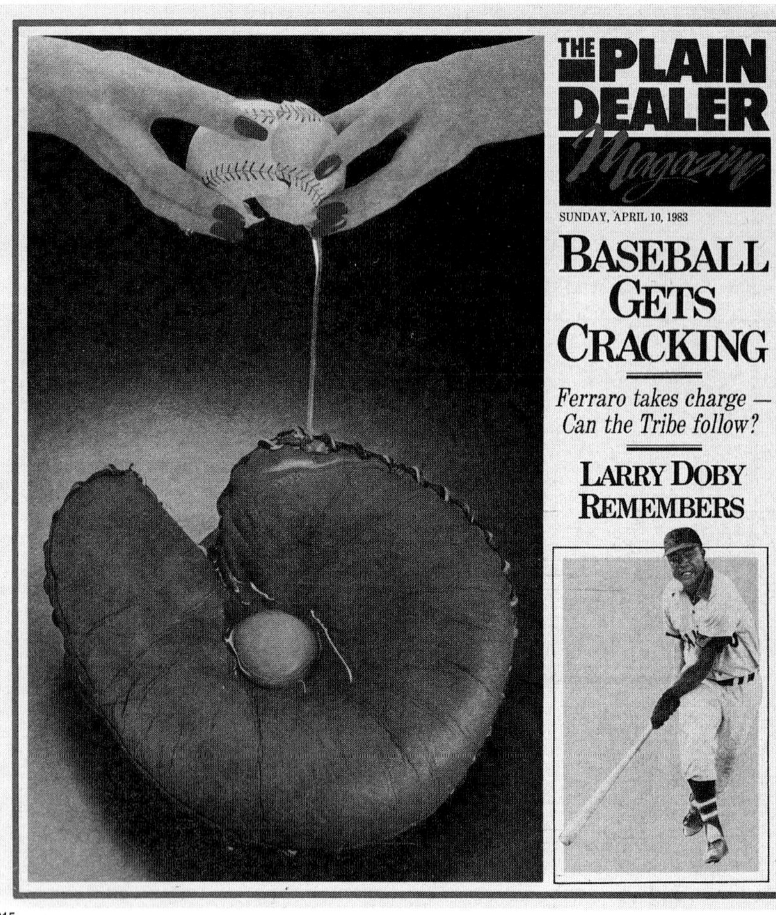
THE PLAIN DEALER Magazine

SUNDAY, APRIL 10, 1983

BASEBALL GETS CRACKING

Ferraro takes charge — Can the Tribe follow?

LARRY DOBY REMEMBERS

315

PHOTOGRAPHER / PHOTOGRAPH / PHOTOGRAPHE:

315 Robert Holcepl
316 Heribert Brehm
317–320 Christian von Alvensleben

DESIGNER / GESTALTER / MAQUETTISTE:

315 Greg Paul

ART DIRECTOR / DIRECTEUR ARTISTIQUE:

315 Greg Paul
316 Jürgen Hellge
317–320 Angelica Blechschmidt

PUBLISHER / VERLEGER / EDITEUR:

315 The Plain Dealer Publishing Co.
316 Jahreszeitenverlag
317–320 Condé Nast Verlag

315 Complete cover of *The Plain Dealer Magazine*, with photography that is a visual pun of the headline. (USA)
316 Double spread for a magazine article about shoes in *Petra*. The trick here was achieved during exposure; the shot (in full colour) needed no later manipulation. (GER)
317–320 Food shown in still-life studies ("Foodstills") is the subject of these photographs published by *Vogue* magazine. (GER)

315 Vorderseite des *Plain Dealer Magazine*. Die Farbaufnahmen beziehen sich auf einen Artikel über Baseball. (USA)
316 Doppelseite für einen Beitrag über Schuhe in *Petra*. Der Phototrick ist direkt bei der Aufnahme entstanden, ohne nachträgliche Manipulation. In Farbe. (GER)
317–320 Stilleben mit Lebensmitteln («Foodstills») sind Thema dieser Aufnahmen, die in der Zeitschrift *Vogue* erschienen sind. (GER)

315 Page de couverture du *Plain Dealer Magazine*. Les photos couleur se rapportent à un article traitant le sujet de base-ball. (USA)
316 Double page d'un article de *Petra* sur des chaussures à la mode. L'astuce de la photo ne résulte pas d'un montage, mais de l'environnement original. En couleur. (GER)
317–320 Des natures mortes à base de légumes («Foodstills»), voilà le sujet de ces photos publiées dans le magazine *Vogue*. (GER)

Marilyn liebte sie, und auch Doris Day schwörte auf die erotische Wirkung der spitzen Stöckel, die in den 50er Jahren getragen wurden. Lange Zeit waren sie fast verschwunden, nun sind die frechen Hohen wieder da – heiß begehrt von denen, die sie noch nie getragen haben, und von denen, die nicht nur Flache mögen. Ein aktueller modischer Tip: Pointer-Pumps oder Stilettos zum frechen Mini oder zum Petticoat-Rock.

Hoch hinaus mit neuen Pumps

★ Gelbe Pumps mit Pepitamuster; Free Lance, ca. 170 DM.
★ Velourlederpumps mit Schlangenleder; Nord-West-Ring, ca. 70 DM.
★ Superhohe Lackpumps; Sergio Rossi, ca. 210 DM.
★ Als Gag eine goldene Metallspitze; Colette, ca. 140 DM.
★ Verspielt und originell: Lackpumps mit Schleife; Deichmann, ca. 50 DM.
★ Edle Schwarze mit Spaghetti-Bändern; Servas, ca. 100 DM.
★ Schwarzes Pepita-Muster, diesmal auf Giftgrün; Free Lance, ca. 170 DM.
★ Schlangenleder-Optik in frechen Farben; Gabor, ca. 100 DM.

50 petra

petra 51

316

317

318

319

Courtesy Vogue, München – Copyright © by Condé-Nast Verlag

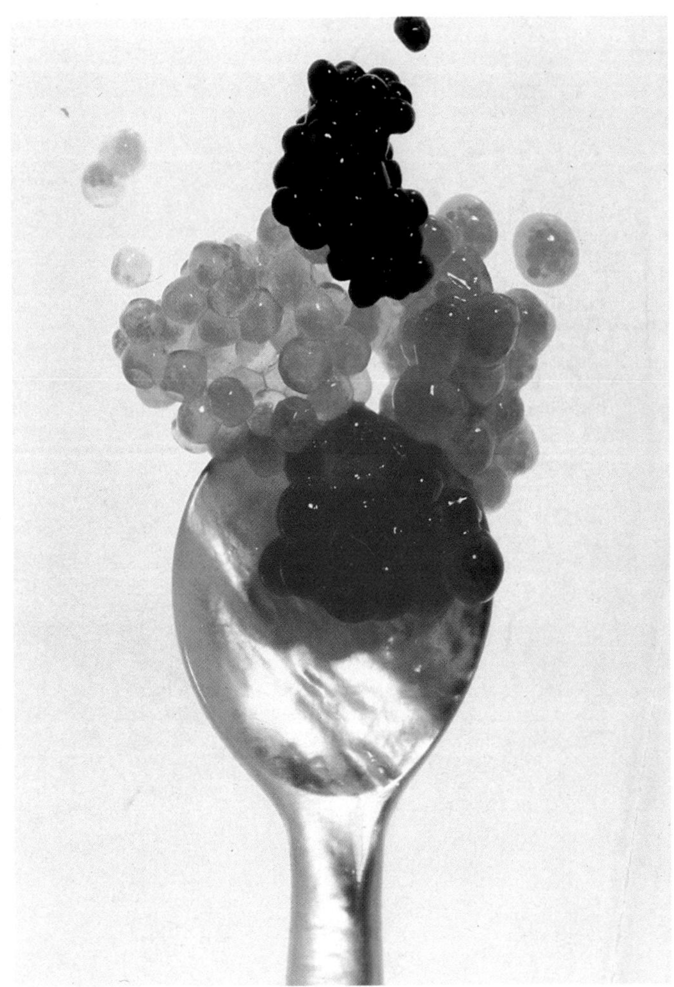
320

321

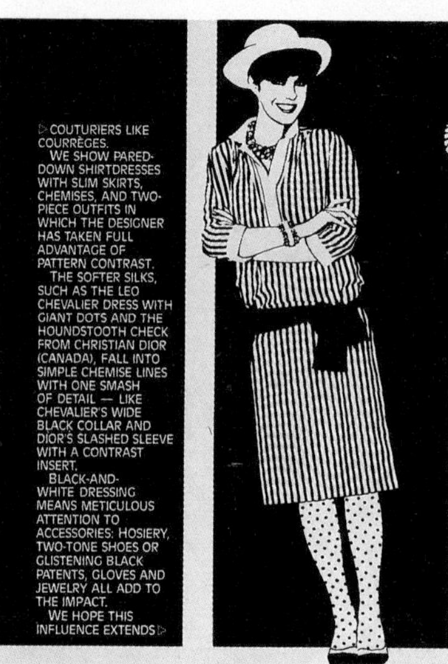

322

323

324

321, 322 Line conversion of photographs in black and white, as used by *Homemaker's Magazine* for its article on fashions in the same colours. (CAN)

323, 324 Complete colour pages from a *Stern* article on fantasy figures in paper and cardboard created by dress designers at a Cologne art school. Fig. 324 shows a creation from cardboard used for paper rolls and, left, Oskar Schlemmer is behind the robot. (GER)

325, 326 Double spreads from an article in *Twen* magazine: "When fashion dolls dance." (GER)

327 A *Penthouse* feature on the Ferrari car was introduced on this double spread. (AUS)

328 Double spread in full colour from a *Town & Country* feature on make-up creations by cosmetic manufacturers. The model has her face made up by two of them: by *Dior*, on the left side of her face, and by *Chanel* on the right. (USA)

321, 322 Schwarzweiss-Aufnahmen, strichumgesetzt, für einen Artikel in *Homemaker's Magazine* über Mode in Schwarzweiss. (CAN)

323, 324 Doppelseiten zu einem Beitrag im *Stern*, in dem phantasievolle Modelle aus Papier vorgestellt werden, Kreationen der Kostümbildner der Kunsthochschule Köln. Bei dem Roboter in Abb. 324 stand Oskar Schlemmer Pate, rechts im Bild ein Kostüm aus Toilettenpapierrollen. (GER)

325, 326 Doppelseiten aus einem Beitrag über Mode in *Twen*: «Wenn Modepuppen tanzen.» (GER)

327 Einleitende Doppelseite für einen Artikel über Autos in *Penthouse*. (AUS)

328 Doppelseite mit Farbaufnahme aus *Town & Country*, für einen Beitrag über Make-up-Creationen der verschiedenen Hersteller; das Make-up der linken Gesichtshälfte ist ein Vorschlag von *Dior*, das der rechten von *Chanel*. (USA)

325

326

TAKE IT AS RED

For performance, refinement and pose value, nothing beats a Ferrari.

327

321, 322 Photos noir et blanc transposées en dessins au trait, pour un article de mode en noir et blanc dans *Homemaker's Magazine.* (CAN)
323, 324 Doubles pages d'un article du *Stern* présentant des modèles en papier sortis de l'imagination des costumiers de l'Université des Beaux-Arts de Cologne. C'est Oskar Schlemmer qui a inspiré le robot de la fig. 324; à droite, un costume en rouleaux de papier hygiénique. (GER)
325, 326 Doubles pages d'un article de mode de *Twen*: «Quand les poupées de mode dansent.» (GER)
327 Double page initiale d'un article de *Penthouse* consacré aux voitures racées. (AUS)
328 Double page, illustrée en couleur, de *Town & Country,* présentant des propositions de maquillage des maisons de cosmétiques. La moitié gauche du visage porte un maquillage *Dior,* la moitié droite s'inspire d'un projet de maquillage *Chanel.* (USA)

328

Editorial Photography

PHOTOGRAPHER / PHOTOGRAPH / PHOTOGRAPHE:

321, 322 Jim Allen
323, 324 Karin Rocholl
325, 326 Conny Winter
327 Tandy Rowley
328 Victor Skrebneski

DESIGNER / GESTALTER / MAQUETTISTE:

321, 322 Shari Spier
323, 324 Dietmar Schulze
325, 326 Heinz Schwan
327 Stephen Costello
328 Melissa Tardiff

ART DIRECTOR / DIRECTEUR ARTISTIQUE:

321, 322 Ursula Kaiser
323, 324 Rolf Gillhausen
327 Stephen Costello
328 Melissa Tardiff

AGENCY / AGENTUR / AGENCE – STUDIO:

321, 322 Homemaker's Magazine

PUBLISHER / VERLEGER / EDITEUR:

321, 322 Comac Communications
323, 324 Gruner & Jahr AG & Co.
325, 326 Fuss Verlag
327 Australian Penthouse
328 Hearst Corporation

329

PHOTOGRAPHER / PHOTOGRAPH:
329 Heribert Brehm
330 Norman Parkinson
331 Tim Saunders
332–334 Conny Winter

DESIGNER / GESTALTER:
331 Shari Spier
332, 333 Wolfgang Weiss
334 H. P. Bauer

ART DIRECTOR:
329 Gudrun Hänsel
330 Jocelyn Kargère
331 Ursula Kaiser
334 H. P. Bauer

AGENCY / AGENTUR / AGENCE:
331 Homemaker's Magazine
332, 333 CC-Marketing

329 Double spread from an article in *Gala* showing the comparison between the 1983 *Charles Jourdan* shoe collection and those collected by André Pérugia for more than 40 years. (GER)
330 Double spread in black and white for a fashion article in *Vogue.* (FRA)
331 Opening double spread to an article in *Homemaker's Magazine.* (USA)
332, 333 Double spreads in *Creation* linked fashion trends with furniture design of *Rolf Benz.* Fig. 332: Navy look and white sofa; Fig. 333: Shades of grey, beige; bright yellow. (GER)
334 Sample from a series on original situations shot around the car. (GER)

329 Doppelseite aus einem Beitrag in *Gala,* in dem die Schuhkollektion von *Charles Jourdan* im Rahmen von Modellen aus einer über 40 Jahre alten Sammlung von André Pérugia gezeigt wird. (GER)
330 Doppelseite mit Schwarzweiss-Aufnahme aus einem Modebeitrag in *Vogue.* (FRA)
331 Einleitende Doppelseite zu einem Artikel über Parfum in *Homemaker's Magazine.* (USA)
332, 333 Doppelseiten aus einem Bericht in *Creation* über Möbeldesign von *Rolf Benz* und Mode. Abb. 332: Marine-Look und weisses Sofa, Abb. 333: Grau- und Beigetöne mit hellem Gelb. (GER)
334 Beispiel aus einer Serie von Aufnahmen origineller Situationen rund um das Auto. (GER)

330

331

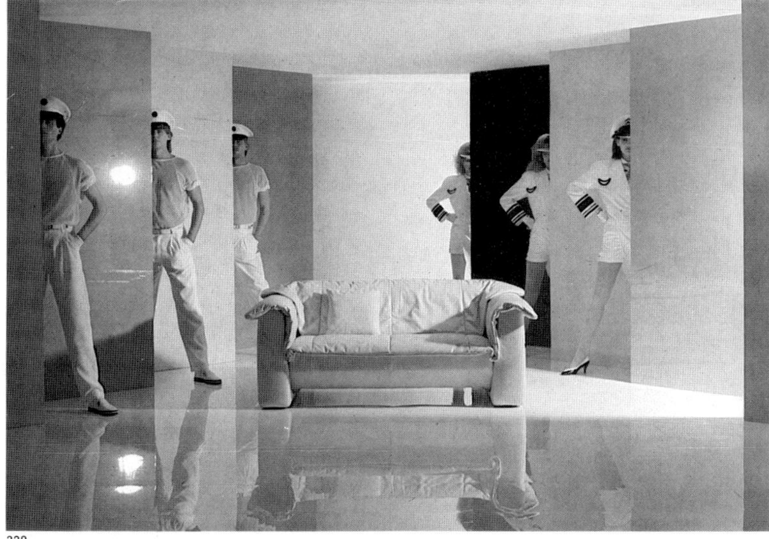

332

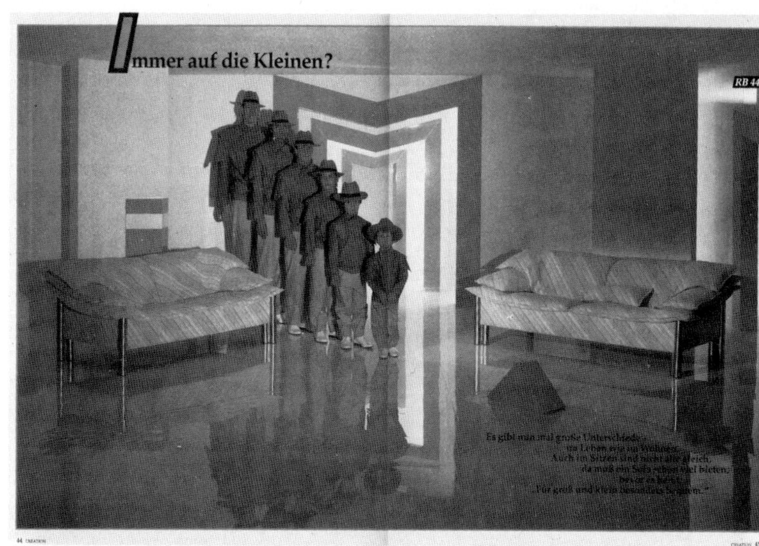

333

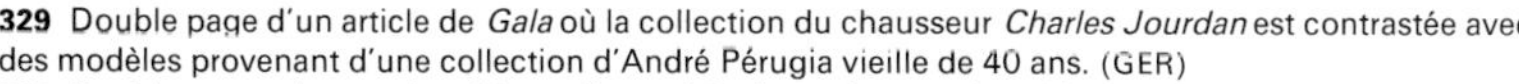

329 Double page d'un article de *Gala* où la collection du chausseur *Charles Jourdan* est contrastée avec des modèles provenant d'une collection d'André Pérugia vieille de 40 ans. (GER)
330 Double page, photo noir et blanc, d'un article de mode paru dans *Vogue.* (FRA)
331 Double page en tête d'un article du *Homemaker's Magazine* sur les parfums. (USA)
332, 333 Doubles pages d'un article de *Creation* sur les créations de meubles de *Rolf Benz* et la mode. 332: style marine et sofa blanc, 333: gris et beiges, avec du jaune lumineux. (GER)
334 Exemple d'une série de photos présentant des situations originales autour d'une voiture. (GER)

PUBLISHER / VERLEGER / EDITEUR:
329 Gala Verlag GmbH
330 Condé Nast SA
331 Comac Communications
332, 333 Rolf Benz
334 A. Würth GmbH

Editorial Photography

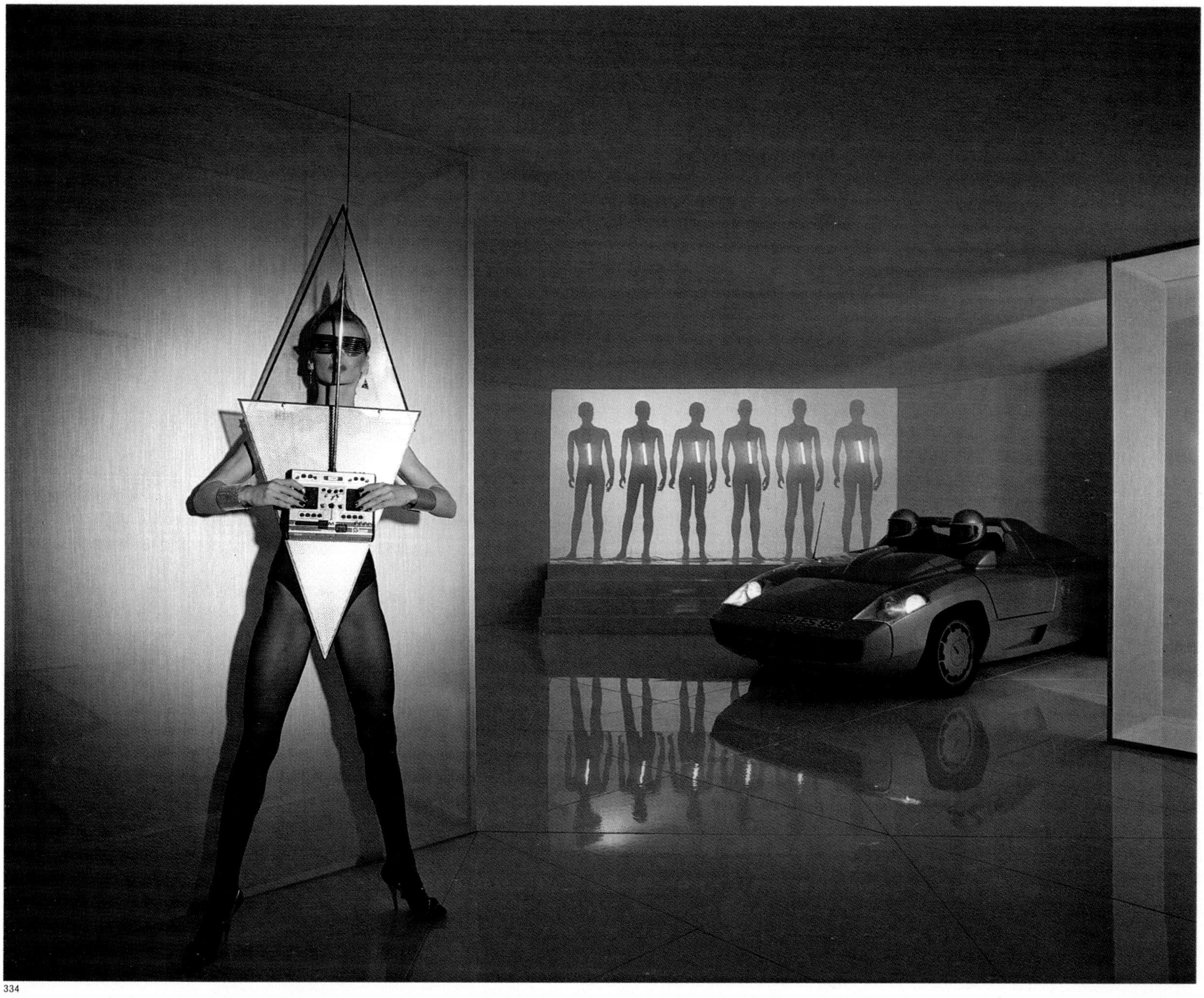

334

335

335–337 Double spreads and a full-page illustration of a *Stern* report on the project realized by Christo Javacheff: his "Surrounded Islands" off the Florida coast. Fig. 335: Helpers join up the floating sheets of pink plastic. Fig. 336: One of the 11 "estranged" islands. Fig. 337: The launch of the project: a motor boat tows a plastic boom into position. (GER)

338–340 Colour double spreads from a *Stern* report on the treks of the gnu. Fig. 338: series of shots show how two cheetahs kill a gnu too big for either of them alone. The close-up shows one of them after the shared meal. Fig. 339: The herd instinct drives the gnus headlong into a lake in their path, wherein hundreds drown. Fig. 340: In search of fresh grazing, the gnus trot in columns that stretch for miles across the steppes—often side by side, as here. (GER)

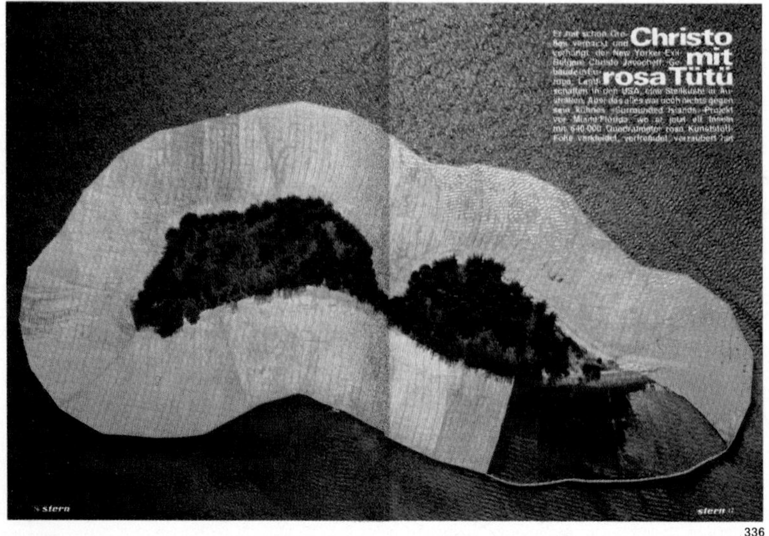

336

337

PHOTOGRAPHER / PHOTOGRAPH:

335–337 Wolfgang Volz
338–340 Reinhard Künkel

DESIGNER / GESTALTER / MAQUETTISTE:

335–337 Dieter Busch
338–340 Wolf Dammann

ART DIRECTOR / DIRECTEUR ARTISTIQUE:

335–340 Rolf Gillhausen

PUBLISHER / VERLEGER / EDITEUR:

335–340 Gruner & Jahr AG & Co.

PHOTOGRAPHER / PHOTOGRAPH:

341, 341 a Heribert Brehm
342 Karl Hugo Schmölz
343 Dennis Manarchy

ART DIRECTOR / DIRECTEUR ARTISTIQUE:

341, 341 a Claus Seitz
342 Manfred Glemser
343 Eric Colmet Daage

PUBLISHER / VERLEGER / EDITEUR:

341, 341 a Art Press Verlag GmbH
342 Union Verlag
343 Publications Filipacchi

342

341, 341a Photograph and complete cover of the magazine *Zoom*. Various photographic tricks were used to achieve a brilliance and directness reminiscent of the photo realists. (GER)
342 From the pages of international magazines on home interiors: a *Draenert* table, depicted as the central point of meetings and conversation. (GER)
343 Double-spread photo for an article on the photographer Dennis Manarchy in the French edition of *Photo*. Pink, red and silver, 1959 Cadillac, on reddish ground with blue and black. (USA)

341, 341a Aufnahme und vollständiger Umschlag der Zeitschrift *Zoom*. Durch verschiedene photographische Tricks wird hier eine Brillanz und Direktheit erreicht, die an den Photorealismus erinnert. (GER)
342 In internationalen Wohnzeitschriften erschienene Aufnahme eines *Draenert*-Tisches, dargestellt als Ort der Zusammenkunft und des Gesprächs. (GER)
343 Doppelseitige Aufnahme aus einem Artikel in der französischen Ausgabe von *Photo* über den Photographen Dennis Manarchy. Das Cadillac-Modell stammt aus dem Jahre 1959. In Pink und Rot mit Silber, Hintergrund rötlich, blau und schwarz. (USA)

341, 341a Photo et couverture complète de la revue *Zoom*. Diverses astuces photographiques ont permis d'obtenir un brillant et une immédiateté rappelant les photoréalistes. (GER)
342 Photo d'une table *Draenert* publiée dans des magazines internationaux de l'habitat et présentant un lieu de réunion et de conversation. (GER)
343 Photo double page d'un article de l'édition française de *Photo* consacré au photographe Dennis Manarchy. La Cadillac est un modèle de 1959. Réalisé en rose et en rouge, avec de l'argent, sur fond rougeâtre, bleu et noir. (USA)

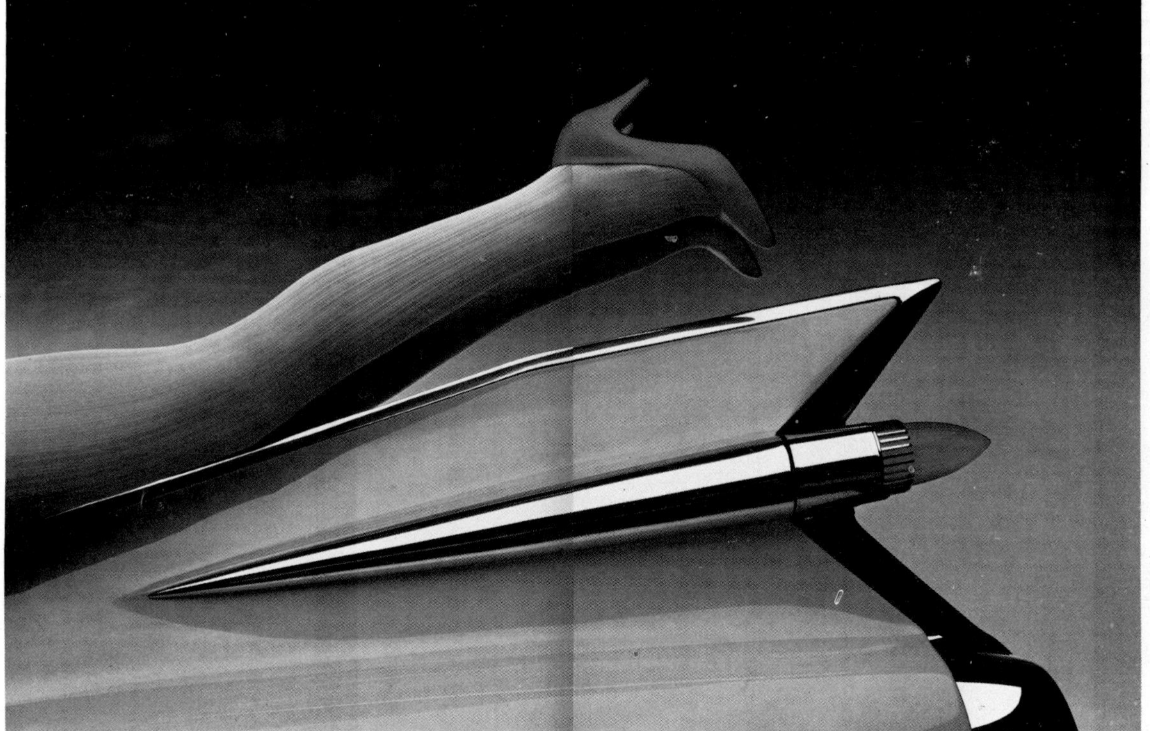

343

341a

Editorial Photography

PHOTOGRAPHER / PHOTOGRAPH / PHOTOGRAPHE:

344 Gerhard Vormwald
345–348 Robert Lebeck
349–351 Peter Lindbergh

DESIGNER / GESTALTER / MAQUETTISTE:

344 Jan Görlich
345–348 Herbert Suhr
349–351 Max Lengwenus

ART DIRECTOR / DIRECTEUR ARTISTIQUE:

344 Franz Epping
345–351 Rolf Gillhausen

PUBLISHER / VERLEGER / EDITEUR:

344–351 Gruner & Jahr AG & Co.

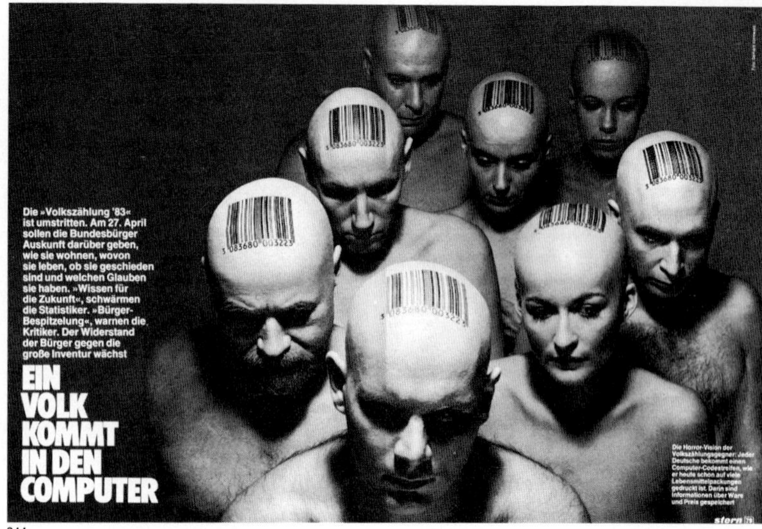

344

344 Complete double spread in black and white from *Stern* magazine that opened its feature on the then pending 1983 national census, "A People is put into the Computer". It effectively visualized the worst fears of opponents to the census and its aim, showing Germans stripped naked, with their privacy revealed to all, by the proposed new form of identity card—here represented by the computer-code strip. (GER)
345–348 From a *Stern* report in black and white on impressions of West Germany. Fig. 345: Still bearing its burden of the nazi swastika; Fig. 346: Its dying forests; Fig. 347: Cologne Cathedral during carnival; Fig. 348: A hospital's futuristic entrance. (GER)
349–351 Full-colour spreads from the fashion pages of *Stern* magazine featuring the Japanese "Tramp Look". (GER)

345

346

347

348

349

350

344 Schwarzweiss-Doppelseite aus der Zeitschrift *Stern* zum Thema der bundesdeutschen Volkszählung. Die Horror-Vision der Volkszählungsgegner, dass jeder Deutsche einen Computer-Codestreifen bekommt, hat seine Wirkung nicht verfehlt. (GER)
345–348 Aus einer Schwarzweiss-Reportage im *Stern* über deutsche Impressionen. Abb. 345: Wir tragen noch immer am Hakenkreuz; Abb. 346: Zum Thema Waldsterben; hier bedrohte Bäume im Schwäbischen Wald, die numeriert wurden. Abb. 347: Der Kölner Dom nach dem Rosenmontagszug; Abb. 348: Futuristische Eingangshalle zu einem Krankenhaus. (GER)
349–351 Mehrfarbige Doppelseiten aus dem Mode-Teil der Zeitschrift *Stern*, in dem der japanische Vagabunden-Look vorgestellt wird. (GER)

344 Double page noir et blanc du magazine *Stern* sur le sujet controversé du recensement en République fédérale. La vision d'horreur propagée par les adversaires de cette opération – chaque Allemand étant doté d'un code d'ordinateur comme le sont les produits d'alimentation sur les rayons des supermarchés – a prouvé toute son efficacité. (GER)
345–348 Dans ce reportage photo du *Stern*, on analyse la réalité allemande d'aujourd'hui. Fig. 345: la croix gammée pèse encore; 346: la mort des forêts; 347: la cathédrale de Cologne après le cortège du Lundi gras; 348: hall d'entrée futuriste d'un hôpital allemand. (GER)
349–351 Doubles pages polychromes dans la section Mode du magazine *Stern* où l'on présente le style «vagabond japonais» qui fait fureur. (GER)

351

PHOTOGRAPHER / PHOTOGRAPH:

352 Michael George
353 James Wojcik
354, 355 Amyn Nasser
356 Chris Wahlberg
357 Heribert Brehm
358 Richard Fegley
359 Chris Dickson

DESIGNER / GESTALTER:

353 Michael Grossman/ Arlene Lappen
354, 355 Russ Willms
356 Robert J. Post
357 Heribert Brehm
359 Stephen Costello

ART DIRECTOR:

353 Michael Grossman
354, 355 Russ Willms
356 Robert J. Post
357 Bärbel Miebach
358 Tom Staebler
359 Stephen Costello

AGENCY / AGENTUR / AGENCE:

354, 355 West Can Communications
356 Chicago Magazine

PUBLISHER / VERLEGER / EDITEUR:

352 Avenue Magazine
353 National Lampoon
354, 355 AADAC
356 WFMT, Inc.
357 Fuss Verlag
358 Playboy Enterprises, Inc.
359 Australian Penthouse

352

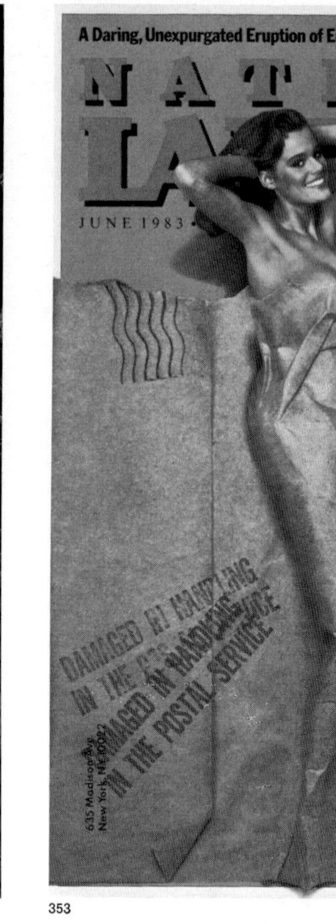

353

356

357

352 Cover of the magazine *Avenue*: green and black, white lettering. (USA)
353 The brown wrapper on the cover of *National Lampoon* is stamped with a warning that it was damaged in transit. (USA)
354, 355 Front and back cover of a youth magazine: on brown wrapping paper, overprinting in various colours—which is reversed on back cover. (CAN)
356 Full-colour cover of *Chicago* magazine. The photo relates to the question posed by the main article: "How will blacks and Hispanics vote?" (USA)
357 Cover of *Twen* magazine's December issue: "Hot Snow." (GER)
358 James Bond's new partner, Kim Basinger, was the cover girl of a *Playboy* issue and the subject of an eight-page article inside. (USA)
359 Cover of the Australian edition of *Penthouse*: bright red with black, overprinted in white. (AUS)

352 Umschlag der Zeitschrift *Avenue*. Grün und schwarz, Schrift weiss. (USA)
353 Für eine Ausgabe der humoristischen Zeitschrift *National Lampoon* über Sex: «Im Postverkehr beschädigt.» (USA)
354, 355 Vorder- und Rückseite des Umschlags einer Jugendzeitschrift. Braunes Packpapier, Schrift, auf der Rückseite spiegelverkehrt, in Farbe. (CAN)
356 Umschlag der Zeitschrift *Chicago*, der sich auf einen Artikel über das Wählerpotential der hispanischen und schwarzen Bevölkerung bezieht. (USA)
357 Umschlag für die Dezemberausgabe der Zeitschrift *Twen*. (GER)
358 Kim Basinger, die neue Partnerin von James Bond, auf dem Umschlag des Herrenmagazins *Playboy*. (USA)
359 Umschlag der australischen Ausgabe des *Penthouse*. Leuchtendes Rot und Schwarz, Schrift in Weiss. (AUS)

354

355

358

359

352 Couverture du magazine *Avenue.* Vert et noir, texte blanc. (USA)
353 Pour un numéro du magazine satirique *National Lampoon* où il est question de sexe: «abîmée dans le trafic postal.» (USA)
354, 355 Première et dernière page de couverture d'un magazine pour les jeunes. Papier d'emballage brun, texte polychrome (inversé en 4e page). (CAN)
356 Couverture du magazine *Chicago.* La photo illustre un article sur le poids électoral des Noirs et des Hispano-Américains. (USA)
357 Couverture du numéro de décembre du magazine *Twen.* (GER)
358 Kim Basinger, la nouvelle partenaire de James Bond, en couverture du magazine masculin *Playboy.* (USA)
359 Couverture de l'édition australienne de *Penthouse.* Rouge vif et noir, texte figurant en blanc. (AUS)

Ein Tag so traurig wie der andere

Wer jahrelang im Irrenhaus gelebt hat und von Wärtern wie ein Möbelstück hin- und hergeschoben wurde, nimmt eine starre, teilnahmslose Haltung an. Aus dieser Erkenntnis heraus beschloß die italienische Regierung vor vier Jahren, die Tore der Anstalten zu öffnen

Dieser Mann ist geisteskrank. Jahrelang saß er hinter den geschlossenen Toren eines Irrenhauses bei Venedig. Die Umgebung machte ihn stumpfsinnig. So zog er sich in sich selbst zurück. Heute lebt er – befreit vom brutalen Milieu der Anstalt – in einer Wohngemeinschaft. Sein Leiden hat sich gebessert

Seit 1978 gibt es in Italien keine geschlossenen psychiatrischen Anstalten mehr. Die Kranken werden ambulant betreut – mit guten Ergebnissen

FREIHEIT HEILT

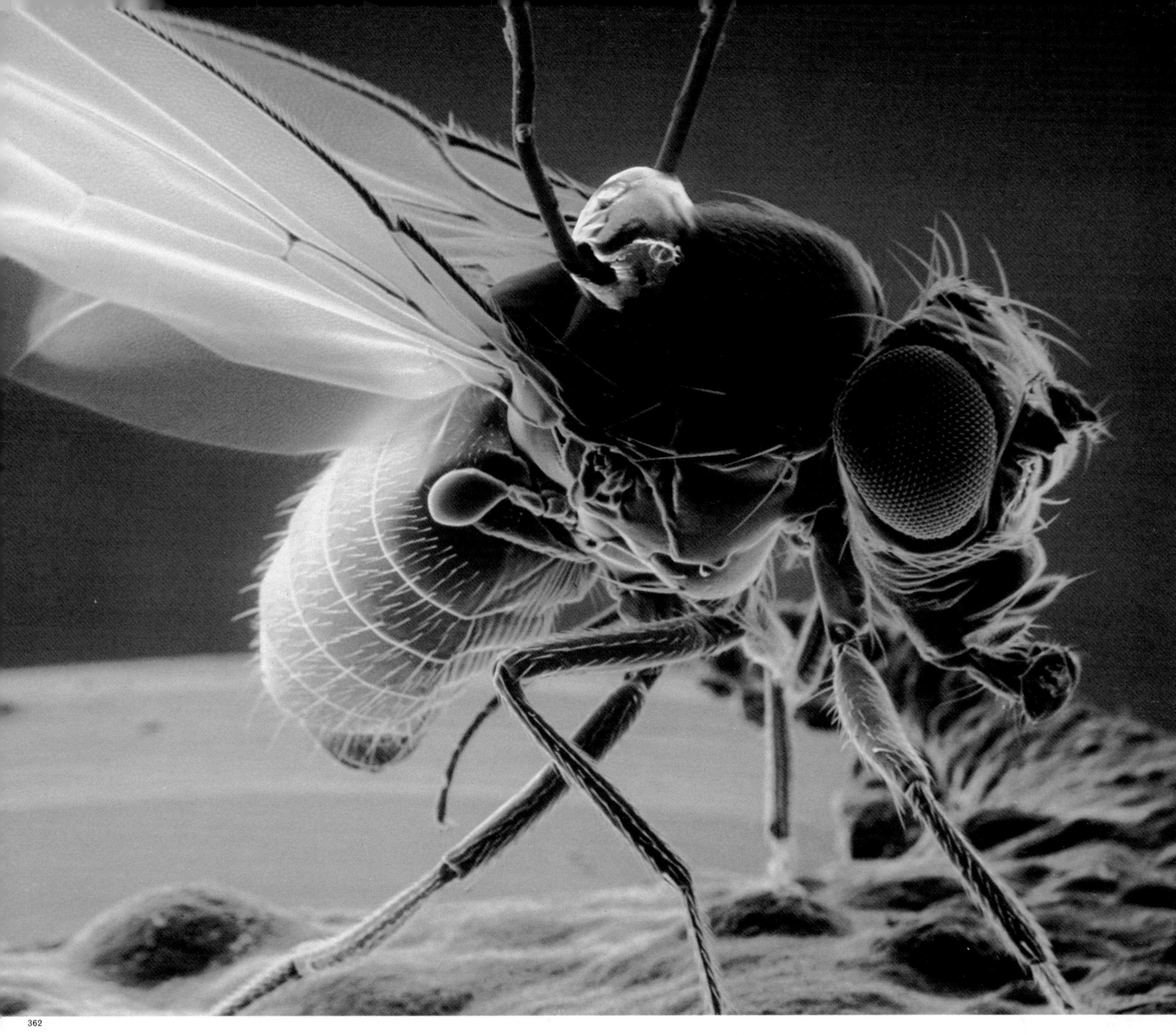

362

PHOTOGRAPHER / PHOTOGRAPH / PHOTOGRAPHE:

360, 361 Raymond Depardon
362 Manfred Kage

DESIGNER / GESTALTER / MAQUETTISTE:

360, 361 Jan Görlich

ART DIRECTOR / DIRECTEUR ARTISTIQUE:

360, 361 Rolf Gillhausen
362 Manfred Glemser

PUBLISHER / VERLEGER / EDITEUR:

360, 361 Gruner & Jahr AG & Co.
362 Union Verlag

360, 361 Double spreads in black and white from an article in *Stern* magazine. Headlined "Freedom Heals", it was featured on the fact that there is now no confinement of patients in Italy's institutes for psychiatric treatment. These were of the "closed" type, as in these photographs, up until 1978. Now those in need of such care are all treated, successfully, as out-patients. (GER)
362 Double-spread shot from a research report that depicted the complexity of brain structures, using this fly as an example. The photograph was taken, with additional lighting, through a screened electronic microscope. (GER)

360, 361 Doppelseiten in Schwarzweiss aus einer Reportage in der Zeitschrift *Stern* zur Tatsache, dass es seit 1978 in Italien keine geschlossenen psychiatrischen Anstalten mehr gibt. Die ambulante Behandlung von Patienten hat sich als erfolgreich erwiesen. Die beiden Aufnahmen zeigen, wie es vor der Aufhebung von psychiatrischen Anstalten aussah. (GER)
362 Doppelseitige Aufnahme aus einem Forschungsbericht über die Darstellung der Komplexität von Gehirnstrukturen am Beispiel einer Fliege. Das Photo entstand mit Hilfe von Licht und einem Raster-Elektronenmikroskop. (GER)

360, 361 Doubles pages en noir et blanc d'un reportage paru dans le magazine *Stern* sur les conditions d'hospitalisation des malades mentaux en Italie. Depuis 1978, les divisions fermées ont été supprimées, et le traitement ambulatoire s'est avéré un plein succès. Les deux photos illustrent la condition du malade avant la fermeture des hôpitaux psychiatriques. (GER)
362 Photo double page illustrant un rapport scientifique sur la représentation de structures cérébrales complexes, par l'exemple d'une mouche. Cette photo a été réalisée avec l'aide de la lumière et d'un microscope électronique à balayage. (GER)

Editorial Photography

PHOTOGRAPHER / PHOTOGRAPH:

363 Heribert Brehm
364 Torkil Gunadson
365 Piet van Leeuwen
366–368 Reinhart Wolf

DESIGNER / GESTALTER / MAQUETTISTE:

364 Laurie Rosenwald
365 Louis Voogt
366–368 Norbert Kleiner

ART DIRECTOR / DIRECTEUR ARTISTIQUE:

363 Manuel Ortiz
364 Paula Greif
365 Hans van Blommestein
366–368 Rolf Gillhausen

PUBLISHER / VERLEGER / EDITEUR:

363 Bauer Verlag
364 Condé Nast Publications Inc.
365 De Geillustreerde Pers
366–368 Gruner & Jahr AG & Co.

363

Bathing beauties—
indulgences for the bathroom,
all at bargain prices

A sleek, oval-design bathroom scale to help keep you in sleek shape, too! With an easy-to-read dial, padded vinyl platform. In white or brown. By Robert Krups of North America, $50.

Super-looking checked and striped toothbrushes in colorful combinations of black, blue and red. From Harry D. Koenig, $3.95 each.

Macaroni-shaped soap! It has a light, clean scent, looks appealing piled into a bowl or basket. From Caswell-Massey, $10 a package.

Before bathing or after, snuggle up in a knee-length bathrobe of pure cotton terry cloth. Notched-collar robe, in pink, blue or white, by Joan Sayour for Saybury, $32.

Natural-bristle nailbrushes in funny animal shapes—great for grown-ups as well as kids! Bear, duck and pig brushes come in blue, green and yellow. From Kent of London, $4 each.

A must for every bathing beauty: An inflatable bath pillow sticks in place with suction cups, lets you soak in comfort. Comes in a variety of colors. From The Elegant John, $9.75.

FOR DETAILS, SEE FINDS SPECIFICS, NEXT-TO-LAST PAGES

TORKIL GUDNASON

364

WINA BORN/FOTOGRAFIE PIET VAN LEEUWEN

DE STERREN VAN MICHELIN

VOEDSEL VOOR DISCUSSIE

De discussie over de sterren van Michelin is op dit moment weer in volle gang. Waarom krijgt dit restaurant er wel een en dat andere niet? En hoe kan het dat er in Frankrijk zoveel worden uitgedeeld? Wina Born over de terechte en onterechte kritiek op de Guide, plus receptuur van De Swaen in Oisterwijk, een restaurant dat volgens haar twee sterren verdient.

Gelijk met de kievitseitjes verschijnen de nieuwe rode Michelingidsen en het eerste waar iedereen onmiddellijk naar kijkt is: de sterren. Een verrukkelijke en tot ver in het jaar voortdruppelende bron van gesprek. Want hoe heerlijk kunnen we hierover onze eigen mening verkondigen. Altijd is er verbazing en verontwaardiging; soms zijn we het roerend eens met Michelin, soms hebben we ernstige kritiek. Er is vreugde bij wie een ster kreeg en verdriet bij wie er een verloor – ook al gaan wij nog niet zo ver als die Parijse restaurateur die in de Seine sprong of als Maxim's die helemaal niet meer in de Michelin vermeld wenste te worden toen hij van drie tot twee sterren teruggebracht werd.
Ook de Franse sterrenregen wordt uitvoerig becommentarieerd, en ook hiermee zijn we het vaak oneens. Dan krijg ik brieven van mensen die niet begrijpen dat X of Y nog altijd die drie sterren heeft terwijl het niet kan tippen aan Z in Nederland die er nog altijd maar een kan tonen. Er wordt geschamperd over de drie sterren van Lasserre en over de twee van Lucas-Carton („volkomen uit de tijd, zo»

365

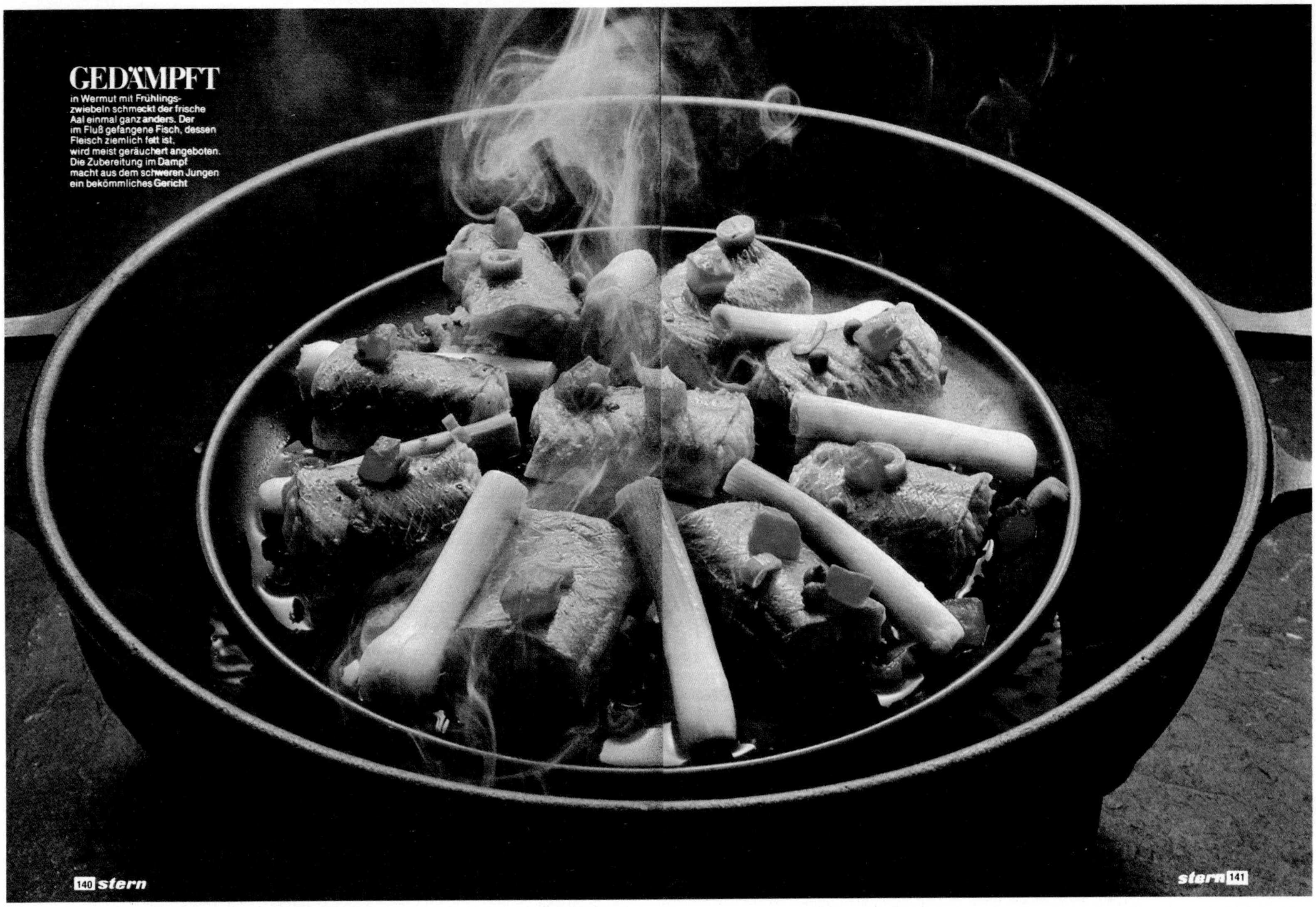

GEDÄMPFT
in Wermut mit Frühlingszwiebeln schmeckt der frische Aal einmal ganz anders. Der im Fluß gefangene Fisch, dessen Fleisch ziemlich fett ist, wird meist geräuchert angeboten. Die Zubereitung im Dampf macht aus dem schweren Jungen ein bekömmliches Gericht
140 stern
stern 141
366

363 Full-colour shot to illustrate a *Playboy* article on summer styles. It was taken at a boxing gym in the Reeperbahn district of Hamburg. (GER)
364 Page from an article in *Mademoiselle* on products and accessories for the bathroom. (USA)
365 Complete double spread in full colour for the opening pages of a critical article in *Avenue*. It discussed the merits and demerits of the Guide Michelin's system of awarding stars. (NLD)
366–368 Double spreads in full colour from the "Eating and Drinking" feature pages of *Stern*. Fig. 366 shows a cooked dish of fresh eel and spring onions, Fig. 367 a perch-type fish dressed with limes, and Fig. 368 shows the most common fresh-water fish found in Germany. (GER)

363 Aufnahme für einen Beitrag über Sommermode im Magazin *Playboy*. Als Kulisse diente ein Boxlokal an der Hamburger Reeperbahn. (GER)
364 Seite aus einem Beitrag mit Produktempfehlungen für das Bad; aus *Mademoiselle*. (USA)
365 Einleitende Doppelseite zu einem Artikel, der sich mit aktueller Kritik am Guide Michelin auseinandersetzt. Erschienen in *Avenue*. (NLD)
366–368 Doppelseiten mit Farbaufnahmen aus dem Sektor «Essen und Trinken» im *Stern*. Abb. 366 zeigt ein Gericht aus frischem Aal und Frühlingszwiebeln, Abb. 367 einen Zander mit Limettenscheiben und Abb. 368 die am häufigsten in deutschen Flüssen, Seen und Teichen vorkommenden Fische. (GER)

363 Photo pour un article de modes d'été publié dans le magazine *Playboy*. Le décor est planté dans une salle de boxe de la Reeperbahn, à Hambourg. (GER)
364 Page de *Mademoiselle;* l'article en question recommande divers produits pour le bain. (USA)
365 Double page initiale d'un article où sont mises en discussion les indications contenues dans le guide Michelin. Publié dans *Avenue*. (NLD)
366–368 Doubles pages illustrées en couleur, section «Boire et manger» du *Stern*. La fig. 366 montre un plat d'anguille fraîche et d'oignons printaniers, la 367 une sandre garnie de tranches de limette, la 368 les poissons usuels des rivières, lacs et étangs d'Allemagne. (GER)

JOURNAL ESSEN & TRINKEN
JEDER FISCH EIN FEST
GEGART
367

GEFORMT
368

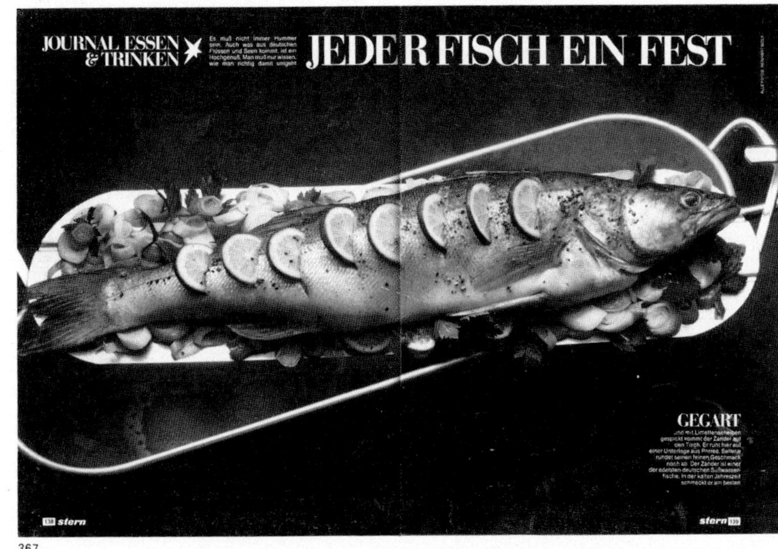

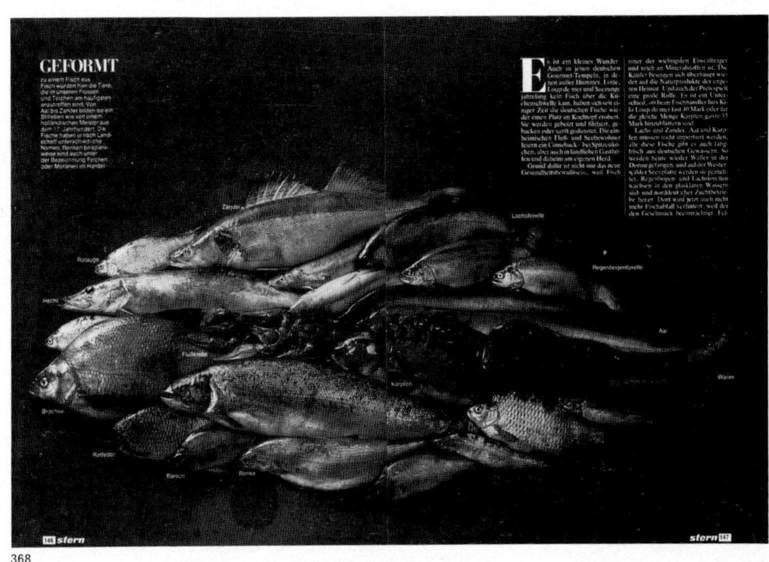

369

Trade Magazines
Fachzeitschriften
Revues professionnelles

369 Double-spread shot used by the magazine *American Photographer* for its printed interview with the American photographer Jay Maisel. (USA)
370 Full-colour shot highlighting points discussed—shapely legs and elegant shoes—in an article on the photographer Guy Bourdin by *Photo* magazine. (GER)
371 Full-colour cover of the magazine *Architectural Record.* See also Fig. 372. (USA)
372 Double-spread shot from a report in the magazine *Architectural Record* on showrooms for furniture and textiles. Here, an example of one of the various showrooms that architect Michael Graves designed for *Sunar.* (USA)

369 Doppelseitige Aufnahme aus einem Interview mit dem amerikanischen Photographen Jay Maisel in der Zeitschrift *American Photographer.* (USA)
370 Mehrfarbige Aufnahme aus einer Reportage über den Photographen Guy Bourdin in der Zeitschrift *Photo:* Mädchenbeine und elegante Schuhe sind das Thema. (GER)
371 Umschlag des Magazins *Architectural Record.* Siehe auch Abb. 372. (USA)
372 Doppelseitige Aufnahme aus einer Reportage im Magazin *Architectural Record* über Showrooms für Möbel und Textilien. Hier als Beispiel ein Raum des Architekten Michael Graves, der verschiedene Ausstellungsräume für die Firma *Sunar* konzipiert hat. (USA)

369 Photo double page illustrant une interview du photographe américain Jay Maisel dans le magazine *American Photographer.* (USA)
370 Photo polychrome pour un reportage du magazine *Photo* sur les travaux du photographe Guy Bourdin. Sujet: des jambes de femmes et des chaussures élégantes. (GER)
371 Couverture du magazine *Architectural Record.* Cf. la fig. 372. (USA)
372 Photo double page pour un reportage que le magazine *Architectural Record* consacre aux salles d'exposition de textiles et d'ameublements. On voit ici une décoration réalisée par l'architecte Michael Graves, auteur de diverses expositions *Sunar.* (USA)

371

Trade Magazines
Fachzeitschriften
Revues professionnelles

370

372

PHOTOGRAPHER / PHOTOGRAPH:

369 Jay Maisel
370 Guy Bourdin
371, 372 Barbara Karant

DESIGNER / GESTALTER:

369 Sean Callahan
371, 372 Massimo Vignelli

ART DIRECTOR:

369 Will Hopkins
370 Karl-Heinz Wendlandt

PUBLISHER / VERLEGER / EDITEUR:

369 CBS Publications
370 NewMagazines Verlags-gesellschaft mbH
371, 372 McGraw-Hill, Inc.

373

374

Weekend Supplements
Wochenendbeilagen
Suppléments dominicaux

375

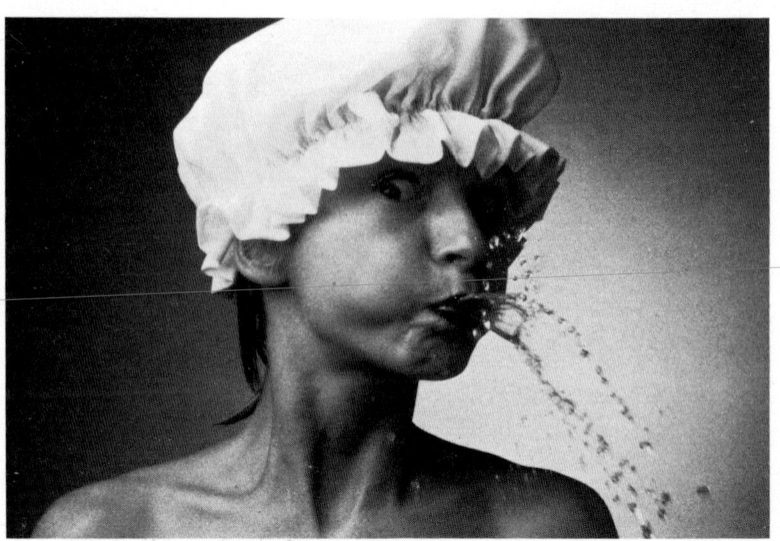

376

PHOTOGRAPHER / PHOTOGRAPH:

373 Steve Hill
374, 377 John Goodman
375, 376 Detlef Odenhausen
378 James Scherer

DESIGNER / GESTALTER / MAQUETTISTE:

373 Greg Paul
374, 377, 378 Ronn Campisi
375, 376 Karin Gerlach

ART DIRECTOR / DIRECTEUR ARTISTIQUE:

373 Greg Paul
374, 377, 378 Ronn Campisi
375, 376 Manfred Manke

PUBLISHER / VERLEGER / EDITEUR:

373 The Plain Dealer Publishing Co.
374, 377, 378 The Boston Globe
375, 376 Zeitverlag Gerd Bucerius KG

377

378

373 Opening full-colour page of an article in *The Plain Dealer Magazine* on crime in homosexual circles. (USA)
374, 377, 378 Full-colour pages from *The Boston Globe Magazine* with articles on the following: Fig. 374, a young, successful chef; Fig. 377, the man who wants to establish an Albert Einstein museum; Fig. 378, a recipe for lamb chops. (USA)
375, 376 Full-colour shots from a humorous feature in *Zeitmagazin* on the quaint and queer in head-gear: a wide-brimmed summer hat of handwoven straw and granny's bathing cap. (GER)

373 Einführende Seite des *Plain Dealer Magazine* zum Thema der Kriminalität unter Homosexuellen. Farbaufnahme. (USA)
374, 377, 378 Mehrfarbige Seiten aus dem *Boston Globe Magazine*. In Abb. 374 handelt es sich um einen Beitrag über einen jungen, erfolgreichen Koch, in Abb. 377 um einen Mann, der ein Albert-Einstein-Museum gründen möchte, und in Abb. 378 um Kochrezepte. (USA)
375, 376 Aufnahmen aus einem humorvollen Beitrag im *Zeitmagazin* über alte Hüte und Mützen – und was darunter steckt. Abb. 375 mit handgeflochtenem Hut, der für die Fahrt ins Grüne empfohlen wird: «Die breite Krempe schützt vor Strahlen und verbürgt allemal ein verschmitztes Schattendasein»; Abb. 376 zeigt Omas konservatives Mützchen: «Hinein in den Morgen mit neuer Frische.» (GER)

373 Page initiale du *Plain Dealer Magazine*. Il y est question de la criminalité qui sévit parmi les homosexuels. Photo couleur. (USA)
374, 377, 378 Pages polychromes du *Boston Globe Magazine*. La fig. 374 illustre un article sur un jeune cuisinier à succès; la fig. 377 évoque un citoyen qui voudrait fonder un musée à la gloire d'Einstein; la fig. 378 se rapporte à des recettes de cuisine. (USA)
375, 376 Photos accompagnant un article humoristique du *Zeitmagazin* au sujet des vieux chapeaux et casquettes et de ce qui se cache dessous. Fig. 375: chapeau tressé main recommandé pour les parties de campagne: «le large bord protège du soleil et garantit à coup sûr une vie rieuse et ombragée»; la fig. 376 montre le bonnet traditionnel des mémées: «Abordons la matinée en toute fraîcheur.» (GER)

379

PHOTOGRAPHER / PHOTOGRAPH:

379 Bruno Zehnder
380 Jost Wildbolz
381 Jacques Alexandre
382 Amyn Nasser
383 Hans Feurer

DESIGNER / GESTALTER / MAQUETTISTE:

379, 381, 382 Christian Guillon
380 Lisa Enderli

ART DIRECTOR / DIRECTEUR ARTISTIQUE:

379, 381, 382 Joël Laroche
380 Jost Wildbolz
383 Eric Colmet Daage

PUBLISHER / VERLEGER / EDITEUR:

379, 381, 382 Publicness
380 Tages-Anzeiger AG
383 Publications Filipacchi

379 Complete cover in full colour of *Zoom* magazine showing a Kabuki player preparing for his role. (FRA)
380 Full-page shot in black and white for a feature in *Annabelle* on fashionable jersey materials. (SWI)
381 Complete cover of *Zoom* magazine. (FRA)
382 Full-page colour shot for a *Zoom* feature on the photographer Amyn Nasser. (FRA)
383 Complete cover of *Photo* magazine relating to its feature on the photographer Hans Feurer, who took this colour shot. It was one of a series that was intended for use in a calendar. (FRA)

379 Ein Kabuki-Darsteller auf dem Umschlag einer Japan-Sondernummer von *Zoom*. In Farbe. (FRA)
380 Ganzseitige Aufnahme für einen Modebeitrag in *Annabelle*: «Jersey, berückend dekolletiert.» (SWI)
381 Umschlag der Monatszeitschrift *Zoom*. (FRA)
382 Ganzseitige Aufnahme aus einem Beitrag über den Photographen Amyn Nasser in *Zoom*. (FRA)
383 Umschlag einer Ausgabe von *Photo*, die einen Artikel über den Photographen Hans Feurer enthält. Die Aufnahme stammt aus einer Serie, die er ursprünglich für einen Kalender aufnahm. (FRA)

379 Un acteur kabuki à l'honneur sur la couverture d'un numéro spécial de *Zoom* consacré à l'archipel nippon. En couleur. (FRA)
380 Photo pleine page pour un article de mode dans *Annabelle*: «en jersey – un décolleté fascinant.» (SWI)
381 Couverture du magazine mensuel *Zoom*. (FRA)
382 Photo pleine page illustrant un article que *Zoom* consacre au photographe Amyn Nasser. (FRA)
383 Couverture d'un numéro de *Photo* contenant un article sur le photographe Hans Feurer. La photo figurait à l'origine dans une série réalisée pour un calendrier *Mintex* dans le paradis des Seychelles. (FRA)

380

381

382

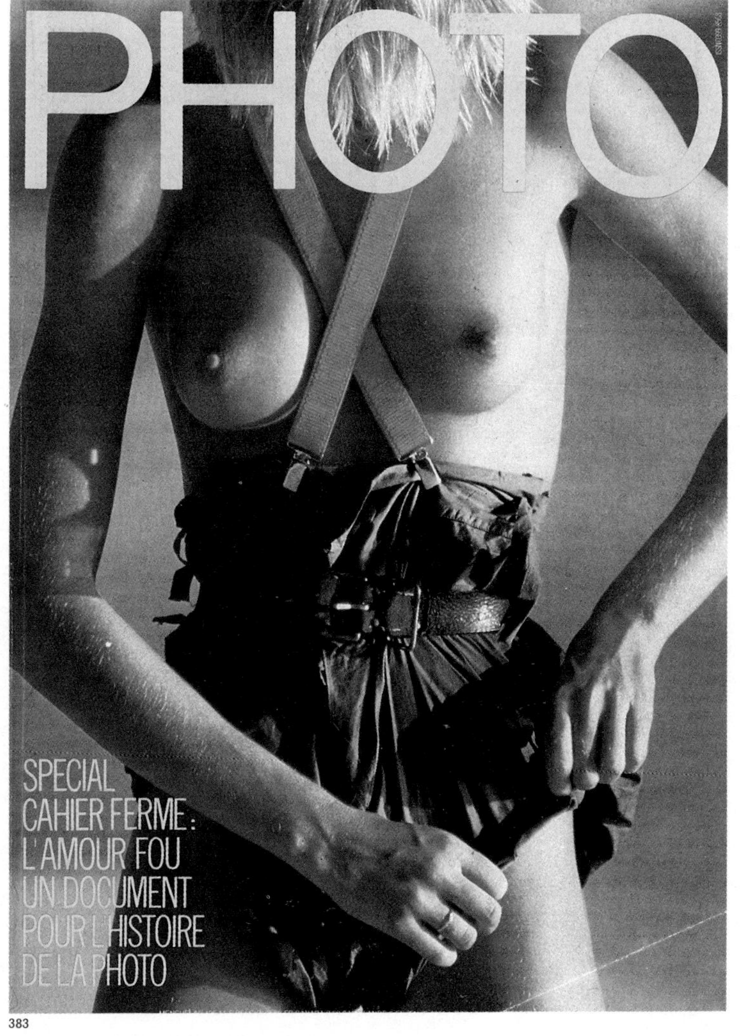

383

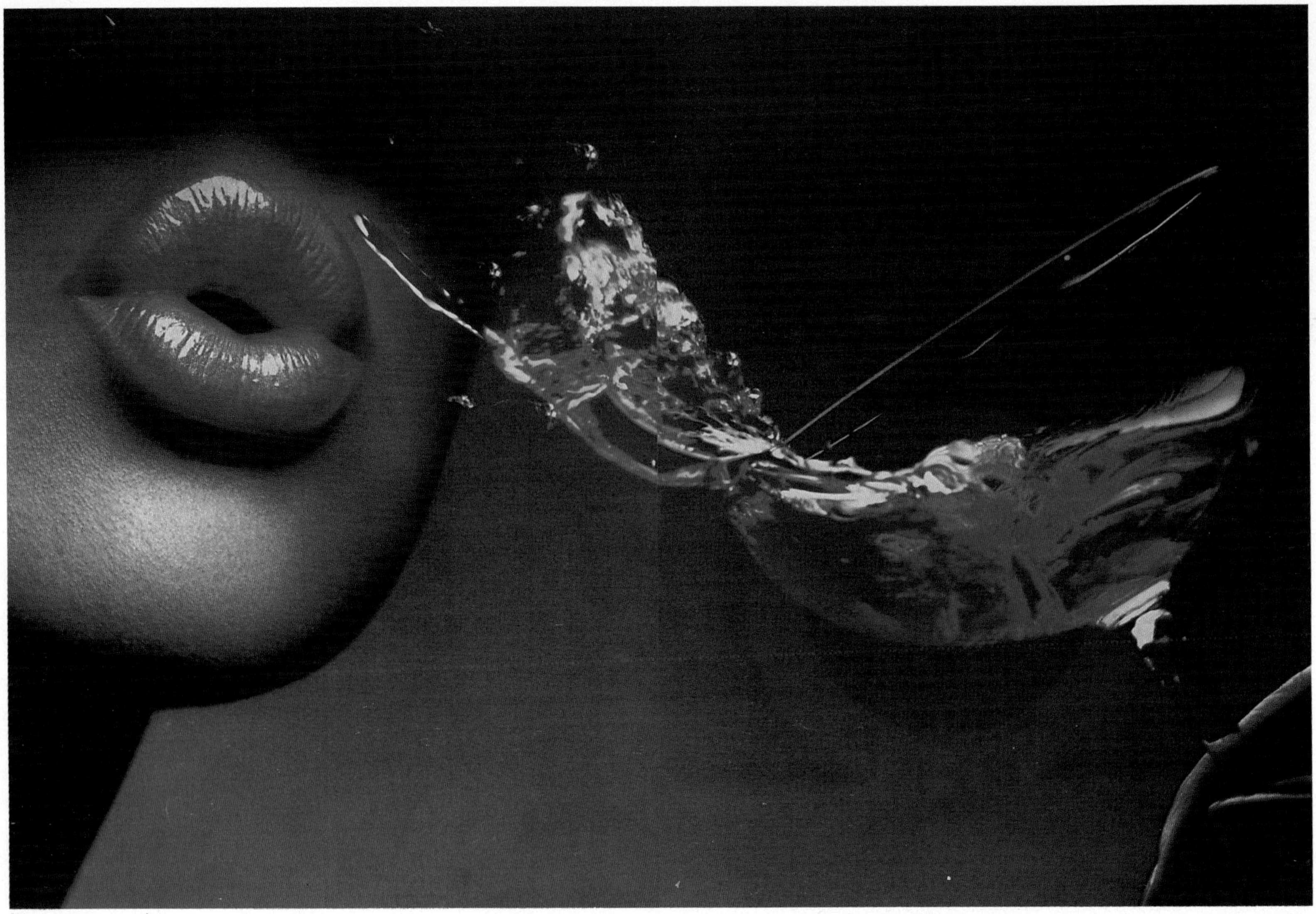

384

Editorial Photography

PHOTOGRAPHER / PHOTOGRAPH / PHOTOGRAPHE:

384 Dennis Manarchy
385 Heribert Brehm
386 Hiroyuki Yamamoto
387 Hiroshi Sugiyama

DESIGNER / GESTALTER / MAQUETTISTE:

387 Masanori Mizushima

ART DIRECTOR / DIRECTEUR ARTISTIQUE:

384 Eric Colmet Daage
385 Axel Gauguin
387 Masatoshi Toda

PUBLISHER / VERLEGER / EDITEUR:

384 Publications Filipacchi
385 Medien Verlagsgesellschaft
386 Canon Sales Co., Inc.
387 Bijutsu Shuppan-sha

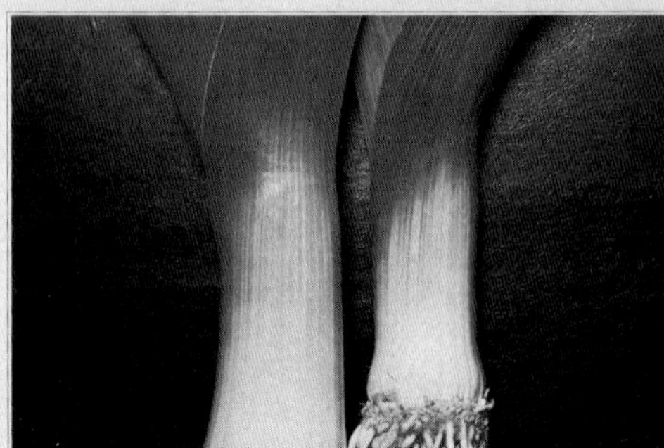

386

385

384 Double spread shot from an article in *Photo* on the photographer Dennis Manarchy. (FRA)
385 Trick shot to illustrate an article in *Cosmopolitan.* The broom was jammed vertically between floor and ceiling, the model climbed up on it and became the "flying witch" in this shot—which was then turned by about 70 degrees. (GER)
386 Full-colour shots in a double spread from *Canon Circle,* a trade magazine published by the *Canon* camera company. (JPN)
387 Black-and-white shot of moss-covered wood as used on the cover of the *1983 Annual of Advertising Art in Japan.* (JPN)

384 Doppelseitige Aufnahme aus einem Artikel über den Photographen Dennis Manarchy in *Photo.* (FRA)
385 «Toll treiben es die jungen Hexen.» Aufnahme für einen Beitrag in *Cosmopolitan.* Bei diesem Trickphoto hängt die «Hexe» wie an einer Kletterstange an dem Besen, der zwischen Boden und Decke eingeklemmt ist. Das Bild wurde um ca. 70° gedreht; dadurch scheinen Haare und Kleid im Flugwind zu flattern. (GER)
386 Doppelseite mit Farbaufnahmen aus *Canon Circle,* eine Fachzeitschrift des Kameraherstellers *Canon.* (JPN)
387 Umschlag mit Schwarzweissaufnahme von vermoostem Holz für ein japanisches Jahrbuch der Werbegraphik (*Annual of Advertising Art in Japan 1983*). (JPN)

384 Photo double page pour un article de *Photo* présentant le photographe Dennis Manarchy. (FRA)
385 «Elles en mènent une vie, les jeunes sorcières!» Photo pour un article de *Cosmopolitan.* Dans ce truquage, qui montre la «sorcière» accrochée à son balai coincé entre le plafond et le plancher, la photo a été tournée d'environ 70°. (GER)
386 Double page illustrée de photos couleur tirée de *Canon Circle,* revue du producteur d'appareils photo *Canon.* (JPN)
387 Couverture ornée d'une photo de bois moussu en noir et blanc pour un annuel japonais de l'art publicitaire, l'*Annual of Advertising Art in Japan 1983.* (JPN)

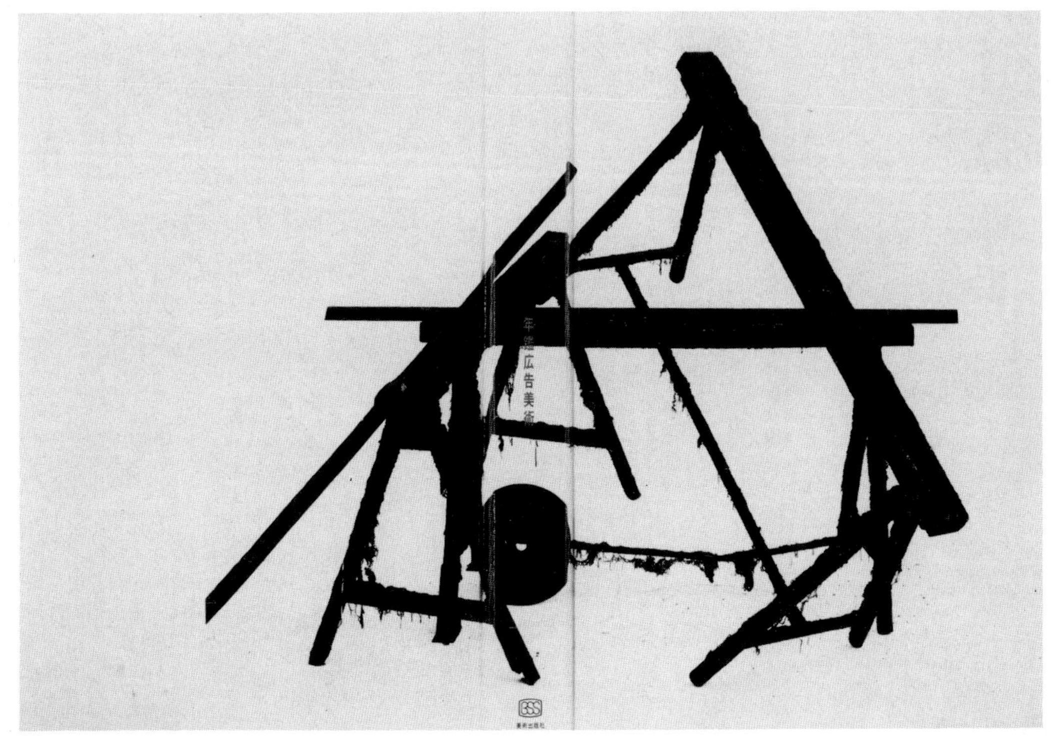

387

388

389

Book Covers
Buchumschläge
Jaquettes de livres

PHOTOGRAPHER / PHOTOGRAPH / PHOTOGRAPHE:

388, 389, 391 Holger Matthies
390 Hans Jürgen Rau
392 Fabio Santagiuliana

DESIGNER / GESTALTER / MAQUETTISTE:

388, 389, 391 Holger Matthies
390 Hans Jürgen Rau
392 Giancarlo Alesiani

ART DIRECTOR / DIRECTEUR ARTISTIQUE:

388, 389, 391 W. L. Siegmund
390 Hans Jürgen Rau

AGENCY / AGENTUR / AGENCE – STUDIO:

390 Studio Rau

PUBLISHER / VERLEGER / EDITEUR:

388, 389, 391 Siegmund Verlag
390 Edition Rau
392 Biblos Edizione

388, 389, 391 Photographic detail and complete book covers in a series on advertising agencies, one for those specializing in cosmetics and pharmaceuticals, the others being active in the fields marked by the seven blossoms on its cover. (GER)
390 Cover of the book on graphic designers "Wanted", with subject-field index. (GER)
392 Book jacket for an album of nude photography in black and white by the Italian Fabio Santagiuliana. (ITA)

388, 389, 391 Aufnahme und vollständige Umschlagseiten von Büchern aus einer Reihe, in der Werbeagenturen präsentiert werden. Hier ein Band über Kosmetik und Pharmaka und einer über sieben verschiedene Bereiche, die auf dem Umschlag angegeben sind. (GER)
390 Umschlag für ein Buch über Graphik-Designer, mit Suchliste nach Fachgebieten. (GER)
392 Schutzumschlag für ein Buch mit Aktaufnahmen des Photographen Fabio Santagiuliana, in Schwarzweiss. (ITA)

388, 389, 391 Photo et couvertures complètes de livres parus dans une série présentant diverses agences publicitaires. Il s'agit ici d'un volume sur les cosmétiques et les pharmaceutiques et d'un volume sur sept branches différentes figurant en couverture. (GER)
390 Couverture d'un répertoire de graphistes, avec un index par spécialisations. (GER)
392 Jaquette d'un album de nus du photographe Fabio Santagiuliana en noir et blanc. (ITA)

390

391

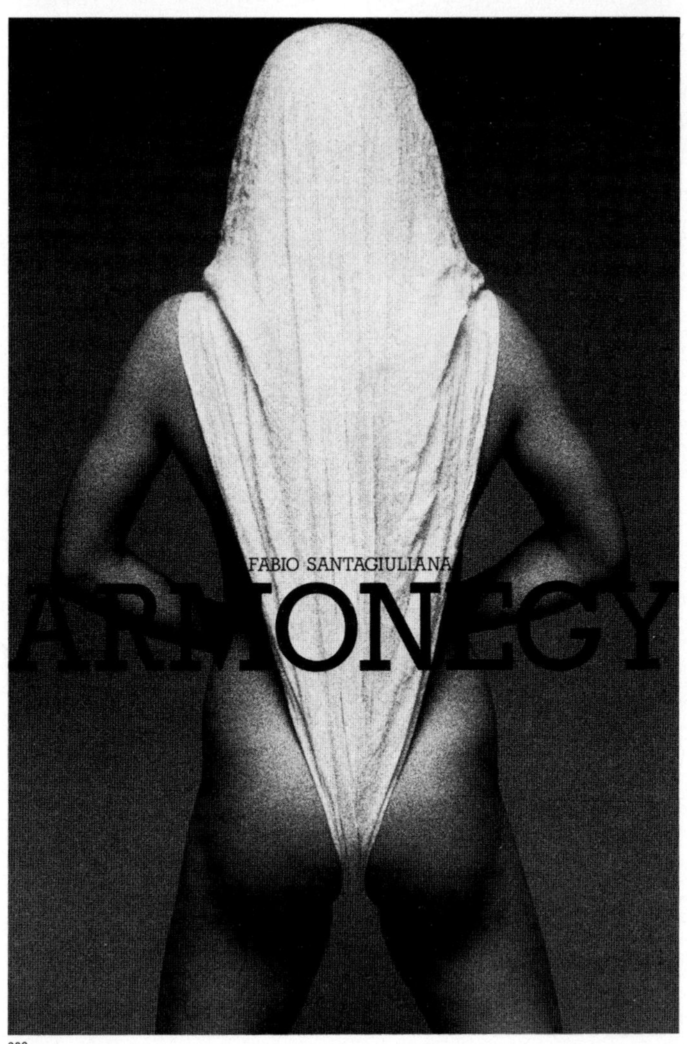

392

PHOTOGRAPHER / PHOTOGRAPH:

393, 394 John Alderson
395 Gerd Messerschmidt
396 François Robert
397 Henry Brimmer

DESIGNER / GESTALTER:

393, 394, 396 Bruno Ruegg
397 Bill Withers

ART DIRECTOR:

393, 394, 396 Bruno Ruegg
395 Hans-Peter Schmid
397 Walter Herdeg

AGENCY / AGENTUR / AGENCE:

393, 394, 396 Sieber & McIntyre
395 Züllig & Kiefer

PUBLISHER / VERLEGER / EDITEUR:

393, 394, 396 PCA Division of Sieber & McIntyre
395 Nikon AG
397 Graphis Press Corp.

393

394

395

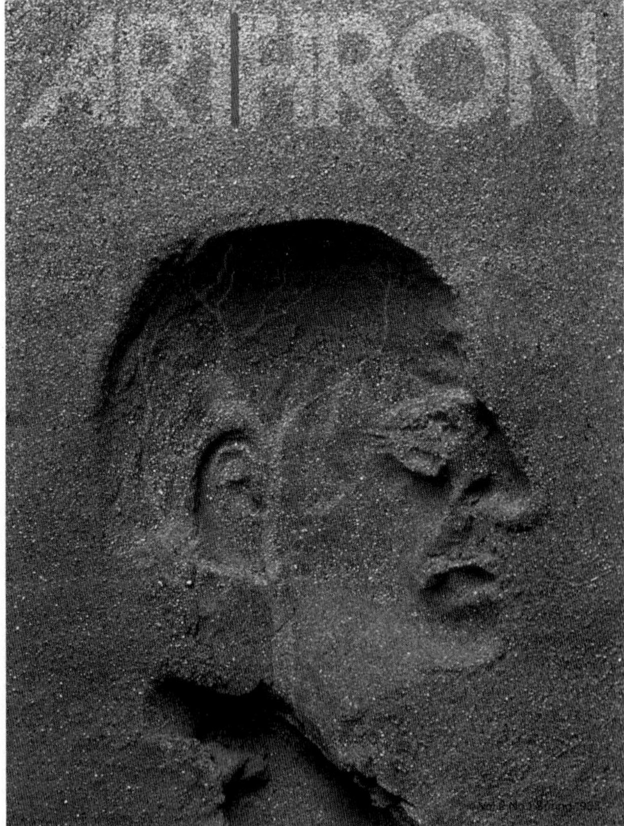

396

393, 394 Complete covers in full colour from the Japanese edition of the medical journal *Current Concepts in Hypertension.* (JPN)
395 Complete cover of the German-language edition of *Nikon-News.* (SWI)
396 Cover of the medical journal *Arthron*: sandy brown, with two red spots indicating blood-vessel inflammations that cause headaches. (USA)
397 Full-page shot of a window display at *Macy's* department store in San Francisco. From a *Graphis* article on "Window Impressions". (SWI)

393, 394 Für japanische Ausgaben der medizinischen Fachzeitschrift *Current Concepts in Hypertension,* deren Thema zu hoher Blutdruck ist. (JPN)
395 Umschlag einer Ausgabe der *Nikon-News.* (SWI)
396 Für die medizinische Fachpublikation *Arthron.* Hier Kopfschmerzen verursachende entzündete Blutgefässe eines älteren Patienten. Braun mit Rot. (USA)
397 Aufnahme eines Schaufensters von *Macy's* in San Francisco, in dem sich die städtische Umwelt spiegelt. Aus einem Artikel in *Graphis.* (SWI)

393, 394 Pour des numéros japonais de la revue médicale *Current Concepts in Hypertension* consacrée à l'hypertension essentielle. (JPN)
395 Couverture d'un numéro des *Nikon-News.* (SWI)
396 Pour la publication médicale *Arthron.* On voit ici des vaisseaux sanguins enflammés, cause de la migraine d'un patient âgé. Brun et rouge. (USA)
397 Photo d'une vitrine de chez *Macy's* à San Francisco, où se reflète l'environnement urbain. Cette photo illustre un article de *Graphis.* (SWI)

397

318

PHOTOGRAPHER / PHOTOGRAPH / PHOTOGRAPHE:

398 Henry Brimmer
399 Holger Matthies
400–402 Daniel Gil

DESIGNER / GESTALTER / MAQUETTISTE:

398 Larry Stripling
399 Holger Matthies
400–402 Daniel Gil

ART DIRECTOR / DIRECTEUR ARTISTIQUE:

398 Walter Herdeg
399 Holger Matthies

PUBLISHER / VERLEGER / EDITEUR:

398 Graphis Press Corp.
399 Staatliche Schauspielbühnen Berlin
400–402 Alianza Editorial S. A.

398 Full-page photo by the designer and photographer Henry Brimmer from an article in *Graphis* on "Window Impressions in San Francisco", here a window display at *Jeanne Marc's.* (SWI)
399 Cover shot in full colour from the promotional "newspaper" of Berlin's state theatres: "We'll open your eyes!" (GER)
400–402 Full-colour jackets for *Alianza* books. (SPA)

398 Aufnahme aus einem Artikel in der Zeitschrift *Graphis* über Schaufenster-Eindrücke in San Francisco (hier bei *Jeanne Marc*) des Designers und Photographen Henry Brimmer. (SWI)
399 Umschlagphoto einer Theaterzeitung der Staatlichen Schauspielbühnen Berlin. Motto: «Wir öffnen Ihnen die Augen!» (GER)
400–402 Mehrfarbige Buchumschläge des *Alianza*-Verlags. (SPA)

398 Photo illustrant un article du bimestriel *Graphis* consacré aux impressions de vitrines rassemblées à San Francisco par le designer-photographe Henry Brimmer. Ici de chez *Jeanne Marc.* (SWI)
399 Photo de couverture d'un journal des Théâtres d'Etat berlinois. La devise illustrée: nous vous ouvrons les yeux! (GER)
400–402 Couvertures polychromes de livres des Ed. *Alianza.* (SPA)

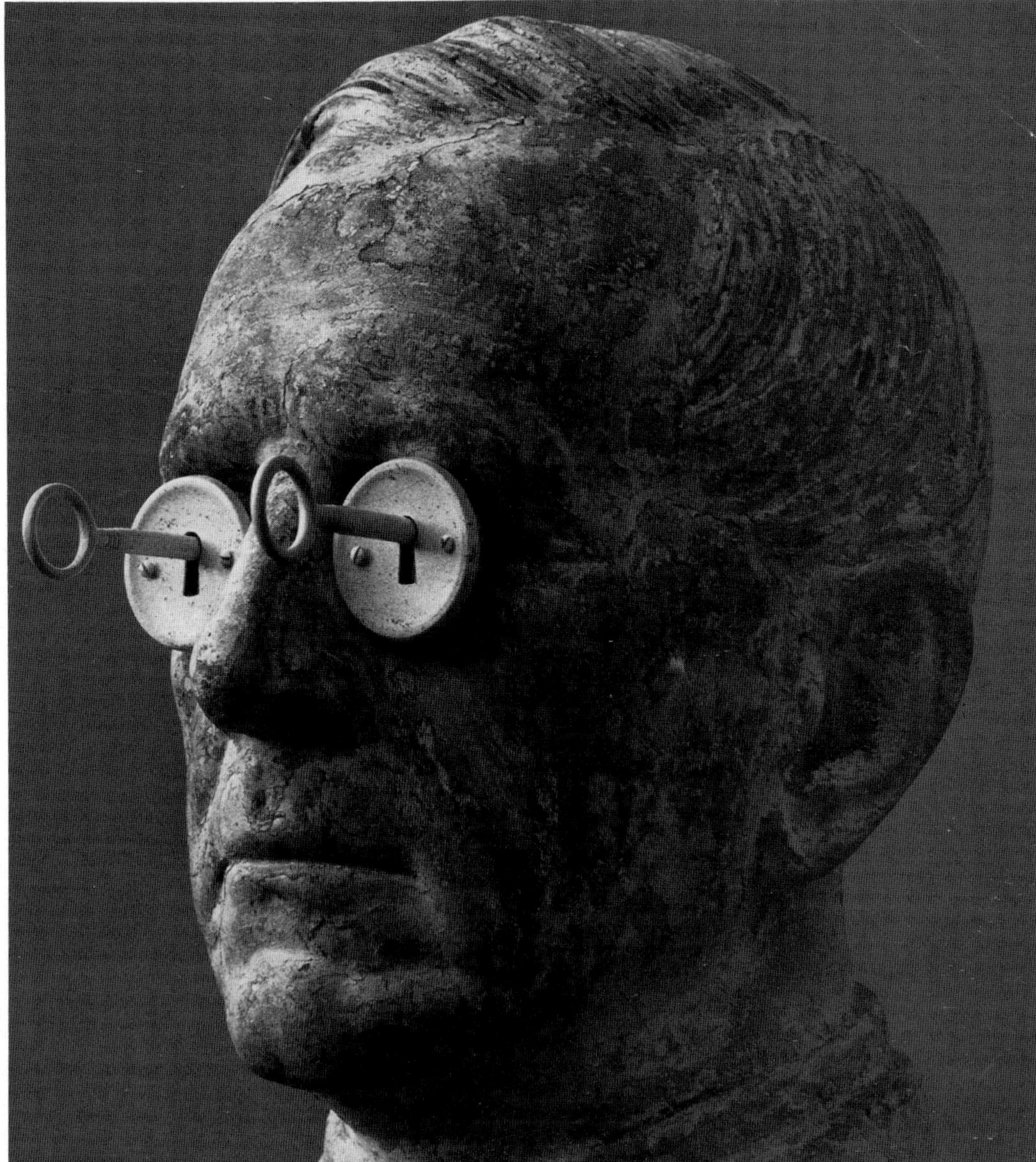

399

400

401

402

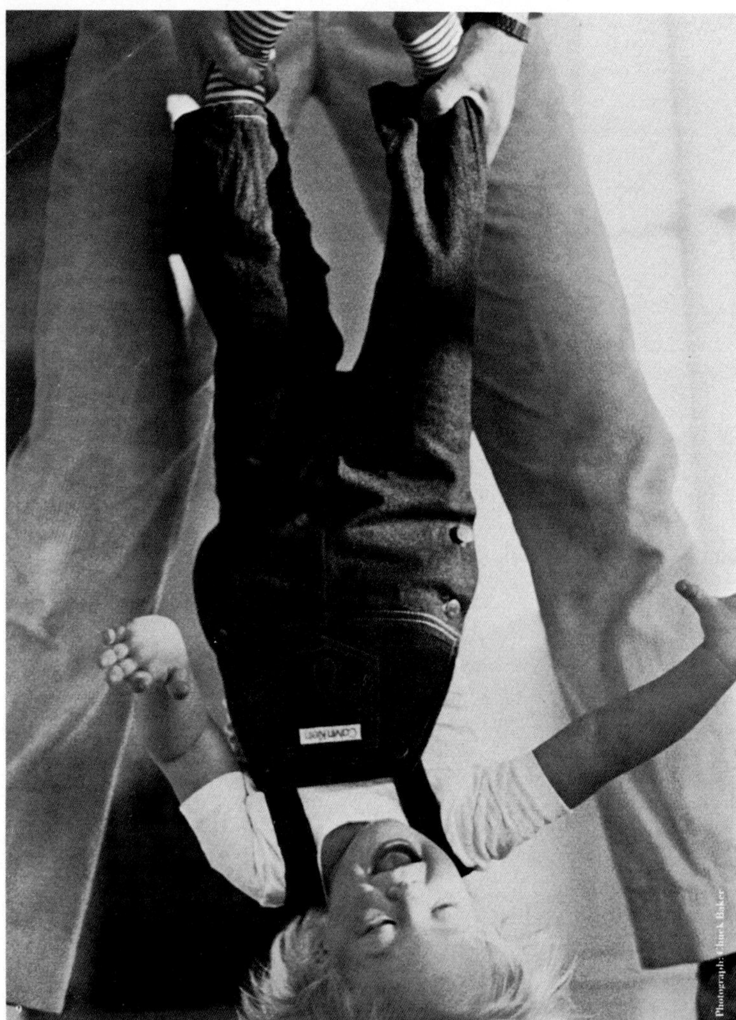

403

404

407

Annual Reports
Jahresberichte
Rapports annuels

PHOTOGRAPHER / PHOTOGRAPH / PHOTOGRAPHE:

403 Chuck Baker
404 Richard Avedon
405, 406 Greg Booth
407–409 Jeff Smith

DESIGNER / GESTALTER / MAQUETTISTE:

403, 404 Peter Laundy
405, 406 Stephen P. Miller
407–409 Larry Tierney

ART DIRECTOR / DIRECTEUR ARTISTIQUE:

403, 404 Lella Vignelli
405, 406 Stephen P. Miller
407–409 Leslie A. Segal/Larry Tierney

AGENCY / AGENTUR / AGENCE – STUDIO:

403, 404 Vignelli Associates
405, 406 Richards, Sullivan, Brock & Associates
407–409 Corporate Annual Reports, Inc.

403, 404 Complete full-colour pages from an annual report of *Puritan Fashions* with models displaying the jeans fashions of designer *Calvin Klein.* (USA)
405, 406 Complete full-colour pages from an annual report of Lomas & Nettleton Financial Corporation visualizing a student's dream of a home of one's own. (USA)
407–409 Complete double spread and full-colour pages showing photographs from a *Sperry* annual report relating to (Fig. 408) an advanced photolithographic process, and (Fig. 409) analysing in an anti-echo chamber. (USA)

403, 404 Ganzseitige Farbaufnahmen aus dem Jahresbericht von *Puritan Fashions,* hier mit Modellen des amerikanischen Modeschöpfers *Calvin Klein.* (USA)
405, 406 Beispiele von ganzseitigen Farbaufnahmen aus einem Jahresbericht einer Hypotheken-Bank. Thema der Aufnahmen ist der Wunsch junger Erwachsener nach einem eigenen Haus, hier in Form von Interviews mit Universitäts-Absolventen dargestellt. (USA)
407–409 Vollständige Doppelseite und ganzseitige Aufnahmen aus dem Jahresbericht 1983 von *Sperry,* Hersteller elektronischer Systeme. (USA)

403, 404 Photos couleur pleine page illustrant le rapport annuel de *Puritan Fashions,* ici par des modèles du grand couturier américain *Calvin Klein.* (USA)
405, 406 Exemples des photos pleine page en couleur illustrant le rapport annuel d'une banque hypothécaire. Le sujet central, c'est le désir qu'ont les jeunes d'avoir une maison à soi; à cet effet, on a interviewé ici des étudiants de l'université en fin d'études. (USA)
407–409 Double page complète et photos pleine page du rapport annuel pour 1983 de *Sperry,* fabricant de systèmes électroniques. (USA)

405

406

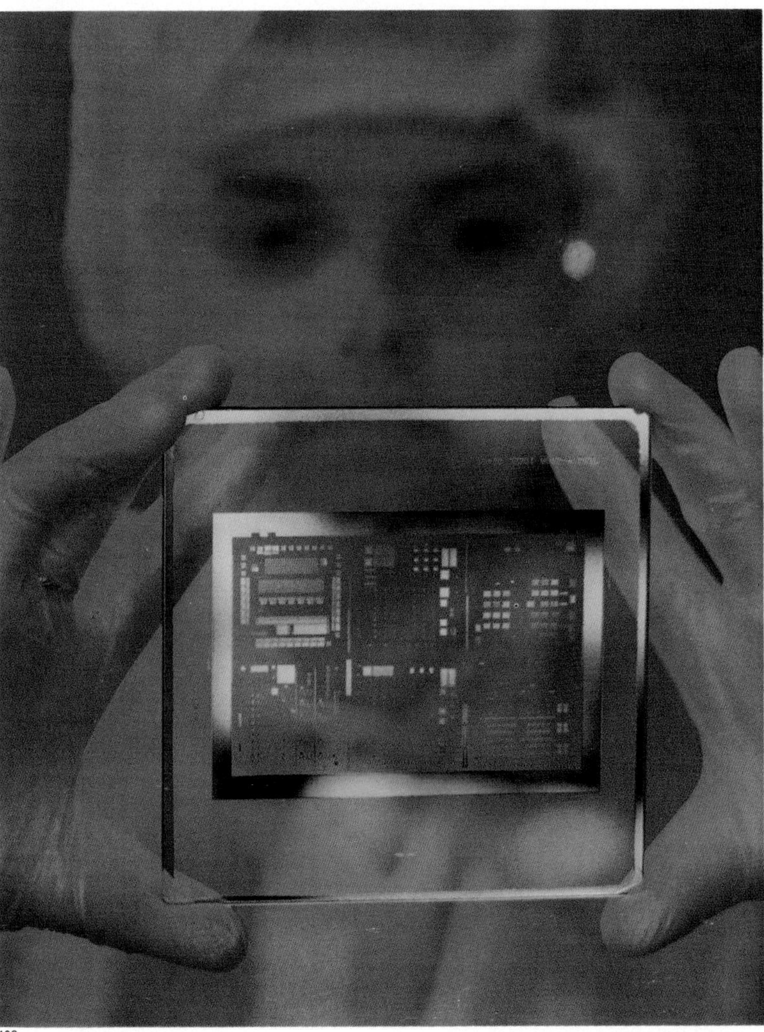
408

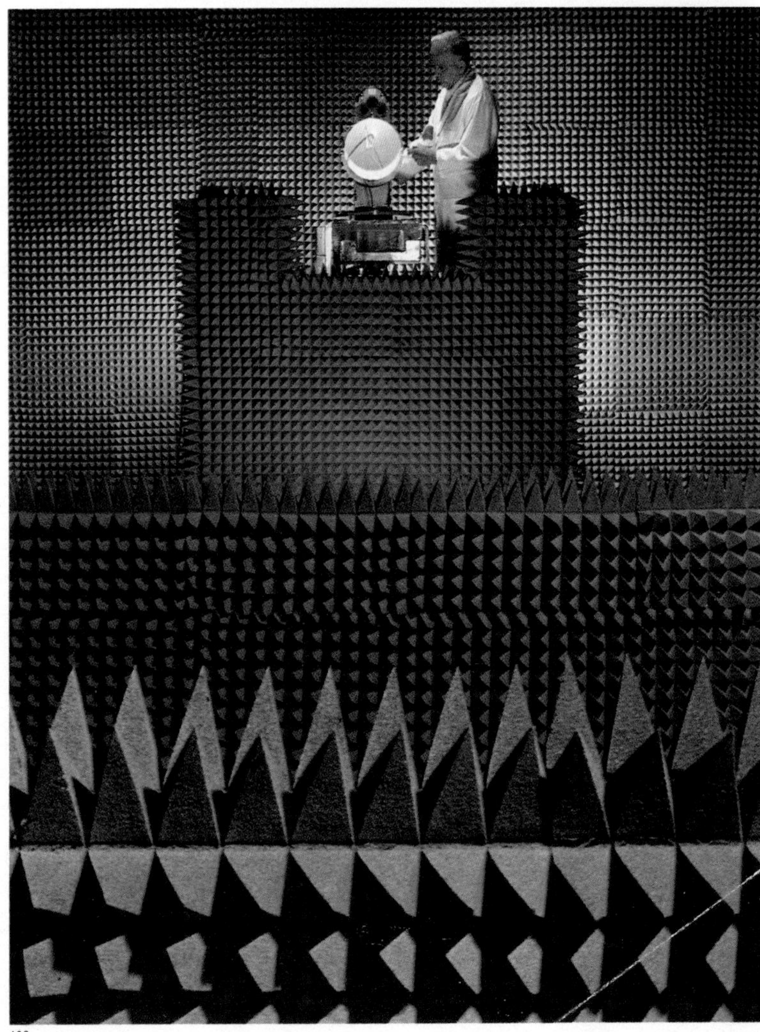
409

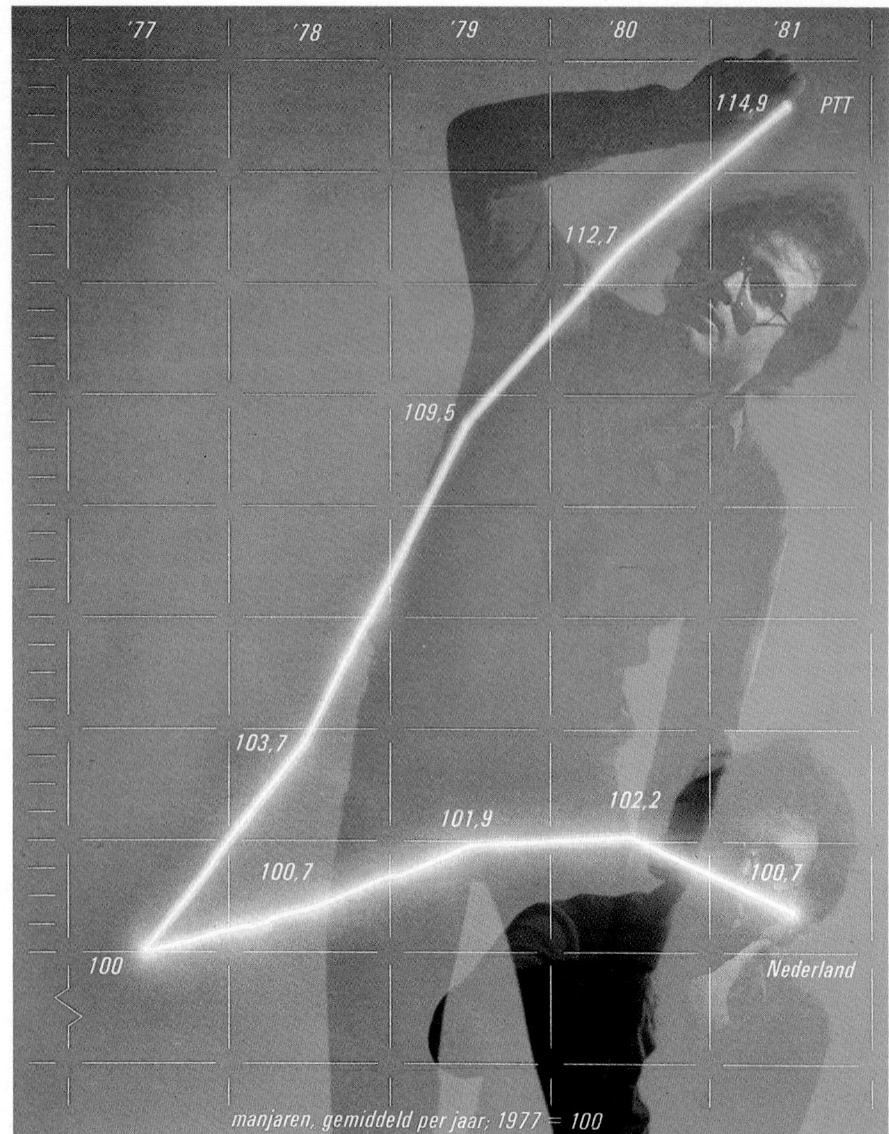

410

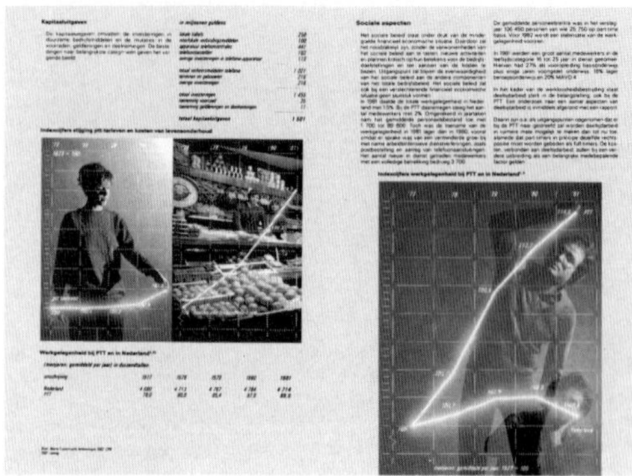

411

410, 411 Photo and complete double spread of the annual report, by the Dutch post office, in which it appeared. Its neon graph outlines a five-year comparison of the job market, nationally and with the post office. (NLD)
412 Full-colour cover of a promotional booklet published by *Frito-Lay,* which makes snacks e.g. from potatoes and maize. (USA)
413 From a promotional booklet by the Textile Rubber & Chemical Co. (USA)
414, 415 From a promotional booklet by *Westineon,* which specializes in neon advertising, synthetics and interior-lit signage systems. Fig. 414: Lettering made of synthetic material; 415: Cover showing shaped neon tubes. (SWI)

410, 411 Aufnahme und vollständige Doppelseite aus einem Jahresbericht der niederländischen PTT. Die graphische Darstellung zeigt die Zunahme der Stellenangebote. (NLD)
412 Mehrfarbiger Umschlag einer Firmenbroschüre, mit der sich der Snack-Hersteller *Frito-Lay* vorstellt. (USA)
413 Photo aus einer Firmenbroschüre der Textile Rubber & Chemical Co. (USA)
414, 415 Aus einer Broschüre der Firma *Westineon,* die sich auf Lichtwerbung, Kunststoffe und Signale spezialisiert hat. Abb. 414: Kunststoff-Buchstaben; Abb. 415: Verformte Neonröhren auf dem Umschlag der Firmenbroschüre. (SWI)

410, 411 Photo et double page complète d'un rapport annuel des PTT néerlandais. La graphique montre l'accroissement des offres d'emploi dans cette grande administration publique. (NLD)
412 Couverture polychrome d'une brochure d'entreprise servant à la présentation du fabricant de petits gâteaux *Frito-Lay.* (USA)
413 Photo illustrant une brochure de la Textile Rubber & Chemical Cie. (USA)
414, 415 Illustrations photo d'une brochure de la *Westineon* spécialisée dans la publicité lumineuse, les plastiques et les signaux. Fig. 414: lettres plastiques; fig. 415: néons tordus en couverture de la brochure. (SWI)

412

413

414

415

PHOTOGRAPHER / PHOTOGRAPH / PHOTOGRAPHE:

410, 411 Lex van Pieterson
412 Mike Haynes
413 Walter Bibikow
414, 415 Fernand Rausser

DESIGNER / GESTALTER / MAQUETTISTE:

410, 411 Michel de Boer/Rik Comello
412 Dick Mitchell
413 Walter Bibikow
414, 415 Fernand Rausser

ART DIRECTOR / DIRECTEUR ARTISTIQUE:

410, 411 Abe van der Werff
412 Dick Mitchell
413 John Donovan
414, 415 Eugen Götz-Gee

AGENCY / AGENTUR / AGENCE – STUDIO:

410, 411 Studio Dumbar
412 Richards, Sullivan, Brock & Associates
413 First National Bank of Boston/Design
414, 415 Didier Weiss

17

Chef Pierre
Leadership in Customer Service

Customer service at Chef Pierre has many definitions. It can mean rerouting trucks to respond to an emergency; providing custom packaging to accommodate special requests; even making product adjustments to accommodate taste in a specific geographic region.

Whatever customer service requires, Chef Pierre delivers.

"That's why Chef Pierre is the leading supplier of frozen pies to the foodservice industry," says Donald J. Childers, a salesman who covers Florida, Tennessee, and North and South Carolina.

Because he could plug directly into the Chef Pierre delivery system and get immediate results, Childers was able to open a last-minute new account at the Knoxville World's Fair.

"A week before the fair opened, we went to the main food concessionaire. Our competition had been there first, but the concession staff realized we had a superior product. They said we would get the business if we could deliver 600 cases before the fair opened. That was a Thursday. They had pies the following Tuesday, and the fair opened on Wednesday. We had another 25 cases from a nearby distributor on hand, too, just in case," Childers states.

It is this type of service that has increased Childers' sales substantially. This year, he will sell 800,000 cases. That compares with 550,000 cases last year and 375,000 cases two years ago.

Another part of the Chef Pierre customer service formula is close contact with distributors and food brokers. Selling business prospects for distributors and giving seminars for nutritionists and dieticians are all part of the job. Childers also keeps small accounts active through regular contact with brokers, an unusually conscientious practice in the foodservice industry, he asserts.

Of course, consumer feedback is also essential. Childers cites the example of how his third-best-selling item was created.

"We introduced lemon icebox pie and my customers told me it just would not sell in the Southeast without vanilla wafers around the side. They were right. So we figured out how to add wafers and supply special pies to that region.

"We made the change in only three weeks. That's the kind of flexibility that will continue to give us substantial market gains."

416

Annual Reports
Jahresberichte
Rapports annuels

416, 417 Double spreads from an annual report of *Consolidated Foods*, a diversified company that produces women's hosiery as well as food and beverages: Fig. 416 relates to its *Chef Pierre* frozen pies, and Fig. 417 to the production of *Hanes* pantyhose. (USA)
418–420 Double spreads and complete cover, all in full colour, of an annual report by *Norton*, manufacturer of abrasive tools and materials: Fig. 418 shows a high-performance grinding wheel in action, and (Fig. 19) the sockets that will hold the synthetic diamonds which are the "teeth" of a compact drill. Fig. 420: The cover's sheaf of spaghetti is actually fluoropolymer tubing, cut after extrusion. (USA)
421 Double spread in full colour from an annual report of *Gannett*, the American communications group, on aspects of Washington state: Mt. Rainer, a yacht haven and one of the group's presses. (USA)

416, 417 Doppelseiten aus einem Jahresbericht der *Consolidated Foods*, ein diversifiziertes Unternehmen, das hauptsächlich auf dem Lebensmittelsektor tätig ist. Abb. 416 bezieht sich auf das Geschäft mit tiefgefrorenen Fruchtkuchen, Abb. 417 auf die Herstellung von Strumpfwaren der Marke *Hanes*. (USA)
418–420 Doppelseiten und Umschlag eines Jahresberichts von *Norton*. Wie aus den Abbildungen ersichtlich, handelt es sich um die Fabrikation von Industrieprodukten; die Umschlagaufnahme zeigt fertiggeschnittene Polymer-Röhrchen. (USA)
421 Beispiel von Doppelseiten mit Farbaufnahmen, die verschiedenen Orten der USA gewidmet sind; hier der Ort Olympia, Washington, mit dem Mount Rainier und Bootshafen. Aus einem Jahresbericht von *Gannett*, ein Unternehmen auf dem Gebiet der Informationsmedien. (USA)

418

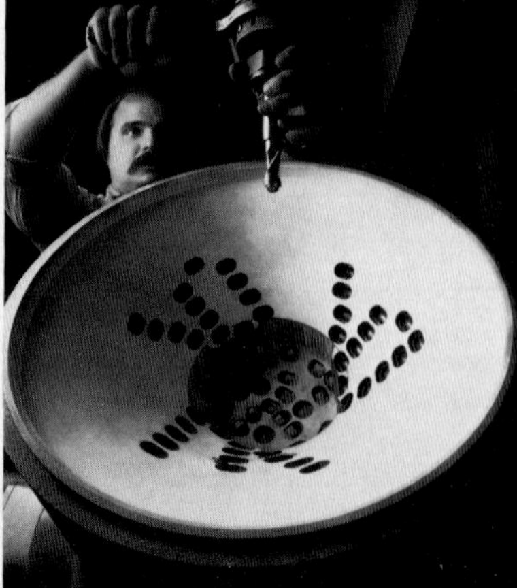

419

13

Hanes Group
Leadership in Product Innovation

The story of the Hanes Group, the leading U.S. manufacturer of women's hosiery products, is a story of leadership in product innovation.

From creation of the flagship *Hanes* hosiery brand to today's diversified product line, Hanes has set the pace for the entire hosiery industry through innovative products such as *L'eggs, Underalls* and *Hanes Too!*

One of the most distinctive Hanes innovations was the *L'eggs* brand from L'eggs Products, a division of the Hanes Group. L'eggs revolutionized women's hosiery buying patterns by making quality hosiery available in food, drug and mass merchandising outlets instead of the traditional department and specialty stores.

Hanes was the first to get creative with a product which for years had seemed as "predictable as a loaf of bread," according to Bob Simms, vice president of marketing for Hanes Hosiery, another one of the companies in the Hanes Group.

"For years, people had been saying, 'What could be new under the sun in pantyhose?' Hanes was there, carving out niches, pulling away from the competition by using disciplined consumer research to uncover new needs in the pantyhose market."

Simms calls the new *Hanes Too!* line an innovative answer to the needs of working women. Available in department and specialty stores, it is a mid-priced alternative to the more elegant *Hanes* line.

"*Hanes Too!* hosiery is less sheer and more durable, and it stretches for everyday work," says Simms.

Hanes Too! products exceeded sales projections by 10% during the first year they were marketed.

Another striking example of Hanes innovation, says Simms, is *Underalls* pantyhose. Before introducing the first no-panty-line pantyhose in 1976, Hanes tested three marketing concepts: price, convenience and comfort, and no-panty-lines. Researchers found the no-panty-lines positioning motivated women to buy the product.

"The *Underalls* brand, packaged with distinctive, memorable graphics, was a rapid success," Simms says.

"There will be other successes for Hanes as the companies in the group continue to break new ground," Simms asserts. "Finding innovative solutions to consumer problems and needs is our specialty, and Hanes products will continue to be leaders in the hosiery industry."

417

416, 417 Doubles pages d'un rapport annuel de *Consolidated Foods*, une entreprise diversifiée travaillant surtout dans la branche alimentaire. La fig. 416 se rapporte à la commercialisation de gâteaux aux fruits surgelés, la fig. 417 à un autre secteur d'activité, la fabrication de bonneterie sous la marque *Hanes*. (USA)
418–420 Doubles pages et couverture d'un rapport annuel de *Norton*. Comme on le voit par les illustrations, il s'agit de la fabrication de produits industriels; la photo de couverture montre des tubes de fluoropolymère coupés à la longueur voulue après l'extrusion. (USA)
421 Exemple des pages doubles illustrées de photos couleur de diverses localités américaines: ici, Olympia dans l'Etat de Washington, avec le Mount Rainier et le port de plaisance. Rapport annuel de *Gannett*, entreprise spécialisée dans les médias. (USA)

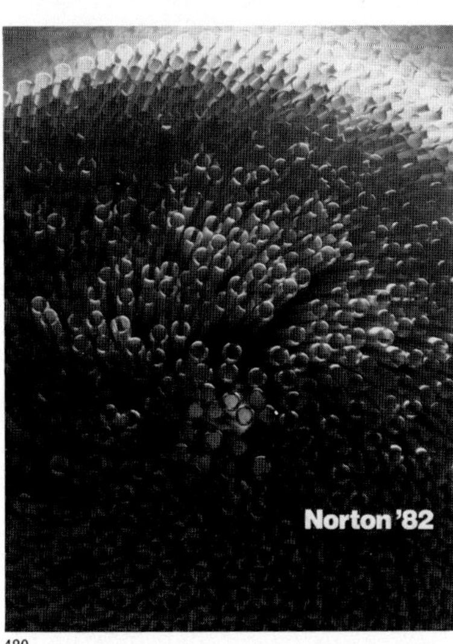

420

PHOTOGRAPHER / PHOTOGRAPH:

416, 417 Peggy Barnett/Bill Ray
418–420 Mason Morfit/Jerry Sarapochiello
421 Jay Maisel

DESIGNER / GESTALTER / MAQUETTISTE:

416, 417 James Hatch
418–420 Robert Jakob
421 Robert Myers

ART DIRECTOR / DIRECTEUR ARTISTIQUE:

416, 417 Bennett Robinson
418–420 Arnold Saks
421 Robert Myers

AGENCY / AGENTUR / AGENCE – STUDIO:

416, 417 Corporate Graphics Inc.
418–420 Arnold Saks Associates
421 Robert Myers Design

421

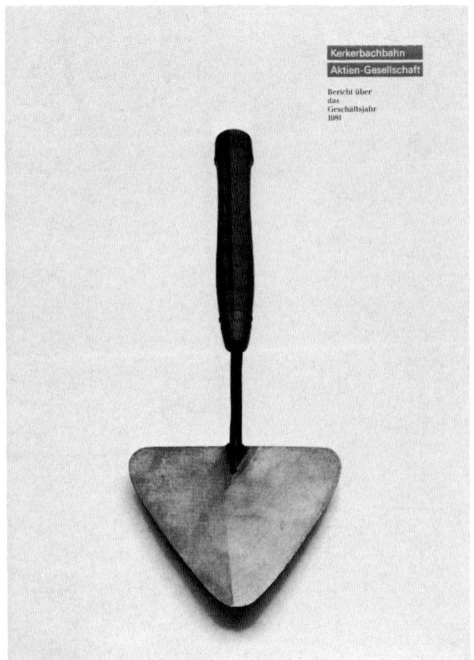

422

423

424

Annual Reports

PHOTOGRAPHER / PHOTOGRAPH / PHOTOGRAPHE:

422 Stefan Blume
423, 424, 426 Jim Barber

DESIGNER / GESTALTER / MAQUETTISTE:

422 Axel Gottschall
423, 424, 426 Leslie A. Segal/ Wayne Roth
425 Joseph M. Essex/Marilyn Lurie

ART DIRECTOR / DIRECTEUR ARTISTIQUE:

422 Axel Gottschall/ Gudrun Martens-Gottschall
423, 424, 426 Wayne Roth
425 Joseph M. Essex

AGENCY / AGENTUR / AGENCE – STUDIO:

422 Gottschall & Martens
423, 424, 426 Corporate Annual Reports
425 Burson-Marsteller

422 Full-colour cover of an annual report by *Kerkerbachbahn*, constructor of apartment blocks. (GER)
423, 424 Full-colour double spreads from a *Rexham* annual report (see also Fig. 426), showing in Fig. 423 a gyroscope, and in Fig. 424 rolls of film, with a coating as thin as .0007 of an inch, used to make the printed circuit on the right. (USA)
425 Complete cover of an annual report by the Union Special Corporation, manufacturer of sewing machines. (USA)
426 Cover in actual size of an annual report of the Rexham Corporation. See also Figs. 423 and 424. (USA)

422 Umschlag mit Farbaufnahme für den Geschäftsbericht der Kerkerbachbahn AG, ein Wohnungsbau-Unternehmen. (GER)
423, 424 Doppelseiten aus dem Jahresbericht eines Herstellers von Packungsmaterial und Maschinen. In Abb. 423, mit Gyroskop, geht es um Qualitätskontrolle, in Abb. 424 um technisches Können und Präzision. (USA)
425 Vollständiger Umschlag eines Jahresberichtes der Union Special Corp., Hersteller von Nähmaschinen. (USA)
426 Umschlag in Originalgrösse von einem Jahresbericht der Rexham Corporation. Siehe auch Abb. 423, 424. (USA)

422 Couverture avec photo couleur pour le rapport annuel de la Kerkerbachbahn AG, un promoteur immobilier. (GER)
423, 424 Doubles pages du rapport annuel d'un fabricant de matériaux d'emballage et de machines. La fig. 423 montre un gyroscope et illustre le contrôle de la qualité, la fig. 424 le savoir-faire et la précision techniques. (USA)
425 Couverture complète d'un rapport annuel de l'Union Special Corp., fabricant de machines à coudre. (USA)
426 Couverture au format original d'un rapport annuel de la Rexham Corporation. Cf. les fig. 423, 424. (USA)

425

426

427

Northwest Pipeline

The Opal, Wyoming extraction plant is undergoing a $30 million expansion in 1983, which will increase processing capacity substantially. The Opal plant extracts liquid hydrocarbons from natural gas produced from the Big Piney Field and from smaller fields in the Overthrust Belt and the Green River Basin. New centralized computer facilities installed in 1982 monitor and control plant operations (lower photo).

location in the center of the Overthrust Belt and the Rocky Mountain sedimentary basins to sign long-term contracts to transport gas supplies for other purchasers. These contracts represent reserves in excess of one trillion cubic feet. These contracts allow Northwest Pipeline to utilize its transmission and gathering system more efficiently to reduce the unit cost of transportation to its existing customers and to expand its gathering system into promising areas. Volumes for transport are expected to increase as development continues in the Overthrust Belt and the sedimentary basins near Northwest Pipeline's transmission system.

Northwest Pipeline's total proved gas reserves were 6.9 trillion cubic feet as of the end of 1982. This gives Northwest Pipeline a reserve to production ratio of 23.8 years, the highest of any major natural gas transmission company in the United States. Major U.S. natural gas supplies come from the San Juan Basin (27%), the Big Piney Field of Wyoming (14%) and various other Rocky Mountain gas fields (18%). The remaining supplies come from Canada.

Northwest Pipeline is planning to install turbo-expander facilities, costing $87 million, to improve efficiency at both the Opal, Wyoming and Ignacio, Colorado liquids extraction plants on the Northwest Pipeline system. These plants extract natural gas liquids—primarily butane, propane and natural gasoline—from the gas stream before it enters the main transmission line. The Opal project will be completed in 1983 and the Ignacio project is expected to be completed in 1984. The new facilities will permit processing of higher gas volumes and recovery of additional liquid products. In 1982, recovery of natural gas liquids at these two plants amounted to 106.1 million gallons, compared with 96.4 million in 1981.

16 17

428

Baxter Travenol Laboratories, Inc.
1982 Annual Report

429

Annual Reports
Jahresberichte
Rapports annuels

PHOTOGRAPHER / PHOTOGRAPH / PHOTOGRAPHE:

427 Gregory Heisler
428 Mark Godfrey/Burk Uzzle
429 Ron Seymour

DESIGNER / GESTALTER / MAQUETTISTE:

427, 428 Ingo Scharrenbroich
429 Hank Robertz/Paul Schulte

ART DIRECTOR / DIRECTEUR ARTISTIQUE:

427, 428 Arnold Saks

AGENCY / AGENTUR / AGENCE – STUDIO:

427, 428 Arnold Saks Associates
429 Robertz/Webb & Co.

427 Full-page photograph in actual size from an RCA annual report. The structure under completion here, one of the largest of its kind in the United States, is an environmental test chamber for satellites. (USA)
428 Complete full-colour double spread from an annual report by *Northwest Energy*, active in oil and gas areas. (USA)
429 Full-colour cover of the report by Baxter Travenol Laboratories, manufacturer of medical-care products. This shot, in bluish grey, shows a technician monitoring a production process. (USA)

427 Ganzseitige Aufnahme in Originalgrösse aus einem Jahresbericht der RCA. Hier eine von der Firma hergestellte Umgebungs-Testkammer für Satelliten, eine der grössten dieser Art in den Vereinigten Staaten. (USA)
428 Doppelseite mit Farbaufnahme aus einem Jahresbericht der Northwest Energy Company, ein Unternehmen für die Energieversorgung mit Erdgas. (USA)
429 Umschlag des Jahresberichts eines Herstellers medizinischer Produkte und Geräte. Die Aufnahme, in hellem Graublau, zeigt einen Techniker bei der Arbeit in einem der Herstellungslabors. (USA)

427 Photo couleur au format original illustrant un rapport annuel de RCA. On voit ici une salle d'essai pour satellites simulant l'environnement spatial, l'une des plus grandes aux Etats-Unis. (USA)
428 Double page illustrée en couleur, dans un rapport annuel de la Northwest Energy Company, société spécialisée dans l'acheminement du gaz naturel. (USA)
429 Couverture du rapport annuel d'un fabricant de produits et équipements médicaux. La photo gris bleu clair montre un technicien contrôlant avec soin le processus de fabrication dans l'une des usines du groupe. (USA)

Corporate Publications
Firmenpublikationen
Publications d'entreprise

430

Our tools for cardiovascular, and other, research include an extensive library of scientific data from around the world(1) and read-outs from sophisticated computers that show test animal systolic blood pressure(2) and other hemodynamics(3).

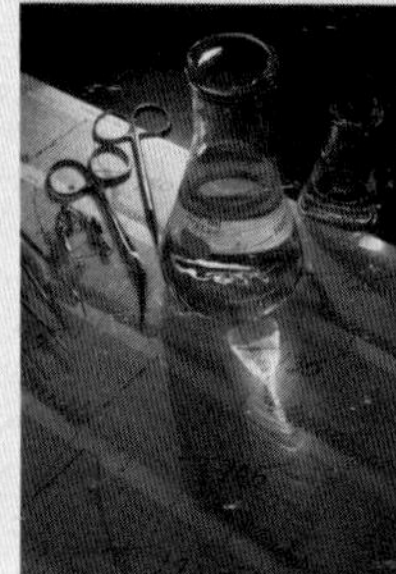

2

3

4

angiotensin II, which triggers high blood pressure.

In a continual search for more keys to the treatment of hypertension, heart failure, angina, arrhythmias and the broad category of vascular disease, Institute researchers from many disciplines are joined in the study of the body's complicated vascular, pulmonary and renal functions.

Their work, fruitful in the creation of a once-a-day beta adrenergic blocking agent for the treatment of hypertension and angina pectoris, continues in that important therapeutic area, and also on a variety of second-generation ACE inhibitors of differing molecular structures.

Further basic research focuses on compounds to combat arrhythmias and necrosis which often occur in the wake of heart attacks, and on new drugs which influence the prostaglandin and other body systems.

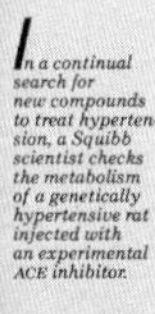

In a continual search for new compounds to treat hypertension, a Squibb scientist checks the metabolism of a genetically hypertensive rat injected with an experimental ACE inhibitor.

5

431

In the rapidly expanding area of diagnostic equipment, our researchers are developing an infusion system to inject radioisotopes into patients for cardiac imaging(1), and a fiber optic pH sensor for prenatal care(2) shown in the foreground of an optical bench(3).

1

3

16

life, assuring a fresh supply when needed for diagnoses.

Research at The Institute is ongoing in the field of radioimmunoassays, laboratory tests which enable physicians to measure quantities of therapeutic drugs, hormones and other biochemicals in body fluids. The automation by our scientists of instrumentation for these assays was an important step to time and cost savings in both hospitals and research laboratories.

2

The Institute's developments in diagnostic imaging made through pharmaceutical research also interrelate with and benefit the research programs of other Squibb subsidiaries that create sophisticated electronic screening and monitoring equipment. Together, the equipment and image-enhancing agents provide both physicians and patients with the parallel benefit of faster and more accurate treatment.

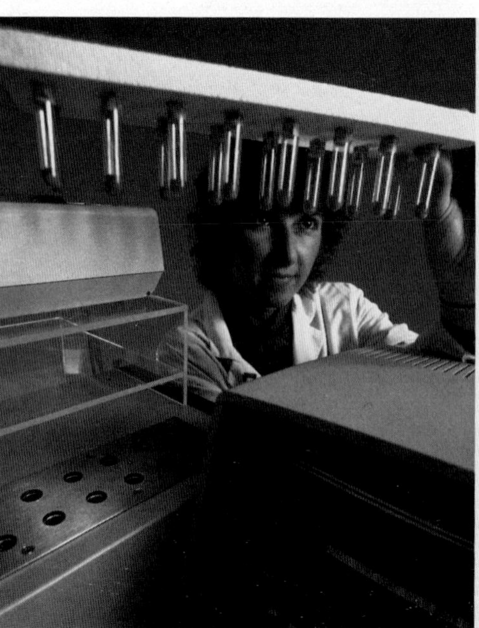

A Squibb researcher tests a new generation counter-top gamma counter capable of simultaneously providing clinical information from 16 different patient samples.

17

432

PHOTOGRAPHER / PHOTOGRAPH:

430 Arthur Meyerson
431, 432 Mark Godfrey
433 Hansa Luftbild

DESIGNER / GESTALTER / MAQUETTISTE:

430 Chris Hill
431, 432 Ingo Scharrenbroich
433 Hans Versteeg

ART DIRECTOR / DIRECTEUR ARTISTIQUE:

430 Chris Hill
431, 432 Arnold Saks
433 Hans Versteeg

AGENCY / AGENTUR / AGENCE – STUDIO:

430 Hill Design
431, 432 Arnold Saks Associates
433 Dots Design

430 Complete cover of a promotional booklet on the Houston construction company *Harvey*. Yellow crane against blue sky. (USA)
431, 432 Complete full-colour spreads from a promotional booklet on the research done by *Squibb*, a pharmaceuticals company. (USA)
433 Full-page aerial view in black and white (here, of railway tracks) from the series used in a promotional booklet by *Arsycom* to emphasize the planning that goes into its computerised systems. (NLD)

430 Vollständiger Umschlag der Firmenbroschüre eines Bauunternehmens in Houston. Gelbe Kräne vor blaugrauem Himmel. (USA)
431, 432 Doppelseiten mit Farbaufnahmen aus einer Firmenbroschüre des Pharmakonzerns *Squibb*, die der medizinischen Forschungsarbeit des Unternehmens gewidmet ist. (USA)
433 Eine von verschiedenen ganzseitigen Luftaufnahmen in Schwarzweiss aus der Firmenbroschüre von *Arsycom*, die verdeutlichen soll, wo Computer bei Planungen helfen können, hier zum Beispiel bei der Bahn. (NLD)

430 Couverture complète de la brochure de présentation d'un entreprise de construction de Houston. Grues jaunes, ciel bleu gris. (USA)
431, 432 Doubles pages illustrées de photos couleur dans une brochure du groupe pharmaceutique *Squibb* consacrée à la recherche médicale au sein du groupe. (USA)
433 L'une des vues aériennes pleine page en noir et blanc qui démontrent, dans une brochure *Arsycom*, l'utilité de l'ordinateur dans la planification et l'urbanisme, ici par l'exemple des chemins de fer. (NLD)

433

434

435

436

437

434, 435 Double spreads from the annual report of 1982 by GTE (when it officially shortened its name from General Telephone & Electronics Corp.) which show executives in work areas. (USA)
436, 437 Full-page colour shots in double spreads of *Annual Report Trends* by the S.D.Warren Company with descriptions of many annual reports. Fig. 437: An anti-echo chamber. (USA)
438, 439 Photograph in actual size and complete double spread from a GTE report which referred to its interconnect systems. (USA)

434, 435 Doppelseiten aus einem Jahresbericht der GTE, ein Unternehmen der Kommunikationstechnik. Die Farbaufnahmen zeigen Mitarbeiter und ihren Arbeitsbereich. (USA)
436, 437 Ganzseitige Farbaufnahmen aus verschiedenen Jahresberichten, einer Publikation über beispielhafte Gestaltung von Jahresberichten entnommen. Abb. 437: eine Anti-Echo-Testkammer. (USA)
438, 439 Aufnahme in Originalgrösse und vollständige Doppelseite aus einem Jahresbericht der GTE. Thema sind Überbrückungsteile und Verbindungen bei elektronischen Systemen. (USA)

434, 435 Doubles pages d'un rapport annuel de GTE (techniques de communications). (USA)
436, 437 Photos couleur pleine page illustrant divers rapports annuels dans un manuel enseignant l'art de produire de tels rapports. Fig. 437: chambre d'essai anti-échos. (USA)
438, 439 Photos au format original et double page complète d'un rapport annuel de GTE (cf. les fig. 434–435). Il s'agit d'éléments d'interconnexion pour systèmes électroniques. (USA)

Annual Reports
Jahresberichte
Rapports annuels

PHOTOGRAPHER / PHOTOGRAPH:

434, 435 Bruce Davidson
436 Ken Whitmore
437 Ted Polumbaum
438, 439 François Robert

DESIGNER / GESTALTER:

436, 437 Tom Laidlaw
438, 439 Gene Rosner

ART DIRECTOR:

434, 435 Leslie Smolan
436, 437 Michael Weymouth
438, 439 Gene Rosner

AGENCY / AGENTUR / AGENCE:

434, 435 Corporate Annual Reports, Inc.
436, 437 Weymouth Design, Inc.
438, 439 Brown & Rosner

438

439

PHOTOGRAPHER / PHOTOGRAPH / PHOTOGRAPHE:

440 Jay Maisel
442, 443 Le Lièvre
444 Burt Glinn/Magnum
445, 446 Gary Gladstone/Barry Rabinowitz

440

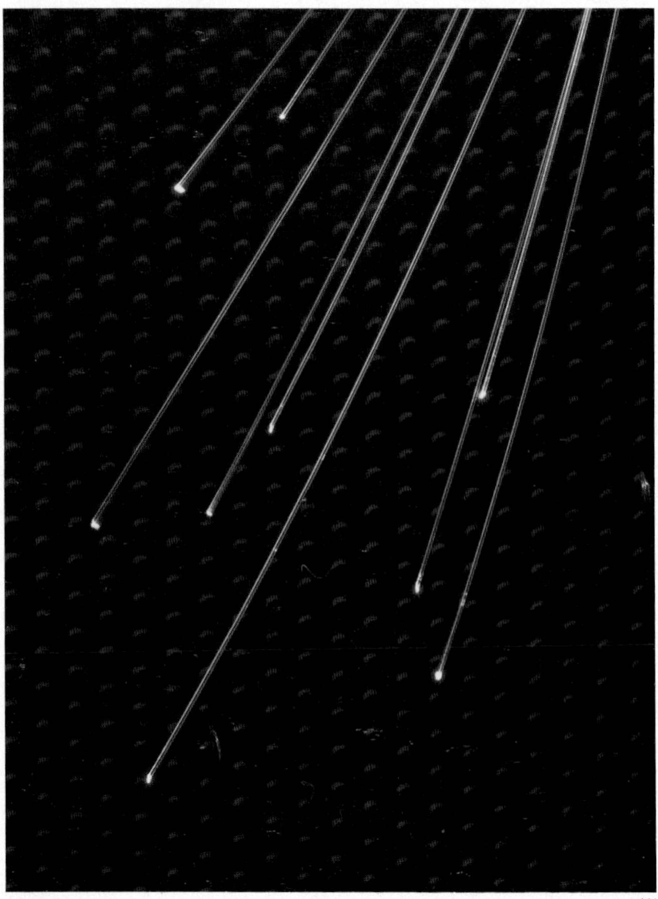

441

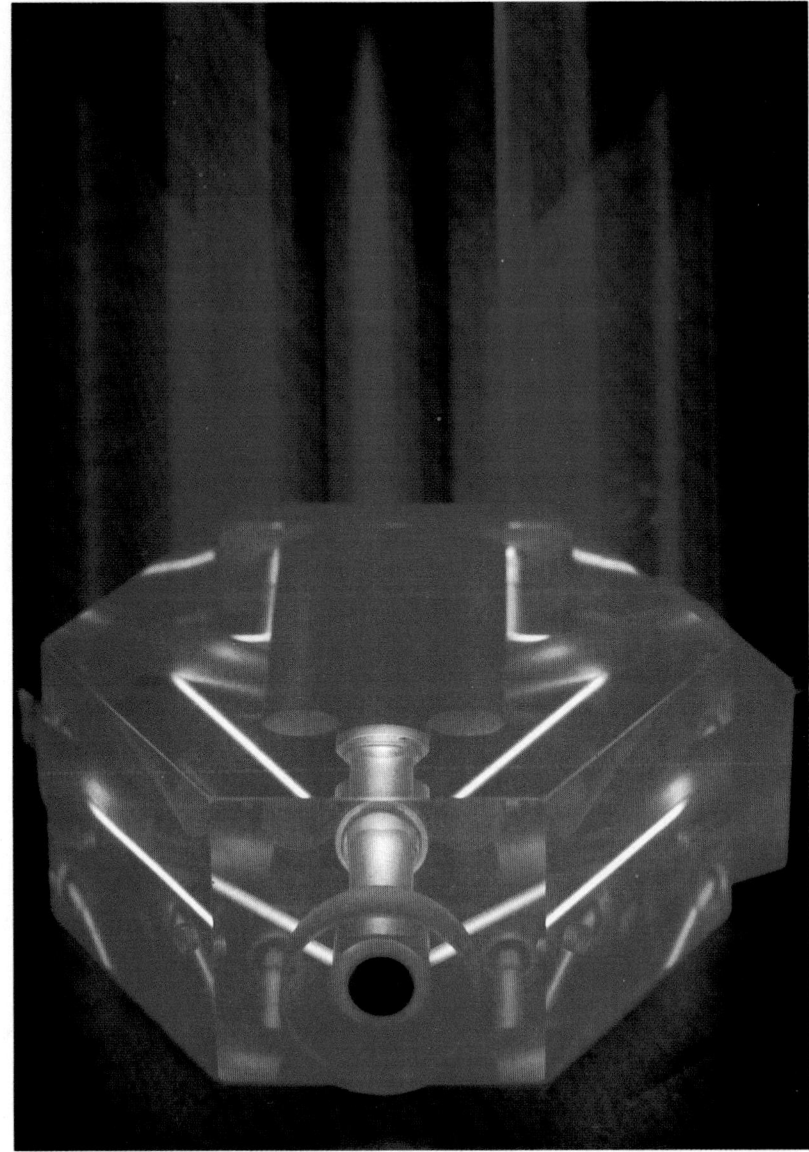

442

DESIGNER / GESTALTER / MAQUETTISTE:

442, 443 Michel Redon
444 John Laughlin
445, 446 Michelle Roberge

ART DIRECTOR / DIRECTEUR ARTISTIQUE:

440 Beverly Schrager
442, 443 André Paulet
444 Arnold Saks
445, 446 Leslie A. Segal/Beverly Schrager

440 Cover of an annual report by *Chesebrough-Pond's* on its diversified consumer markets. (USA)
441 From a report by *Northern Telecom*, manufacturer of electronic communication systems, showing optical fibres as the transmission media of the future. (USA)
442, 443 Full-page photograph and double spread from a promotional booklet by SFENA, manufacturer of aerial navigation systems. (FRA)
444 Double spread with snapshots of staff at work for investment consultants *Goldman Sachs*. (USA)
445, 446 Double spreads from a report by *Scovill*, producer of diversified consumer goods. (USA)

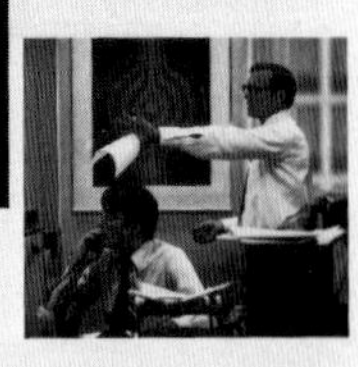

444

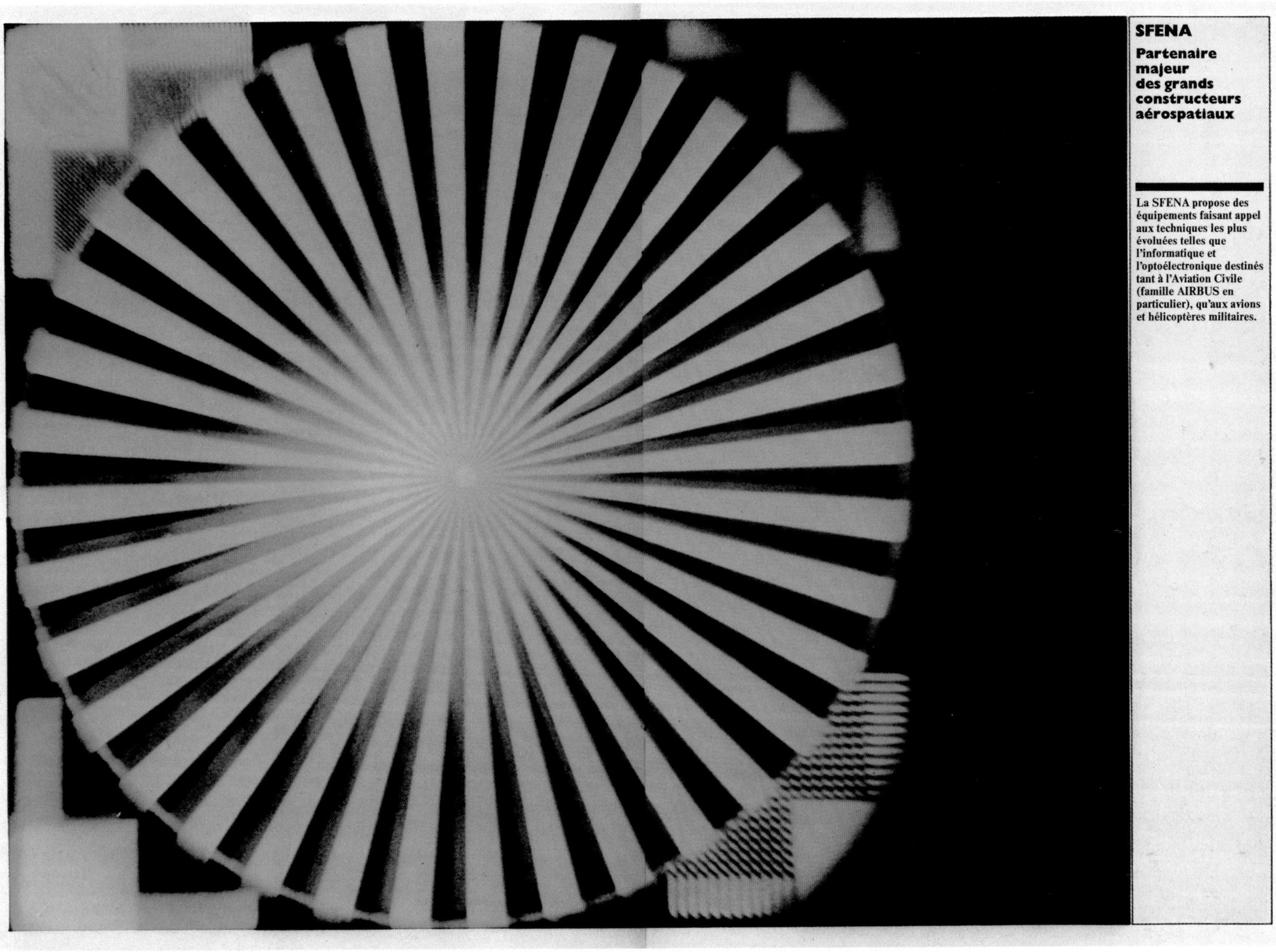

SFENA

Partenaire majeur des grands constructeurs aérospatiaux

La SFENA propose des équipements faisant appel aux techniques les plus évoluées telles que l'informatique et l'optoélectronique destinés tant à l'Aviation Civile (famille AIRBUS en particulier), qu'aux avions et hélicoptères militaires.

443

AGENCY / AGENTUR / AGENCE – STUDIO:

440, 445, 446 Corporate Annual Reports, Inc.
441 Cabana, Séguin Design Inc.
442, 443 Studio des Grands Augustins
444 Arnold Saks Associates

440 Umschlag des Jahresberichtes eines Unternehmens der Konsumgüterbranche. (USA)
441 Aufnahme aus einer Firmenbroschüre der *Northern Telecom*, Hersteller elektronischer Kommunikationssysteme; hier das Übermittlungs-Medium der Zukunft auf der Basis von Licht. (USA)
442, 443 Ganzseitige Aufnahme und Doppelseite aus einer Firmenbroschüre der SFENA, Hersteller von Navigations-Ausrüstungen für die Luftfahrt. (FRA)
444 Doppelseite mit Photos der Mitarbeiter. Jahresbericht einer Anlageberatungsfirma. (USA)
445, 446 Doppelseiten aus dem Jahresbericht eines Unternehmens der Konsumgüterbranche. (USA)

440 Couverture du rapport annuel d'un groupe diversifié dans les biens de consommation. (USA)
441 Photo illustrant une brochure d'entreprise de *Northern Telecom* (systèmes de communication électroniques). Il s'agit ici du moyen de transmission de l'avenir, les fibres optiques. (USA)
442, 443 Photo pleine page et double page d'une brochure de présentation de la SFENA, qui fabrique des équipements de navigation pour l'aéronautique. (FRA)
444 Double page illustrée d'instantanés du personnel d'une société d'investissements. (USA)
445, 446 Doubles pages du rapport annuel d'une entreprise de biens de consommation. (USA)

445

446

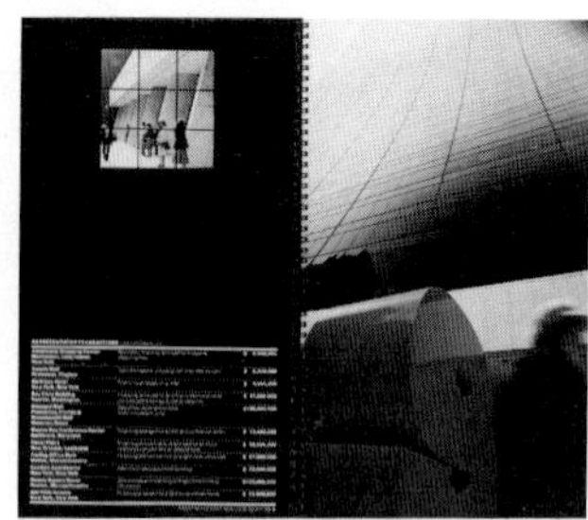

448

PHOTOGRAPHER / PHOTOGRAPH:

447, 448 Stan Ries/Cheryl Rossum
449 Thomas Höpker

DESIGNER / GESTALTER / MAQUETTISTE:

447, 448 Jonson Pedersen Hinrichs Shakery
449 Franz Merlicek

ART DIRECTOR / DIRECTEUR ARTISTIQUE:

447, 448 B. Martin Pedersen
449 Franz Merlicek

AGENCY / AGENTUR / AGENCE – STUDIO:

447, 448 Jonson Pedersen Hinrichs Shakery
449 Demner & Merlicek

447

447, 448 Photograph in actual size and complete double spread from a corporate borchure by *Sonnenblick-Goldman,* real-estate agents and financiers. The entire booklet is illustrated with colour photographs of New York buildings and their details—as here, at 9 West 57th Street. (USA)
449 Double spread with colour photograph from a promotional booklet on the Creditanstalt, Vienna, with information on the investment potentials in Austria. (AUT)

447, 448 Aufnahme in Originalgrösse und vollständige Doppelseite aus einer Unternehmensbroschüre der Firma *Sonnenblick-Goldman,* eine Immobilien- und Finanzierungsgesellschaft. Die ganze Broschüre ist mit Farbaufnahmen von New Yorker Gebäuden und Details davon illustriert; hier die Adresse 9 West 57th Street. (USA)
449 Doppelseite mit Farbaufnahme aus einer Unternehmensbroschüre der Creditanstalt, Wien, die über die Anlagemöglichkeiten in Österreich informiert. (AUT)

447, 448 Photo au format original et double page complète d'une brochure d'entreprise *Sonnenblick-Goldman,* une société immobilière et financière, illustrée de vues en couleur de buildings et détails d'immeubles newyorkais. On voit ici l'adresse 9 West 57th Street. (USA)
449 Double page avec photo couleur, dans une brochure de présentation de la Creditanstalt de Vienne renseignant notamment sur les possibilités d'investissement en Autriche. (AUT)

Corporate Publications
Firmenpublikationen
Publications d'entreprise

"Careful learning of the lessons of history has brought Austria to the state of prosperity which she currently enjoys."

(International Currency Review, No. 6 Vol. 12/ December 1980)

20

21

449

450

Corporate Publications
Firmenpublikationen
Publications d'entreprise

PHOTOGRAPHER / PHOTOGRAPH / PHOTOGRAPHE:

450, 453, 454 Tom Vack
451, 452 John Hill/Fred Ohringer

DESIGNER / GESTALTER / MAQUETTISTE:

450, 453, 454 Paul Bussman
451, 452 Diana Graham

Project Financing and Financial Systems

Richard L. Fisher

"We have an unusual degree of financial sophistication. But the most important factor in our work is the freedom that comes with financial strength."

Project financing and overall asset management for Fisher Brothers are the responsibilities of Richard L. Fisher, Chief Financial Officer for the firm. From initial estimates of project costs to long-term projections of return on investment capital, he provides Fisher Brothers with the experience demanded by the volatile real estate and financial markets.

In coordination with Fisher Brothers' project-initiation team and the firm's own construction company, Mr. Fisher and a staff of financial analysts prepare detailed studies on construction budgets, buy-outs and other expenses related to project development. In tandem with these projections, estimates are formulated for rental levels required to meet expenditures and the cost of financing, while still providing for an adequate return on the project. Once precise financial requirements have been determined, a coordinated effort is launched in the capital markets to arrange construction financing, permanent mortgage financing and lines of credit on terms favorable to successful project completion. In doing so, Fisher Brothers relies on an extensive range of working relationships with banks, mortgage and insurance companies and other major financial institutions. After construction has commenced, a fully computerized cost-accounting system custom-developed by Fisher Brothers continuously monitors project budgets as compared with actual expenditures.

Beyond the specific financial needs of new developments, Fisher Brothers' own material financial position has enabled the firm to develop a special expertise in the areas of asset management and money-market operations. The same levels of sophistication and experience that are employed on behalf of Fisher Brothers' substantial liquid and property assets are also utilized for each of the projects it undertakes, principally in the development of forecasting models that measure long-term trends in costs, profit performance and asset valuation.

Fisher Brothers' IBM 38 computer system continuously monitors construction and operating budgets

Bankers Trust Plaza

451

452

453

ART DIRECTOR / DIRECTEUR ARTISTIQUE:

450, 453, 454 Paul Bussman
451, 452 Diana Graham

AGENCY / AGENTUR / AGENCE – STUDIO:

450, 453, 454 Burson-Marsteller
451, 452 Gips & Balkind & Associates

450, 453, 454 Double spreads from a corporate brochure on *MCC Powers,* manufacturer of control systems for power supplies in buildings. Fig. 450: Photograph in shades of green, with details of the systems' suitability for use in new buildings, and their adaptability to existing ones; Fig. 453: Here the theme is flexibility and careful workmanship; Fig. 454: Staff know-how was the subject visualized here. (USA)

451, 452 Double spread with full-colour photograph and the introductory illustration to a promotional booklet on *Fisher Brothers,* a company specializing in planning, building and managing of high-rise blocks for office accomodation (a 30-year total of more than 8 million square feet). Fig. 451 shows one of their New York buildings. (USA)

450, 453, 454 Doppelseiten aus einer Unternehmensbroschüre für *MCC Powers,* Hersteller von Energie-Kontrollsystemen für Gebäude. Abb. 450: Aufnahme in Grüntönen, mit Hinweis auf die Eignung der Kontrollsysteme für den Einsatz in Neubauten sowie für die Anpassung an bestehende Gebäude; Abb. 453: Das Thema ist sorgfältige Bearbeitung und Flexibilität; Abb. 454: Darstellung der Sachverständigkeit des Personals. (USA)

451, 452 Doppelseite mit Farbaufnahme und Aufnahme als einleitende Illustration zu einer Firmenbroschüre für *Fisher Brothers,* eine Firma, die sich mit der Planung, dem Bau und der Verwaltung von Bürogebäuden befasst. Abb. 451 zeigt eines der Gebäude in New York. (USA)

450, 453, 454 Doubles pages d'une brochure de présentation de *MCC Powers,* producteur de systèmes de contrôle énergétique pour immeubles. Fig. 450: photo aux tons verts; le texte souligne l'adaptabilité des systèmes de contrôle aussi bien aux constructions existantes qu'aux constructions nouvelles. Fig. 453: le thème en est la personnalisation de la commande et les soins voués à son exécution. Fig. 454: compétence des collaborateurs de la firme. (USA)

451, 452 Double page avec photo couleur et photo en tête d'un texte dans une brochure de *Fisher Brothers,* entreprise spécialisée dans la conception, la construction et l'administration d'immeubles de bureaux. La fig. 451 représente l'un de ces immeubles à New York. (USA)

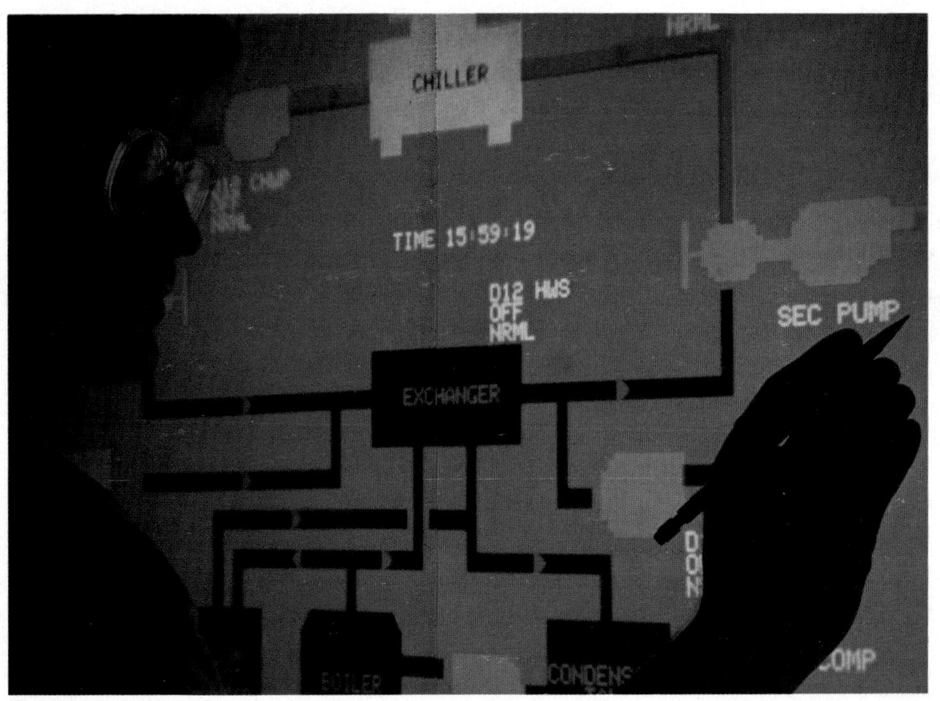

454

455

456

455–457 Complete cover and its photographs (in almost actual size here) from a promotional brochure for the architects Anshen + Allen of San Francisco. The cover photograph in Fig. 456 was taken at the Lawrence Memorial Hall of Science in Berkeley, Fig. 457—as an example of remarkable renovation—inside the U. S. Court of Appeals, San Francisco. (USA)

455–457 Vollständiger Umschlag und Aufnahmen (ca. Originalgrösse) für eine Firmenbroschüre der Architekten Anshen + Allen. Die Umschlagaufnahme in Abb. 456 zeigt die Lawrence Memorial Hall of Science, Berkeley, die Aufnahme in Abb. 457 den U. S. Court of Appeals, San Francisco; letzteren als Beispiel für gelungene Renovation. (USA)

455–457 Couverture complète et photos approximativement grandeur nature pour une brochure de présentation du bureau d'architecture Anshen + Allen. L'illustration de couverture (fig. 456) représente le Lawrence Memorial Hall of Science de Berkeley, la photo de la fig. 457 la Cour d'appel fédérale (U. S. Court of Appeals) de San Francisco, un exemple réussi de rénovation immobilière. (USA)

PHOTOGRAPHER / PHOTOGRAPH:
455–457 Charly Franklin

DESIGNER / GESTALTER:
455–457 Michael Manwaring

ART DIRECTOR:
455–457 Michael Manwaring

AGENCY / AGENTUR / AGENCE:
455–457 The Office of Michael Manwaring

457

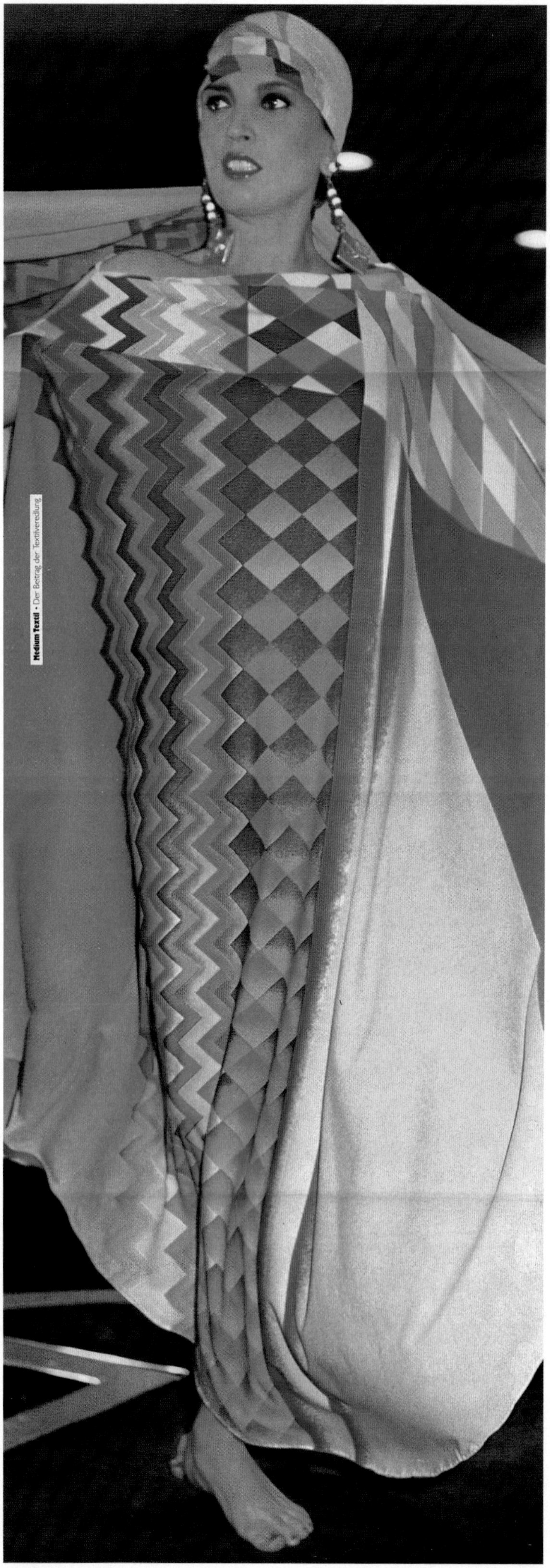

458

459

458, 459 Dust jacket—here, completely unfolded, and as used on the cover—of a promotional book published by the General Association of German Textile Industries (GdT). (GER)
460 Double spread from the GdT book (see Figs. 458, 459) with a full-page colour photograph to exemplify "Fashion in White". (GER)
461, 462 Photograph and complete double spread from a promotional brochure for the real-estate agency Edward S. Gordon. The double spread's theme is glass in architecture. (USA)
463 Double spread with full-colour photograph from a promotional brochure by a transport company. The explanatory text is given on the narrow inside page as shown here. (USA)

458, 459 Vollständig auseinandergefalteter Umschlag und Präsentation der Vorderseite für eine Image-Broschüre des Gesamtverbandes der deutschen Textilindustrie. (GER)
460 Doppelseite aus der Image-Broschüre der deutschen Textilindustrie (s. Abb. 458, 459), mit ganzseitiger Farbaufnahme als Beispiel für «Mode in Weiss». (GER)
461, 462 Aufnahme und vollständige Doppelseite aus einer Firmenbroschüre für Edward S. Gordon, ein Immobilienunternehmen. Glas in der Architektur ist das Thema dieser Doppelseite. (USA)
463 Doppelseite mit Farbaufnahme aus der Firmenbroschüre eines Speditionsunternehmens. Erklärender Text steht jeweils auf einer schmaleren Innenseite, wie hier gezeigt. (USA)

458, 459 Couverture entièrement dépliée et présentation de la première page de couverture d'une brochure de prestige de l'Union allemande des industriels du textile. (GER)
460 Double page d'une brochure de prestige de l'industrie textile allemande (cf. les fig. 458, 459), avec une photo couleur pleine page illustrant «la mode en blanc». (GER)
461, 462 Photo et double page complète d'une brochure de la société immobilière Edward S. Gordon. Le sujet de cette double page est l'utilisation du verre en architecture. (USA)
463 Double page illustrée en couleur, dans la brochure de présentation d'une maison d'expéditions. Le texte explicatif figure sur des pages intérieures plus étroites. (USA)

PHOTOGRAPHER / PHOTOGRAPH / PHOTOGRAPHE:

458, 459 Hans-J. Richter
460 Peter Lindbergh
461,462 Ernst Haas
463 Paul Fusco

DESIGNER / GESTALTER / MAQUETTISTE:

458–460 Uwe Lohrer
461, 462 Ivan Chermayeff/Steff Geissbuhler
463 Sidjakov Berman & Gomez

benötigt, bei denen die Textilveredlung etwa durch Heißsiegel-Ausrüstung Verarbeitungsvorteile für die Konfektion schafft. Und natürlich ist immer eine Vielfalt von Accessoires mit im modischen Spiel – wie Stoffknöpfe, Stoffgürtel, Litzen, Tressen, Biesen, Borten, Reißverschlüsse, Nähseide. Alles braucht Textilveredlung.

Es versteht sich, daß Mode auch immer die inneren Werte moderner Bekleidung mitbringen soll, die das gute Gefühl, gut angezogen zu sein, erst vollkommen machen: Sie soll bei Hitze und Kälte eine angenehme Körpertemperatur gewährleisten, etwa durch Wärmerückhaltevermögen und Luftdurchlässigkeit. Sie soll die vom Körper abgegebene Feuchtigkeit schnell nach außen transportieren. Sie darf nicht empfindlich sein gegen Einflüsse wie Licht, Wasser, Schmutz und Flecken. Sie muß pflegeleicht sein, zum Beispiel durch eine Wash-and-wear-Ausrüstung. Tragekomfort, Gebrauchstüchtigkeit und modischer Chic – die besonderen Leistungen der Textilveredlung werden auf allen Seiten sichtbar und spürbar.

Professor René König – Autor von Büchern über das Phänomen Mode – stellt fest, sie sei »zu einem der wesentlichsten Medien für die Selbstgestaltung der großen Massen geworden«. Aus dieser modernen Funktion der Mode ist allen, die in der europäischen Textilindustrie zusammenwirken – vom Faserhersteller bis zum Konfektionär – eine anspruchsvolle Aufgabe erwachsen. Weil sie im schnellen Rhythmus ihrer Zeit lebt, weil sie eine fast unendliche Bandbreite textiler Gestaltungsformen ermöglicht, trägt die Textilveredlung entscheidend dazu bei, das starke Bedürfnis nach Mode zu erfüllen. *Durch Mode kann der Mensch auch in Zukunft einer nicht immer erfreulichen Welt eine sehr schöne Seite abgewinnen.*

460

461

ART DIRECTOR / DIRECTEUR ARTISTIQUE:

458–460 Uwe Lohrer
461, 462 Ivan Chermayeff/Steff Geissbuhler
463 Jerry Berman/Jerry Leonhart

AGENCY / AGENTUR / AGENCE – STUDIO:

458–460 PS-Marketing Kurt F. Steiner
461, 462 Chermayeff & Geismar Assoc.
463 Burger Felix & Wood

462

463

4

Calendars

Record Covers

Kalender

Schallplatten-Umschläge

Calendriers

Pochettes de disques

PHOTOGRAPHER / PHOTOGRAPH / PHOTOGRAPHE:

464, 465 Otto Kasper
466 Gregory Heisler
467, 467a David Burnett

DESIGNER / GESTALTER / MAQUETTISTE:

464, 465 Joseph Pölzelbauer
466–467a Steve Orant

ART DIRECTOR / DIRECTEUR ARTISTIQUE:

464, 465 Joseph Pölzelbauer
466–467a Leslie Smolan

AGENCY / AGENTUR / AGENCE – STUDIO:

466–467a Gottschalk & Ash Int'l

464, 465 Air space, in German, is "air room"—the theme of these sheets visualized by Joseph Pölzelbauer and photographer Otto Kasper. Fig. 464: Air as a cause of movement; Fig. 465: Air as a force. The calendar, entitled "Air is Life", was published by the pharmaceuticals company Byk Gulden. (GER)
466–467a From the calendar "A Day in the Life of Australia" (first in a planned series with photographs from the book of that title). Fig. 466: A young mineworker; Figs. 467, 467a: A detail of Ayer's Rock and complete front sheet. (AUS)

464, 465 Kalenderblätter mit «Lufträumen», visualisiert von Joseph Pölzelbauer und dem Photographen Otto Kasper. Abb. 464: Luft, die Bewegung schafft; Abb. 465: Luft, die Kraft beweist. Titel des Kalenders für Byk Gulden: «Luft ist Leben.» (GER)
466–467a «Ein Tag im Leben von Australien» lautet das Thema dieses Kalenders. Geplant ist eine jährliche Ausgabe mit Photographien aus dem gleichnamigen Buch. Abb. 466: Junger Minenarbeiter auf dem Februar-Blatt 1983: Abb. 467, 467a; Detailaufnahme des Ayer Rock und vollständige Kalendervorderseite. (AUS)

464, 465 Feuillets de calendrier comportant des «espaces aériens» visualisés par Joseph Pölzelbauer et le photographe Otto Kasper. Fig. 464: l'air qui crée le mouvement; 465: l'air qui démontre la puissance. Calendrier «L'air, c'est la vie» pour Byk Gulden. (GER)
466–467a «Une journée dans la vie de l'Australie». C'est ainsi que s'intitule ce calendrier illustré de photos tirées du livre du même nom, qui doit encore fournir la matière d'autres calendriers annuels. Fig. 466: jeune mineur, feuillet de février 1983; 467, 467a: détail d'Ayer Rock et recto complet du calendrier. (AUS)

464

465

466

467a

467

468

469

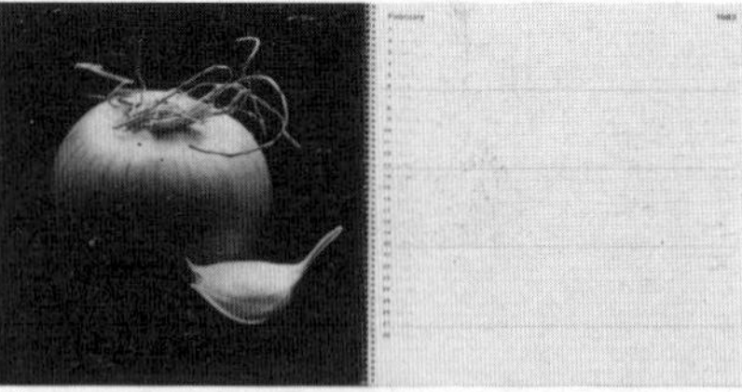

470

471

PHOTOGRAPHER / PHOTOGRAPH / PHOTOGRAPHE:

468–470 Arthur Beck
471, 472 Christian Küenzi

DESIGNER / GESTALTER / MAQUETTISTE:

468–470 Roger Cook/Don Shanosky
471, 472 Christian Küenzi

ART DIRECTOR / DIRECTEUR ARTISTIQUE:

468–470 Roger Cook/Don Shanosky
471, 472 Christian Küenzi

AGENCY / AGENTUR / AGENCE – STUDIO:

468–470 Cook & Shanosky Assoc., Inc.
471,472 Heller, Stillhard, Brönnimann AG

468–470 Photographs and complete double-spread from a table-top diary published by the printers *S. D. Scott* showing still lifes with fruits and vegetables. (USA)
471, 472 Complete sheet and photographic detail of a wall calendar for *Sycotronic* on the subject of light and its colours. As it has shorter light waves, violet shows up more intensely than red in the spectral colours of white light when—as here—it is refracted by a prism. (SWI)

468–470 Aufnahmen und eine Doppelseite aus einer Tischagenda der Druckerei *S. D. Scott*, mit Stilleben von Früchten und Gemüsen. (USA)
471, 472 Vollständiges Blatt und Detail der Aufnahme aus einem Wandkalender für *Sycotronic*. Das Thema ist Licht / Lichtfarben; hier ein Prisma, das aufgrund der unterschiedlichen Brechung der verschiedenen Wellenlängen weisses Licht in die Spektralfarben zerlegt. Dabei wird violettes Licht, wegen seiner kürzeren Wellenlänge, stärker gebrochen als rotes Licht. (SWI)

468–470 Photos et une double page d'un agenda de bureau de l'imprimerie *S. D. Scott*: natures mortes de fruits et légumes. (USA)
471, 472 Feuillet complet et détail de la photo d'un calendrier mural pour *Sycotronic*. Le thème en est la lumière et les couleurs du prisme. On voit ici un prisme décomposant la lumière blanche en rayons lumineux de couleur différente selon les différents indices de réfraction. Du fait de sa longueur d'onde plus courte, la lumière violette subit une réfraction plus forte que la rouge. (SWI)

472

473

474

475

Calendars / Kalender / Calendries

PHOTOGRAPHER / PHOTOGRAPH / PHOTOGRAPHE:

473, 477 Christina Herzberger
474, 475 Horst F. Neumann
476 Andreas Schirmer

DESIGNER / GESTALTER / MAQUETTISTE:

473–477 Klaus Winterhager

473–477 Five motifs from a German calendar, winner of a 1983 *Kodak* award for colour photography. Both the calendar and its theme, "Administration", were suggested by a chief administrator in Nordrhein-Westfalen—its Minister of Science and Research—to students of graphic design at Wuppertal University. They responded with a total of 58 motifs, all of which were reproduced in various sizes. (GER)

473–477 Fünf Motive aus einem anlässlich des *Kodak*-Farbphoto-Kalender-Wettbewerbs 1983 ausgezeichneten Kalenders. Der Minister für Wissenschaft und Forschung des Landes Nordrhein-Westfalen bat Graphik-Design-Studenten der Universität-Gesamthochschule Wuppertal um die Gestaltung dieses Kalenders zum Thema Verwaltung. Das Resultat waren 58 Motive, die alle im Kalender reproduziert sind, entweder als ganze Blätter oder in kleinerem Format. (GER)

473–477 Cinq motifs d'un calendrier primé lors du concours *Kodak* du meilleur calendrier photo couleur 1983. Le ministre de la Science et de la Recherche du Land allemand de Rhéanie-du-Nord-Westphalie avait demandé aux étudiants d'art graphique de l'Université de Wuppertal de créer ce calendrier sur le thème de l'administration. Il en résulta 58 motifs qui furent tous reproduits dans le calendrier sous forme de feuillets ou dans un format plus réduit. (GER)

476

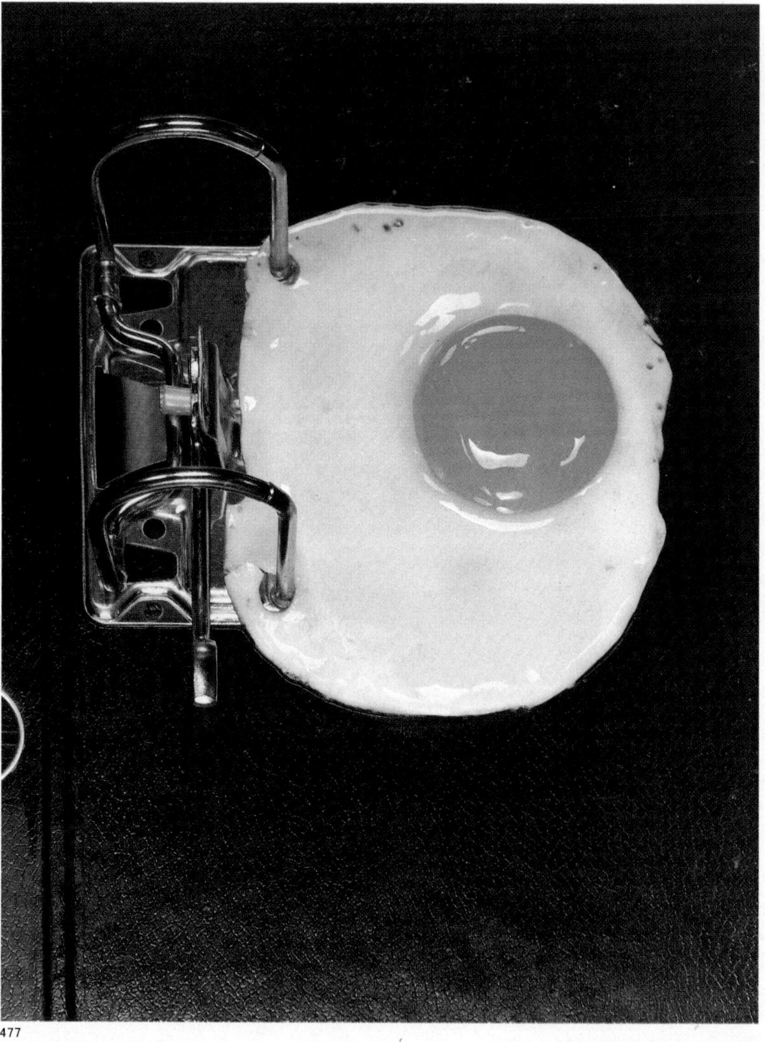

477

PHOTOGRAPHER / PHOTOGRAPH / PHOTOGRAPHE:

478 Yoshikatsu Shirakawa
479, 480 Maximilian Bruggmann

ART DIRECTOR / DIRECTEUR ARTISTIQUE:

478–480 Emil Schulthess

478

478–480 Details of the photography and a complete sheet from the 1983 *Swissair* calendar. Fig. 478: In Egypt, at the Pyramids of Giseh near Cairo, the setting sun is caught between the Cheops and Chephren pyramids (right to left), ca. 2550–2450 BC. Fig. 479: In Africa, the dunes of Temet, Niger. In front of the Massif de l'Aïr, the desert winds have swept up a range of sickle-shaped dunes. (SWI)

478–480 Aufnahmen und vollständiges Blatt aus dem Kalender 1983 der schweizerischen Luftverkehrsgesellschaft *Swissair.* Abb. 478: Sonnenuntergang zwischen den Pyramiden von Giseh bei Kairo, Aegypten. Rechts die Cheops-, links die Chephrenpyramide (ca. 2550–2450 v. Chr.). Abb. 479: Dünen von Temet, Niger, Afrika. Im Hintergrund das Massif de l'Aïr, vorne durch den Wind gehäufte Sicheldünen, die ein neues «Gebirge» gestalten. (SWI)

478–480 Photos et feuillet complet du calendrier pour 1983 de la compagnie aérienne suisse *Swissair.* Fig. 478: coucher de soleil entre les pyramides de Gizeh près du Caire (Egypte). A droite la pyramide de Kheops, à gauche celle de Khephren (vers 2550–2450 av. J.-C.). Fig. 479: dunes de Temet, au Niger, Afrique. Au fond, le massif de l'Aïr, au premier plan, des dunes en forme de faucille édifiées par le vent et entremêlées jusqu'à former une nouvelle «montagne». (SWI)

479

480

481

482

PHOTOGRAPHER / PHOTOGRAPH / PHOTOGRAPHE:

481–484 Albrecht Brugger

DESIGNER / GESTALTER / MAQUETTISTE:

481–484 CeveyKeller

ART DIRECTOR / DIRECTEUR ARTISTIQUE:

481–484 G.O. Hübner

AGENCY / AGENTUR / AGENCE – STUDIO:

481–484 CeveyKeller

483

Calendars
Kalender
Calendriers

481–484 Samples of the aerial photography used in a wall calendar for the Südwestbank, Stuttgart. Fig. 481: "The Love-sick Farmer", as motif for the front sheet; Fig. 482: "Field Paths near Engstingen", motif for the April sheet; Figs. 483, 484: "Harvesting Grain near Korntal-Münchingen"—complete sheet for August and photographic detail. (GER)

481–484 Aus einem Wandkalender mit Luftaufnahmen für die Südwestbank, Stuttgart. Abb. 481: "Der verliebte Bauer" als Motiv für die Vorderseite; Abb. 482: "Feldwege bei Engstingen", Aufnahme für das April-Blatt; Abb. 483, 484: «Getreideernte bei Korntal-Münchingen», vollständiges August-Blatt und Detail der Aufnahme. (GER)

481–484 Calendrier mural illustré de vues aériennes pour la Südwestbank de Stuttgart. Fig. 481: «le paysan amoureux», motif du recto; fig. 482: «chemins vicinaux près d'Engstingen», photo pour le feuillet d'avril; fig. 483, 484: «moisson près de Korntal-Münchingen», feuillet complet du mois d'août et détail de la photo. (GER)

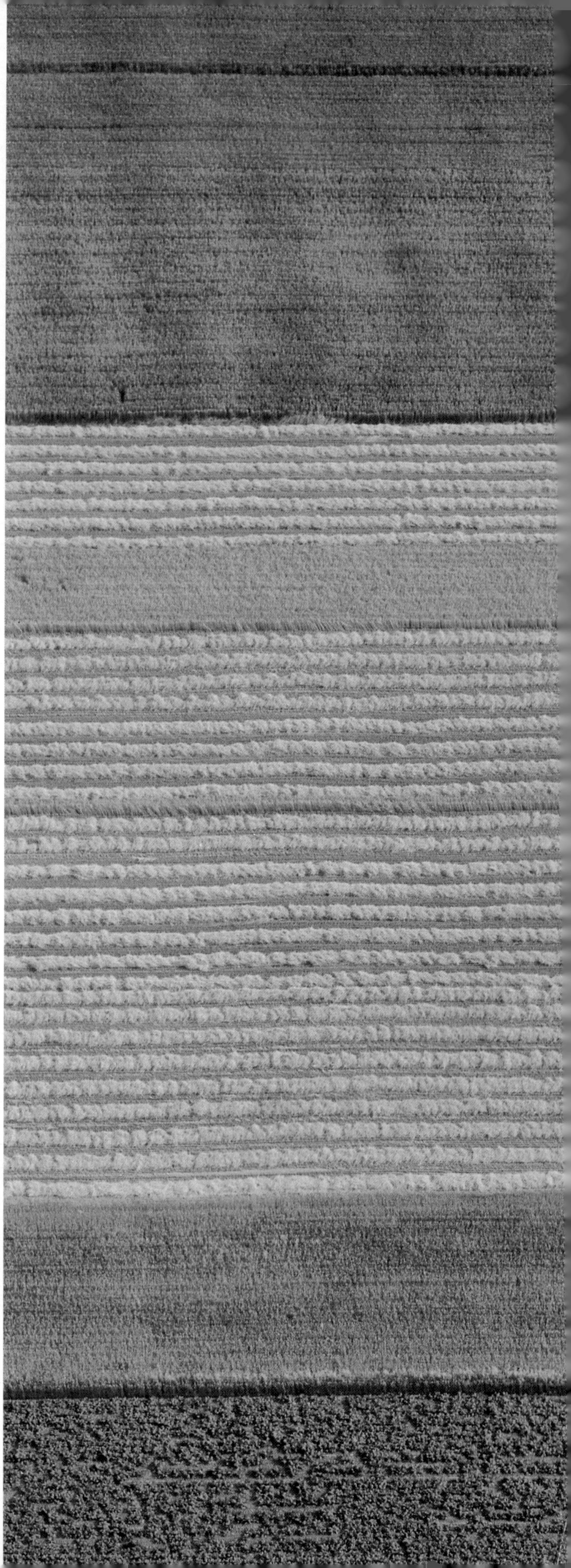

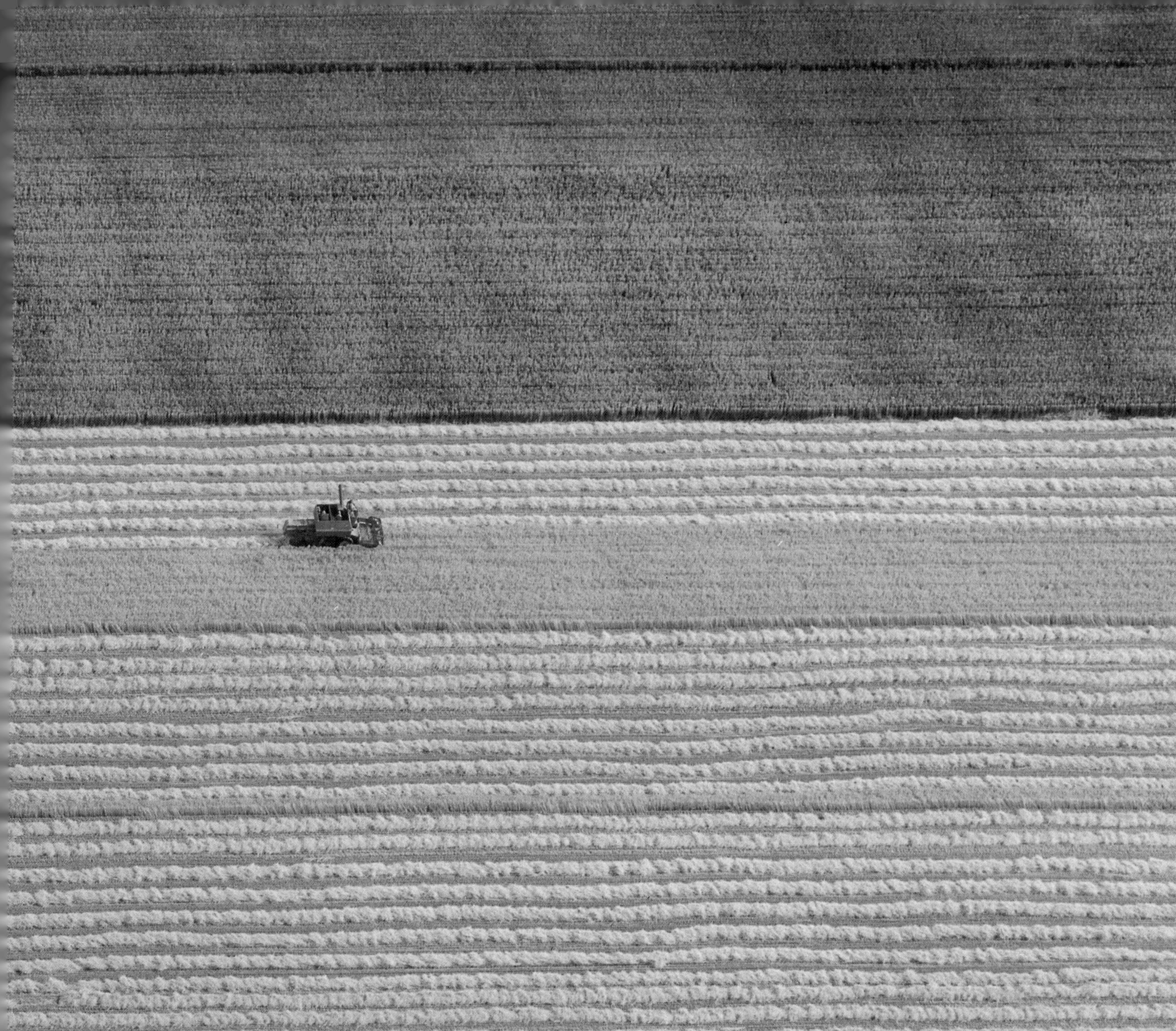

PHOTOGRAPHER / PHOTOGRAPH / PHOTOGRAPHE:

485 Hideki Fujii
486 Otto Hoernisch

DESIGNER / GESTALTER / MAQUETTISTE:

495 William Wilkens
486 Carl Zeiss/Werbeabt.

AGENCY / AGENTUR / AGENCE – STUDIO:

486 Carl Zeiss/Werbeabt.

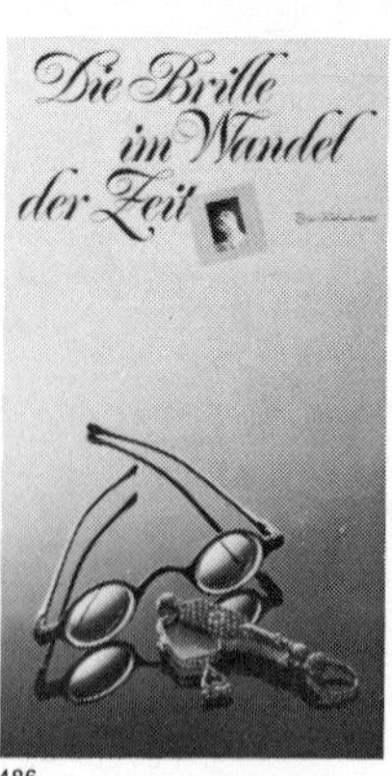

486

485 From a calendar issued by the Olympus Optical Co., Hamburg. The photograph was taken by Hideki Fujii, whose work is rooted in the Japanese tradition. (GER)
486 Cover and photograph from a *Zeiss* calendar about glasses through the ages. The full-page reproduction shows glasses as used by Chinese mandarins, who banned their use by the common people. (GER)

485 Aufnahme aus einem Kalender der Olympus Optical Co., Hamburg. Der Photograph Hideki Fujii ist stark mit der japanischen Tradition verbunden. (GER)
486 Umschlag und Aufnahme aus einem *Zeiss*-Kalender mit dem Titel «Die Brille im Wandel der Zeit». Das grosse Bild zeigt eine chinesische Brille, Symbol des Gebildeten. (GER)

485 Photo pour un calendrier de l'Olympus Optical Co. de Hambourg. Le photographe Hideki Fujii est fortement imprégné de la tradition japonaise. (GER)
486 Couverture et photo du calendrier *Zeiss* publié sous le titre «Les lunettes au cours des âges». La grande photo montre des lunettes chinoises, symbole du lettré. (GER)

485

487

PHOTOGRAPHER:

487 Giorgio Balmelli
488–492 Terry Heffernan/
Light Language

DESIGNER / GESTALTER:

487 Urs Bachmann
488–492 Kit Hinrichs/Nancy Koc

ART DIRECTOR:

487 Peter Linsin
488–492 Kit Hinrichs

AGENCY / AGENTUR:

487 Directa
488–492 Jonson Pedersen
Hinrichs & Shakery

487 Sheet for three months from a calendar by photographer Giorgio Balmelli. (SWI)
488–492 Full-colour motifs from a calendar published by *American President Lines*. Figs. 488, 491: Complete sheet and photographic detail on the subject of shipping perishable goods; Figs. 489, 490: Complete sheet and photographic detail; Fig. 492: Photographic detail of one of the heavy-duty multi-strand synthetic ropes used by its ships. (USA)

487 Dreimonats-Blatt aus einem Kalender des Photographen Giorgio Balmelli. (SWI)
488–492 Mehrfarbige Motive aus einem Kalender der *American President Lines*. Abb. 488, 491: Vollständiges Blatt und Aufnahme, die sich auf die Verschiffung verderblicher Lebensmittel bezieht; Abb. 489, 490: Vollständiges Umschlagblatt und Detail der Aufnahme; Abb. 492: Aufnahme der synthetischen Hochleistungstaue, die diese Reederei verwendet. (USA)

487 Feuillet trimestriel d'un calendrier du photographe Giorgio Balmelli. (SWI)
488–492 Motifs polychromes d'un calendrier des *American President Lines*. Fig. 488, 491: feuillet complet et photo montrant l'expédition de denrées alimentaires périssables; fig. 489, 490: couverture complète et détail de la photo; fig. 492: photo des cordages synthétiques très résistants employés par cet armateur. (USA)

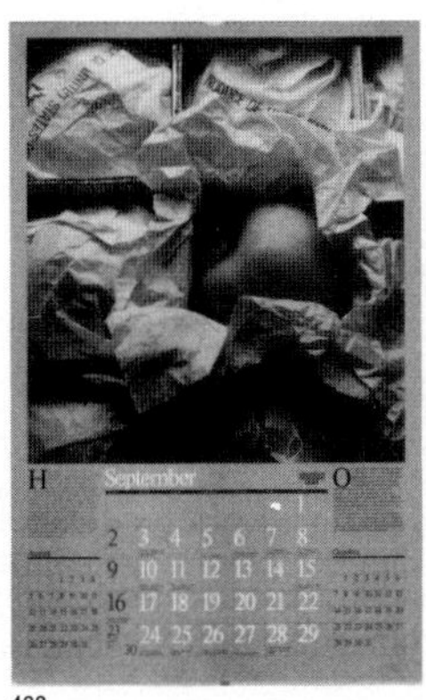

488

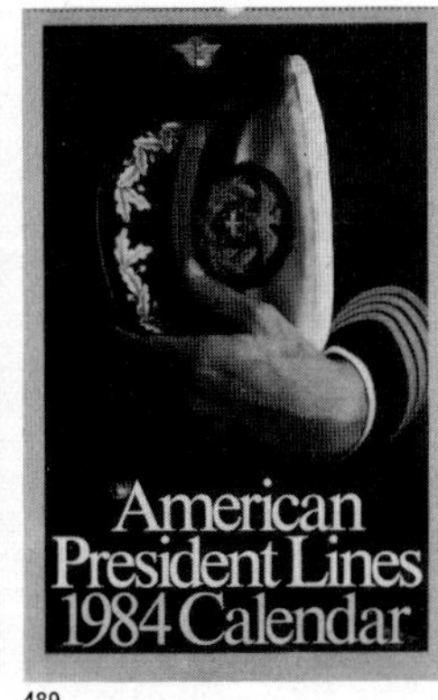

489

490

491

492

493, 494 Complete sheet and photographic detail from a 1983 calendar issued by *Brügmann*, a concern operating in the markets for wood and synthetic materials. (GER)
495–497 From a calendar that portrayed unique events humourously. Fig. 495: Participant with carrier-pigeon at annual show; Fig. 496: The world's most untalented opera diva; Fig. 497: A couple (after Grant Wood's "American Gothic") during national chewing-gum week. (USA)

493, 494 Vollständiges Blatt und Aufnahme aus dem 1983er-Kalender, herausgegeben von der im Holz- und Kunststoffbereich tätigen Unternehmensgruppe *Brügmann*. (GER)
495–497 Aus einem humoristischen Kalender mit eigenartigen Anlässen. Abb. 495: Teilnehmer am jährlichen Brieftauben-Show-Weekend; Abb. 496: Der Welt unbegabteste Opernsängerin; Abb. 497: Paar (nach Grant Woods Bild «Amerikanische Gothik») während einer Kaugummiwoche. (USA)

493, 494 Feuillet complet et photo du calendrier pour 1983 du groupe d'entreprises *Brügmann* dont les activités se situent dans les domaines du bois et des matières plastiques. (GER)
495–497 Calendrier satirique aux illustrations insolites. Fig. 495: participant au week-end annuel de présentation des pigeons voyageurs; fig. 496: la cantatrice d'opéra la moins douée du monde; fig. 497: couple évoquant Grant Wood lors de la semaine nationale du chewing-gum. (USA)

Calendars

PHOTOGRAPHER / PHOTOGRAPH:

493, 494 Siegfried Himmer
495–497 Larry Kunkel/Hillary Turner

DESIGNER / GESTALTER:

493, 494 Klaus Winterhager
495–497 Joseph Rozon

ART DIRECTOR:

493, 494 Siegfried Himmer
495–497 Joseph Rozon

AGENCY / AGENTUR / AGENCE:

495–497 VICOM Associates

493

494

495

496

497

498

PHOTOGRAPHER / PHOTOGRAPH:

498–501 Miker Chesser

DESIGNER / GESTALTER / MAQUETTISTE:

498–501 Peter Sargent

ART DIRECTOR / DIRECTEUR ARTISTIQUE:

498–501 Keith Bright/Peter Sargent

AGENCY / AGENTUR / AGENCE – STUDIO:

498–501 Bright & Associates

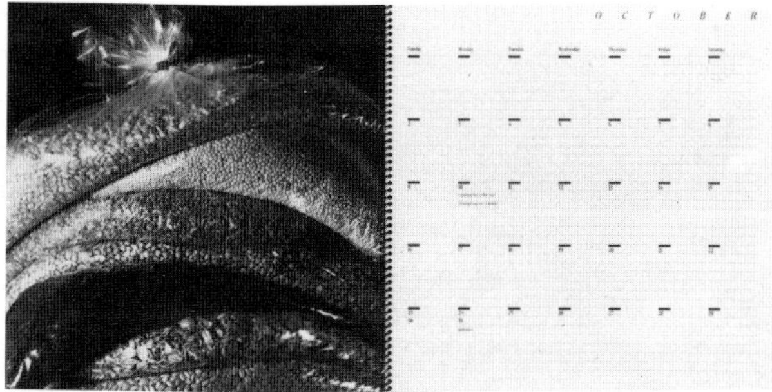

499

498–501 Colour sheets and a double spread from the 1983 table-top calendar of the Saga Corporation, California. It used twelve striking photographs of basic foods to illustrate its theme: proper nourishment. (USA)
502 Front cover of a *Lucra* desk diary. (NLD)

498–501 Farbseiten und eine Doppelseite aus dem Tischkalender 1983 der kalifornischen Saga Corporation. Thema ist die Bedeutung richtiger Ernährung. Es wurden zwölf wirkungsvolle Aufnahmen von wichtigen Grundnahrungsmitteln verwendet. (USA)
502 Vorderseite des Umschlags einer *Lucra*-Tischagenda. (NLD)

498–501 Pages couleur et double page du calendrier de table de la Saga Corporation de Californie pour 1983, sur le thème de l'alimentation correcte. Ce calendrier est illustré de douze photos saisissantes d'aliments de base essentiels. (USA)
502 Première page de couverture d'un agenda de bureau *Lucra*. (NLD)

502

500

501

504

Calendars
Kalender
Calendriers

506

PHOTOGRAPHER / PHOTOGRAPH:

504 Claes Westlin
505–508 Gert Wagner

DESIGNER / GESTALTER / MAQUETTISTE:

505–508 Michael Stahl

ART DIRECTOR / DIRECTEUR ARTISTIQUE:

504 Tord Elfwendahl
505–508 Michael Stahl

AGENCY / AGENTUR / AGENCE – STUDIO:

504 Ogilvy & Mather
505–508 Hopf & Stahl

504 Three-month sheet from an *Allmänna Brand* calendar with colour shots of old-timers. (SWE)
505–508 Three of twelve shots and a complete sheet from BMW Classics, the calendar that won an award for colour photography in the 1983 *Kodak* calendar competition. Fig. 505: shows a 1961 four-cylinder BMW 1500 (car in beige, white balloons, blue ground); Figs 506, 507: a 1937 six-cylinder 328 Sport; Fig. 508: a 1934 six cylinder 319/1 model. (GER)

504 Dreimonatsblatt aus einem Wandkalender mit Farbaufnahmen von Oldtimers von *Allmänna Brand*. (SWE)
505–508 Drei von zwölf Aufnahmen und ein komplettes Blatt aus dem BMW Classic-Kalender, der beim *Kodak*-Farbphoto-Kalender-Wettbewerb 1983 ausgezeichnet wurde. Hier ein 4-Zylinder BMW 1500, 1961, (Abb. 505) mit weissen Ballonen, blauem Hintergrund und beigefarbenem Wagen, ein 6-Zylinder 328 Sport von 1937 (Abb. 506, 507) und ein 6-Zylinder 319/1, 1934 (Abb. 508). (GER)

504 Feuillet trimestriel d'un calendrier mural *Allmänna Brand* en couleur: vieilles voitures. (SWE)
505–508 Trois des douze photos et feuillet complet du calendrier BMW Classic primé lors du concours *Kodak* du meilleur calendrier photo couleur 1983: 4-cylindres BMW 1500 de 1961 (fig. 505) avec ballons blancs, fond bleu et voiture beige; 6-cylindres 328 sport de 1937 (fig. 506, 507); 6-cylindres 319/1 de 1934 (fig. 508). (GER)

505

507

508

509

510

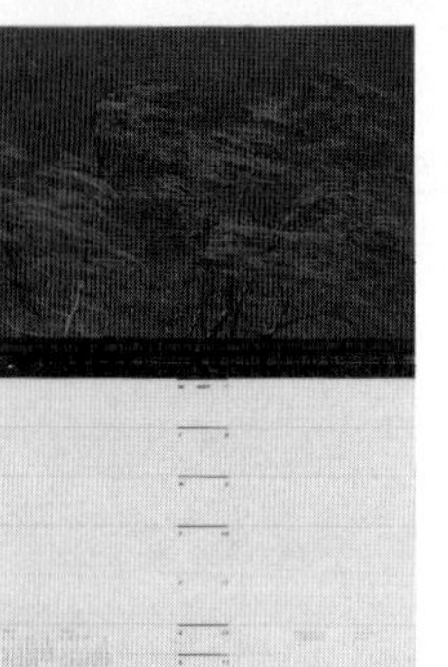
513

PHOTOGRAPHER / PHOTOGRAPH:

509, 513 Tom Kochel
510 Craig Aurness
511 Greg Pease
512 Martin Rogers
514, 515 Tommy Ewasko
516 Balfour Walker

DESIGNER / GESTALTER / MAQUETTISTE:

509–513 Jack Beveridge
514, 515 Glenn Kroepil/Warren Moeckel/ Marilyn Vancleave
516 Kurt Gibson

ART DIRECTOR / DIRECTEUR ARTISTIQUE:

509–513 Jack Beveridge
514, 515 Warren Moeckel
516 Kurt Gibson

AGENCY / AGENTUR / AGENCE – STUDIO:

509–513 Beveridge & Associates Inc.
514, 515 Intergraphic Design Inc.
516 IBM Tucson Design Center

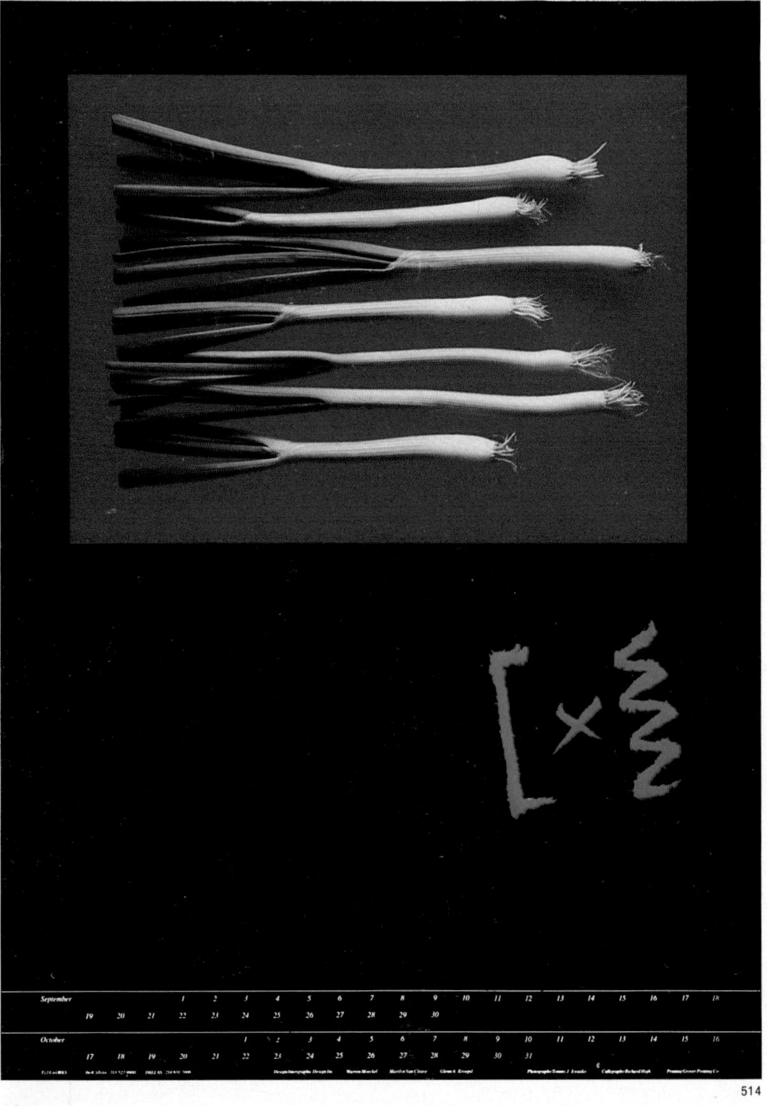
514

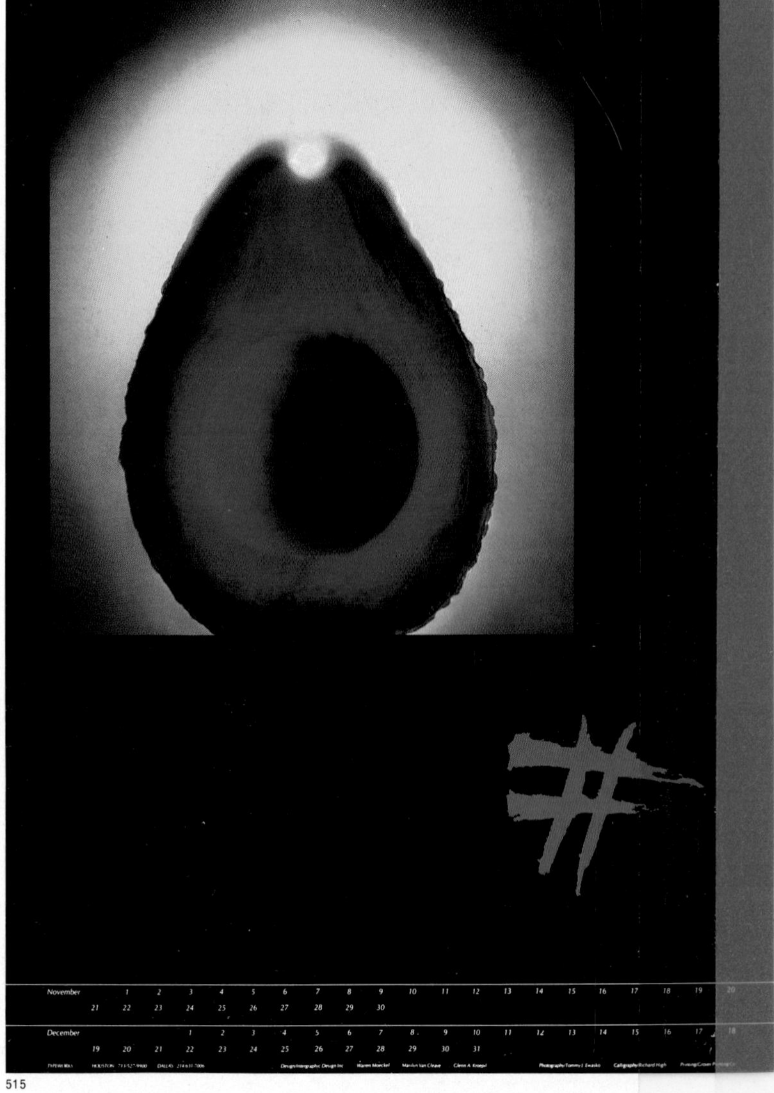
515

511

512

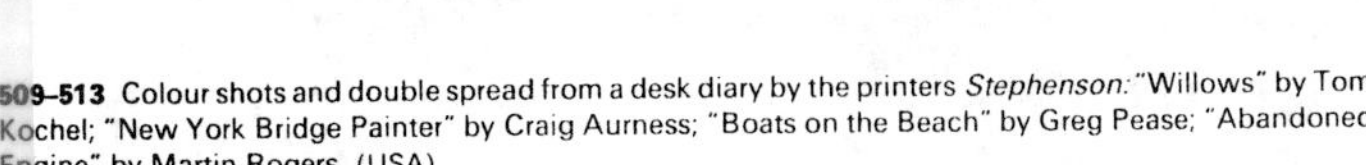

509–513 Colour shots and double spread from a desk diary by the printers *Stephenson:* "Willows" by Tom Kochel; "New York Bridge Painter" by Craig Aurness; "Boats on the Beach" by Greg Pease; "Abandoned Engine" by Martin Rogers. (USA)
514, 515 Two of six sheets from a calendar for Typeworks, Inc., in which each sheet consists of a graphic illustration of one of the marks made by proof-readers. (USA)
516 Photographic detail from the October sheet of an IBM calendar showing dozens of new eraser-tipped pencils, still unsharpened. (USA)

509–513 Farbaufnahmen und eine vollständige Doppelseite aus einer Tischagenda der Druckerei *Stephenson.* Die Motive, Weiden, ein New Yorker Brückenmaler, Boote am Strand und eine verlassene Lokomotive (Spitzbergen), wurden von verschiedenen Photographen aufgenommen. (USA)
514, 515 Zwei von sechs Blättern eines Kalenders für Typework Inc., mit photographischen Illustrationen von Korrekturzeichen, wie sie von Korrektoren auf Abzügen verwendet werden. (USA)
516 Illustration des Oktoberblattes eines grossen IBM-Kalenders. (USA)

509–513 Photos couleur et page double complète d'un agenda de bureau de l'imprimerie *Stephenson.* Divers photographes se sont partagé les sujets: une saulaie; un peintre sur un pont de New York; des barques sur la plage; une locomotive abandonnée dans l'archipel du Spitzberg. (USA)
514, 515 Deux des six feuillets composant un calendrier réalisé pour Typework, Inc. et illustré d'illustrations photographiques de signes de correction typographique qu'emploient les correcteurs chargés de lire des épreuves d'imprimerie. (USA)
516 Illustration du feuillet d'octobre d'un calendrier IBM au grand format. (USA)

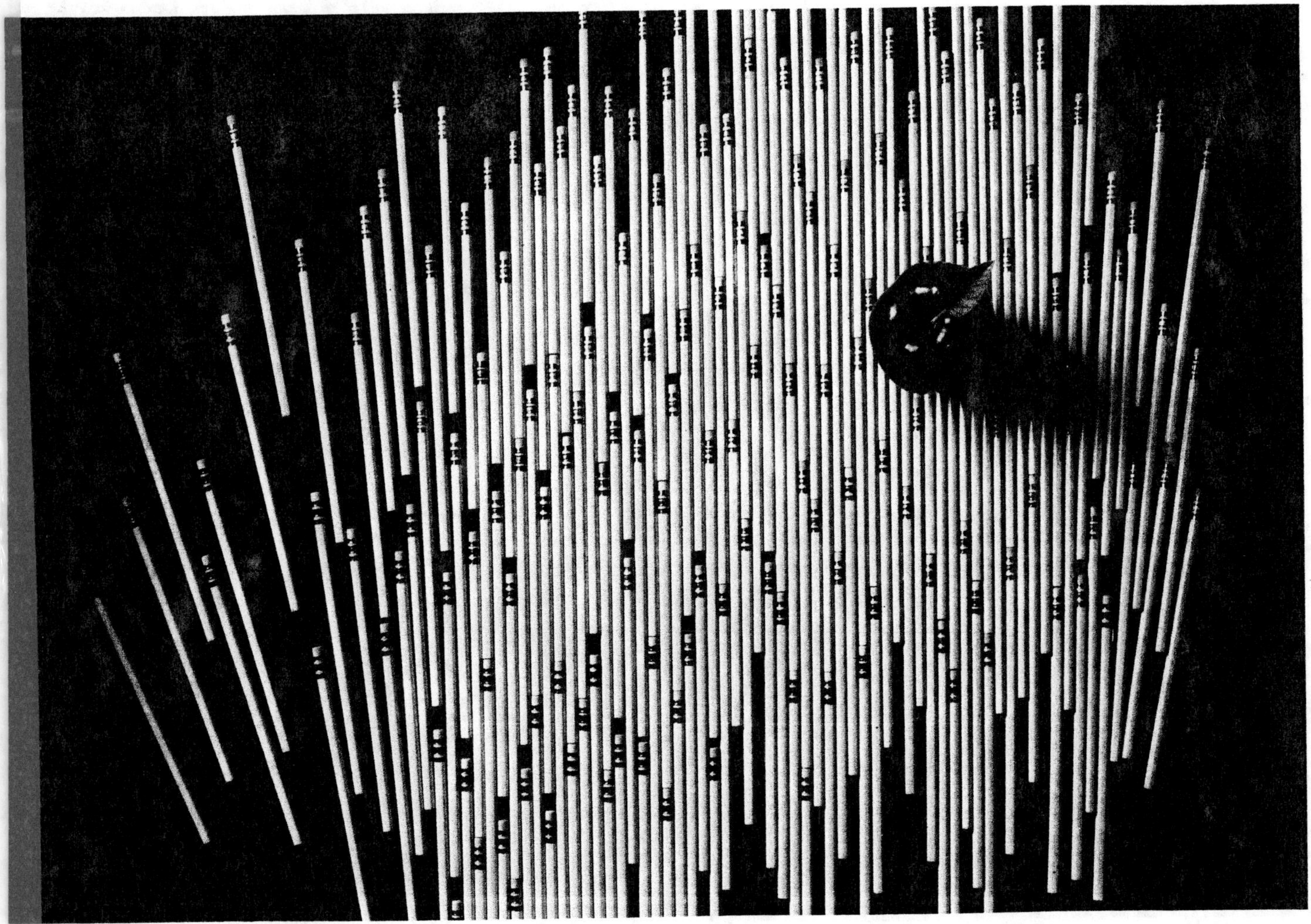

516

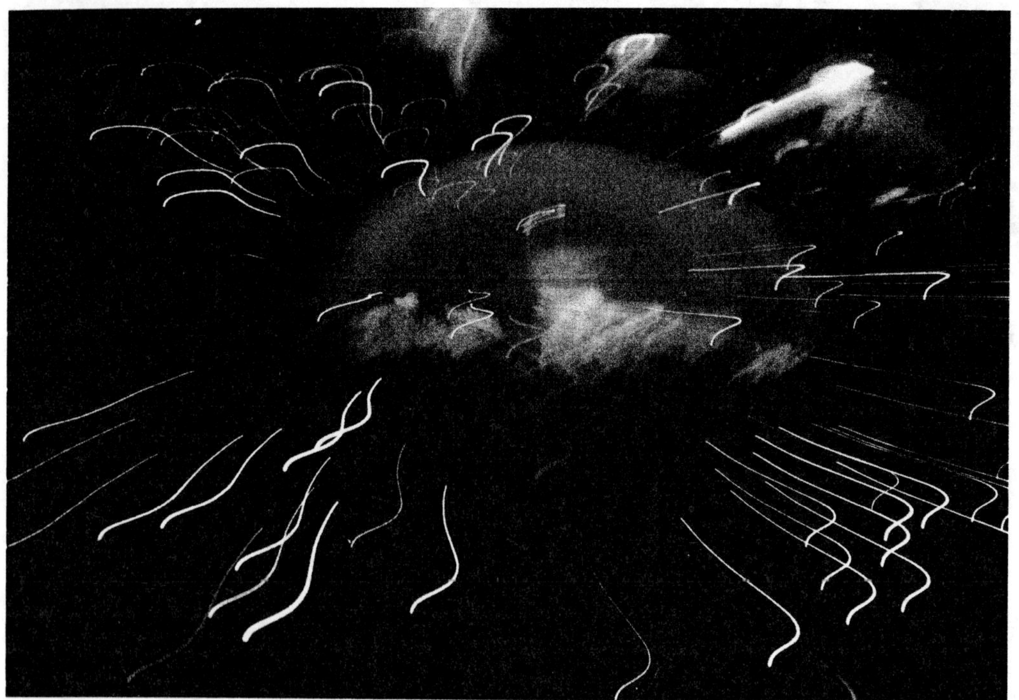

517

Calendars

PHOTOGRAPHER / PHOTOGRAPH:

517 P. Andras Dancs
518, 519 Sam Haskins
520 Tom Tracy
521, 522 Terry Heffernan/Light Language

DESIGNER / GESTALTER / MAQUETTISTE:

518, 519 David Pratt
520–522 Kit Hinrichs/Lenore Bartz

ART DIRECTOR / DIRECTEUR ARTISTIQUE:

518, 519 Sam Haskins
520–522 Kit Hinrichs

AGENCY / AGENTUR / AGENCE – STUDIO:

517 North Light
520–522 Jonson Pedersen Hinrichs & Shakery

518

519

520

521

517 "Cities in Flight": Detail from the promotional calendar by photographer P. A. Dancs. (CAN)
518, 519 Complete sheet and shot (yellow shades with black) from a *Pentax* calendar. (GBR)
520–522 Interpretations, with complete sheet, on the theme of "Time" in a *Champion Papers* calendar. Fig. 521: The beautifully chambered shell of the Nautilus, symbol of eternity. (USA)

517 «Städte im Flug.» Aufnahme aus dem Eigenwerbungskalender des Photographen P. A. Dancs. (CAN)
518, 519 Vollständiges Blatt und Aufnahme (Gelbtöne und Schwarz) für einen *Pentax*-Kalender. (GBR)
520–522 Interpretationen und vollständiges Blatt aus einem Kalender zum Thema Zeit von *Champion Papers*. Der Nautilus, seit dem Erdaltertum fast unverändert, als Symbol für eine Ewigkeit. (USA)

517 «Villes au vol.» Photo d'un calendrier autopromotionnel du photographe P. A. Dancs. (CAN)
518, 519 Feuillet complet et photo (divers jaunes et noir) pour un calendrier *Pentax*. (GBR)
520–522 Interprétations et feuillet complet d'un calendrier sur le thème du temps publié par *Champion Papers*. Le nautile, qui existe depuis l'ère primaire, symbole de la pérennité. (USA)

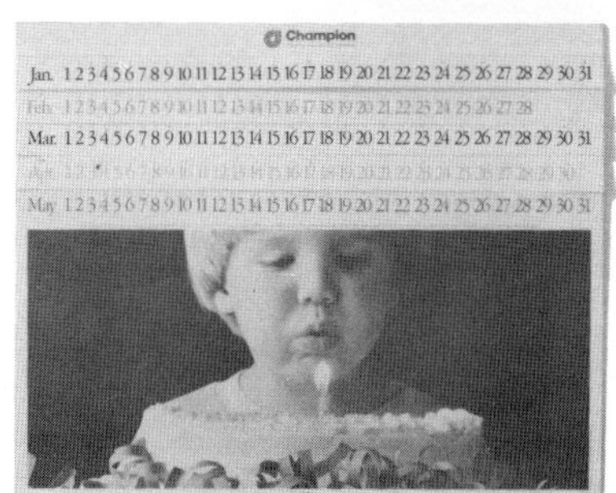

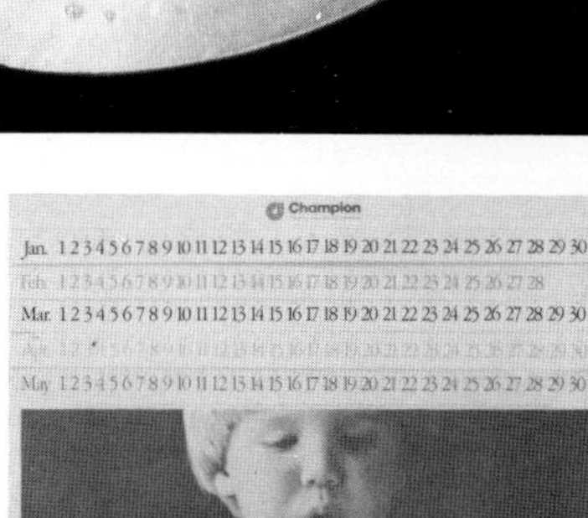

522

523 Cover of a record by the famous guitarist Eric Clapton. (USA)
524 Linda Ronstadt in a dress of red with white spots—colours reversed on background. (USA)
525 Cover of a songs record by Paul Simon, who wrote the music and lyrics and sang them. (USA)
526 Cover (mainly red and green) of a record by Dexy's Midnight Runners. (GBR)
527, 528 Complete cover with photographic detail of the record entitled "Love doesn't grow on Trees" by the Waldo group. (USA)

523 Hülle einer Schallplatte mit Aufnahmen des berühmten Gitarristen Eric Clapton. (USA)
524 Linda Ronstadt im roten Kleid mit weissen Punkten, Hintergrund umgekehrt. (USA)
525 Für eine Schallplatte mit von Paul Simon komponierten, getexteten und gesungenen Liedern. (USA)
526 Vorwiegend in Grün und Rot gehaltene Schallplattenhülle für Dexys Midnight Runners. (GBR)
527, 528 Vollständige Plattenhülle und Detailaufnahme davon für die Gruppe Waldo. «Liebe wächst nicht auf Bäumen» heisst der Titel der Schallplatte. (USA)

PHOTOGRAPHER / PHOTOGRAPH:

523 Graham Hughes
524 Aaron Rappoport
525 E.K.T.V.
527, 528 Bill King

DESIGNER / GESTALTER / MAQUETTISTE:

523 Ian Murray/Acrobat Design
524 Kosh/Ron Larson
525 Jeri McManus
527, 528 Karen Katz

527

523

524

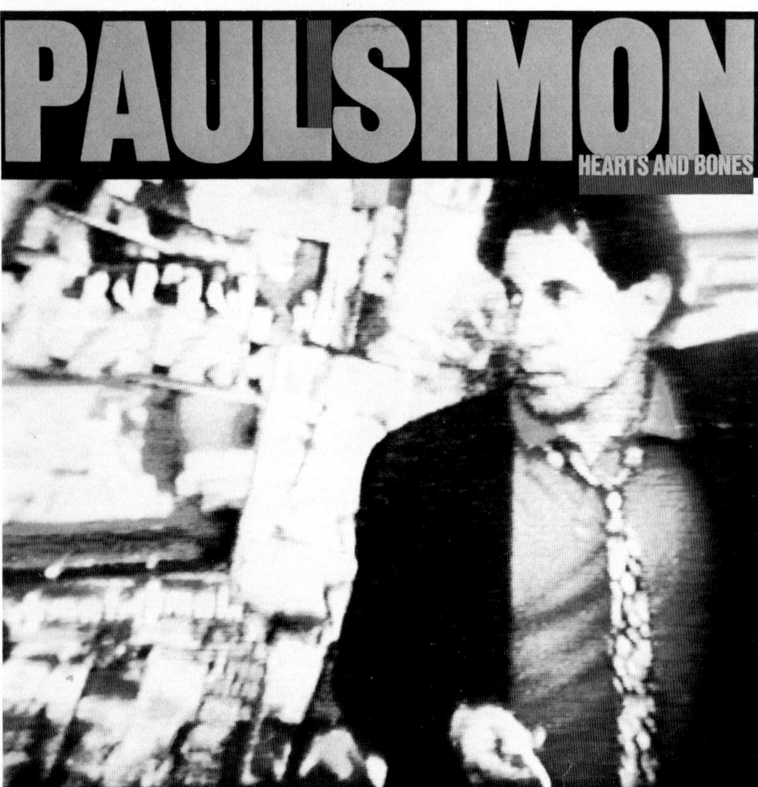

525

526

528

Record Covers
Schallplattenhüllen
Pochettes de disques

ART DIRECTOR / DIRECTEUR ARTISTIQUE:

523 Graham Hughes
524 Kosh/Ron Larson
525 Jeffrey Kent Ayeroff/Paula Greif
527, 528 Karen Katz

PUBLISHER / VERLEGER / EDITEUR:

523, 525 Warner Bros. Record Inc.
524 Elektra/Asylum Records
526 Emi Records Ltd.
527, 528 CBS Records

523 Pochette de disque pour les enregistrements du célèbre guitariste Eric Clapton. (USA)
524 Linda Ronstadt en robe rouge à pois blancs sur fond de couleur inverse. (USA)
525 Pochette d'un disque de Paul Simon qui en est le compositeur, le parolier et le chanteur. (USA)
526 Pochette de disque aux tons verts et rouges prédominants, pour Dexys Midnight Runners. (GBR)
527, 528 Pochette de disque complète et détail, pour le groupe Waldo. Le disque est intitulé «L'amour ne pousse pas sur les arbres». (USA)

529

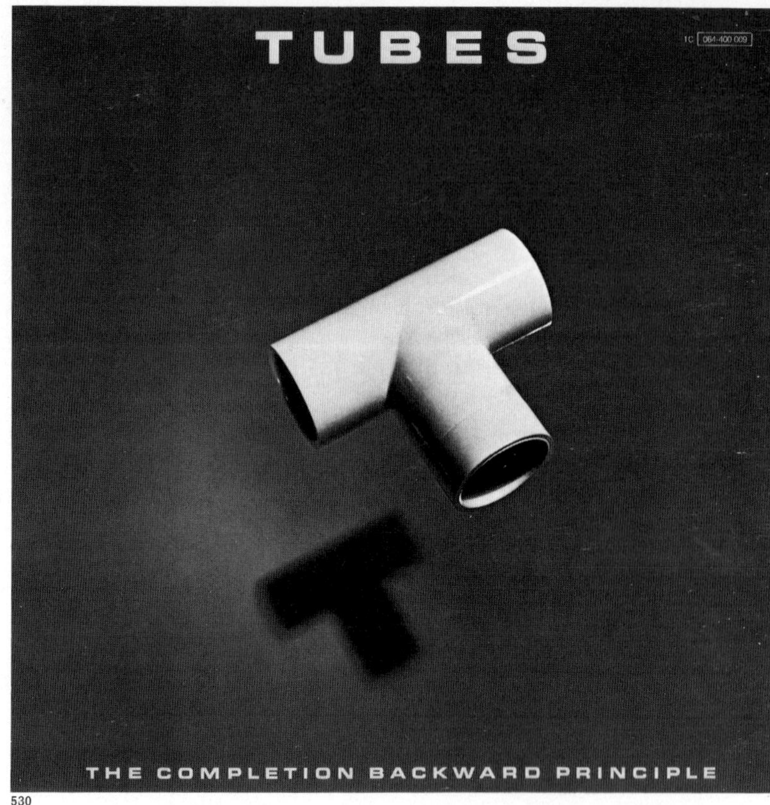

530

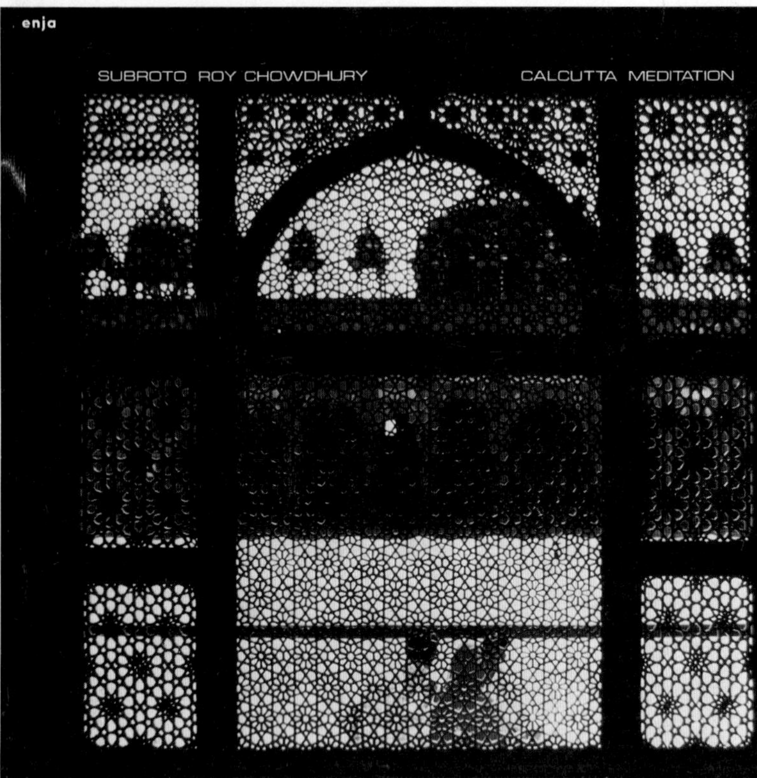

531

532

PHOTOGRAPHER / PHOTOGRAPH / PHOTOGRAPHE:

529 John Paul Endress
530 Cotten/Prince Design
531 Gerhard Koch
532 Dimke-Fotografie
533 Jim Shea
534 Linda McCartney

DESIGNER / GESTALTER / MAQUETTISTE:

529 Bob Heimall
530 Cotten/Prince Design
531 Elisabeth Winckelmann
532 Sabine Sörensen
533 Jeff Adamoff
534 Linda McCartney

ART DIRECTOR / DIRECTEUR ARTISTIQUE:

529 Peter Paul
530 Roy Kohara
533 Jeff Adamoff

PUBLISHER / VERLEGER / EDITEUR:

529, 530 EMI/Capitol Records, Inc.
531 ENJA Records
532, 534 EMI/Electrola
533 Warner Bros. Records Inc.

533

529 Recto of the cover for a record by Earl Klugh and Bob James. (USA)
530 White on blue ground: the cover of a record cut by the Tubes group. (USA)
531 Cover for a record of Raga music from India. It featured the well-known sitar player Subroto Roy Chowdhury. (GER)
532 A typical French cock, the "chanteclair", on the cover for a record of French songs. (GER)
533 The wax seal, red on white, is the cover visualization of the record title "Seal in Red" by the American group Rufus. The back of the cover carries a visual pun on the double meaning of the title, showing the aquatic seal—also in red. (USA)
534 Complete cover, back and front, of the "Pipes of Peace" by Paul McCartney. (USA)

529 Hüllenvorderseite einer Schallplatte mit Aufnahmen von Earl Klugh und Bob James. (USA)
530 Plattenumschlag für die Gruppe Tubes. Weiss auf blauem Grund. (USA)
531 Hülle für eine Schallplatte mit indischer Raga-Musik. Subroto Roy Chowdhury ist ein bekannter indischer Sitar-Spieler. (GER)
532 Vorderseite einer Hülle für eine Schallplatte mit französischen Liedern. (GER)
533 Schallplattenhülle für Aufnahmen der amerikanischen Gruppe Rufus. «Siegel (Seehund) in Rot» ist der Plattentitel. Rotes Siegel auf weissem Grund; auf der Hüllenrückseite ist ein roter Seehund abgebildet, in Anlehnung an die Doppelbedeutung des englischen Wortes «seal». (USA)
534 Vollständiger Plattenumschlag für Paul McCartneys «Friedenspfeifen». (USA)

529 Recto de la pochette d'un disque réunissant Earl Klugh et Bob James. (USA)
530 Pochette de disque pour le groupe Tubes. Blanc sur fond bleu. (USA)
531 Pochette pour un disque de musique raga indienne. Subroto Roy Chowdhury est un sitariste indien très connu. (GER)
532 Recto de la pochette d'un disque de chansons françaises. (GER)
533 Pochette de disque pour des enregistrements du groupe américain Rufus intitulés «Seal in red»: comprenez «cachet en rouge» et «phoque en rouge», d'où le cachet rouge sur blanc et le phoque rouge figurant au verso de la pochette, conformément au double sens de «seal». (USA)
534 Pochette complète de disque pour les «calumets de la paix» de Paul McCartney. (USA)

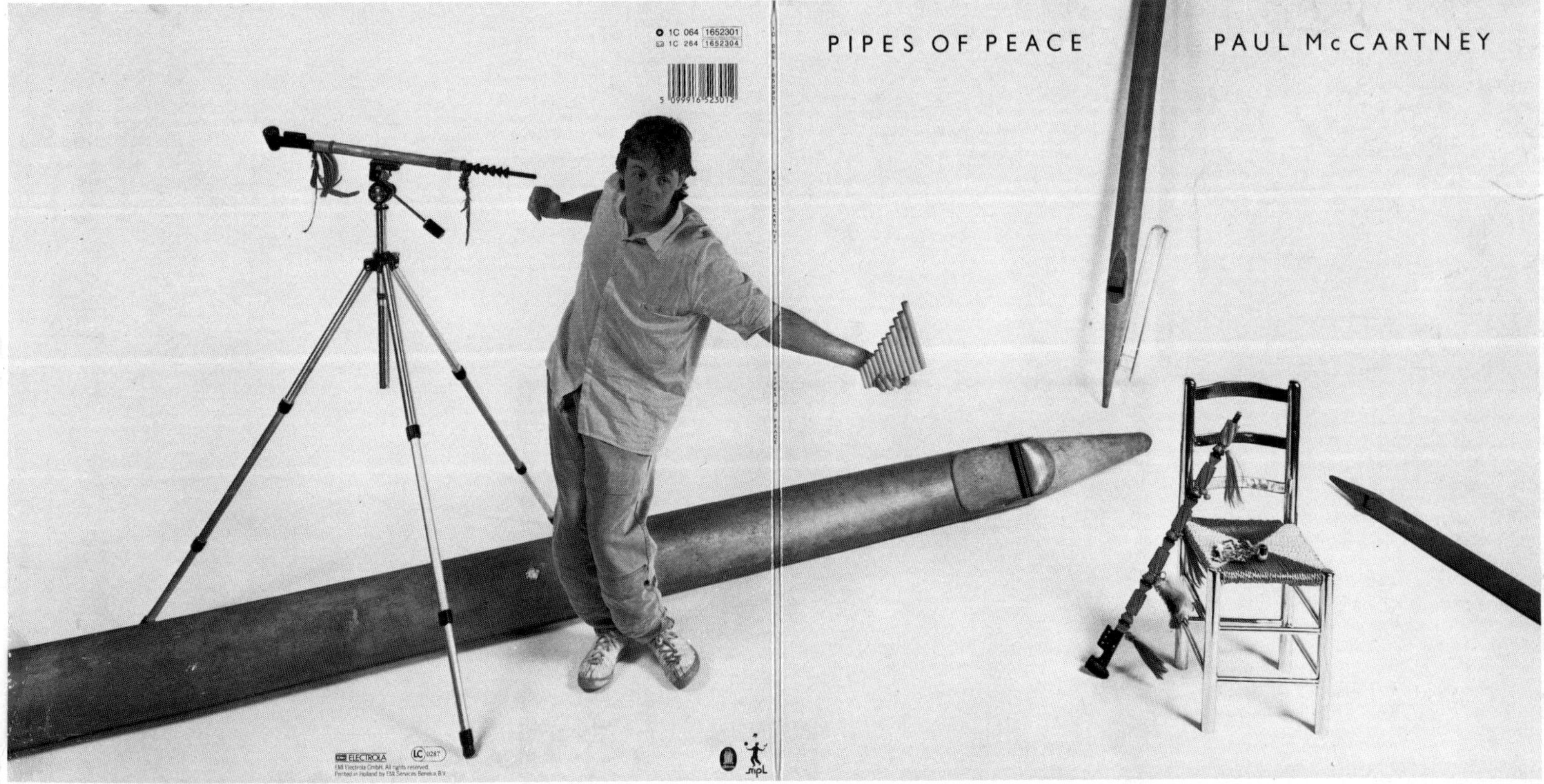

534

Paper / Papier: Papierfabrik Biberist–Biber art paper, super white, glaced, 130 gm² and Biber Offset SK3, pure white, machine-finished, 140 gm² / Biber-Kunstdruck ultra weiss, glaciert, 130 gm² und Biber-Offset SK3, hochweiss, maschinenglatt, 140 gm²

Printed by / gedruckt von: Sigg Söhne AG, Winterthur (Colour pages and dust jacket / Farbseiten und Schutzumschlag), Merkur AG, Langenthal (black and white / schwarzweiss)

Typesetting / Lichtsatz: Sauerländer AG, Aarau (Univers, MONOTYPE-Lasercomp)

Binding / Einband: Maurice Busenhart SA, Lausanne

Glossy lamination / Glanzfoliierung: Durolit AG, Pfäffikon SZ

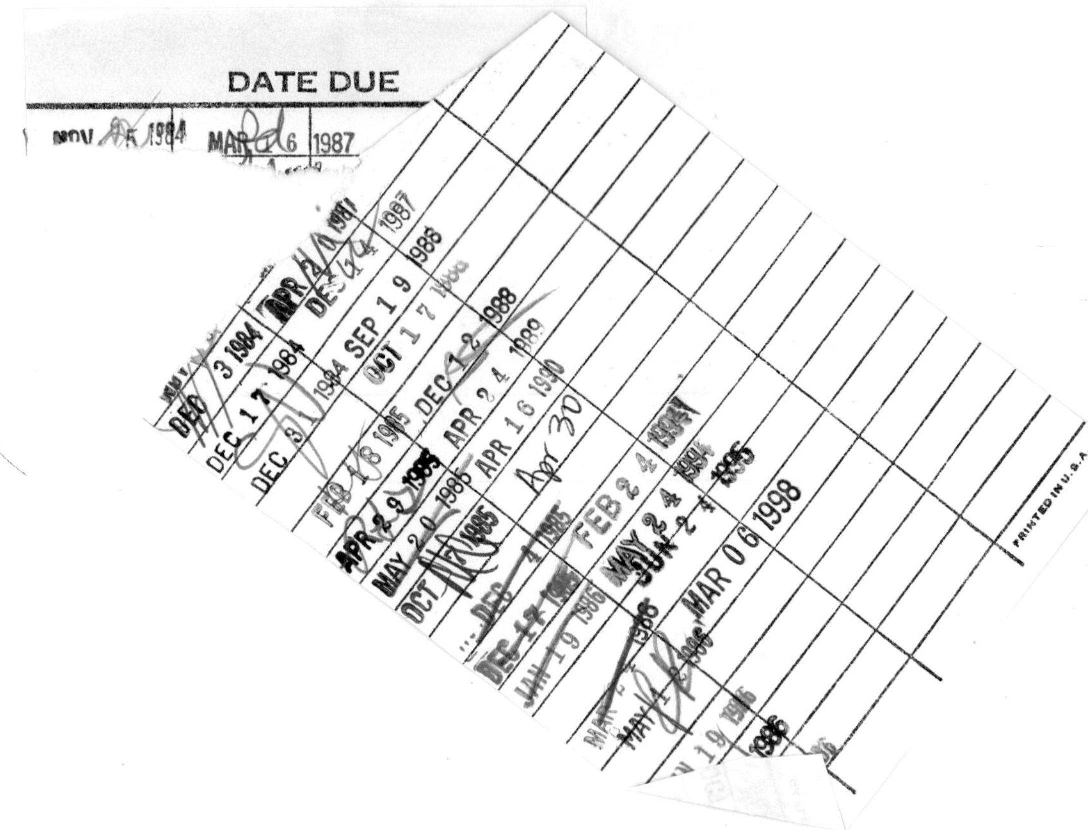
DATE DUE
PRINTED IN U.S.A.